FLORIDA SHERIFFS:

A HISTORY 1821–1945

By

William Warren Rogers

and

James M. Denham

Sentry Press
Tallahassee, Florida

Copyright © 2001 by Sentry Press

All rights reserved
Manufactured in the United States of America
First printing
10 09 08 07 06 05 04 03 02 01
5   4   3   2   1

Designer: Frank J. Jones
Typeface: Times Roman and Baskerville
Typesetter: Frank J. Jones
Printer and binder: Rose Printing Company

Library of Congress Cataloging-in-Publication Data
William W. Rogers and James M. Denham

ISBN 1-889574-11-2

FRONT COVER - Figures named clockwise starting with upper left are: Joseph S. Sanchez, Sheriff of St. Johns County 1845; Emmanuel Fortune, town marshal of Jacksonville during Reconstruction; Napoleon Bonaparte Broward, Sheriff of Duval County 1888; Robert C. Baker, Sheriff of Palm Beach County 1920; Celia Atkinson, Sheriff of Walton County 1938; David William Mizell, Sheriff of Orange County 1868; Elias E. Blackburn, U. S. Marshal 1854; center figure on horse, Lewis Washington Fennell, Sheriff of Alachua County 1890. Dust jacket design by Frank J. Jones.

TABLE OF CONTENTS

Preface		i
Introduction		1
Chapter 1	Sheriffs and Lawmen In Territorial Florida	6
Chapter 2	From Statehood to Civil War	32
Chapter 3	Sheriffs During the Civil War	56
Chapter 4	The Hard Years of Reconstruction 1865-1877	82
Chapter 5	Closing the Nineteenth and Into the Twentieth Century, 1877-1900	118
Chapter 6	The Ku Klux Klan and the Endemic Problem of Violence	152
Chapter 7	The First Two Decades of the Twentieth Century	178
Chapter 8	Bob Baker and the Ashley Gang	210
Chapter 9	Boom Times and the Great Depression	232
Chapter 10	Wartime Florida, 1941-1945	266
Appendix		284
Notes		end of each chapter
Bibliography		310
Index		325

PREFACE

There are not many monographs that study the office of sheriff and the men who held the position, but there are some. The overall situation is improving as witnessed by Thad Sitton's excellent book, *The Texas Sheriff Lord of the County Line*, recently published by the University of Oklahoma Press. Similar works on southern sheriffs in individual states or the South as a region would be welcome, and this book on Florida lawmen is one attempt to answer the need.

Fortunately, a number of studies on the multiple aspects of Florida sheriffs and the office are available in scholarly articles and books that are readily obtainable. Many county histories contain valuable information on sheriffs, and the growing shelflist of Floridiana is similarly important in dealing with various aspects of the sheriffs' history. Primary materials in the form of newspapers, journal proceedings, letters, diaries, manuscript collections and archival records in courthouses, sheriffs' offices, libraries (public and private), and court cases are available. The book could not have been written without the assistance of librarians and archivists, professional colleagues, and friends. Particularly useful in this study were the sheriffs, other personnel in sheriffs' offices, and former sheriffs. They shared their records and gave extremely useful interviews. In many Florida counties the sheriffs' offices forwarded manuscript and published material on their counties that was difficult to assemble and available nowhere else. These records were kindly forwarded to the Florida Sheriffs Association offices in Tallahassee for the authors' use.

The writers owe a large debt to numerous persons and institutions that have provided help and financial assistance for this project. We wish to acknowledge some of them but want to emphasize that the list is by no means exhaustive. We thank all of the many people who helped. J.M. "Buddy" Phillips, Executive Director of the Florida Sheriffs Association, conceived the project and convinced the FSA to underwrite publication costs. His staff in Tallahassee, especially Gary E. Perkins, Deputy Executive Director; Marti Moore Stover, Executive Assistant to the Director; Julie Bettinger, editor of *The Sheriffs Star*; Frank Jones, Director of Publications; Tom Berlinger, Director of Operational Services; and former Executive Director Carl Stauffer whose knowledge of Florida sheriffs and their history is unmatched, never failed to offer help or to believe in the project. Laurie Lore of Tallahassee was an early supporter and helped with interviews. We also thank Karen Wells, expert grammarian and computer wizard. Canter Brown opened his voluminous files, shared his expertise on Florida history, and offered useful advice. The authors are grateful to Larry Rivers of Florida Agricultural and Mechanical University; David J. Coles (previously archivist at the Florida State Archives and currently professor at Longwood College); William Wilbanks of Florida International University, author of the invaluable reference book, *Forgotten Heroes: Police Officers Killed in the Line of Duty, 1840*-1925, who shared his research and command of the subject; and William Warren Rogers, Jr., of Gainesville College. Others who generously read all or portions of the manuscript are Canter Brown, Tallahassee; Richard Buckelew, Bethune-Cookman College; Jerrell H. Shofner, professor-emeritus of the University of Central Florida; and Bertram Wyatt-Brown, University of Florida.

James M. Denham thanks Florida Southern College for granting him a sabbatical leave of absence during the spring 2000 semester to finish the manuscript. He also thanks Rand Sutherland, Francis Hodges, Barbara Giles, and John Santosuosso who filled in for him during his absence.

We are indebted for their contributions and assistance to Patrick Anderson, Florida Southern College; Nancy Aumann, Florida Southern College; Joe Knetsch, Bureau of Land Archives, Tallahassee; Leslie Lawhorn, Florida State Archives; Randall MacDonald, Florida Southern College; Joan Morris, Florida State Archives; Boyd Murphree, Florida State Archives; Jody Norman, Florida State Archives; Andrew Pearson, Florida Southern College; Vernon Peeples, Punta Gorda; Thomas L. Reuschling, president of Florida Southern

PREFACE

College; Jack and Jane Spencer, Florida Southern College; Ada Coats Williams, Ft. Pierce; Sally Hadden, Florida State University; Lucy Patrick, Florida State University; John Hebron Moore, Professor Emeritus Florida State University; Lorraine Smith, Historical Society of Palm Beach County; Don Moreland, United States Marshals Service, Middle District of Florida; and Ted Calhoun, Historian, U.S. Marshals Service, Washington, D.C.

Numerous people supplied detailed information on their counties, and among them are Robert Crowder, sheriff of Martin County; Bob Neumann, sheriff of Palm Beach County; Edward Brooks, Assistant Director of Information and Technology, Palm Beach County Sheriffs Office; Laura Tierney, Executive Secretary, Palm Beach County Sheriffs Office; W. A. Woodham, sheriff of Gadsden County; the late Otho W. Edwards, sheriff of Gadsden County from 1944 to 1968; Stephen M. Oelrich, sheriff of Alachua County; Larry Campbell, sheriff of Leon County; the late Ed Blackburn, former sheriff of Hillsborough County; Colonel M. F. Mann, undersheriff of Martin County; Beverly Auer, Executive Assistant, Martin County Sheriffs Office; Cal Henderson, sheriff of Hillsborough County; Fred Taylor, former Director Metro-Dade Police Department; Gail A. Tierney, Public Information Officer, Citrus County Sheriffs Office; the late Robert Smith, Volusia County Sheriffs Office; Helen Tragus, Research and Development Director, Broward County Sheriffs Office; Joan Heller, Brevard County Sheriffs Office; Ann Tankersley, Sheriff's Office, Walton County; Phyllis J. Norris, Administrative Secretary, Hardee County; Tamera Rogers, Lake County Sheriffs Office; Robert L. Vogel, sheriff/director of Volusia County; Robert D. Smith, Historian, Volusia County Sheriffs Office; Susan C. McVeigh, Executive Assistant, Lee County Sheriffs Office; and Sergeant Robert Snell, Sarasota County Sheriff's Office.

None of these people are responsible for errors of omission or those of commission that occur in this book. Such mistakes are solely the fault of the authors.

INTRODUCTION

Because of the media, especially movies and television, the southern sheriff has often been depicted as an evil figure. A number of disparaging words and images have been used to describe the men who wore and wear the sheriff's star. No honest white southerner, no matter how paranoid personally, or how non-critical of white law officials, can deny that some of the bad repute has been earned and is true. Yet, the concept of the southern sheriff as a stereotypical sadist has been largely overdrawn. Historically, the sheriffs have been important as enforcers of the law and protectors of the public safety. They are the individuals who have carried out the process of law, that is, they have served summons, writs, warrants, and other official documents. They have routinely acted as court officials, often been tax collectors, conducted public auctions, been personally responsible as executioners of persons convicted of capital crimes, foreclosed mortgages, labored as timber agents and game wardens, and worked as election officials. The above list is by no means comprehensive.

The southern sheriff has been unique largely because the region has been unique. He (and now, sometimes, she) has reflected and embodied the region's environmental, cultural, racial, urban-rural, geographical, political, and religious paradoxes and points of view. Beyond that, each southern state has its own idiosyncratic qualities and aspects. More specifically, each southern state has been "different" enough (sometimes dramatically so) to frame its own set of characteristics. This book is about the sheriff in Florida, the second largest state (after Georgia) east of the Mississippi River. It is also about much more, especially the Florida Sheriffs Association founded in 1893, and an increasingly effective spokesman for the lawmen in the following years. Present day Florida has sixty-seven counties, but after it was transferred by Spain to the United States in the summer of 1821 and prior to being organized as a territory in 1822, it had only two: Escambia and St. Johns. Before the Civil War Florida was the South's most rural state, much of it sparsely settled frontier. In the twenty-first century it is the most urban. That metamorphosis and how the county sheriffs helped shape it is part of this study.

INTRODUCTION

Any understanding of the Florida sheriff has to take into account that he was an elected county official, except during Reconstruction when he was appointed by the governor. As a person who depended on public approval of his performance, the sheriff had to develop the skills necessary to win elections. He had to become a politician. Dependency on popular election greatly influenced how the sheriff performed his duties. The lawman's personality and his qualities as a man were other factors that helped determine whether he remained in office. Often a sheriff emerged as a county's single most powerful and important individual. Far more than most public officials, the sheriff was able to manipulate his power and create a facade of honesty and conscientiousness that did not always exist. Fortunately, a majority of the state's lawmen were men of integrity. Most sheriffs were ordinary people, many with only the rudiments of public education. Still, as time passed and the job became larger, more demanding, and more sophisticated, sheriffs became better educated and equipped in order to deal with the modern intricacies of administration and the precise world of communication made possible by technical equipment and machines. Modern methods of criminal detection advanced rapidly, and required trained technicians and administrators.

It was the rule of all southern states, and noticeably so in Florida, that the office of sheriff had a familial aspect. It was common for a sheriff to have a son to succeed him, a process that continued through several generations. Not only that, but a sheriff's deputies and assistants were often brothers or other kinfolk. Holding a county's office of sheriff was family oriented. Often, members of a sheriff's family entered other areas of law enforcement, becoming detectives, policemen, highway patrolmen, or entered various specialized fields relating to crime and criminology.

Physical danger differentiated the sheriff from most county, state, and national officials. The story of sheriffs who gave their lives or were badly injured in the line of duty is a long, grim, and never-ending one. Risk was inherent in the job, and the position called for a person familiar with firearms, one who accepted danger that was both unpredictable and potentially always present. Because an encounter with a criminal could result in death or injury to the sheriff and the lawbreaker, a successful lawman needed sound judgment. The risk factor was a major reason why many men declined to make careers out of being sheriffs. Another reason was the low salary. Many lawmen had to seek additional money from farming and other jobs. From the earliest times, Florida sheriffs were primarily dependent for their income on the bewildering and ever broadening fee system. A sheriff received many small fees of varying amounts, as well as certain fines, for carrying out his multiple responsibilities. Florida had no salary system for sheriffs until well into the twentieth century, and even then the pay varied greatly from county to county. The state's official records, especially those of the nineteenth century, are replete with examples of various sheriffs seeking compensation from the legislature for services rendered but for which they were refused payment. In many cases their appeals were successful.

Certain conditions in nineteenth-century-Florida were beyond the sheriff's capacity to influence, and they greatly affected his job. The large, underpopulated, and undeveloped state had massive problems of communication and transportation. In the early years some sheriffs served more than one county. The official was an isolated individual who had difficulty communicating with his fellow sheriffs in other counties. Transporting prisoners was a dangerous and arduous mission. The advantages of eluding their pursuers lay heavily with the felons. Once captured, their delivery to the nearest jail was uncertain. If they were tried, found guilty, and incarcerated the chances of escape were great, and the likelihood of recapture improbable. In addition, unlike other southern states such as Georgia and Alabama, Florida had no state penitentiary until after the Civil War. Local jails, always scandalously insecure and often nonexistent, were the rule.

Through time certain civil and criminal transgressions have continued. For example, in criminal annals such illegal acts as rape, murder, arson, theft, and assault have always been present. Yet, other categories of crime and control, either small before or entirely new, have emerged. The broad scale crisis of drugs in the twentieth- and twenty-first centuries is the most striking example. The sheriff's duties increased to meet the needs created by an industrialized society. Unknown to the nineteenth century, but becoming vitally important in the early twentieth century, was the need to regulate the use of automobiles. Sheriffs became a part of the solution to controlling the many problems—criminal, civil, and social—related to traffic congestion. Yet, in 1939 the creation of the Florida Highway Patrol established another and separate law enforcement agency. The highway patrol was tangible proof of the importance that automobiles, trucks, and other vehicles had assumed in the lives of Floridians. Most recently, costly crime in the computer world of communication threatens corporate America.

Through it all, the sheriff in Florida has had a place. This study is a documented account of how the sheriffs office operated from the creation of the territory to the end of World War II in 1945. It is a chronological account that goes beyond the limits imposed by institutional history. The focus is on sheriffs in detail and in general. Within a broad scope and with varying emphasis, it examines and evaluates the roles of various deputies, county traffic officers, constables, prison personnel, United States marshals, and highway patrolmen. Because the story of the Florida Sheriffs Association after its founding was inseparable from that of individual sheriffs, close attention has been paid to it. At the very least the complicated and important history of the Florida sheriff and the office he held was closely related to every aspect of state government and to the lives of the people.

CHAPTER I

SHERIFFS AND LAWMEN IN TERRITORIAL FLORIDA

ales of sheriffs in Florida can be traced back virtually to the moments when the one-time Spanish colony found itself under the stars and stripes. The story began when President James Monroe appointed Andrew Jackson as Commissioner and Governor. More accurately, he became the provisional or military governor and only for a brief period. Old Hickory's resignation from the army and his appointment as governor were closely paired. The president wrote Jackson, "I have confidence that your appointment will be immediately & most beneficially felt. Smugglers & slave traders will hide their heads; pirates will disappear & the Seminoles cease to give trouble."[1] Ceremonies handing over the jurisdiction of East Florida took place at St. Augustine on July 10, 1821, and, a week later, on July 17, Jackson himself accepted the transfer of West Florida at Pensacola.[2]

Before the territory was formally organized by Congress on March 30, 1822, Jackson exercised his authority with verbal commands and, more importantly, by issuing ordinances. The first mention of a sheriff in Florida came in Section 4 of a lengthy ordinance promulgated by the governor on July 21, 1821. It provided that a sheriff and a clerk would be appointed for the courts of the territory's first two counties: Escambia and St. Johns. The two officials were "to exercise the process thereof." The term "process" meant the total of the summons directing a defendant to appear in court, and process was the variety of writs, suits, and other documents involved.[3]

Although it was not spelled out in the ordinance, later statutes

 Andrew Jackson, depicted here in his general's uniform served as provisional governor of the territorial Florida, 1821. (Courtesy of the Florida State Archives).

assigned the sheriff a myriad of duties encompassing the broader sweep of what the word "Sheriff" implied. He was a man who enforced the law. The job also involved prisoners, jails, taxes, various aspects of county government, and interaction with other judicial and administrative officials. The sheriff's work went beyond what the law said and included what individual lawmen interpreted as their basic obligations.

Under Jackson's ordinance of 1821 the two sheriffs were appointed by him and paid by the court. Both the sheriff and the clerk had to give bond to the presiding justice. Less than a month later, on August 4, 1821, a St. Augustine paper, the *Florida Gazette*, published a list of newly appointed public officials. Eight police officers and their deputies were included. One of them, Joseph Sanchez, a prominent Creole, later served both as federal marshal for the Eastern Judicial District of Florida (1837-1842) and as sheriff of St. Johns County (1845-1847). In all likelihood the eight men were the territory's first law enforcement officials.[4] What laws they were to enforce remained unclear until the legislative council began to function. Until then, the men and their fellow public officials operated within the confusion of the transfer from Spanish to American control.

The sheriff in Florida emerged as a law enforcement officer, keeper of the peace, and protector of the people. He was to ensure that laws—whether local, territorial, or national—were obeyed. He understood less well (but neither did anyone else) that he was to act under the common and statute laws of England, so far as they applied to Florida. Statutes relating to crime and lawmen, some so general as to be meaningless, some of utter specificity (embracing disparate topics from wills to the apprehension of criminals) would be enacted by the various sessions of the lawmakers at Tallahassee.[5] Each sheriff came to understand that being designated ex officio for an office often meant actually having to perform the duty. For example, if a person died intestate it was all well and good for the law to require a judge to appoint a curator for the deceased's estate. Yet, if no appointment was made, the sheriff, in his ex officio capacity, had to take charge of the property and inventory it.[6]

A knowledgeable incumbent of the sheriff's office could benefit from traditions and experiences that already were hundreds of years old

 Joseph S. Sanchez of St. Augustine served as federal marshal of the District of East Florida before becoming sheriff of St. Johns County, 1845-1847. (Courtesy of St. Augustine Historical Society).

by the 1820s. The history of the sheriff in America dates to the colony of Virginia in 1635. In that year the sheriff's office absorbed that of the provost marshal. The office had a direct connection with England, and the sheriff became and remains a key figure in American history.[7] In Anglo-Saxon England, centuries before Virginia's settlement, the sheriff was the main link between the king and local government units.[8] Each shire of the county had a leader known as the "reeve" and the term shire reeve gradually evolved into the word "sheriff." One historian, William Alfred Morris, has asserted that "the rise of the sheriff" helped make for "the centralization of local government" in the tenth century. As a key representative of the Crown in local government, the sheriff kept the peace, held court, collected taxes, and commanded the militia.[9] The sheriff's headship of the courts of shire and hundred and his direction of the bailiffs were, Morris contends, "alone sufficient to designate him as the mainspring of local government."[10]

Although the English sheriff's duties changed through time, it was natural that the office would be transported across the Atlantic Ocean to England's colonies in the seventeenth and eighteenth centuries. There the sheriff continued to exercise wide law enforcement authority.[11] According to Cyrus Harreld Karraker's study comparing English sheriffs with their American counterparts in Virginia and Maryland, the differences were due mainly to the environment.[12] Sheriffs on both sides of the Atlantic shared common characteristics: they were the principal keepers of the peace, assembled posses, dispersed and seized rioters, enforced political and religious conformity, and came from the same economic and social groups. Their similarities were much more numerous than their differences.[13]

Yet they differed in that the colonial position was more sought after because it afforded its occupant a substantial income; the colonial sheriff had fewer expenses; his judicial and ceremonial duties were fewer; and in America the sheriff had greater importance as a financial officer. In the colonial environment the sheriff remolded the ancient institution, and it became more provincial, more democratic, and more important in local government. While the office of sheriff rose and declined in England, it never declined in the colonies. Still, with all of the changes

...and Dollars with approved security, conditioned for the performance of the duties of their said offices.

8. Be it further enacted, that the Inferior Courts shall be the offices of original records, for deeds, mortgages and other instruments required by Law to be recorded within their respective Counties.

9. Be it further enacted, that the Inferior Courts shall have power to fine and imprison for Contempts of their Authority, provided the fines do not exceed Twenty Dollars or the imprisonment six days.

10. Be it further enacted, that there shall be appointed a Sheriff for each County who shall perform all the duties required by Law and before entering upon the duties of his office, shall take an oath faithfully to execute the duties required of him without respect of persons, and execute Bond in the office of the Secretary of the Territory in the penalty of Five Thousand Dollars, with approved security, conditioned for the performance of his said office, or at such other place as the Governor shall appoint, which shall not be void upon the payment of the penalty, but remain in full force: and the Sheriff and his Securities shall be liable to the suit of any person upon failure or neglect of his said duties.

11. Be it further enacted, that all causes now depending and undetermined in any of the Courts of this Territory, shall be transferred at the election of the Plaintiff or Complainant to either the Inferior or Superior Court — and it shall be the duty of the Clerk of any of the existing Courts to deliver over all papers relating to said causes to the Clerks of the aforesaid Courts by the direction of the Plaintiff or Complainant, his or her agent or attorney and take their receipt therefor.

12. Be it further enacted...

Territorial statute outlining the duties and responsibilities of sheriffs. (Courtesy of the Florida State Archives).

the American sheriff has always retained "many of his Anglo-Saxon and Normal characteristics...."[14]

The sheriffs in the English seaboard colonies worked with the judiciary and served the process of the courts, kept the peace, maintained jails, and acted as tax collectors. The office was firmly entrenched by the time the colonies won their independence, and the sheriffs continued as important parts of the American judiciary. As the nation expanded into the West and Southwest, the county lawman's place became permanent. Beginning with the Northwest Territory in 1787, subsequent territories passed statutes establishing the post of sheriff and setting up basic rules of operation.[15]

While unversed in the office's historical evolution, Andrew Jackson realized its importance. After serving only eighty days, Old Hickory would resign, and in October 1821, he and his wife Rachel would return to their home, the Hermitage, in Nashville, Tennessee. Despite his short tenure, Jackson appointed Florida's first sheriff: James R. Hanham. The former U. S. Army captain went to St. Augustine in August 1821, and opened an office. After Congress officially created the Territory of Florida,[16] President Monroe appointed William Pope DuVal of Kentucky as the first civilian governor. The durable and iconoclastic DuVal held the position for the next twelve years, during which he would add his own stamp upon the office of sheriff.[17]

Territorial laws passed by Congress affected Florida in many ways. For example, the act of creation called for a court system, an appointed delegate to Congress, an appointed legislative council (the body was later enlarged, made elective, and divided into two houses), and an appointed territorial secretary. George Walton, a disciple of Jackson, filled the post of territorial secretary and served as acting governor until DuVal arrived to take control on April 17, 1822.

Sheriff Hanham served in the first territorial legislative council, but, ironically, the same body rejected his reappointment by DuVal as St. Johns County sheriff. By August 1823, ex-sheriff Hanham was in desperate economic straits. He wrote Governor DuVal that the absence of territorial funds had forced him to purchase provisions on credit to feed prisoners and defray office expenses. Asking for advance money to

 William Pope Duval was Florida's first civil governor, serving, 1822-1834. (Courtesy of the Florida State Archives).

pay his debts, the dejected Hanham explained his bleak situation: "I am in a strange country without means and a family to support and if relief is not soon afforded, what little property I have will be exposed to Sheriff['s] sale to pay Public expense." DuVal, not knowing how to proceed, forwarded Hanham's correspondence and accounts to Secretary of State John Quincy Adams and noted, "the account is large and too important for me to decide." He continued: "I therefore required him to produce his account and vouchers for your inspection. Capt. Hanham as far as I know has done his duty promptly and faithfully—he is distressed by the advances he has made, and his situation requires the speedy settlement of his accounts."[18] Whether former Sheriff Hanham obtained relief is unknown. In his quest for funds he became the first of many lawmen to follow, each with legitimate and often plaintive pleas. Being mired in debt was not uncommon among Florida lawmen.

For the citizens of Florida's counties during the 1820s and 1830s having a sheriff whose activities were limited by a shortage of resources was better than having no sheriff at all. Sparse finances and sparse population meant that every county did not have a sheriff. Of necessity the territorial legislature sometimes assigned a sheriff duties in other counties. In 1824 the Duval County sheriff was empowered to serve writs in Nassau County. Likewise, the St. Johns County sheriff did the same thing in Alachua, Mosquito, and Monroe counties.[19]

Early on and later, how a sheriff actually got his job was unclear. There was no consistently applied procedure. At first the office came by way of appointment, but who did the appointing? Jackson did so initially, but how binding was the precedent? In general, from 1821-1828 the governor appointed sheriffs with the advice and consent of the legislative council. A bill of 1828 required sheriffs and other county officials to be popularly elected and hold office for two years. Governor DuVal disapproved the measure, but it passed over his veto.[20] Earlier, when the territorial chief executive had to approve the appointment, a prospective candidate applied for the position verbally or in writing. He would come to the governor's attention by private recommendations from interested parties. Knowing the governor personally greatly enhanced the applicant's chances for approval. Politics, at least as much as talent and experience, was a powerful factor. For sufficient cause the governor could also remove a sheriff. Before he assumed the post a future sheriff had to take an oath of office and post bond of $5,000 (later $12,000).[21]

By 1834 being sheriff was so demanding that it was clear the typical Florida lawman needed help. That year a welcomed law empowered him to appoint deputies. Wisely, the deputy sheriff was given the same arrest powers as his superior officer.[22]

In lieu of a salary the early Florida sheriff relied on a system of fees and fines—fees came for acts of public service and fines from collecting money for punitive transgressions. The complicated process was made formal and specific by the legislative council and amended and enlarged from time to time. After statehood was achieved in 1845 fees and fines were regulated by the state legislature, officially known as the general assembly. Lawmakers expected the criminal justice system— through the collection of fees and fines—to pay for itself. It never did, and only rarely were lawmakers moved to provide adequate funding. The lack of official commitment weighed heavily on numerous local lawmen who possessed little means to carry out their demanding responsibilities. Many good men were discouraged from serving.

Governor DuVal's executive functions included reviewing acts of the legislative council, and on September 17, 1822, he approved a law that set fees for certain officials, including sheriffs. Until the schedule was enlarged later, sheriffs were rewarded with fees for serving process; removing a prisoner (ten cents a mile); attendance before a judge or justice with a prisoner (two dollars a day); committing a prisoner to jail (one dollar); releasing a prisoner (twenty-five cents); serving a declaration in ejectment (one dollar for each defendant); executing condemned persons (ten dollars); whipping a free person under court order (two dollars—an act of 1823 permitted the sheriff or marshal to employ another person to execute the whipping, but the sheriff or marshal had to be present to oversee the punishment); and whipping a slave (one dollar, to be paid by the owner).[23]

The existence of slavery in the territory created special obligations and special fees for the sheriffs. The individual owner had the authority to punish his or her slaves, while the regulation of slaves on a broader scale was entrusted to local white groups known as "patrols" that had administrative connections to justices of the peace.[24] Yet, the sheriff also had a role. As early as 1822 an act dealt with runaway slaves "laying out" in swamps or other places. If that occurred any two justices of the peace could order a sheriff to gather a posse, find and arrest the fugitives, and commit them to jail to await further trial. If the court directed, the sheriff could sell the runaway slaves, and twenty-five percent of the amount received would go to the county. The remainder went to the slaveholder with the sheriff getting five percent of the owner's share.[25]

Because Florida was a territory under federal jurisdiction, the early sheriffs were not the primary law enforcement officers. That duty was held by U.S. marshals who were government officials appointed by the president. How those federal officers worked both independently and in concert with the sheriff requires separate consideration.

It has been seen that when the United States took possession of Florida there was a pressing need to arrange judicial administration and law enforcement at the federal, territorial, and local levels. Although aware of the great distance between St. Augustine and Pensacola—414 uncomfortable land miles, or the uncertain and longer sea route via the Atlantic Ocean, Straits of Florida, and Gulf of Mexico—President Monroe designated only one U. S. marshal for the territory. New York native James Grant Forbes's appointment required him to live either in St. Augustine or Pensacola and to appoint a deputy to reside at the other place.[26]

Coming to St. Augustine, Forbes received his commission and secured his bond from William Worthington, Jackson's secretary and acting governor of East Florida. Forbes immediately began exercising his authority with wide latitude. His precise duties and compensation as U. S. marshal were as yet undefined. Concerned about "his personal and family obligations," Forbes had a brief interview with the acting governor, and queried Secretary of State John Quincy Adams for more information. Primarily, Forbes was concerned about Worthington's revelation that remuneration was uncertain. "Unless there was a Salary," the marshal wrote Adams, "the appointment would not give me Salt for my Herrings."[27] Forbes suggested that his knowledge of Spanish could be of service. Later, these skills in the language proved valuable both to the government and himself. He frequently accompanied other federal officials to Havana, and, once in Cuba, helped them secure documents relevant to Spanish land grants in Florida.

One of Forbes's principle duties was to monitor the large stands of live oak and cedar that were critical to the nation's ship-building industry. Illegal cutting of timber on public lands was a federal offense, and Forbes was responsible for arresting violators.[28] Because a marshal's duties often required him to handle large sums of money, Jackson ordered acting governor William Worthington to see that Forbes executed a bond sufficient to ensure "perfect security to all and particularly to individuals."[29]

Forbes's responsibilities as marshal and those of his successors applied to Florida, but they were based on a national legacy that had already been established. Statutes dating back to the republic's founding defined their power. The historian Frederick S. Calhoun has shown that the Federal Judiciary Act of 1789 and subsequent legislation gave marshals "extensive authority to support the federal courts within their judicial districts and carry out all lawful orders issued by judges, Congress, or the president." Primarily, they assisted the federal courts, issuing subpoenas, summons, writs, warrants, and other process. They made arrests and handled prisoners, and paid the fees and expenses of court clerks, U. S. attorneys, jurors, and witnesses. Further, they rented the courtrooms and jail space and hired the bailiffs, criers, and janitors. In addition, they took the national census every ten years until 1870. Marshals routinely distributed presidential proclamations, collected statistical information on commerce and manufacturing, and supplied the names of government employees for the national register.[30]

Not unexpectedly confusion arose, and in 1823 the legislative council attempted clarification. An act of that year instructed marshals to perform the duties assigned them by the laws of the United States. They were to be the executive officers of the superior courts within their respective districts. A marshal's pay was determined by the legislative council. Working often in the transfer of prisoners, the hard-pressed marshals were allowed to employ special guards to aid them and receive compensation for their labors.[31]

Marshals were subject to the same penalties as sheriffs, and both sets of officials had similar responsibilities. The clarifying law of 1823 made marshals subject to a loyalty oath and a bond of five thousand dollars. They were instructed to take charge of all prisoners currently incarcerated and to have custody of all future inmates. Even so, sheriffs were to complete the process in civil cases involving them and to receive the accompanying fees.[32] Although the U. S. marshals were the chief law enforcement officers, they were given fewer duties than sheriffs in executions regarding land.[33] Marshals and sheriffs were affected whenever the legislative council passed acts amending the judiciary system. Laws such as a lengthy one in 1828, revised and spelled out their assignments at trials.[34] Marshals attended superior courts in their districts and executed courts' orders. By the time Florida joined the Union in 1845 Congress had created five judicial districts: Western, 1821; Eastern, 1821; Middle, 1824; Southern, 1828; and Apalachicola, 1838. There was a federal judge, district attorney, and marshal in each district.

In carrying out his assignments the marshal received $200 annually and, like the sheriff, was entitled to fees for his services.[35] As he went about his job a marshal was expected to perform labors other than those specifically prescribed. In the best of situations his salary would have been inadequate, but in Florida circumstances sometimes became intolerable. Facing financial ruin, Charles Evans, marshal of the Western Judicial District, resigned his post in 1841. As he explained to President John Tyler:

> I should feel myself honored in continuing [in] the office if Florida was a State and my duties were confined to the laws of the United States only; but being obliged as I am to receive all crimenals [sic] offending against the laws of the Territory, and to defray the expense of their mentaince [sic] from my private funds for want of funds on the part of the Territory, I have not hesitated what course it was most prudent for me to persue [sic].[36]

Surviving federal records provide some insights about the men who served as U. S. marshals during Florida's territorial years. They reveal that marshals differed widely as individuals but shared some things in common. Most were fairly well educated and well-connected politically in their native states. Of the twenty-seven marshals who served, eight were appointed after living for some time in the territory. Their native states are unknown. Of the remaining nineteen, twelve were Southerners, while seven were from the North. These nineteen represented Kentucky (two), North Carolina (two), Virginia (four), Georgia (one), Alabama (two), Tennessee (one), New York (four), Maine (one), Indiana (one) and New Jersey (one). Of the twenty-seven marshals, the longest serving, were James W. Exum (Western Judicial District, 1819-1838); Waters Smith (Eastern Judicial District, 1823-1831); and Thomas E. Randolph (Middle Judicial District, 1831-1837). At least ten of the twenty-seven served four-year terms. Four marshals were removed from office during their tenure.

As presidential appointees, marshals held office at the pleasure of the political party that controlled the White House. Inevitably, the selections often evoked a partisan reaction in district communities. Some local citizens were pleased, but others were outraged by certain appointments. The choices of Joseph Sanchez (Eastern District) and Leigh Read (Middle Florida), both Democrats, were cases in point. In 1840 one prominent Democrat joined Leon County Whigs in deploring Read's appointment, claiming that Read "never was a man of business and possessed neither the capacity nor the common sense sufficient to learn his duties." Read was even more unfit because he was a "man of violent passions and prejudices—and incapable of acting with the impartiality that the office demands."[37]

The same year, 1840, a St. Augustine newspaper denounced Joseph Sanchez's reappointment as marshal because he was a "'loco-foco' [a Democrat who advocated radical policies] and a *notoriously partisan prostituted office holder* of the late Van Buren Party...and a man who on every occasion openly manifested a *total disregard for the rule laid down by the present Administration for the regulation of officeholders.*"[38] The outburst had an impact. Within a year Sanchez was replaced by John Beard.

Politically appointed for a nonpartisan job, a marshal found it difficult to avoid criticism. That the criticism could have a sound base was seen in the case of U.S. Marshal Henry Wilson of the Southern Judicial District. An angry and prominent citizen of Key West complained to Washington authorities in 1829 that Wilson used the "power and influence" of his office against those who would "not yield to his...capricious and partisan whims and inclinations." Wilson continually showed both "*favoritism*...to his *party* friends" and "malice and hatred...to those who will not be subservient to him." The marshal's "general conduct," the petitioner complained, "is indecorous, immoral, and obnoxious.... The violence of his passions [s]ubjects to gross insults all those having business to contract with him."[39]

Throughout the territorial period the marshals' extensive geographical responsibilities crippled their efficiency. They were unable to meet the needs of all citizens at all times, or even some of them some of the time. Added to the large areas and making them seem even more unmanageable were the hazards of travel. The average citizen took none of these difficulties into account, and complaints against marshals for not being omnipresent were common.

In 1836 John Rodman, Port Collector for St. Augustine, berated marshal Samuel Blair of the Eastern Judicial District. Blair was in town, Rodman charged, only when court was in session, and his deputies were equally negligent. When needed they were not there, according to Rodman, or if there, they could not be relied upon to execute their duties efficiently. A native of New York, Rodman voiced an historic complaint by asserting that metropolitan authorities "are very prompt in doing their official duty, but I am sorry to say, that dilatory and negligent conduct is a prevailing vice in Florida." Blair discounted the accuracy of Rodman's premise, and reminded his superiors of the large area under his jurisdiction. Well he might, since the marshal lived forty miles from St. Augustine on the St. Johns River, and his district extended 150 miles from east to west and 200 miles north to south. He attended four different superior courts. Besides that, Blair claimed Rodman's charges were false and stemmed from the arrest of one of his slaves on charges that she was consorting with the Seminoles.[40]

On occasion, a marshal sought to trade his specific job but keep his profession by running for sheriff. Joseph Sanchez has been mentioned as serving first as U. S. marshal and then as sheriff of St. Johns County. Although born in Maine, Ebenezer Dorr became a dual law official in Florida. Between 1841-1846 Dorr served simultaneously as marshal of the Western District of Florida and sheriff of Escambia County.

The southern penchant for violence, combined with blatant disrespect for legal authority by some lawless Floridians, resulted in attacks on lawmen, including marshals, sheriffs, and their deputies.[41] The first law enforcement official murdered in Florida was U. S. marshal Leigh Read of the Middle District of Florida. Opposition to his general fitness for the job was widespread, but his death came as the result of a personal political grudge. When he was gunned down in the streets of Tallahassee in 1841 by Willis Alston, it was a matter involving families and unrelated to Read's official duties as marshal.[42]

Given the nature and danger of the marshals' jobs, not surprisingly they were sometimes accused of resorting to excessive force. In 1860 Jason A. Hemingway, a preacher from Columbia County, preferred charges against Elias E. Blackburn, marshal of the Northern District of Florida. The minister charged that Blackburn arrested him and forced him to leave his residence with "force and violence" that included "knives, pistols, sticks, staves, whips, and handcuffs...without any reasonable or probable cause." Further investigation revealed that a U. S. post office employee had charged the Reverend Hemingway with stealing letters from the mails.[43]

Although marshals remained important in territorial Florida, in many ways sheriffs emerged as more significant and identifiable figures in the public eye, even by the mid-1820s. The legislature consistently curtailed the marshals' functions even as it enlarged those of the sheriffs. The act of 1823 relating to marshals was repealed in 1824. A new law expanded the sheriffs' obligations by assigning them custody of all prisoners serving time under Florida's territorial laws. All business previously assigned to marshals was transferred to the sheriffs in individual counties. Even as they completed serving process in civil cases before the superior courts and collected their fees, the marshals were superseded by the sheriffs.[44]

Major changes affecting state and county officers came when Florida joined the Union. The transition involved profound administrative adjustments, and, more important, statehood created a difference in the psychological and emotional makeup of Floridians. Now when they voted, their ballots counted in national elections, and in Florida their votes elected the previously appointed territorial governor. Florida's written document, the St. Joseph constitution, provided lines of government and—slaves and free blacks excepted—guarantees of certain rights. Occurrences in neighboring states and the nation at large affected them more, and they had a voice in what happened. But there was no abrupt transformation. There remained a continuity in the lives of the people, and it was provided by the frontier environment and its restrictions. Transportation and communication remained limited. Not until the 1880s would Florida begin to smooth its rough edges (and, some would argue, not even then).

Yet, there were basic changes. As a state, Florida adopted a new judicial system. The constitution—drafted in 1837 by the convention in St. Joseph, ratified by the people in 1839, but without force until 1845—dropped the territorial superior courts and replaced them with circuit courts.[45] The law of 1845 that organized circuit courts contained a provision for sheriffs. The lawmen were still popularly elected for two-year terms, but their bonds ranged wildly from $2,000 to $20,000. The sheriffs became the circuit courts' executive officers, exercising all the powers held by the marshals in the territorial period. From 1845 forward, the sheriff or his deputy had complete charge of all the process in his county. Because Leon County housed the state capital, the sheriff there was also executive officer of the supreme court and served that tribunal's process.[46]

Soon, additional statutory provisions touched sheriffs. In 1848, for instance, a law of implementation specifically declared the clerk of the circuit court and the sheriff elected officers. They were to give bonds and securities and to serve two-year terms.[47] Florida continued to have U.S. marshals after 1845, but they were concerned with federal matters and no longer carried out some of the duties required of them in the territorial period.

It was necessary to have lawmen, be they U.S. marshals, sheriffs, or, in more limited capacities, justices of the peace. The constable was another historic figure who combined administrative work with that of a law officer. The courts established in 1824 (they met twice a year and justices of the peace were required to attend) were empowered to "appoint as many constables for their respective counties as they deem necessary and the county may require."[48] A more detailed law of 1827 defined a constable's duties. They were to be appointed by the county courts and had to take loyalty oaths and put up bonds of $500. The constable's primary task was to take precepts (written orders, warrants, or writs) and serve them on defendants. The constable's compliance was reinforced by the threat of a fine and loss of office should he fail to return an official document. A constable was authorized to give certain securities and, as a law enforcer, to apprehend and bring to justice felons and disturbers of the peace. He collected fees for his services, and had full power and authority to levy any execution or attachment and to serve and execute warrants or other process within his county.[49]

Laws in Florida sometimes contradicted each other, and those applying to constables illustrated that fact. In 1827, the year that had constables chosen by county courts, another law permitted magistrates (justices of the peace) to appoint them in their respective districts.[50] In 1855 a law applying only to Hamilton County provided that constables would be popularly elected at the same time as justices of the peace and in the same manner.[51]

Like other officials, constables had special duties. In an act of 1828 relating to "negroes and mulattoes," a constable was directed to give information against and prosecute any free black who kept or carried ammunition contrary to law.[52] More often his duties were administrative. Just as sheriffs and marshals summoned grand and petit jurors, constables summoned juries for justices of the peace.[53] Enacted in 1833, one law gave constables power equal to that of sheriffs and marshals in levying on and selling property, and another statute defined their jurisdiction and that of sheriffs in county courts.[54] The official's versatility was seen the next year when he, no less than a sheriff or marshal, was assigned the task of selling property seized from delinquent taxpayers. The auctions occurred in front of courthouses across the territory and made the constable a highly visible man.[55]

The position came with a measure of risk. In 1827 Foster Chapman, an Escambia County constable, was shot while trying to make an arrest. Another Escambia County constable was severely beaten when he tried to apprehend a hog thief. In 1832 Constable James B. Watts attempted to execute an order of the court on John Scott. The latter man "cocked and presented his pistol." A grand jury indicted the uncooperative Scott for resisting process during the Jefferson County superior court's November term. Scott was found guilty but fined only $1.00.[56]

> **PROCLAMATION**
> **BY**
> **GEORGE K. WALKER,**
> *Secretary and Acting Governor of the Territory of Florida.*
>
> WHEREAS, it appears by a verdict of a Jury of Inquest of the county of Jefferson, that one WILLIAM SAFFOLD, of said County, stands charged with the Murder of MARTIN W. CRAWFORD, of said county, by shooting him on the 14th day of the present month—And whereas it has also been certified to me, that said William Saffold has fled from justice:—Now, THEREFORE, in pursuance of law, I do hereby offer a Reward of TWO HUNDRED DOLLARS for his apprehension and safe delivery in any jail in the Middle District of Florida.
>
> And I hereby enjoin all Magistrates and Peace Officers to be vigilant in the apprehension of said fugitive, and bringing him to justice.
>
> Given under my hand at Tallahassee, this 24th day of July, 1834.
> GEORGE K. WALKER.
>
> ☞ Said Saffold is a man of red complexion, light red hair, bald on the top of the head, and about six feet high. {50-6w}

Proclamation for the arrest of William Saffold, July 24, 1834, by acting Governor George K. Walker.

Constables suffered the same personal financial woes as other lawmen. Like a sheriff, he could petition the legislature for help if reimbursement through normal channels was not forthcoming. In December 1827, Foster Chapman, the unfortunate Escambia County constable who had been shot in the line of duty, wrote the legislative council informing its members that he was a de facto jailer who had arrested prisoners at great distances from Pensacola. The "duty has been attended," he explained, "with much labor and expense." He often kept prisoners at his own risk and capital outlay, but had "never received any compensation whatever for his care or for feeding and maintaining prisoners...." In fact, "the state of the Territorial Funds have [sic] been such that no money could be obtained and his vouchers which might be necessary for obtaining the same has [sic] been left with Justices who have either died on removed from the country and left no evidence of the services rendered and the amount due."[57] There is no record that the legislative council ever reimbursed Chapman.

Already important in the territorial period, the constable remained a key figure when Florida became a state. After 1845, instead of being appointed for an indefinite term, taking a loyalty oath, and providing a bond of $500, the constable was appointed for a one-year term by the collecting justice (usually the justice of the peace) in each district. His bond was set between $500 and $1,500. The constable, like the sheriff, had his fees prescribed for him by the legislature.[58]

The economic collapse known as the Panic of 1837 severely hurt Florida's growth, and attendant problems (a crippling banking crisis, accompanied by widespread bankruptcy and foreclosures) were compounded by the Second Seminole War that lasted from 1835 to the early 1840s. Still, statehood promised better times, and the protection that was symbolized by the lawman's metal badge was powerfully re-enforced in 1845 by a cloth star in the U. S. flag that indicated Florida was the twenty-seventh state. On June 25, 1845, an enthusiastic throng braved temperatures in the nineties to see Democrat William D. Moseley take the oath of office as Florida's first governor. Then, on July 4, the official celebration of entry into the Union was held. There was a new surge of optimism among the people.[59]

 William D. Moseley served as governor of Florida, 1845-1849. (Courtesy of the Florida State Archives).

Notes for Chapter I

1. The President to Commissioner and Governor, May 23, 1821, in Clarence E. Carter, ed., *Territorial Papers of the United States*, 26 vols, XXII, 57.
2. Jackson has attracted a large body of historical works. See Robert V. Remini and Robert O. Rupp, *Andrew Jackson A Bibliography* (Newport, Connecticut, 1991). See Robert V. Remini's condensation of his three-volume biography, *The Life of Andrew Jackson* (New York, 1988). For Jackson in Florida see Herbert J. Doherty, Jr., "The Governorship of Andrew Jackson," *Florida Historical Quarterly*, XXXIII (July, 1954), 3-31.
3. For Jackson's ordinance see *Florida Territorial Legislative Council Acts* 1821. For the full ordinance see XX-XXII. Hereafter cited as *FLCA* with appropriate dates and pages.
4. The new police officers and deputies were Anthony Mier, Peter Benet, Roman Rogero, Matthew Solana, John Fontane, Andrew Papy, and John Pelliser. See Temporary Organization of St. Augustine, July 16, 1821, Carter, *Territorial Papers*, XXII, 120.
5. See, as examples, *FLCA 1829*, 108-109, 128-130, 76-77.
6. Ibid., 124-145. See especially 140.
7. Irene Gladwin, *The Sheriff: The Man and His Office* (London, 1974), 9-13, 383-384.
8. Ibid., see also Roger Wayne Smith, "The Medieval English Sheriff In The Reign Of King Henry II," Unpublished M. A. thesis, Florida State University, 1986, 1.
9. William Alfred Morris, *The Medieval English Sheriff To 1300* (Manchester, England), 2. See also Gladwin, *The Sheriff*, 15-33.
10. Ibid., viii.
11. Larry D. Ball, *Desert Lawmen: The High Sheriffs of New Mexico and Arizona, 1846-1912* (Albuquerque, 1992), 1.
12. Cyrus Harreld Karraker, *The Seventeenth-Century Sheriff A Comparative Study of The Sheriff In England And The Chesapeake Colonies 1607-1689* (Chapel Hill, 1930), vii.
13. Ibid., 147-15.
14. Ibid., 152-159.
15. See James M. Denham *"A Rogue's Paradise: Crime and Punishment in Antebellum Florida, 1821-1861* (Tuscaloosa, 1997), 26-27, 141-154; Herbert A. Johnson and Nancy Travis Wolfe, *History of Criminal Justice* (Cincinnati, 1996); Michael Hindus, *Prison and Plantation: Crime, Justice, and Authority in Massachusetts and South Carolina, 1767-1878* (Chapel Hill, 1980), 26-29, 203-204; Frank Richard Prassel, *The Western Peace Officer: A Legacy of Law and Order* (Norman, 1972), 26-30; Philip D. Jordan, *Frontier Law and Order: Ten Essays* (Lincoln, 1970), 109; Lawrence M. Friedman, *Crime and Punishment in American History* (New York, 1993), 28-29; David R. Johnson, *American Law Enforcement: A History* (Arlington Heights, Illinois, 1981), 1-9.

16. *United States Statutes At Large, 1822-1823*, 654-659.
17. See W. T. Cash, "William Pope DuVal," *Tallahassee Historical Society Annual*, I (1934), 10-13; and James Owen Knauss, "William Pope DuVal, Pioneer and State Builder," *Florida Historical Quarterly*, XI (January, 1933), 95-139.
18. Carter, *Territorial Papers*, XXII, 134, 171n, 422-423, 727.
19. *FLCA 1824*, 12.
20. Ibid., 212-218, see especially 216.
21. Ibid.
22. Ibid., *1834*, 19.
23. Ibid., *1822*, 171-172. See ibid., *1823*, 128. Still another law of 1823, 132-138, listed fees of various officials, including sheriffs, marshals, and constables. For similar acts see ibid., *1832*, 96-101, especially 98-99, and *1834*, 19-24, especially 20-21.
24. Julia Floyd Smith, *Slavery and Plantation Growth in Antebellum Florida 1821-1860* (Gainesville, 1973), 204, 210, mentions slave patrols only briefly. More detail can be found in Larry E. Rivers, *Slavery in Florida: From Territorial Days to Emancipation* (Gainesville, 2000). Depending on the state, patrols were closely tied to the county courts or to the militia. See Sally Hadden, "Law Enforcement in a New Nation: Slave Patrol and Public Authority in the Old South, 1700-1865," Ph.D. dissertation, Harvard University, 1993.
25. *FLCA 1822*, 181-185.
26. Carter, *Territorial Papers*, XXII, 45, 51 Benjamin Robertson was the original appointment for the Western District. His appointment was May 7, 1822. See "United States Marshals Service Middle District of Florida, List of United States Marshals in Florida." Document in possession of the authors.
27. James Forbes to the Secretary of State, July 14, 1821, ibid., 117.
28. James Forbes to Acting Governor William Worthington, March 5, 1822, ibid., 376-377.
29. Andrew Jackson to Acting Governor William Worthington, July 26, 1831, ibid., 135.
30. Frederick S. Calhoun, *The Lawmen: United States Marshals and Their Deputies, 1789-1989* (Washington, 1989), 2-3. See also Larry D. Ball, *The United States Marshals in the New Mexico and Arizona Territories, 1846-1912* (Albuquerque, 1978); Robert Sabbag, *Too Tough to Die: Down and Dangerous with U. S. Marshals* (New York, 1992); Johnson, *American Law Enforcement*, 96-97; and Prassel, *The Western Peace Officer*, 220-243. On U. S. Marshals in Florida see Denham, *Rogue's Paradise*, 141-145.
31. *FLCA 1828*, 59-61.
32. Ibid.
33. The marshals' duties were spelled out as part of a larger act passed June 28, 1823. See ibid., 64-66.

Chapter 1 - Sheriffs and Lawmen in Territorial Florida

34. Ibid., *1828*, 90.
35. Leslie A. Thompson, *A Manual or Digest of the Statute Law of the State of Florida, of a General and Public Character, in Force at the End of the Second Session of the General Assembly of the State, on the Sixth Day of January, 1847* (Boston, 1848), 592.
36. Charles Evans to the President, April 20, 1841, Carter, *Territorial Papers*, XXVI, 301.
37. William P. DuVal to B. Penrose, February 19, 1841, Carter, *Territorial Papers*, XXV, 272-273.
38. St. Augustine *News*, November 6, 1841.
39. John Whitehead to the Secretary of State, May 29, 1829, Carter, *Territorial Papers*, XXIV, 221-222.
40. John Rodman to the Secretary of State, July 23, 1836, and Samuel Blair to the Acting Secretary of State, August 25, 1836, ibid., XXV, 320-321, 328-331.
41. At the local level one town marshal was beaten up by a slave in 1846 when he attempted to arrest him. See Frank Hatheway Diary, January 25, 1846, Special Collections, Robert Manning Strozier Library, Florida State University, Tallahassee.
42. Read had killed Alston's brother in a duel. See James M. Denham, "The Read-Alston Duel and Politics in Territorial Florida," *Florida Historical Quarterly*, LXXVI (April, 1990), 442-443; see also Clifton Paisley, *The Red Hills of Florida 1528-1865* (Tuscaloosa, 1989), 100-102.
43. Warrant for the Arrest of Jason A. Hemingway, January 1, 1860, C. C. Yonge Papers, box 3, P. K. Yonge Library, University of Florida.
44. *FLCA 1824*, 173.
45. See F. W. Haskins, "The St. Joseph Convention; the Making of Florida's First Constitution," *Florida Historical Quarterly*, XVI (July, 1937), 33-43; (October, 1937), 97-109; (April, 1938), 242-250; XVII (October, 1938), 125-13 See also Dorothy Dodd, *Florida Becomes a State* (Tallahassee, 1945).
46. *Florida General Assembly Acts and Resolutions 1845*, 8-12. Hereafter cited as *FA* with appropriate dates and pages.
47. Ibid., *1847-1848*, 29-30.
48. *FLCA 1824*, 247-251.
49. Ibid., *1827-1828*, 49-55.
50. Ibid., *1828*, 91-104.
51. *FA 1855*, 47.
52. *FLCA 1855*, 174-179.
53. Ibid., *1828*, 147-150.
54. Ibid., *1833*, 30-34, 46-47.
55. Ibid., *1834*, 13-14. The day could be changed by mutual agreement between the erstwhile owner and county officials.
56. See *Territory vs. William Mimms*, 1827, Escambia County Case Files and Minutes

of the Escambia County Superior Court, Book I, 325, 343, 406; *State vs. Charles Brightly*, 1851, Escambia County Case Files; Minutes of the Circuit Court, Book A, n. p., Escambia County Courthouse, Pensacola; *Territory vs. John B. Scott*, 1832, Jefferson County Case Files. See also Jefferson County Minutes of the Superior Court, Book 1, 62, 76, Jefferson County Courthouse, Monticello.

57. Petition of Foster Chapman, September 3, 1827, Territorial Legislative Council, Unicameral, RG 910, series 876, box 2, folder 3, FSA.
58. *FLCA 1845*, 15; ibid, *1847*, 16-17.
59. William Warren Rogers, *200 Years of Independence Tallahassee Celebrates the Fourth of July, 1976* (Tallahassee, 1976). This sixteen page pamphlet notes that when a territory became a state, its star was added to the flag on the following July 4. See 4.

CHAPTER II

FROM STATEHOOD TO CIVIL WAR

After becoming a state Florida had scarcely more than a decade and a half before casting its fate with a new country, the Confederate States of America. In that period important developments took place regarding the sheriff and the evolution of his office, although on a larger scale, Florida did not establish a state penitentiary. In carrying out their duties sheriffs were governed by state laws which they interpreted to fit local conditions. Sheriffs were as provincial as their constituents, making his individual judgment and character vital to the county's well being.

During the first half of the nineteenth century improving prison systems was a powerful reform idea that became popular in the United States. Southern states such as Georgia and Alabama became a part of the move, but in Florida, safety and security were more important than reform. The new state, much of it still a frontier, faced the complicated process of building prisons, incarcerating prisoners, and keeping them locked up. Such demands took precedence over working out and implementing broad theories of penology.

Even so, a joint resolution of Florida's legislative council in 1841 recognized that the "peace and security of the country demand [that] a general and sufficient jail should be built in each of the judicial districts of this Territory." "Should be" was only a concept and vastly different from the real situation. Yet, the need was painfully there, and, looking for financial backing beyond their own resources, the Florida lawmakers asked Congress to appropriate $5,000 for a jail in each judicial district. The chance of receiving such largess was remote, but the legislative council went even further. Declaring that the "present good and future hopes of Florida" required a penitentiary, the solons instructed their Washington delegation to ask Congress to set aside two townships of land in the territory for such an institution. An agent of the governor would select the site.[1] Nothing came of the proposal.

Down to the Civil War Florida's sheriffs were almost entirely non-professionals. A sheriff carried out his responsibilities without much training and supplemented his income through additional work. Requirements for the sheriff's badge were mainly reliability, honesty, good character, and a willingness to take on dangerous tasks. Most sheriffs were also engaged in farming. Possession of bondsmen was a measure of wealth, and of the 160 sheriffs who served the state from 1845 to 1861, 70 owned slaves. Wealth or well-established credit was necessary to post the office's required bond. Some sheriffs doubled as tradesmen. Haley Blocker, sheriff of Leon County from 1851 to 1857, was a surveyor and also operated a livery stable in Tallahassee. Sheriff Thomas Land of Calhoun County (1852-1855) was a shoemaker. In Franklin County Clinton Thigpen was sheriff through most of the 1850s. He was a butcher by trade. The absence of a salary caused a number of potentially good lawmen to seek other fields of work.[2]

Fortunately, a number of men were not deterred by the low prospects for financial remuneration. Once the office became elective, another problem faced the would-be lawmen. Those seeking the post had to canvass their counties for votes. Capturing votes, like capturing criminals, required special talents that did not necessarily complement each other. Some men were equipped to do so, some were not, but, in any case, the turnover rate was high. Ralph Wooster's historical study of antebellum officials in the Gulf states revealed that few sheriffs served more than one term.[3]

Florida's experience was typical. Most surviving evidence points to a rapidly changing force. Only forty-three (roughly twenty-seven percent) of the state's antebellum sheriffs held office more than one two-year term. The greatest stability occurred in Nassau, Leon, and Gadsden counties where a total of seven sheriffs served the entire period. For reasons difficult to discern, continuity was difficult in the counties of Alachua, Duval, Hamilton, St. Johns, and, especially, Escambia which had nine. Sumter County had the most instability, averaging one sheriff a year from its founding in 1853 to the outbreak of the Civil War.[4] Their brief tenures may have been partly the result of having to perform duties that seemed unrelated to protecting citizens. Many sheriffs found themselves required to assess and collect taxes. For example, poll taxes designed to raise revenue had been enacted in colonial America, and that was the purpose of Florida's poll tax of 1823. The measure required all white males twenty-one and older to pay a poll tax of twenty-five cents. Owners (apparently regardless of their sex or age) of all "able bodied" slaves between seventeen and fifty-years-old had to pay a similar levy on their chattels. Collecting the poll taxes became the duty of the county sheriff. He had to give advance notice by way of newspaper advertisements citing the time and place where collections would be made. Eligible men and slaveowners had to register with the county clerk who, in turn, supplied the sheriff with a list of their names. At least the sheriff received in payment three percent of the amount he collected, and the clerk received two percent. Failure to pay meant that one's property could be seized and sold at public auction.[5]

The sheriffs' hard work in capturing felons resulted in widespread psychological disappointments when prisoners found it so easy to escape from Florida's inadequate prisons. The jails were so makeshift and insecure as to invite prisoners to breakout. Felons availed themselves of the invitation early and often. Jackson County's security system was an embarrassment. In early 1840, King Gill, a young man of nineteen whose actions belied his years (juvenile crime was not a major problem), killed William Raffenburg and was confined to jail in Marianna on a murder charge. He escaped within a few days, and Governor R. R. Reid offered a $200 reward for his capture. Bryant Meredith was jailed on a similar charge a few months later, and within a short time left an empty cell behind him. Meredith's flight was followed by the familiar governor's proclamation offering a reward for his capture. In 1844 John G. Stafford killed George W. Folsum, but fled the country before the Jackson County sheriff could arrest him. Despite the

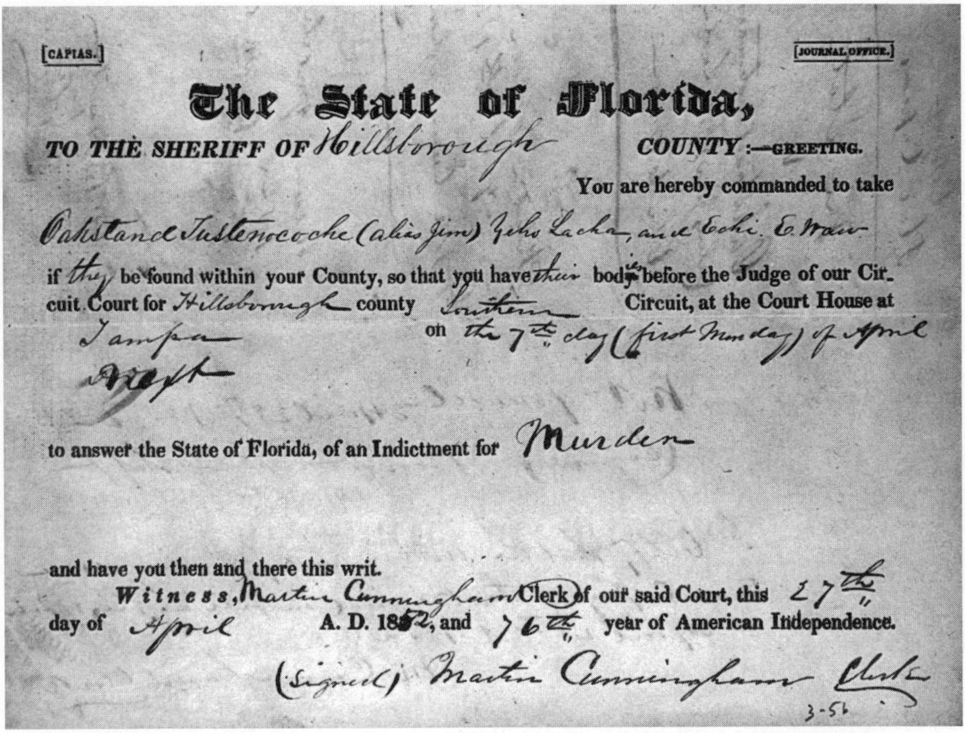

 Throughout Florida's antebellum years sheriffs served arrest warrants like the one depicted here. (Courtesy of the Florida State Archives).

rewards, few escapees were ever recaptured. It was too easy for them to flee the state or go to another Florida locale and adopt a new identity and a new life.[6]

Jails rarely gained mention in legislative council statutes or, later, in those of the legislature. An exception came in an 1831 law when a jail in Key West was provided for, but no territorial funds were mentioned.[7] Although Franklin County was created in 1832, provision for a courthouse and jail was not made until 1838. Construction began the next year and was paid for by a special local tax.[8]

Sheriffs and marshals were able to use the jails to supplement their incomes, although the amount earned was small. The lawmen were entitled to thirty-seven-and-a-half cents per day for maintaining prisoners, and were reimbursed twenty-five cents a day when keeping slaves taken by execution of process. A law stipulated that slaves were "allowed half a pound of salt meat or beef per day, and one peck of

Chapter 2 - From Statehood To Civil War

good Indian corn per week, or such other rations as may be equivalent thereto."[9] While citizens considered the pay for keeping prisoners adequate, the law officials did not. In 1840 Peter Gautier, who served as editor of the St. Joseph *Times* and U.S. marshal of the newly created Apalachicola Judicial District, argued unsuccessfully in his own publication that the amount should be raised to seventy-five cents per day.[10]

Florida's frontier status hampered measures to apprehend lawbreakers and made escapes easy. Poor transportation and almost nonexistent communication facilities further conspired to thwart the escapee's capture or recapture. Newspapers published gubernatorial proclamations providing information and offering rewards. Territorial and state executives struggled constantly to aid in the arrest of fleeing criminals and to inform the public of their misdeeds. Emergency situations required deputizing special guards and assistants. More often than not prisoners were transported back and forth from jail to court over extensive uninhabited regions. The result was a law of 1828 that permitted a justice of the peace to "direct the sheriff...to deliver offenders to the sheriff of the next adjoining county where a jail or place of safekeeping may be." If the sheriff needed extra guards, as he frequently did, he was authorized to hire them, but had to provide a documented record before being compensated.[11]

Florida lawmen received pay for many of their tasks, and most important was the hiring of guards and maintaining prisoners. Typically, Sheriff D. B. Cappleman of Marion County sent a note in 1850 to Comptroller Theodore Brevard explaining his contingent expenses for a term of the "Sircit Caort" [*sic*]. Cappleman asked the state to pay an extra "Gard" [*sic*] for Garding [*sic*] the prisoners in our jail which we consider unsafe without a gard [*sic*]. I hope you will remit the money as I have paid it out of my pockett [*sic*]."[12]

Not all attempts at obtaining reimbursement were successful. In 1857 a heated exchange occurred between James Johnson, a Marion County official, and Comptroller Brevard over compensation for Robert Bulloch. When Bulloch received no pay for guarding the Ocala jail, Johnson protested that only recently Brevard had paid someone else for a similar service. "Now Sir," Johnson remonstrated, "why you can allow this favoritism, I do not know, nor do I care—but I do say it is despicable in a public officer." He added, "I have little more to say [but your] favoritism shall be showed [sic] in every paper printed in the State of Florida."[13]

Columbia County Sheriff Arthur Wright's woes were revealing examples of a lawman's financial ordeals relative to jails, guards, and prisoners. On May 26, 1855, Circuit Judge William Forward specifically ordered Wright to hire an extra guard for the county jail: "Have several prisoners in jail for capital offenses and it [has] been made to appear they are desperate men with outside accomplices and will if possible break jail, and learning from you as well as the citizens generally that the jail is insecure without [a] guard, you are hereby authorized to employ a suitable guard." Forward directed Wright to consult with Solicitor James Baker about "the necessity and continuance of said guard." In an appeal to the comptroller for payment, Wright enclosed his correspondence with the circuit judge and the solicitor, noted that he had hired six guards at $1.50 a night, properly identified the guards, and put his expenses at $217.50. In seeking compensations the sheriff described the arduous responsibilities of the guards:

> They guarded...and watched the jail all night and in the morning until the people of the village was [sic] up and then commenced to Guard again in the evening before the night as to prevent the friends of the band from breaking [them] out of jail. The Guards could not be reasonable [sic] expected to guard all the time and sleep none.... In the night they were armed with guns on strict duty [;] in the day they were ready near by the jail at all times doing nothing else as their services was [sic] more at night than any other time to prevent this band of *robbers* from coming in the night and Breaking the jail and taking out their comrades.... I hope you will allow the account [because] the men done [sic] good and faithful service, and are entitled to their pay.[14]

Whatever the outcome of Sheriff Wright's appeal, there was no doubt about the strength of his argument.

William Forward served as Circuit Court Judge for the Eastern Judicial Circuit of Florida, 1853-1857. (Courtesy of the Florida Supreme Court).

James M. Baker served as Solicitor of the Eastern Judicial Circuit, 1853-1856 and Judge of the Supreme Circuit Court, 1859-1861.

Sheriffs spent a large part of their time transporting prisoners back and forth between a safe jail and court. On April 4, 1857, Alexander J. Braddock, sheriff of Nassau County, wrote Comptroller Brevard seeking immediate authorization for a draft from a Jacksonville bank. Braddock complained that shifting prisoners around "broak [sic] me entirely. Irish

Chapter 2 - From Statehood To Civil War

men in our county will brak [sic] the state of Florida down after a while in carrying them back and forth to Duvall [sic] Jail."[15]

In a similar vein, the Sumter County clerk wrote the comptroller on May 16, 1860, regarding Sheriff W. B. Story's unpaid accounts. "I am fully aware," he commented, "that there was considerable travel" involved in the murder case of Robert Noble. No one had been paid. "Mr. Story and I were of the opinion," the clerk wrote, "that Sheriffs were entitled to milage [sic] to and from the court house or place of holding court to every witness[']s house that was subpoenaed even if he subpoenaed everyone together." A problem arose when the state and the court issued subpoenas at different intervals: fees for travel time were doubled. The remedy was to serve the subpoenas at one term of court. The pessimistic clerk lamented that in "this section of the country where milage [sic] is charged it is altogether gueswork [sic] any way as none of the roads are posted. If Mr. Story can not get his pay this time he will certainly have to give the matter up."[16]

The need for jails that were physically secure, for sufficient guards, and for the safe transport of prisoners were overcome with the passage of time. Yet, other problems remained. Adequate housing for a growing number of prisoners coming from a growing state population would be a chronic problem in the next century.

In some ways Florida's transition to statehood brought dramatic change. In particular, the sheriff's job became more complicated. Overall there were duties common to all sheriffs, but they also varied from county to county. Sometimes a special fee was established for a particular county. In 1839 Sheriff Christopher H. Edwards was paid five cents a head for taking the census of Madison County. The sheriff of Hillsborough County was compensated in 1859 for summoning grand and petit jurors. Similar situations in other counties were not uncommon.[17]

With Florida as a state, the sheriff's role in the arcane world of taxation was increased. A general law of 1845 declared that if a tax assessor became unable to function (whatever the causes), the sheriff was to take over his duties. Beyond that, all sheriffs were declared ex-officio collectors of county taxes and were required to put up additional bonds. The lawmen were further obligated to conduct public auctions at the various courthouses for the property of delinquent taxpayers.[18]

Chapter 2 - From Statehood To Civil War

Collecting taxes bore heavily on sheriffs throughout the antebellum period, but 1859 was especially troublesome. In that year the sheriff of Wakulla County was affirmed as the ex-officio tax assessor and tax collector; he was given the same designation in Lafayette, Taylor, and Broward counties, and in Escambia County he was assigned the duty of collecting the road tax. It seemed abnormal when Calhoun was declared a county where the office of sheriff was specifically separated from that of tax assessor and tax collector.[19]

As a state, Florida broadened its fee schedule for sheriffs. Beginning in 1847 the expanded area of process, as well as other duties, was itemized. More than ever the sheriff became the instrument of enforcing laws that reflected raw frontier punishment, and fees were his payment. For whipping a prisoner under court sentence he was paid two dollars. The lawman got the same amount for containing a person in a pillory (a device with holes for the head and hands in which petty criminals were locked and exposed to public scorn). His fee was upped to three dollars for nailing a prisoner's ears to a post and to five dollars for branding. The ultimate punishment, hanging, commanded a fee of ten dollars.[20]

The expanding labors of a Florida sheriff could be traced through the acts of the legislative council and, later, the state legislature. The lawmaking body enacted statutes listing crimes and specifying their punishments. Some of the acts were later abandoned as impracticable or inapplicable, but each session always passed new laws with new punishments to replace the obsolete ones. The sheriff's responsibilities were always increased; they were never decreased. As early as 1824 the legislative council specified a long list of punishments for various crimes. To its credit the same session abolished imprisonment for debt. The historic penalty was done away with never to be reenacted.[21] The act of 1824 enumerating crimes and penalties was amended and expanded in 1827. An act of 1828 repealed existing legislation and dealt with the entire mode of criminal proceedings.[22] The trend continued, and in statehood the situation became one where a lawman, besides executing laws, had trouble knowing which laws to execute.

Life on the Florida frontier followed the cruel reality of survival of the fittest. The typical sheriff availed himself of existing fines and "special" fees to improve his frequently depleted personal finances. Such endeavors began during territorial days. Elections meant extra work and extra rewards. That fact was recognized in the 1820s—for carrying elections returns for the delegate to Congress more than ten miles the sheriff was compensated four cents a mile.[23] By 1838 each clerk of the county court had to provide the sheriff with a list of the road commissioners. The sheriff then had ten days to avoid a $50 fine by notifying the commissioners of their appointments. For every notice delivered he received fifty cents and the mileage allowed by law.[24] After 1845 whenever there was a presidential election the sheriff and the elections inspectors worked with the county poll books. Among other things, the sheriff took charge of the records two days before the votes were cast (his fee was $3). After the elections he delivered the poll books to the secretary of state's office and was paid ten cents a mile.[25]

Unless he broke the law to benefit himself, a sheriff had to depend for his income on statutes that might or might not work for his economic good. Other than through the accident of personal acquaintance, he had no one to speak for him or his interests to the Tallahassee solons. There was no statewide sheriffs association or lobbying group. A sense of justice in framing acts by the framers themselves was the sheriffs' main hope. After the legislature switched to biennial sessions in 1847-1849 (a practice adhered to, except for the Civil War years, through 1958), a sheriff had to wait two years for glaring and often unintentional flaws in acts to be corrected.[26]

By and large, a sheriff accepted most legislative acts affecting him as neutral and fair. No lawman objected to a statute of 1848 that forbade him, a deputy sheriff, or a constable from receiving fees for collecting money under execution or attachment unless the money had actually been collected and received. That same year the law enforcers universally approved an act making them responsible, if ordered by a probate judge, to act as administrators ex officio for the estates of deceased persons. That was because they received compensation for services rendered to a probate judge at the same rate as their services to circuit courts and county commissioners.[27]

41

Chapter 2 - From Statehood To Civil War

A sheriff had another recourse when he believed himself due a special fee. Like any citizen, he could appeal for a special legislative act addressing his case. Depending on the facts, he might be compensated. In 1848 Sheriff Alfred A. Fisher and Circuit Clerk Daniel McRaney of Leon County claimed that certain "articles" they had submitted to the circuit court entitled them to fees. When they were turned down, the two appealed to the legislature. That body ordered the state comptroller to examine their case and evaluate its validity.[28] Sometimes the report of a sheriff's payment was favorable but failed to explain why the decision was reached. In 1849 Jefferson County's Sheriff, James R. Tucker, was paid $12.58 in addition to his regular fees, but what the award was for went unrecorded.[29] Nor was it ever made clear why sheriff Joel T. Walker of Jefferson County merited a special act in 1857 awarding him $32.40.[30]

Mostly, the acts appropriating money to individual sheriffs were specific in their language. In 1850 the circuit judge of Washington County ordered Sheriff Levi F. Miller to confine a prisoner. The fee was $92.50. Sheriffs who were awarded sums after they left office considered the belated payments as being better late than never. Sheriff A. E. Geiger of Alachua County was given credit for $30 that he forwarded to the comptroller in Tallahassee. Since it never arrived, he was not reimbursed. Geiger finally collected in 1851 when he no longer wore a badge. In Jacksonville John B. Hardin broke out of jail before paying $155 in fines. His escape was not the fault of Sheriff Thomas Ledwith, but the Duval County sheriff was forced to begin paying Hardin's fines. The legislature disagreed, and had the comptroller return $83.33 that the grateful sheriff had already paid.[31]

Most of the special fees requested by sheriffs involved routine matters. In 1840, for example, the legislative council compensated the heirs of deceased Calhoun County Sheriff Francis A. Ross who was still owed money when he died for "apprehending and guarding certain persons charged with offenses against the laws of the territory."[32] In 1855 Haley T. Blocker, sheriff of Leon County, collected $112 from the state for hiring extra guards and paying them with his own money. He had a slightly more difficult time the next year when a law allowed him fifty

TRANSFERABLE ONLY BY WRITTEN ENDORSEMENT.

N₀. 24 152 **STATE WITNESS' CERTIFICATE.** $ 12.35

COUNTY OF HILLSBOROUGH,
...... Fall ...... Term, 1859.

This Certifies THAT THE STATE OF FLORIDA IS INDEBTED TO Richard V. Buffum, in the sum of Eight 75/100 Dollars for attendance in the Circuit Court of said County at said Fall Term, 1859 as a WITNESS in behalf of the State vs. George M. Buckley from the 19th to the 25th day of October inclusive 1859. Mileage 36 miles @ 10¢ $3.60.

And in Testimony that the said Claimant did actually, to our personal knowledge, so attend and serve; and that said Claimant has not, to our knowledge, any claim against the State for attendance, during any part of said period, in any other capacity; and that the said amount is legally, and in all respects justly due, we, the undersigned, Sheriff and Clerk of said County, have hereunto set our hands, and I, the said Clerk, have also hereunto set my Seal of Office, this 12th .... November .... 1859.

William A. Lively, Clerk.
By J. M. Hayman D.C.
Wm. S. Spencer, Sheriff.

Sheriff William S. Spencer of Hillsborough County authorizes payment for witness. (Courtesy of the Florida State Archives).

William S. Spencer served as sheriff of Hillsborough County, 1858-1865 and was sheriff when the warrant was issued. (Courtesy of the Hillsborough County Sheriffs Office).

cents a day for maintaining a lunatic for three months. The state paid, but required the comptroller to audit Blocker's account for claims of $8.25 to buy clothes for the afflicted man.[33] Sheriff Blocker learned that persistence, plus having a strong argument, paid off. When the state supreme court refused to him per diem for his services to the justices in the mid-1850s, Blocker appealed to the legislature. An act subsequently directed the comptroller to pay him the per diem.[34] The sheriff of Santa Rosa County, J. C. McArthur, had far less difficulty in 1859 collecting $612 from the state for supporting a certain deranged person under court order.[35]

Overall, the hiring of supporting personnel was allowed without protest. After he left office Sheriff John H. Patterson of Madison County was repaid $52 for hiring extra bailiffs under orders from a circuit judge.[36] State payments were usually forthcoming without legislative action. Former Santa Rosa County Sheriff Isiah Cobb received $82.10 in 1856 for his earlier labors in taking the census of county children.[37] Even so, to gain relief a lawman had to present the necessary vouchers, receipts, and other documentary evidence to support his plea. For instance, in 1859 Sheriff J. C. Crosby of Escambia County had to offer documentary evidence before he was paid for committing prisoners to jail.[38] The legal backing was welcomed by lawmen when they received commissions after making levies by executions, or when a sheriff obtained his percentage for protecting and disposing of wrecked and derelict goods.[39]

If the fee system was a large part of any sheriff's economic salvation, it could also play a role in his frustration and damnation. The problem was that the fee system confounded those with little education or administrative skills. Account schedules had to be filled out carefully, certified by a judge, and forwarded to the territorial auditor or state comptroller for reimbursement. Through inept or neglectful record keeping some sheriffs lost out on fees they rightfully deserved: the most unfortunate ones left office with their accounts in arrears.

Newly elected Sheriff J. C. Stewart of Orange County became hopelessly lost. On New Year's Eve 1859 Stewart wrote state Comptroller Theodore G. Brevard from Mellonville that instead of for-

Hernando County Sheriff Charles J. McMinn authorizes the payment of a juror. (Courtesy of the Florida State Archives).

warding his official accounts directly to Tallahassee, he had sent them to St. Augustine for the circuit judge's approval. The sheriff wanted the balance due him "half at a time, as there is so much uncertainty in the mails at this time." There were problems, Stewart explained, in collecting taxes. He complained that many people moved out of the county just before "pay day" confronted them. As to where they had gone, "some of [them] have moved into unorganized counties and some have left the state." Stewart admitted that he was "behind the time of settlement with the Treasury but it is not from choice, the causes are that I have had too much to do in the sheriff's office in criminal cases that I have been compelled to leave the revenue settlement until [now].... At this time I am on my way with a criminal to Ocala jail."[40]

Sheriffs dismissed critics who accused them of scrambling for fees. They pointed out that lawmen were subject to possible imprisonment and a fine of $100 for each failure to execute or return process. Since the 1820s they and marshals had faced dismissals from office, fines, and imprisonments for a litany of illegal acts: stealing, embezzling, and aiding in escapes, not to mention extortion and the vast range of "malpractice."[41] Nor, they claimed, should there be criticism when there was special compensation for a sheriff's services that did not involve people. In the late 1850s when Sheriff James M. Smith obtained and guarded medical and surgical aid for a prison, the state paid the Gadsden County lawman $131.50 for his work.[42]

As local officials sheriffs were able to have their pleas answered or at least heard by fellow Floridians who made up the legislature. That was not true of U. S. marshals who were dependent on Washington to answer their requests for extra compensation. Even so, there was one case whose details demonstrated Florida's concern with the welfare of a federal officer. As has been seen, U. S. marshals were far less numerous than sheriffs and became secondary in importance to them after 1845. Still, they were involved in federal cases and were court officers in federal lawsuits. In the late 1850s thieves forcibly entered the Tallahassee offices jointly occupied by the clerk of the circuit court and the district U. S. marshal. Both the circuit clerk and the marshal, who rented the space, were robbed of valuable records. The U. S. judge for the northern district ordered Elias E. Blackburn, resident marshal, to make the repairs necessary to increase security.[43] Because no contingency funds were available, Blackburn spent $178 of his own money. When the marshal presented his bill to the Washington accounting offices, payment was refused. The amount of $178 was a considerable sum, and since Blackburn was the loser, the State of Florida took action. With understandable self-righteousness the legislature passed a joint resolution declaring its unwillingness "that a faithful public servant [Marshal Blackburn] shall suffer so great [an] injustice" and granted him the amount of his expenditures. Florida's congressmen and senators were instructed to demand that the federal government refund the state $178.[44]

It was assumed that sheriffs and clerks of the circuit court would

Elias E. Blackburn (1808-1872), served in the Florida legislature before his appointment as United States Marshal in 1854. (Courtesy of Mrs. Frederick Lee Cook).

maintain their offices in county seat towns, but applying such logic was not always desirable or possible. Beyond assumption and rationale, there was the law. An act of 1834 specifically stated that the sheriffs and clerks of the court were to keep their offices in the county seats.[45] Still, that was a territorial law, and that confusion could sometimes cloud the issue was seen in Orange County where circumstances were at best uncertain. Mosquito, as Orange County was known prior to 1845, first boasted county seats at New Smyrna and also at Enterprise (Benson Springs). The future Orlando (Fort Gatlin) came into existence in 1838 as a military post and later as the homestead of Aaron Jernigan and his family. With the Second Seminole War in progress, such records as the county had were removed in 1838 to St. John's County for safekeeping. They were not returned until 1843.[46]

Holmes, established in 1848, had its county seat located at Hewett's Bluff. The problem of having no town there was solved when the new post office was named Cerro Gordo (the name honored General Winfield S. Scott's defeat of Santa Anna the year before in the Mexican War). Eleven years later Bonifay became the permanent county seat. Throughout the antebellum period Holmes was the only county that permitted the sheriff and the clerk of the circuit to keep their offices in a town other than the county seat.[47]

In compartmentalizing the separate demands of his job, the Florida sheriff, not unexpectedly, found law enforcement the most difficult category. An unusual law, one that may have been enforced, applied only to St. Johns County. There, a slave or slaves could not hunt hogs or cattle on Sunday unless accompanied by a white person. The statute was intended to placate white owners who claimed that slaves used their day off to steal livestock.[48] Statewide, sheriffs were supposed to see to it that no white person played "cards or shot dice with a Negro, Mulatto, Quadroon, or any other persons of color." If caught, the white man was fined from $20 to $500 or jailed from thirty days to three months.[49] In Monroe County a state law that had only local application required the sheriff to make sure that all stores were closed on the Sabbath. Should they remain open the lawman was entered as the prosecutor against them and received a fee of $10 with each conviction.[50]

Detailed and demanding administrative duties aside, the Florida sheriff faced the constant danger of being wounded or killed while keeping the peace. In 1854 Robert Potts assaulted Jefferson County's sheriff Joel Walker and his assistant Asa May at Monticello. They testified before Justice of the Peace Thomas Chance that Potts "drew his knife against them and told them he would have them before he left town." Once Walker and May finally took Potts into custody, Judge Chance remanded him to "jail, he being in a state of intoxication and entirely unmanageable."[51] Sometimes juries failed to support lawmen. In 1850 an Escambia County grand jury indicted John Kelly for rescuing and "putting at large" a man named James A. Guilford who was in the lawful custody of Sheriff A. J. Collins. Although found guilty of "Rescuing Prisoner from Sheriff," Kelly was fined only five cents.[52] Law officers were sometimes dismayed and angered at the lack of compassion they received when wounded. Sheriff John Delany, a law officer in Alligator (Lake City), sought compensation after he was shot while performing his duty. He wrote Governor Thomas Brown in 1841, "I have received your letter and was disappointed at not being released of my costs when others been so—and especially...one J. Tyne who attempted my life and has rendered me a cripple for life, by shooting me in the hand with a pistol."[53]

The first Florida lawman to suffer death in the line of duty in the post-colonial era was a sheriff. Lewis Williams, believed to have been sheriff of Jackson County, was shot and killed in 1844 by William Watson, a member of a notorious gang led by James Avant.[54] If Williams was a lawman, then Watson, who escaped and assumed a new identity in Alachua County, holds the dubious distinction of killing two Florida sheriffs. Though seriously wounded in the shoulder, Watson lived to kill another day. Before that occurred, Watson's partner Avant met the kind of fate that he had fashioned for himself. Avant and an accomplice were captured in a swamp by a self-appointed posse of Jackson County citizens, taken to Marianna, and hanged on June 20, 1845 without a trial.

As fate would have it, on April 4, 1848, Watson (now known as Black) resurfaced to kill another sheriff—not in the line of duty—but in a poker game at a Newnansville inn. As the Jacksonville *News* reported on April 15, a dispute began during a card game between Watson (Black) and Alachua County Sheriff William Gibbons. When the sheriff "called for his pistols," Watson went out on the piazza and challenged Gibbons to follow him. A shot rang out and the party found Gibbons shot dead through the side. Watson fled the scene. Before fleeing himself, another man in the game admitted that Watson (Black) was actually his own son and had changed his name to Black to escape prosecution in Jackson County. A posse eventually apprehended Watson, identified him by the gunshot scar on his shoulder, and turned him over to the authorities for trial. Watson eventually escaped, however, and all accounts of his prosecution in the courts have been lost.[55]

In 1859 a deputy sheriff in Washington County, one John Joyner, was stabbed to death while trying to arrest Enoch Johns and his son during court proceedings in Vernon. Notified of the outrage, Sheriff G. F. Gainor organized a posse, and the fugitives were captured in Marianna. The outcome of the affair is unclear to historians, but it was clear to contemporaries that the deceased lawman left a "large family with scarcely any means of support."[56]

Given the difficulties, uncertainties of pay, and dangers to life and limb, some citizens were unwilling to become lawmen. Even so, many did, and Florida benefited from their service. Despite imperfections in the system sometimes the sheriffs received public recognition for efficient service. By the 1850s many Floridians had begun to acknowledge, if not fully appreciate, their lawmen. On March 5, 1853, the editor of the Pensacola *Gazette* published a "tribute justly due" to Escambia County Sheriff Francis Maury. The upholder of the law was commended for "dispatch[ing] with promptitude and fidelity...all business that has been confided to him." Such praise was far better than condemnation, even though it fell short of what might have been said of Maury and others like him. The majority of Florida's lawmen took their jobs seriously and worked hard to perform them.

Since the 1820s the southern and the northern sections of the United States had been drifting apart. Their differences included issues as specific as the tariff and as general as industrial versus agrarian concepts of society and culture. Yet, nothing was so divisive as the issue of slavery. By the latter 1840s the slave South and the Free North found their animosities exacerbated by the entry of the West into the equation. The decade of the 1850s witnessed a series of crises—the Compromise of 1850, the Kansas-Nebraska Act that resulted in "Bleeding Kansas," the rise of militant abolitionism, the publication of Harriet Beecher Stowe's *Uncle Tom's Cabin*, John Brown's raid, the Dred Scott decision—all tied to the question of slavery. The coming presidential election of 1860 would decide, many people thought, the future of the republic. The long discussed possibility of secession with its distinct

A PROCLAMATION.

STATE OF GEORGIA;
By George W. Crawford, Governor of said State.

HAVING received information that a murder was committed on the first day of August, in the County of Lowndes, upon the body of Samuel Maulden, by DAVID W. KING, who has fled from justice, I have thought proper to issue this, my Proclamation, offering a reward of ONE HUNDRED DOLLARS to any person or persons, who may apprehend and deliver said fugitive from justice to the Sheriff or Jailor of Lowndes County.

And I do, moreover, charge and require all officers civil and military, to be vigilant in endeavoring to apprehend the said King, in order that he may be tried for the offence with which he stands charged.

GIVEN under my hand and the great seal
L. S. of the State, at the Capitol, in Milledgeville, this 15th day of September, A. D., 1845.   GEORGE W. CRAWFORD.

By the Governor:
N. C. BARNETT, Secretary of State.

DESCRIPTION.

The said King is about twenty-three years of age, thin visage, swarthy complexion, blue eyes, dark hair, has a down look, and is about six feet high.

In addition to the Governor's reward, we will pay

250 Dollars

for the delivery of said David W. King to any one of us, or the Sheriff or Jailor of Lowndes County.

The "FLORIDIAN" will please copy for six months, unless otherwise instructed, and forward account to the subscribers, at Grooversville, Ga., for payment.

☞The New-Orleans "PICAYUNE" will please copy weekly, for two months, unless otherwise instructed, and forward account as above.

ABRAHAM MAULDEN,
JAMES GROOVER,
THOMAS J. DENMARK,
MALACHI GROOVER,
JOHN LEE,
J. S. GROOVER.

Grooversville, Georgia, Oct. 14, [21,] 1845. 6m

Proclamations by out-of-state governors like this one for Georgia fugitive David W. King issued by Georgia Governor George W. Crawford, appeared often in Florida newspapers. (Tallahassee Florida *Sentinel*, November 4, 1845; Tallahassee *Floridian*, November 1, 1845).

$100 REWARD.

PROCLAMATION BY JAMES E. BROOME, GOVERNOR OF THE STATE OF FLORIDA.

WHEREAS it has been made known to me that ELY STEPHENS, charged with the murder of JOHN STEWART, has absconded, and is a fugitive from justice,

Now, therefore, I, JAMES E. BROOME, Governor of the State of Florida, by virtue of the authority vested in me by law, do hereby offer a reward of one hundred dollars for the apprehension of said Stephens, and his safe delivery to the Sheriff of Hillsborough County.

Mem.—Said Stephens is about 5 feet 8 inches high, of dark complexion, black hair and eyes.

Witness my hand and the Great Seal of the State of Florida. Done at the [SEAL.] Capitol, in the City of Tallahassee, this 17th day of May, A. D. 1854.
JAMES E. BROOME,
Governor of Florida.

ATTEST:—F. L. VILLEPIGUE,
Secretary of State.

May 29, 1854.   29   3t

☞ *Sentinel*, Tampa *Herald* and Ancient City publish 3 times.

Proclamation for the arrest of Ely Stephens, a fugitive from Hillsborough County. (Tallahassee *Floridian*, May 20, 1854).

51

Chapter 2 - From Statehood To Civil War

potential of Civil War had become probability. It seemed that the fate of the nation lay with the election's outcome. The Civil War that had been predicted did come, and Florida's participation in it was limited but significant. The conspicuous role that the sheriffs played during the four years of conflict (1861-865) was about to unfold.

Florida on the eve of the Civil War.

Notes for Chapter II

1. *FLCA 1841*, 70.
2. U. S. Manuscript Census, Population, 1850, Leon, Calhoun, and Franklin counties.
3. Ralph Wooster, *People in Power: Courthouse and Statehouse in the Lower South* (Knoxville, 1969), 162-163.
4. See Denham, *A Rogue's Paradise*, 146-147.
5. *FLCA 1824*, 206-233. In neighboring Alabama the poll tax on slaves was that state's major source of income for the antebellum period. See J. Mills Thornton III, *Politics and Power in a Slave Society Alabama, 1800-1860* (Baton Rouge, 1978), 100-101.
6. See Jerrell H. Shofner, *Jackson County, Florida–A History* (Marianna, 1985), 170; Denham, *Rogue's Paradise*, 159.
7. *FLCA 183* 28-29.
8. Ibid., *1838*, 62; ibid., *1839*, 30.
9. Tallahassee *Floridian*, March 6, 1832, citing act of the *FLCA*.
10. St. Joseph *Times*, January 8, 1840.
11. See "An Act for the Apprehension of Criminals and the Punishment of Crimes and Misdemeanors," section 7, in John Duval, *Compilation of the Public Acts of the Legislative Council of the Territory of Florida Passed Prior to 1840* (Tallahassee, 1840), 162-163.
12. D. B. Cappleman to Theodore W. Brevard, December 22,1859, State Comptrollers Correspondence, RG 350, series 554, box 2, folder 5, FSA.
13. James H. Johnson to Theodore Brevard, August 21, September 10, 1857, box 2, folder 2, ibid.
14. William Forward to Arthur Wright, May 26, 1855, and Arthur Wright to Theodore W. Brevard, October 22, 1855, Comptrollers Vouchers 1846-1862, Criminal Prosecutions, RG 350, series 565, box 1, folder 6, Columbia County, FSA.
15 A. J. Braddock to Theodore Brevard, April 4, 1857, State Comptrollers Correspondence, RG 350, series 554, box 2, folder 2, FSA.
16. David Leigh to T. W. Brevard, May 26, 1860, State Comptrollers Correspondence, RG 350, series 554, box 2, folder 6, FSA.
17. *FLCA 1839*, 56; *FA 1848-1849*, 22-23.
18. *FA 1845*, 25-32.
19. Ibid., *1859*, 53, 138-139, 62, 52.
20. Ibid., *1846*, 13-15.
21. *FLCA 1824*, 206-233; 174-178.
22. Ibid., *1827-1828*; ibid., 91-92.
23. Ibid., *1828*, 248-253.
24. Ibid., *1838*, 8.
25. *FA 1846*, 7-10.

Chapter 2 - From Statehood To Civil War

26. Ibid., *1847-1848*, 1-2.
27. Ibid., 32, 28-29.
28. Ibid., 58. There is no record of the comptroller's decision.
29. Ibid., *1848-1849*, 102-103.
30. Ibid., *1856*, 67.
31. Ibid., *1850-1851*, 168-169.
32. See St. Augustine *Florida Herald and Southern Democrat*, September 11, 1840. In 1841 both the governor and the legislative council ordered payment of $250 to Leon County sheriff Alfred A. Fisher for renting a room, using it as a jail, and guarding two prisoners four years earlier. See ibid., November 26, 1841.
33. *FA 1855*, 39.
34. Ibid., *1859*, 76.
35. Ibid., *1858*, 159-160.
36. Ibid., 137.
37. Ibid., *1856*, 64.
38. Ibid., *1859*, 102. The money was for putting in jail certain "Negro thieves."
39. Ibid., 19, and ibid., 20-21.
40. J. C. Stewart to T. W. Brevard, December 31, 1859, State Comptrollers Correspondence, RG 350, series 554, box 2, folder 5, FSA.
41. *FLCA 1834*, 48-78, and see especially 6, 64. See ibid., 27-44.
42. *FA 1858*, 134.
43. Ibid., *1859*, 152.
44. Ibid.
45. *FLCA 1834*, 13-14.
46. Ibid., *1838, 14-15*; ibid., *1842*, 2 Mosquito was divided in 1856 between Volusia and Orange. Jernigan, renamed Orlando the next year, became the county seat of Orange. The courthouse was an old, deserted two-room log house with a dirt floor and no windows. A permanent courthouse—one with one door and two rooms, one down and one up—was not built until 1863. See William Warren Rogers and Canter Brown, Jr., *Florida's Clerks Of The Circuit Court Their History And Experiences* (Tallahassee, 1996), 34-35.
47. *FA 1858*, 52. The act passed January 12, 1859. See also E. W. Carswell, *Homesteading The History of Holmes County, Florida* (Chipley, 1986), 320-321.
48. Ibid., *1853*, 137-138.
49. Ibid., *1854*, 62. The act passed January 6, 1855.
50. Ibid., 87.
51. Potts stayed in jail for eight days while awaiting bail. See *State vs. Potts*, 1854, Jefferson County Case Files. Potts pleaded guilty to one count of assault and battery and one count of assaulting an officer. He was fined five cents for each county. See Jefferson County Minutes of the Circuit Court, Book B, 16, 86, Jefferson County Courthouse, Monticello.

52. *State vs. John Kelly*, 1850, Escambia County Case Files, Escambia County Courthouse, Pensacola.
53. John Delany to Thomas Brown, January 27, 1851, Official correspondence of Thomas Brown, 1849-1853, RG 101, series 755, box 2, folder 1, FSA.
54. See Pensacola *Gazette*, October 12, 1844; June 28, 1845; *State vs. William Watson*, 1844, Comptrollers Vouchers, Criminal Prosecution, RG 350, series 565, box 3, folder 6, Jackson County, FSA. See also Proclamation for the Arrest of James Avant and William Watson, September 19, 1844, in Office of the Governor, Letterbooks 1836-1909, RG 101, series 32, vol 2 np, FSA.
55. See Jerrell H. Shofner, *Jackson County* (Marianna, 1985), 170; Proclamation for the Arrest of William H. Watson, alias James Black, January 5, 1849, in Book of Record (Proclamations), RG 156, Ser. 13, Box 1 no. 92, 74, FSA: Marianna *Florida Whig and Workingman's Advocate,* January 13, 1849; Tallahassee *Florida Sentinel*, January 9, 1849; Tallahassee *Floridian and Journal*, January 6, 1849; Jacksonville *News,* January 13, 1849; Pensacola *Florida Democrat and Workingman's Advocate*, January 18, 1849; Jacksonville *News*, April 15, May 13, June 3, 1848.
56. Tallahassee *Floridian and Journal*, April 2, 1859, quoting Marianna *Patriot*.

CHAPTER III

SHERIFFS DURING THE CIVIL WAR

When news reached Florida in November 1860, of Abraham Lincoln's election to the presidency, public meetings erupted simultaneously throughout the state. The Illinois rail-splitter's Republican party had pledged itself to halt the spread of slavery in the territories, although Lincoln's personal position on the issues facing the country remained unclear. He had stated that the nation could not continue to exist half slave and half free. Yet, throughout the campaign Lincoln had asserted that neither he nor his party had plans or the constitutional right to tamper with slavery where it already existed. Even so, Republicans opposed the "Peculiar Institution," and Lincoln's victory portended dire consequences for Florida. Like situations existed in other southern states. Even if the slave-holding states' immediate fears were exaggerated, the threat seemed stark and real to most white southerners.

The animus against Lincoln ran statewide to greater and lesser degrees. In Florida's plantation belt counties surrounding Tallahassee, where the institution of slavery undergirded the cotton-based economy, plans for resisting Lincoln's election began at once.[1] Indignation meetings in the Red Hill counties of Leon, Madison, and elsewhere championed secession as the only remedy for protecting southern rights. In late November 1860, Major Haley Blocker, Eighth Regiment, Florida militia, led his men into the Florida House of Representatives just as resolutions calling for a state convention to determine Florida's course "in the emergency now existing" were being considered. As the Tallahassee

Floridian reported, Blocker's command "numbering several hundred men, ...with trailed arms ...thundered forth one unanimous Aye in their favor [of secession]."[2] Springing from the yeoman ranks, Blocker had moved to Tallahassee in the 1840s, and in 1851 had been elected sheriff of Leon County. Serving until 1857, he left office with an excellent reputation. Blocker was one of many past and present sheriffs who would answer Florida's call to arms.

As respected citizens, Florida's sheriffs naturally played key roles inside and outside of their counties during the war. Some resigned their positions and marched off to fight. Others stayed home, struggling to maintain some semblance of civil government. Often, they were all that stood between their fellow citizens and anarchy. As the figure most responsible for enforcing the law, the sheriff occupied a critical position. In the event of a military threat to a particular locale, "home guards"—usually composed of men too old and boys too young for active service—were organized in Florida's towns and communities. The part played by the antebellum patrols as defensive units is not known, but it was limited. With so many men away in the service, fear of a slave insurrection was always present. Early in the war, the apprehension was high. In 1861 a Jefferson County newspaper called on Justice of the Peace James Ellenwood to have the patrol posted every night from 9 p.m. to 4 a.m.[3] As time passed and the insurrections did not occur the patrols became less active.

Sheriffs filled other vital functions, and that of collecting taxes soon emerged as one of the most important. In some counties sheriffs themselves were responsible for tax collection; in others they assisted. Massive conflicts cannot be waged without money, as Florida's wartime experience would prove. With funds needed for supplies, guns, ammunition, food, and soldiers' pay the sheriff's skills in collecting revenues were crucial.

When Florida seceded the state's population was 140,424. The figure included 77,747 whites of whom 41,228 were males and 36,619 were females. There were 61,745 slaves who were almost evenly divided between 31,348 men and 30,397 women. The 932 "free colored," an anachronistic minority, numbered 454 males and 478 females.[4] Most of the state's wealth was concentrated in the counties of Middle Florida, the area between the Suwannee and the Apalachicola rivers. The region was home to the majority of the state's slaves and slaveholders. Overall, owners of slaves were a minority, but they wielded political, economic, and social influence far in excess of their numbers.

In other parts of the state's sparsely settled counties, pockets of prosperity were evident. Hillsborough, Orange, Hernando, and four-year-old Manatee County (with the Seminoles removed or else pushed south to the Everglades after the Billy Bowlegs War of 1855-1858) attracted settlers. Some of the pioneers were cattlemen driving their herds south from Duval, Columbia, and Alachua counties. The East Florida migrants braved harsh frontier conditions to establish homesteads on tracts that had been vacant a decade earlier.

In 1860 Florida's present was good, and its future was even more promising. Older towns such as Key West, St. Augustine, Pensacola, Jacksonville, Lake City, Tallahassee, Quincy, Apalachicola, and Marianna prospered. Economic challenges were coming from newer towns—Tampa, Ocala, Gainesville, Mellonville, Enterprise, and Orlando. River travel helped link the state's urban centers, as did improvements in the rude system of roads. Even more important, railroads connecting Jacksonville with Lake City and Tallahassee to the west, and Fernandina with Cedar Key on the Gulf of Mexico, were beginning operations.

A war that Florida was not prepared to fight put prosperity on hold. The strains of military commitment would sorely test not only law and order but civil government itself in many Florida counties. Each county and locale was affected differently, but all felt the ever increasing shortages, first of luxuries, then of necessities. Not least of the home front shortages was manpower. "A Citizen," worried about conditions, wrote from the state capital in 1862. "In many counties in the State, both civil and militia offices have been vacated," he declared, "not from an disinclination on the part of those who hold offices to serve the public, but from patriotic ardor to serve during the war against the United States upon the battle field, in vindication of the sacred right of self government and constitutional liberty."[5]

Floridians watched many of their sons, brothers, fathers, kin, and friends leave home. The pain of death and deprivation eventually touched all. Factors such as periodic Union occupation of coastal areas, disaffection from the Confederate cause, and intra-county conflict among militant Confederate, passive Confederate, and pro-Union elements resulted in unsettled local conditions. Even before the war, outbreaks occurred in Calhoun, Duval, and Alachua counties. They were based largely on disagreements over secession, but often involved personal and other partisan issues. The difficulties damaged the fabric of society and exacerbated already uncertain conditions.[6] The discord served as prelude to what lay ahead.

From the last half of the twentieth century and into the next one, historians debated the degree of unanimity in Florida for secession. The degree of support or lack of support for the Confederacy was based on a complex mixture of partisan politics, differing definitions of patriotism, personalities, place of birth, length of residence in Florida, economic factors, and local conditions.[7] Nevertheless, on January 11, 1861, the delegates assembled at Tallahassee, having debated the issues, signed an Ordinance of Secession. Governor Madison Starke Perry, who relinquished the governor's chair to John Milton in October, began organizing the state's defenses.

Despite the excitement that followed secession—patriotic rhetoric, militia musters, forming units, procuring arms, obtaining uniforms, presentations of company flags, and the like—county government functioned much as it had before. This was especially true in the more prosperous counties with larger populations. In them the sheriff's office operated fairly efficiently during the Civil War. Up to the end of 1862, for example, Leon County's Sheriff Richard Saunders dutifully filed his accounts with the comptroller's office. In Tallahassee itself crime was under control and limited to minor disturbances. Despite the tranquility, a local editor exaggerated with his complaint in 1862 that a house break-in and other crimes—one involving a good watch that was stolen and another relating to the theft of chickens—were alarming, "Time was," he observed, "when a man might go to sleep and leave his house open with impunity in this city, but we fear that time has passed away."[8]

  John Milton served as governor of Florida during the Civil War, 1861-1865. (Courtesy of the Florida State Archives).

The relative order in Leon County was reflected by conditions in Jefferson, Jackson, and Madison counties at least until the war's closing stages. In all of them wealth, stability, and isolation from federal incursions kept civil government, despite shortages and increasing manpower demands, functioning. In Jefferson County W. H. Ellis looked after routine matters throughout 1861, holding sheriff's sales as required. When the county officers were elected in October, the office of sheriff was considered so desirable that at least four aspirants announced their candidacies. The Monticello *Family Friend* remarked: "There may be other gentlemen in the race. *Rumor* says there are, but we do not know it to be the case."[9]

Confederate sympathies were strongest in Middle Florida's plantation belt. Other counties contained more people who had opposed secession initially and remained unsure about the decision. Sometimes more anti-Confederate than Unionist, these citizens occasionally resisted with violence efforts by Confederate and state officials to collect taxes, impress property, and conscript troops. The disorder compounded law enforcement difficulties. Sheriffs were not conscription officers, but their jobs were made more difficult by those who refused to enter the armed forces. The sheriff of Walton County surely took some wry pleasure in developments there. In 1861 a number of men refused to organize a company of volunteers for any purpose other than home defense. At that, a group of women organized the Venetian Guards and offered to go anywhere to fight in defense of their liberties.[10]

United States soldiers, operating as part of the Gulf Coast Blockading Squadron (GCBS), aided and assisted anti-Confederate elements in coastal counties. By late 1862 Union raiding parties had gone ashore in Escambia, Walton, Washington, Taylor, Hernando, Hillsborough, and Manatee counties on the Gulf coast. A loyal Confederate from Levy County reported in 1864 that his area "was in a continuous excitement about deserters and their movements." He continued, "They pass through on their way to Cedar Key, almost every day, and it will not be long before they will have a heavy force here if they have not already got one."[11] The deserters concentrated on stealing slaves. Since slaves were valuable property, the sheriff's duties increased largely.

Chapter III - Sheriffs During The Civil War

Probing the Atlantic coastal areas of Nassau and Duval counties early in the war, the Federals gained permanent possession of Fernandina and St. Augustine during 1862. Jacksonville, dubbed the "Yankee Hell-Hole" by some Rebels, was occupied four times in less than two years.[12] In the south, Key West remained in Union hands throughout the conflict, although a sizeable number of its citizens refugeed to the Tampa Bay region rather than live under Union rule. United States naval operations on the St. Johns and St. Marys rivers made raids possible in St. Johns, Alachua, and Marion counties.[13] In those areas poverty, uncertainty of the currency, slave unrest, and growing disaffection made tax collection, law enforcement, and even rudimentary operation of county government nearly impossible.

By the war's second year deserters and "lay outs" (those who avoided service illegally) formed bands that sometimes disrupted civil government. Loyalty to the Union was part of their motive, but some dissidents harbored prior grievances against the constituted authorities. "These organized bands were especially strong in Lafayette, Walton, Taylor, Levy, and Washington counties...and in the part of Southwest Florida from Tampa south to Fort Myers," according to one historian.[14] Sheriffs and state officials stoically attempted to cope with the degenerating situation. In such a state of flux juries could not be called. Courts were often suspended. County business came to a standstill. Rows of blank pages in county record books for the years 1863-1865 appear paradoxical, their blankness telling an unwritten and grim story.

Still, letters and private correspondence between county sheriffs and authorities in Tallahassee demonstrate that many mundane affairs continued with little interruption in some counties. Sheriffs maintained jails and guarded prisoners. They opened and closed courts. They sold property under court order. Complying with directions from state authorities, sheriffs traveled to neighboring states with requisitions for fugitives. Governor Milton had more pressing demands but, when called upon, dutifully ordered county law enforcement authorities to apprehend criminals fleeing Florida.[15] Before the Civil War the General Assembly had passed a law requiring the state to pay for the maintenance of "lunatics" in asylums in other states. The statute remained in effect during the war, and various sheriffs transported the mentally afflicted to asylums in Georgia and South Carolina.[16]

Inevitably, wartime conditions caused confusion between sheriffs and Confederate authorities. When necessary, the governor served as arbitrator. An exchange of correspondence between Milton and a Confederate colonel illustrated the problem. When the colonel asked him to order sheriffs to incarcerate deserters in county jails, the governor hesitated. Ever mindful of local concerns not only of state's rights but also of "county rights," he replied that the law did not authorize him to act. Instead, Milton promised to "recommend to the county authorities with whom...the jurisdiction in this matter rests...that they comply with your desires in this respect and offer such assistance as they can for the efficient administration of the Confederate laws."[17] The potential problem of what to do with a civilian arrested by a military officer was easily solved. A state law required the arresting officer to turn his captive over to a commissioner of the Confederate states, to "the civil authorities" (sheriffs and their deputies) of the county, or to the authorities in the next county for examination.[18] With the unavoidable overlapping of authority between Confederate and state officials, there was need for clarification. That came in 1863 with a joint resolution by Florida's House and Senate. "The civil authority is the supreme and paramount power in this State, to which the military authority [*is*] in all cases strictly and absolutely subordinate," the solons declared.[19]

As noted in previous chapters, most sheriffs had groaned beneath the pre-war burden of collecting taxes and forwarding the revenues to Tallahassee. The practice continued and expanded during the Civil War. Some sheriffs blamed subsequent financial problems on the confused wartime conditions, but Santa Rosa County's Sheriff Isaiah Cobb had troubles that preceded the fighting. Cobb's failure to provide the comptroller with his revenues for 1860 prompted a series of threatening letters from Tallahassee. In March 1861 Comptroller R.C. Williams warned Cobb that unless he forwarded his "tax book" immediately, the "law makes it my imperative duty to [bring] suit...on your official bond...." Cobb employed one John Chain to answer the official. Cobb's candid explanation, wrote Chain, was the "deranged condition of the

63

County" which had "produc[ed] tightness in money matters,...provisions and supplies." The surrogate afterward speculated that Cobb's difficulties stemmed from "the result of his drinking too much liquor." Otherwise, Chain continued, Cobb was "a very Correct Officer."[20]

As often proved the case when sheriffs grappled with the state bureaucracy, the matter did not end there. Apparently acting as county clerk, the straightforward Chain next wrote Williams that Cobb blamed the comptroller's office. Cobb claimed to have forwarded his books to the state capital. "It is surprising that there is such crooked work about the Tax Book. I do not understand it," Chain complained. "There must be a screw loose somewhere." He predicted that more confusion would follow. "What is to be done about the Revenue of 1861—no one is acting— Cobb is doing the sheriff's business, [but] the coroner does not act—No election is ordered—What is to be done?" Despite Williams's continuing letters to Cobb and Chain, he received no adequate reply and decided to take action. In July he informed Chain that he had "written Mr. Cobb several times in regard to the Book of 1860, and indulged him a great deal, and I can not indulge him any longer." Williams added, "I am now compelled to order his official Bond sued upon for the Revenue of 1860 for Santa Rosa County."[21] Out of a sense of duty to the South, or to escape his financial burdens, probably both, Cobb enlisted in the Confederate army. He suffered death in one of the war's last engagements. According to a comrade's account, the former sheriff was "hit near the shoulder in the back as we were retreating towards the works."[22]

In counties where citizens were evenly divided over secession, sheriffs discovered that the word "justice" had several meanings, both personally and for the broader context of the times. Manatee County provides an example. It abutted the limitless Everglades where hiding places abounded. Most of its settlers clustered around the river settlement of Manatee (later Bradenton) or else near the Peace River in today's Hardee County where cattle herdsmen and small farmers had also taken up lands in the interior. Manatee County was large, settlement sparse, and travel difficult. Partisan politics further complicated county administration. James D. Green, elected sheriff in 1858, was a recognized leader. A cattleman with Unionist leanings, Green would become a Republican after the war. He continually clashed with secession-minded locals. Green's two years as sheriff were sandwiched between the administrations of W. H. Whitaker and John W. Whidden, who became Confederate stalwarts. Whidden, who was Green's brother-in-law, was actually elected sheriff, but was declared ineligible because he was not of age.[23] Under such circumstances tax collection was haphazard at best. In 1861 a county official wrote the comptroller explaining conditions. The sheriff was making an effort to collect back taxes but with little success. "Some of our people," a citizen explained, "object to paying taxes for 1860 upon the ground that there was no officer to assess and collect them."[24]

The Manatee turmoil persisted when a new sheriff took office. Joel J. Addison informed the comptroller that since the last election "this County has bin [*sic*] lying perfectly lawless." Seeking no "indulgences, only time," the new sheriff promised to do his best. He reminded the

Joel Jackson Addison served as Manatee County sheriff, 1861-1869. (Courtesy of Ferguson Addison).

Chapter III - Sheriffs During The Civil War

state official that the "County is large and the People badly scattered." In fact, the county's most prominent taxpayer had left the state, and others refused to pay simply because they had no money. Equally bad, Judge Thomas King had refused to preside in 1860 because, as one local man put it, "there was no legally authorized officer to open court." Addison faced numerous quandaries. If no taxes were collected in 1860, he asked, "can the new elected sheriff assess and collect for the year 1860. And if so ought he be required to furnish an additional bond to collect such taxes[?]." Lamenting the disarray of financial and legal affairs, he concluded, "I have nothing new to communicate to you from this distant and isolated place. War and rumors of War is all the topic at this present time."[25]

Addison and his deputy D. L. Hawkins persevered. Eventually Manatee County's revenue for 1860 reached Tallahassee. The order in county government proved short-lived. By 1864 the sheriff reported, "There is over half the Taxpayers of this County gone to the Yankees." As if that were not bad enough, Addison added, "One of our county commissioners has gone to the Yankees...."[26]

In antebellum times many sheriffs served brief tenures, but during the war a surprising number remained in office for the duration. The conscription laws partly explained the anomaly. Sheriffs and other county officers enjoyed exemptions from Confederate military service. Beyond that, the men considered their sheriffs' positions no less significant than those of soldiers and often just as dangerous. At least eight lawmen remained in office the entire four years of the conflict. Sheriff James J. Ward of Lafayette County held office from 1860 to 1865 in adverse conditions in a divided county. Lafayette received heavy criticism from some quarters for its disloyalty to the Confederate cause. "A Citizen," who strongly resented such slanders, wrote the Tallahassee *Floridian & Journal* in 1863. He admitted that in local elections Unionist candidates drew strong support. Yet, according to him, that did not mean disloyalty "because [some] men will not vote for those strong advocates of secession. I do not call them Union, but, on the contrary, advocates of justice."[27]

Alachua County's S. W. Burnett, Hillsborough County's William S.

Spencer, and Holmes County's Daniel J. Brown occupied their offices from 1857 to 1865. Richard Saunders, the successor to Leon County's Sheriff Blocker, upheld the law from 1857 to 1867. Sheriffs Daniel Williams and Edward Jordan (Taylor County) manned their posts from 1859 to 1865, although both saw temporary duty in military units. Such men are part of the little known record of Florida sheriffs who were exemplars of the positions they held. Yet the case of Alexander Bell, sheriff of Hamilton County, illustrates the ironic twists and turns that befell lawmen who had to deal with the sometimes contrasting demands of their private convictions and their public duties.

Bell's official story began with his election as sheriff in 1859. Although a captain in the Florida militia and a veteran of the recent Seminole war, he never served in any of the numerous Confederate units organized in his region. Some speculated that he opposed secession. Though Bell's two younger brothers were Confederate soldiers, he never openly supported the southern cause. Even his precise tenure as sheriff is unclear. Some evidence suggests that Bell ceased his official functions in the war's later stages. His situation was further complicated by sharp divisions of loyalty in Hamilton County. Perhaps a majority of residents favored the Confederacy, but one observer insisted that it was "the strongest Union county in the State." In the ensuing four years of competing allegiances Sheriff Bell struggled to maintain stability. He provided food and other services to the suffering families of Confederate soldiers and was himself listed among the war refugees at Cedar Key when the conflict ended. Although branded a radical sympathizer, Bell remained a life-long Democrat. As a final irony, one of his Confederate veteran brothers, Thomas Bell, served as Hamilton County sheriff during Reconstruction—as a Republican.[28]

The disruptions of wartime Florida sometimes impacted directly on a sheriff's tenure in office. Sheriffs in Brevard, Clay, Franklin, Gadsden, Jackson, Levy, Liberty, Marion, Nassau, and Orange counties either died in office, were killed during the war, were forced out of office by Union occupations, or were defeated in one of the few normal wartime elections. When a sheriff failed to appear in court for whatever reason or failed to send a deputy, the circuit judge was empowered to

Chapter III - Sheriffs During The Civil War

appoint a successor with all the powers of the missing lawman.[29] The sheriff of Duval County was elected in 1863, but because he "had been in the enemy's lines since February 1864 and [was] still there with no prospect of returning," a special election was held in October and a new official took over.[30]

Of the sheriffs who died while in uniform, Jonathan C. Stewart of Orange County was unrivaled for the difficulties that attended his career. A native of Ware County, Georgia, Stewart resided in Hamilton and Marion counties before settling in Orange County in 1854. An able public servant, Stewart still was unable to avoid the pitfalls that could beset a sheriff.[31] In 1858 the lawman became embroiled in a troublesome case involving a man named William Tyler. Ultimately convicted of manslaughter in April 1860, for his part in a "general fight" at the Orlando post office, Tyler was fined $200 and sentenced to thirty days in jail.[32] Because the county had no such building, the judge ordered Sheriff Stewart to transport the convicted Tyler and several other suspects to the Marion County jail in Ocala.[33] Tyler escaped and fled the state.

The unfortunate Stewart was held responsible for the unpaid fine and court costs amounting to well over $600. A court order levied against Tyler's Orange County property pitted Stewart and the state against other claimants for the estate sale money. "There is [sic] Individual claimants as well as the state," Stewart recorded, "& until the judge renders his decree in the matter it is quite uncertain whether the state gets any part of it or not—consequently my request to him [was] not to mix up that claim with my other current business, that when it was settled it could & would be broght [sic] in if the individual claimants did not get it." Stewart thereafter sparred with the comptroller in a futile attempt to gain satisfaction from the state. Finally, the legislature intervened to end the sheriff's private war with Florida's officialdom.[34]

Influenced by Stewart's problems and other pending cases involving Florida's lawmen, the legislature soon felt itself compelled to pass a law authorizing the comptroller to relieve "sheriffs and other ministerial officers of the court against whom charges for the non-collection of fines and forfeitures had been made...." Circuit court judges had to cer-

Jonathan Clay Stewart served as Orange County sheriff, 1855-1861, before entering Confederate military service in 1861. He died from wounds sustained in battle in the fall of 1862, sometime between the battles of Antietam and Second Manassas. (Courtesy of the Orange County Sheriffs Office).

tify that the affected officers were insolvent. The statute gave citizens the right to appeal a comptroller's decision directly to a circuit judge.[35] Besides the sweeping general law of 1861, the legislature enacted special laws relieving sheriffs in Levy, Holmes, and Madison counties of outstanding obligations.[36]

Back in Orlando, the beleaguered lawman enlisted on May 17, 1862, and was elected captain of Company G, Eighth Florida Infantry. Before he left his wife and eight children, Stewart hastily asked the state comptroller to hold his treasury warrants until he returned "if he should be so lucky, but should be killed or die," to send them to his wife. Stewart's unit reached Virginia in the fall of 1862. Not long thereafter Stewart sustained serious wounds, and died at Winchester, Virginia, on November 24, 1862. Early the next year, newly appointed Comptroller Walter Gwynn forwarded Stewart's warrants to his widow. Shocked that they amounted only to $365, she complained vehemently that she was due a much greater amount. Sympathetic but unyielding,

Gwynn insisted that he would not have intentionally wronged her. "If I was mean enough," he asked, "what object would I have in doing so? I would not gain for myself one cent. Whilst on the other hand I would be robbing the widow and children of my personal friend who gave his life for his country."[37]

Stewart and Isaiah Cobb were not the only Florida sheriffs to fight or die for the Confederate cause. A number of other sitting and ex-sheriffs volunteered for active duty. They would act in a variety of ways. One of them, Haley Blocker, accepted assignment to assess the condition of the coastal defenses south of Tallahassee. In the war's first months he made several reports to the governor on the condition of Apalachicola Bay, St. George Island, and Dog Island, as well as surrounding areas.[38]

At least fifty-one sitting or ex-sheriffs served in the Civil War. Although the vast majority were Confederate soldiers, a few such as James D. Green (Manatee County) and David J. W. Boney (Hillsborough County) were Unionists. Green and Boney saw service in the Second Florida (U. S.) Cavalry organized in 1864.[39] The soldier-sheriffs represented a diverse set of backgrounds, and a cross-sampling of some of them is revealing. Some stayed in the military for most of the war, while others enjoyed brief enlistments. Four Columbia County sheriffs—perhaps more than in any other county—wore uniforms of gray. Thomas Mickler was sheriff when the war broke out. Enlisting in September 1861, at Fernandina, he was elected first lieutenant of the Tenth Florida Infantry, Company D. He fought in and around Jacksonville early in the war and was eventually promoted to captain. When his unit was transferred to Virginia, Mickler became ill and ended the war hospitalized.[40] Arthur J. T. Wright, sheriff from 1849-1853, attended the secession convention where he voted to secede. Elected lieutenant colonel of the Third Florida Infantry when he enlisted at Fernandina in August 1861, Wright served only briefly before returning to Lake City. Enlisting again in June 1863, he was a member of the Ninth Florida Infantry until his health failed late that year.[41] Reuben Hogans, sheriff in 1854, enlisted as a private in the Eighth Florida Infantry, Company I, at St. Johns Bluff in February 1862. In

Virginia throughout much of the war, Hogans stood among those who surrendered at Appomattox in April 1865. The oldest Columbia County sheriff to volunteer, Asa E. Stewart, was forty-eight when the war began. As captain of the Ninth Florida Infantry, Company E, from February 1863, he served until January of the next year.[42]

In addition to the previously mentioned Isiah Cobb and Jonathon Stewart, at least eleven other sheriffs lost their lives between 1861 and 1865. One was Walton County Sheriff John C. Campbell whose tenure ran from 1855 to 1861. Enlisting at Quincy in the Sixth Florida Infantry on March 15, 1862, Campbell died in Richmond, Kentucky, on January 1, 1863, after being accidentally shot.[43] Six sheriffs, including Stewart, died of disease. Madison County's Edward Vann was captured while on picket duty at Petersburg, Virginia. The ex-sheriff was sent to Point Lookout prison in Maryland where he succumbed on October 26, 1864. Washington County's Levi Miller died in a Vicksburg, Mississippi, hospital in December 1862. Benjamin Edwards of the Jefferson Beauregards also died in a hospital at Lake City in June 1863. The life of Hillsborough County's Edward T. Kendrick ended in Knoxville, Tennessee, on December 12, 1862, only eight months after the former sheriff enlisted. Richard V. Buffum, another Hillsborough County lawman, died of typhoid fever at Richmond General Hospital on October 8, 1862. Two months earlier he had survived the fighting at Second Manassas.[44]

In addition to Santa Rosa County's Isaiah Cobb, at least three other Florida sheriffs were killed in battle. Captain John McNeill of Alachua County was mortally wounded at Olustee on February 20, 1864. Two sheriffs were killed during the battle of Marianna. A native of Jackson County and sheriff of Calhoun County from 1852 to 1855, forty-six-year-old Thomas Jefferson Land suffered fatal wounds when the Federals attacked Marianna on September 27, 1864. Captain Henry O. Bassett resigned as Jackson County sheriff soon after Florida seceded from the Union. Enlisting at Mt. Vernon in the Sixth Florida Infantry, Company E, he served under the overall command of General Jesse J. Finley in Tennessee and Kentucky. Bassett also fought with other Florida troops in the battles of Chickamauga and Chattanooga.

Ironically, the combat veteran was home on furlough when Union forces attacked Marianna. He was killed in the ensuing battle.[45] William G. Parker died either of wounds sustained in battle or of disease, perhaps a combination of both. He had resigned as Suwannee County sheriff to join the fighting as captain of the Columbia and Suwannee Guards. Entering the army at Lake City on May 23, 1861, Parker commanded companies E and K of the Third Florida Infantry during the first battle of Murfreesboro in December 1862. He died of wounds on January 31, 1863, at the Empire House Hospital in Atlanta.[46]

A number of sheriffs who remained at home assumed prominent roles in their towns and counties. Too old to leave their communities, six sheriffs served as captains in home guard units organized at different stages of the war. There may have been more, but it is a matter of record that W. W. Harrison commanded the Santa Rosa Guards and that George Costa formed an auxiliary artillery unit in St. Johns County. Putnam County Sheriffs J. B. Brown and Nathan Norton organized home guard units, as did Captain E. D. Howse (Marion County) and Alfred A. Fisher (Leon County).[47] After Vicksburg fell in the summer of 1863, the desperate Confederate government turned more than ever to Florida to supply hungry Rebel armies with beef. A number of special units were organized into the famed "Cow Cavalry" during the following year. At least five sheriffs buttressed the units and supported their crucial mission.

By late 1863 the struggle between Union and Confederate forces for the cattle of south Florida assumed a new dimension with the organization of the Second Florida (U. S.) Cavalry in the region around Fort Myers. Until then cattlemen had enjoyed a draft exemption, and many of them became alienated when the Confederate government revoked the measure. Prominent among Union-leaning cattlemen was James D. Green, ex-sheriff of Manatee County. Green commanded units that devastated Confederate driving operations.[48]

Given that military duty involved heavy sacrifices including the ultimate possibility of death on the battlefield, civilian service as a sheriff often proved only slightly less hazardous. As the war dragged on counties were drained of manpower. More and more men were called to arms. The Florida legislature adopted means to release additional able-bodied males to serve by consolidating the offices of sheriff, tax assessor, and tax collector. In 1861 Suwannee was the first county to have the offices merged. The trend continued throughout the war. In 1862 the general assembly required sheriffs in Calhoun and Hernando counties to combine the duties into a single office. In Hernando County the sheriff at least received a supplement to his regular salary. Polk County followed suit in 1865.[49]

The wartime legislature passed numerous measures calculated to ease the burdens of sheriffs and other public officials. Salaries for sheriffs were increased in 1863, and all of their fees were doubled. The antebellum practice of appealing to the legislature for compensatory funds was sharply curtailed.[50] Whether out of a concern for runaway inflation or out of a realization that thirty-seven-and-a-half-cents a day was a woefully inadequate allowance to maintain prisoners, jailers were allowed to double the previous reimbursement. Given the obvious exposure of county courthouses to Union attacks or other disruptions, sheriffs and various county officers were allowed to keep their official records at their residences. In 1863 circuit judges were given authority to appoint replacements for sheriffs if they were killed or otherwise failed to carry out their duties.[51]

Despite a desire to ease sheriffs' burdens, the exigencies of war forced the legislature to mandate additional duties. When in 1863 the Tallahassee lawmakers passed a statute preventing the distilling of spirituous liquors, each sheriff was directed to seize all liquor in his county and turn it over to the military for "hospital use." Lawmen who refused to comply were subject to fines and imprisonment "at the discretion of the court." Sheriffs had to help enforce local liquor ordinances such as one passed in Lake City in 1865.[52] Similarly, in December 1864, the legislature imposed even more extra duties (and potential fines) on sheriffs with regard to slaves. By the time the measure was enacted, such laws were all but irrelevant and added confusion to an already chaotic situation. In counties still free of Union occupation the laws were unnecessary; in others they could not be enforced.[53]

The legislature also addressed one benefit that lawmen enjoyed when it prevented able-bodied males from eluding state or Confederate military service by securing appointments as deputy sheriffs or county clerks. An 1862 measure forbade sheriffs and clerks from appointing deputies who otherwise would be subject to conscription. Any confusion about the act's permanence was removed by the statement that it would remain in force "until the declaration of peace between this Government and that of the United States." Conviction under the law meant fines of between $500 and $1,000 and removal from office.[54]

Although much legislation strove to mandate support for the Confederacy, resistance grew through the years of wartime strife and mounting defeats. The Conscription Act (April 1862), the Impressment Act (March 1863), and other unpopular measures alienated large numbers of residents. Many citizens turned against the conflict, and there was outright revolt in a number of regions. In Washington County a sheriff named Abram M. Skipper led the recalcitrant elements against state and Confederate authority. Skipper was legally elected in October 1863, but clashed with the governor who insisted that he take a special oath. Governor Milton appointed a replacement, but Skipper refused to resign and went into hiding.[55] By early 1864 his activities had become so threatening that Milton asked authorities in Richmond to release Edward Perry's brigade from Lee's command. The chief executive wanted the general to restore order in the county. While deploring the overall effects of conscription and other Confederate measures, Milton further justified his request:

> In the counties bordering on the Gulf and especially *Washington County* there are many deserters and many other persons who have fled from other states to avoid conscription. These persons have contaminated large portions of the citizens and constant communication is kept up with the enemy who are massing forces on Santa Rosa Island, evidently with the purpose of making a raid in that portion of the state, which is comparatively defenseless. The sheriff [Skipper] of the county and others who are persons of influence have gone to the enemy, carrying with them their horses etc.

and will pilot them in any raid which may be attempted.

I assert this to be true with full knowledge of the facts.

Later that month Milton requested further military assistance from General P. G. T. Beauregard. The governor reiterated that the disloyal Sheriff Skipper "together with other citizens—and deserters from the armies, who are acquainted with [the] localities, the strength, and [the] positions of troops in that part of the state, have recently gone too, and are now in the service of the enemy."[56]

By 1864 all or portions of several Florida counties were under the control of Union forces. There and elsewhere deprivation, manpower shortages, and overall poverty made collecting taxes a futile effort. The critical stage came when the state's revenue needs were greater than ever. State authorities put even greater pressure on sheriffs to collect monies.[57] One incumbent benefited from the crisis. Ora Carpenter, recently elected sheriff of Volusia County, was serving at Out Post Camp, Army of Florida, and from there informed the state comptroller that he could not comply with his orders. "I am still in Confederate service as private in Capt. James D. [Starke's] company," he explained. "I have made every effort to get discharged and as yet have failed to do so. Consequently, I can not attend to the duties of the office." He added, "Please advise me what steps to take." Gwynn turned the matter over to the governor who immediately provided the Confederate Secretary of War with the proper papers and an appeal for Carpenter's release. Within a month Carpenter was discharged.[58]

Even in counties free of Union penetration, economic conditions deteriorated to the degree that monies could not be collected. As a result, sheriffs found themselves in default. By September 1863, six present and past sheriffs in Gadsden, Madison, and Jefferson counties already were so listed by state authorities. Soon state officials knew, whether they admitted it or not, that it was too late. The vast majority of the state's sheriffs had defaulted on their accounts. Despite the painful difficulties, officials, operating with bureaucratic loyalty, tried to prosecute. They failed.[59]

The most dangerous threat to the sheriffs' abilities to execute their official duties was the potential or actuality of Union attack. Official let-

Chapter III - Sheriffs During The Civil War

ters from sheriffs in Manatee, Hillsborough, Orange, Hernando, and Clay counties described desperate circumstances. On July 5, 1864, Sheriff Joel J. Addison of Manatee County wrote that "Tax payers of this County [have] gone to the Yankees." Several county commissioners had also joined the Union forces. Addison asked the governor to appoint replacements and to have the comptroller "write to me and instruct me how to proceed." He observed: "We are in quite a critical situation in this county[;] we don't know what day or how the Tories will attack us and distroy [sic] all we got [;] if you can invent any plan for the Assessing & Collecting of the Tax please let me know. I am willing to do any thing for the Benefit of the State." The response offered little comfort and no real help. Addison was referred to an 1862 law that authorized him to suspend tax assessment and collection in such emergencies. Remarkably, he was informed, the governor had no power to appoint a county commissioner. The judge of probate had to call an election.[60] Addison persevered, but almost a year later, he averred that affairs had degenerated to the point of anarchy. "It is out of the question for the Tax Collector of this County to come up to the letter of the Law," he wrote. "The men are all soldiers [e]ither for or against us and it is a difficult matter to see the owners of the property to get [their] Tax and if I was to offer Property for sale I would not get a bit and besides the Yankees & Tories are strolling around trying to capture all civil officers."[61]

Neighboring Hillsborough County experienced a similar situation. Sheriff William S. Spencer, writing from Alafia, informed Tallahassee officials in the fall of 1864 that "owing to the broken state of affairs in the County I have not been able to send up my Tax book...." Spencer explained that in his county the people were "much scattered and...in the service and are much opposed to paying any Tax at this time as our County [is] too often disturbed by the enemy and as some of them wilnot [sic] give in their taxes atol [sic]."[62]

In Orange County an official wrote that prominent cattleman-farmer Moses Barber refused to pay his taxes because the enemy had driven off nine hundred head, confiscated his slaves, and burned his farm. In addition, A. K. Simmons had "gone to the Yankees and has left no property behind." The confusing state of the currency was another pressing matter. The same official asked what denomination, date, and discount rate of Confederate bills were acceptable for state obligations. The comptroller's response highlighted the sheriff's dilemma, and was a classic example of bureaucratic language. The "safest money you can receive for Taxes is State Treasury Notes, or new issued Confederate Notes," the official declared. "If you receive an old issue of denomination less than $100 you will incur personally the risk of exchanging for the new issue, as the Treasurer will only receive for it after the exchange has been affected." The comptroller continued, "Of course, those who returned property and have since left the county leaving nothing behind out of which to make their Taxes, must be returned on the list of Insolvencies approved by the Board of County Commissioners."[63]

Writing from Brooksville, a Hernando County official was defiant: the "Civil business gives way before the necessities of the country in a military point of view. My fellow citizens think it of more importance to defend the country than to try to assess taxes which could not be collected if the country fell under the controle [sic] of the enemy in so far as all persons who did not flee up the country had to take up arms in its defense." An attack was expected any minute, and though the county's forces were outnumbered three to one, the official wrote they had plenty of ammunition and were determined to resist.[64]

As the war's final year passed the state's condition worsened. Many Floridians died inside and outside the state before the formal surrender came on May 10, 1865. The four-and-a-half-years of conflict had destroyed the state's economy, decimated villages, towns, and farms, and wrecked civil government. By any measure the physical and economic destruction was catastrophic. The war's toll can best be calculated in human terms. When Florida seceded from the Union the voting population was 14,374. An estimated 16,000 to 17,000 Floridians became part of the Confederacy's military forces. A third of them died. More than 1,200 Floridians enlisted in the Federal commands.[65] The Civil War had set in motion a series of major events. Lincoln's Emancipation Proclamation and the subsequent Thirteenth Amendment (1865) ended slavery. The surrender terminated the Confederate nation's brief life, and freedom came to the state's 61,745 slaves.

Readjustment to a new order would prove complicated and demanding.

Inevitably, the state's criminal justice system would stand at the center of post-war events. Sheriffs had played a large role during the conflict—some had remained in office throughout the conflict, others had entered Confederate service (several of them were killed), and a few had remained loyal to the Union. Their peacetime responsibilities had been significantly increased, especially in the area of collecting taxes. They and their successors were about to enter the Reconstruction era, a time period when the political nature of their job would become more evident than ever.

Notes for Chapter III

1. For mass meetings that demanded immediate secession see Monticello *Family Friend*, November 8, 17, December 1, 8, 1860.
2. Clifton Paisley, *Red Hills of Florida*, 193, quoting Tallahassee *Floridian*.
3. Monticello *Family Friend*, August 10, 186 Generally see Larry E. Rivers, *Slavery in Florida*.
4. *United States Census 1860*, Population, 51, 53.
5. See letter in Tallahassee *Sentinel*, August 5, 1862.
6. For pre-war violence in these counties see Denham, *Rogue's Paradise*, 194-202; William Watson Davis, *The Civil War and Reconstruction in Florida* (New York, 1913), 34-46; Canter Brown Jr., "Politics, Greed, Regulator Violence, and Race in Tampa, 1858-1859," *Sunland Tribune: Journal of the Tampa Historical Society* XX (November, 1994), 25-29; and Kyle Van Landingham, "James T. Magbee: Union Man, Undoubted Secessionist and High Priest in the Radical Synagogue," *Sunland Tribune: Journal of the Tampa Historical Society*, XX (November, 1994), 7-24.
7. See Davis, *Civil War in Florida*; John E. Johns, *Florida During the Civil War* (Gainesville, 1963); William H. Nulty, *Confederate Florida: The Road to Olustee Florida During the Civil War* (Tuscaloosa, 1990); Canter Brown, Jr., "The Civil War in Florida, 1861-1865" in Michael Gannon (Editor), *The New History of Florida* (Gainesville, 1996), 231-248; his *Ossian Bingley Hart: Florida's Loyalist Reconstruction Governor* (Baton Rouge, 1997), 107-120; and his "Tampa's James McKay and the Frustration of Confederate-Cattle-Supply Operations in South Florida," *Florida Historical Quarterly*, LXX (April, 1992), 409-433; David J. Coles, "'A Fight, a Licking, and a Footrace': The 1864 Campaign and the Battle of Olustee," Master's thesis Florida State University, 1985; and his "Military

Operations in Civil War Florida," Ph.D. dissertation, Florida State University, 1997; George E. Buker, *Blockaders, Refugees and Contrabands* (Tuscaloosa, 1993); Robert A. Taylor, *Rebel Storehouse: Florida in the Confederate Economy* (Tuscaloosa, 1995); and William Warren Rogers, *Outposts on the Gulf Saint George Island and Apalachicola from Early Exploration to World War II* (Pensacola, 1986), 50-90.

8. Tallahassee *Florida Sentinel*, August 5, 1862. By 1863 Tallahassee would begin to suffer slave-induced turmoil. See Larry E. Rivers, *Slavery in Florida*.
9. Monticello *Family Friend*, September 28, 1861.
10. Ibid., July 6, 1861, quoting Marianna *Patriot*.
11. Quoted in Gainesville *Cotton States*, June 18, 1864.
12. Numerous scholars had studied Jacksonville during the conflict, but see Richard A. Martin and Daniel L. Schafer, *Jacksonville's Ordeal by Fire A Civil War History* (Jacksonville, 1984).
13. The raids led to the employment of black troops. See David J. Coles, "'They Fought Like Devils': Black Troops in Florida During the Civil War," in Mark I. Greenberg, William Warren Rogers, and Canter Brown, Jr. (Editors), *Florida's Heritage of Diversity: Essays in Honor of Samuel Proctor* (Tallahassee, 1997), 29-42; George E. Buker, *Jacksonville: Riverport-Seaport* (Columbia, South Carolina, 1992), 51-72; Richard Martin and Daniel L. Schafer, *Jacksonville's Ordeal by Fire*.
14. Johns, *Florida During the Civil War*, 16 See also Brown, "The Civil War," 239-241; Davis, *Civil War and Reconstruction*, 256-267. John F. Reiger has a good article on disloyalty and Unionism in Florida: "Deprivation, Disaffection, And Desertion In Confederate Florida," *Florida Historical Quarterly*, XLVIII (January, 1970), 279-298; the second half of the article appears in ibid., L (October, 1972), 28-58. For the situation in the South see Georgia Lee Tatum, *Disloyalty in the Confederacy* (Chapel Hill, 1934).
15. John Milton to Henry J. Stewart, October 5, 1863, Milton Letter Book RG 101, series 32, vol. 7, 3, FSA.
16. See order of Judge Benjamin A. Putnam, December 4, 1862, RG 101, series 577, 1857-1888, box 1 folder 14; Walter Gwynn to Thomas F. Green, January 22, 1862, Comptroller's Correspondence, RG 350, series 554, vol. 4, 244, FSA.
17. John Milton to Henry J. Stewart, October 5, 1863, Milton Letter Book RG 101, series 32, vol 7, 3, FSA.
18. *FA 1864*, 28.
19. Ibid., *1863*, 55-56.
20. R. C. Williams to Isaiah Cobb, March 18, 1861, Comptroller's Correspondence, RG 350, series 554, vol 4, 27; John Chain to R. C. Williams, March 25, 1861, ibid., folder 2; John Chain to R. C. Williams, May 15, 1861, ibid.; Isaiah Cobb to Richard C. Williams, May 30, 1861, ibid.; Richard W. William to Isaiah Cobb, June 6, 1861, ibid., vol. 4, 89; R. C. Williams to John Chain, July 25, 1861, ibid., 123, FSA.

21. Ibid.
22. David W. Hartman and David Coles (Compilers), *Biographical Register of Florida's Confederate and Union Soldiers* (Wilmington, North Carolina, 1996), 1668.
23. *Manatee County Sheriff's Office, 1855-1993* (Dallas, Texas, 1993), 19-21.
24. E. Glazier to R. C. Williams, March 26, 1861, Comptroller's Correspondence, RG 350, series 554, box 3, folder 1, FSA.
25. Joel J. Addison to Richard C. Williams, April 1, 1861, and Archer McNeil to Richard C. Williams, April 27, 1861, Comptrollers Correspondence, RG 350, series 554, box 3, folder 2, FSA. Making further inquiries of the comptroller was deputy sheriff and ex officio tax assessor and collector D. L. Hawkins. See D. L. Hawkins to R. C. Williams, May 1, 1861, ibid.
26. Joel J. Addison to Walter Gwynn, July 5, 1864, Comptroller's Correspondence, RG 350, series 554, box 3, folder 3, FSA. For an overview of conditions see Janet Snyder Matthews, *Edge of Wilderness: A Settlement History of Manatee River and Sarasota Bay* (Tulsa, Oklahoma, 1983).
27. See letter quoted in Tallahassee *Sentinel*, September 29, 1861.
28. James M. Denham interview with Vernon Peeples, August 3, 1997. See also Vernon Peeples, "Alexander Bell," manuscript in possession of James M. Denham. See also Tallahassee *Sentinel*, September 27, 1866, and Tallahassee *Weekly Floridian*, December 24, 1867.
29. *FA 1863*, 16.
30. See legislative resolution in ibid., *1864*, 35.
31. *Orange County Sheriff's Office, Orlando, Florida: 150th Anniversary History Book* (Paducah, Kentucky, 1994), 20.
32. Tyler and six others were indicted in April 1859, for the murder of William Wright. See Orange County, Minutes of the Circuit Court, Book A, 146, 171, 174.
33. Denham, *A Rogue's Paradise*, 179.
34. J. C. Stewart to R. C. Williams, January 29, 1861, March 25, 1861, Comptroller's Correspondence, RG 350, series 554, box 3, folder 1, FSA; *FA 1861*, 61-62.
35. *FA 1861*, 26.
36. Ibid., 63; *1862*, 30-31.
37. Hartman and Coles, *Biographical Register*, 833; Walter Gwynn to Mrs. J. C. Stewart, February 27, 1863, Comptroller's Correspondence, RG 350, series 544, vol. 4, 347, FSA.
38. H. F. Blocker to John Milton, November 20, 1861, Governors' Office Letterbooks, 1836-1909, RG 101, series 32, vol. 6. 82-84.
39. Hartman and Coles, *Biographical Rosters*, 1797-1798.
40. Ibid., 968, 1030.
41. Ibid., 261.
42. Ibid., 927.

43. Ibid., 583.
44. Ibid., 833, 788, 433, 305, 729, 864-865.
45. Ibid., 969, 1478, 621.
46. Ibid., 357.
47. Ibid., 2155, 2088, 2106, 2220, 2164, 2130.
48. For Green's exploits see Canter Brown, *Fort Meade, 1849-1900* (Tuscaloosa, 1995), 42-51, and his *Florida's Peace River Frontier*, 167-17 See also Joe Akerman, *Florida Cowman, A History of Florida Cattle Raising* (Kissimmee, 1976), 84-89, and Robert A. Taylor, *Rebel Storehouse* (Tuscaloosa, 1995).
49. *FA 1861*, 58; *1862*, 10.
50. Ibid., *1863*, 22-23; ibid., *1862*, 10.
51. Ibid., *1862*, 12-13, 32-33; ibid., *1863*, 16.
52. See Lake City *Columbian*, March 15, 1865.
53. *FA 1863*, 45; ibid., *1864*, 13.
54. Ibid., *1862*, 23-24.
55. Carswell, *Washington County*, 107-112, 481.
56. John Milton to James M. Seddon, January 11, 1864, and ibid., to ibid., January 29, 1864, Governor John Milton Letterbook, RG 101, series 32, vol. 7, 18, 25, FSA.
57. See Walter Gwynn to Tax Collectors et al, January 19, 1864, Comptrollers Correspondence, RG 350, series 554, vol. 4, 416, FSA.
58. Ora Carpenter, to Walter Gwynn, March 23, 1864, Comptroller's Correspondence, RG 350, series 554, box 3, folder 3, FSA; Walter Gwynn to Ora Carpenter, April 5, 1864, ibid., vol. 4, 426, FSA. Carpenter entered Confederate service on October 15, 1863, and was discharged on April 27, 1864. See Hartman and Coles, *Biographical Register*, 1668.
59. See Walter Gwynn to L. F. Fleming (Eastern Circuit), E. M. Graham (Suwannee Circuit), James M. Landrum (Western Circuit), and S. B. Stephens (Middle Circuit), September 7-9, 1864, Comptrollers Correspondence, RG 350, series 554, vol. 4, 448-452.
60. J. J. Addison to Walter Gwynn, July 5, 1864, ibid., vol. 4; Walter Gwynn to J. J. Addison, September 6, 1864, ibid., vol. 4, 447.
61. Joel Addison to Walter Gwynn, March 20, 1865, ibid., box 3, folder 3.
62. William S. Spencer to Walter Gwynn, September 11, 1864, ibid.
63. J. Wingord to Walter Gwynn, February 8, 1865, and J. Wingord to Walter Gwynn, March 28, 1864, ibid., and Walter Gwynn to J. Wingard, May 26, 1864, ibid., vol. 4, 431.
64. J. L. Peterson to Walter Gwynn, May 28, 1864, ibid.
65. See Davis, *Civil War and Reconstruction in Florida*, 322-323.

CHAPTER IV

THE HARD YEARS OF RECONSTRUCTION 1865-1877

econstruction is that time period between the end of the Civil War and when native white southerners regained political control of their particular states. Although setting time limits on history is always problematic, Reconstruction lasted roughly from 1865 to 1877. It was an era of profound change in the South. Florida's people and the state's sheriffs shared in that controversial era, contributing their chapter to the story. What follows is an assessment of a complex and important era.

The Civil War's end arrived for Floridians when Brigadier General Edward M. McCook led his Union troops down the dusty road from Thomasville, Georgia, to Tallahassee on May 10, 1865. The young commander was a man with a mission: to receive the formal surrender of Florida to the United States of America. A few days earlier the war had ended for the governor. John Milton had committed suicide at his plantation near Marianna. Abraham K. Allison, president of the state senate, assumed the governor's chair and moved immediately to reestablish normal relations with the Union. McCook's arrival eliminated the new governor's efforts. Reconstruction had begun.[1] During Reconstruction's first phase—known as Presidential Reconstruction—authorities in Washington created the Department of Florida, and stationed United States troops at places that included Tallahassee, Monticello, Lake City, Madison, Gainesville, Palatka, and Tampa. Among the soldiers' ranks were substantial numbers of former slaves. Anxiously viewing events, most white Floridians undoubtedly felt a mixture of anger and relief. If the bluecoats' presence meant defeat and humiliation their arrival also promised a temporary restoration of normality to Florida. For freed slaves there was a powerful sense of elation.

At the local level, what better symbol could there be of Reconstruction than the creation of a new building from which governmental affairs could be conducted? Seeking to achieve that end in 1866, local commissioners in Escambia, Santa Rosa, and Franklin counties were authorized to borrow $15,000 for the construction of new courthouses and jails, and those in Jackson County could borrow $5,000.[2] The idea was good, even noble, but the stark fact of having no money negated those and similar plans. Much of Reconstruction would be like that—brave beginnings and thwarted conclusions.

As it never had before, the office of sheriff would become politicized during Reconstruction. Even so, the fundamental concept of the sheriff's role remained clear. A state law of 1866 proclaimed that it was "the duty of the Sheriff, his Deputies, and the constables in each county to preserve the peace of each county, and to inquire into the violation of criminal laws, and on being informed of such violations, it shall be their duty to take the necessary steps to bring such offenders to punishment."[3]

As the late spring of 1865 turned into summer there arose a host of unanswered political, social, and economic questions. When would Florida be restored to the Union and under what circumstances? Would soldiers and state officials be tried for treason? Slavery was dead, but what would be the precise status of freedmen in the new order? Would the former slaves be granted citizenship and voting rights? In the face of a worthless currency, falling cotton prices, and thousands of liberated bondsmen, how would the state's agricultural economy be put back together? Springtime planting had been neglected, and how now would a farmer—black or white—make a crop? Few people, no matter how depressed, realized that Middle Florida would not reclaim its former prosperity during the nineteenth century or for much of the twentieth.

If economic prospects in the old Black Belt counties of Middle Florida seemed dismal, many natives soon joined northerners in recognizing the potential of the middle and lower peninsula. Florida's Reconstruction and Gilded Age years witnessed the beginning of a demographic shift that continued well beyond 1900. During that time large numbers of whites and blacks abandoned their homes in Middle Florida and the Panhandle to pursue opportunities further south in logging, citrus, cattle, and tourism. They were joined by other southerners and by people speaking in accents that marked them as native to regions outside of Dixie.

Within five years after Appomattox northern entrepreneurs such as Hubbard Hart, Frederick DeBary, and Henry S. Sanford had opened the St. Johns River valley to tourists. Steamboats took passengers as far south as Mellonville (Sanford), and soon thousands of visitors were exploring the natural beauty of the Oklawaha River and Silver Springs. The Indian River area, Tampa Bay, and Sarasota Bay drew both seasonal and permanent settlers from the North. A myriad of publications within and without the state trumpeted Florida's climate, physical attractiveness, and economic potential. The avalanche of propaganda fueled a "Florida Boom" not duplicated until the 1920s. By the 1870s Florida's population had grown to approximately 250,000, and by 1900 its citizenry had more than tripled in size since 1861. Florida's demographic shift was already evident during Reconstruction. While plantation-belt counties edged upward slightly, growth in peninsula counties was astonishing and irreversible.[4]

The surge of Hillsborough County illustrated the trend. In 1860 its population was 2,981 (almost half of whom soon were lost to the new Polk County), but it had 5,814 citizens in 1880 and 14,491 in 1890. The arrival of Henry B. Plant's railroad in 1884, the relocation of Vincente Ybor's cigar operation, and the phosphate boom caused the jump in population. By 1900 Hillsborough's 36,013 people gave it second rank to Duval County. Orange, Brevard, Polk, Manatee, and Dade (which grew nearly 500 percent between 1890-1900) experienced similar increases.[5]

The post-Civil War processes that sparked such dynamic growth began to energize during Reconstruction, which can be broken down into two phases. The first began in July 1865, when President Andrew Johnson appointed New York-born William Marvin as governor. Phase two began after the mid-term elections of 1866 when the Republicans,

William Marvin of Key West served as District Attorney, 1835-1839, and as Judge of he Southern Judicial District. At the end of the Civil War, President Andrew Johnson appointed him provisional governor of Florida. (Courtesy of the Florida State Archives).

James Dopson Green, 1823-1886, early pioneer of the Peace River Valley, served in the Union Army as a captain, and was one of the area's leading Republicans. He served as sheriff of Manatee County, 1858-1859 and 1874-1875. (Courtesy of the Canter Brown Collection).

with veto-proof majorities in both houses of Congress, cast aside the reconstituted "Johnson Governments" and launched congressional ("Radical") Reconstruction. A former district attorney and judge at Key West, Marvin called elections for a constitutional convention and, subsequently, a meeting of the state legislature. Marvin had been a conditional secessionist but not a Unionist. Despite the presence of a few Unionists, such as one-time Manatee County Sheriff James D. Green, ex-Confederates and former slaveholders dominated the proceedings. The structures and laws emanating from the convention and the first legislative session relegated the ex-bondsmen to a condition resembling slavery.

The new constitution of 1865 accomplished many purposes. Positively, it authorized the provisional governor to issue writs of election in Florida's counties for various officers, including sheriffs. The constitution was a conservative document written by whites. It repudiated the Confederate debt but barely mentioned blacks. Article I of the document declared that "no freeman shall be taken, imprisonered, or disseized of his freehold, liberties or privileges, or outlawed or exiled, or in any manner destroyed or deprived of his life, liberty or property, but by the law of the land." Under the "General Provisions" that made up Article XVI, section one outlawed slavery in Florida, and section two permitted blacks to testify in cases involving other blacks. In cases involving whites, they could not testify "unless made competent by future legislation." The first post-war legislature produced the infamous "Black Codes," which, while recognizing the freedom of slaves, kept them distinctly unequal to whites in criminal procedures, labor contracts, and nearly every facet of daily life. The laws were intended to circumscribe the blacks' movements and to put them in a status of legal inferiority.[6]

The reestablishment of a statewide equilibrium that depended on laws, courts, and sheriffs was made difficult by the complex issue of race. Accepting the new dispensation meant adjusting to a revolutionized social situation, and that readjustment was wrenching for white and black Floridians. The legislature moved to reinforce white supremacy. Florida's first post-war legislature passed an act to control

"Vagrants and Vagabonds." It gave "Sheriffs, his Deputies, and Constables" broad powers to "take necessary steps to bring such offenders to punishment." Sheriffs were to hire out vagrants "at public outcry...to any person who will take him or her for the shortest time and pay the fine, forfeiture, and penalty imposed and cost of prosecution."[7] Other Black Codes gave sheriffs the authority to enforce labor contracts. Violators were subject to capture and punishment. When sheriffs moved to enforce the restrictive laws they sometimes confronted a hostile black population that, on occasion, were backed by federal officials ready to intercede.

Some legislative acts had extensive lists of crimes and punishments applying to both races but containing sections that pertained specifically to blacks. A lengthy statute of 1866 had a section that forbade any black, mulatto, or other person of color from possessing a Bowie knife, dirk, sword, firearm, or ammunition of any kind without a license from a judge of probate. Even then, the license applicant had to have "the recommendation of two respectable citizens." Violators were guilty of a misdemeanor and on conviction were subject to standing in the pillory for an hour or receiving thirty-nine lashes. Similar punishment was decreed for blacks who "intruded" on a "for whites only" railroad car or other public vehicle. The latter law had a vice versa application to whites.[8]

The post-war scene was unsettled, but reality could not be ignored. The war was over, the Confederacy was no more, and federal authority had been reinstated. The sooner conditions could be restored to normal the better off Florida and the South would be. Law officials were essential for that goal to be effected. Given the carnage of war, it was important to know how many people lived in Florida. United States marshals assumed their former roles as census takers in 1865. E. E. Blackburn, marshal of the northern district, and his associates performed their duties, but the legislature had to pass a resolution instructing the state's congressional delegation to ask congress to pay them.[9]

The return to stability seemed more assured when the court system resumed its operations. Sheriffs continued their historic roles as important participants in legal procedures. A new county court system was established in 1868 that had concurrent jurisdiction with circuit courts in trying various criminal cases. The difference was that the county courts had no jurisdiction over capital cases. The sheriff was made the ministerial officer, and received the same fees as he did in the circuit courts.[10]

Meanwhile, the northern reaction to Florida and other southern states' passage of the Black Codes was to overturn the governments established under Andrew Johnson. In March 1867 Congress passed the first of its Reconstruction acts, formally beginning Radical Reconstruction. Before it was over blacks were enfranchised and made citizens under the Civil Rights Act and the Thirteenth and Fourteenth amendments to the federal constitution. The Fifteenth Amendment secured, or was supposed to secure, their voting rights. Congressional Reconstruction ushered in a period of Republican party rule. Formerly an alien institution in Florida and the South (Lincoln did not appear on most southern ballots in 1860), the party was composed of a diverse combination of freedmen, northerners, and Unionists or Loyalists. It was an amorphous coalition whose various factions often worked at cross purposes. To sustain itself in power the party relied on large-scale black voting. In 1866 Congress created the Bureau of Freedmen, Refugees, and Abandoned Lands, an agency better and more simply known as the Freedmen's Bureau. It aided the destitute of both races, and it oversaw contractual arrangements between white landlords and black tenants. In 1866 Congress strengthened the Freedmen's Bureau by granting it the power to protect blacks in their rights. Ultimately, the agency became a powerful political force.

The federal courts also prosecuted whites for violating the civil rights of freedmen. Republicans used patronage to build support among loyal whites and blacks. The federal army, though not ever-present, was sometimes summoned to aid civil officials in enforcing laws. In 1871 Congress passed the Enforcement Acts that gave state and federal officials greater authority to attack the Ku Klux Klan. The Klan was a secret para-military society of whites organized throughout the former Confederacy under various names. It resisted Radical Reconstruction by resorting to intimidation and terroristic methods against

Republicans, especially blacks.

Republicans governed Florida under the constitution of 1868, which for the first time in Florida history, concentrated power in the hands of the chief executive. Governors appointed all county officials (including sheriffs) except constables and members of the legislature. As directed by the constitution, each county was to have at least two and no more than twelve popularly elected constables, and, as directed by state law, their terms were for two years. Building on both his personal power and a loyal following locally for the Republican party, newly elected Governor Harrison Reed used his appointive power to effective advantage. The inevitable result was to politicize county office holding on a scale without precedent. Sheriffs were particularly subject to partisanship because they were the indispensable instruments for the enforcement of "Republican" laws in every county.

Florida's notorious convict lease system had its origins during the post-war years of Republican hegemony. Florida did not have a state prison in the antebellum period, but, like the Carolinas, relied on a system of county jails. After the Civil War, blacks, whose punishment had been largely in the hands of the slave owners, were free. That presented a considerable problem for state authorities. There was a rapid overcrowding of the inadequate local prisons, especially by former bondsmen no longer subject to plantation discipline. The ex-slaves were far more likely than whites to be adjudged guilty of crimes and sentenced to jail. In 1868, Republican Governor Harrison Reed saw the need for a state prison. After obtaining the use of the federal arsenal property at Chattahoochee, he supported a bill establishing one for Florida. To offset the costs of maintaining the prison, the convict lease system was begun. As discussed in the next chapter, Florida followed the pattern of other southern states in leasing its convicts to private contractors willing to house and feed them. It was an economic system open for abuse and exploitation. In the name of reducing state expenditures and acquiring a profit for the state, a cruel and inhuman system was instituted. The private firms that "rented" the prisoners for low costs profited as well. Leasing would be expanded and made permanent once the Democrats gained political control of the state. Once leasing came under county as

Chapter IV - The Hard Years of Reconstruction 1865-1877

well as state jurisdiction, sheriffs had a role to play. After the lawmen completed the obligatory functions of arrest and incarceration they continued to participate in the system. Any particular sheriff's job performance was affected to the extent that he became a part of the system.[11]

Not only was the sheriff himself a key county official, he continued to play, as in former years, a critical role as an election official. A law of 1868 required the sheriff to issue proclamations for special elections, circulate lists of legitimate voters, and (along with constables) take disorderly persons into custody on election days.[12] The constitution of 1868 did not neglect the broad subject of law and order. Carrying out the ambitious mandates was another matter, but Article X, "Public Institutions," called for the establishment of a state prison to be maintained as fixed by law. Article XVI, with its catchall "Miscellaneous" designation, was mindful of past confusion and required sheriffs and other county officers to hold their respective offices at the county seats. Beyond that, each county was to build a courthouse and a jail and to maintain them.

Soon after Reed's election, his office received an avalanche of communications from concerned citizens. They informed him of local conditions while stressing the dire need for various appointments. The letters were unsubtle demonstrations of the ties between the appointment process and politics. In 1868 a Quincy citizen wrote Secretary of State George J. Alden requesting J. P. Jordan's reappointment as sheriff of Gadsden County. That Jordan was a good lawman was secondary to his "support of Mr. Reed's administration & [his status] as a [Ulysses S.] Grant man. I desire him to be appointed for the interest of the Republican Party—as he will be of great service to us, & will give strength to Governor Reed's Administration." Alden was cautioned against the appointment of a man named Williams, "who wants the office." Williams was a "Stearns man." Marcellus L. Stearns, a native of Maine and an ambitious Republican politician, later served as governor from 1874-1877. "[Williams] will never be of any benefit to the Party & will make a [sic] inefficient Officer—The negroes also are very much opposed to his appointment—Stearns has played out and I am glad of it."[13]

Harrison Reed served as governor of Florida, 1868-1873. (Courtesy of the Florida State Archives).

PROCLAMATION

FOR, AND
NOTICE OF ELECTION!

To all and singular the Sheriffs of the several counties of the State of Florida:

WHEREAS, Section first of "An Act to provide for holding an election for Representative in Congress," provides that an election shall be held on the last Tuesday in December, A. D. 1868, in the several counties in this State, for a Representative in the Forty-first Congress of the United States; AND, WHEREAS, under the Constitution and laws of this State, vacancies exist in the Legislature of the State of Florida—

Now therefore know ye, That we, Harrison Reed, Governor of Florida, and George J. Alden, Secretary of State, do hereby order and direct, and so notify the Sheriffs of the several counties in this State, that a general election shall be held in each county in this State on

Tuesday, the 29th Day of December, A. D. 1868,

(the same being the last Tuesday in December), for a Representative in the Forty-first Congress of the United States, and that in the several districts and counties in which vacancies in the Senate and the Assembly of the State Legislature exist, an election shall be held to fill such vacancies, to wit:

In the first district, composed of the county of Escambia, a Senator in place of George J. Alden, commissioned Secretary of State.
In the third district, composed of the county of Jackson, a Senator in place of W. J. Purman, commissioned County Judge.
In the fourth district, composed of the counties of Holmes and Washington, a Senator in place of Dallas Wood, resigned.
In the sixth district, composed of the county of Gadsden, a Senator in place of J. E. A. Davidson, commissioned County Judge.
In the ninth district, composed of the county of Jefferson, a Senator in place of Robert Meacham, commissioned Clerk of Court.
In the thirteenth district, composed of the counties of Alachua and Levy, a Senator in place of Horatio Jenkins, Jr., commissioned County Judge.
In the fourteenth district, composed of the county of Columbia, a Senator in place of A. A. Knight, resigned.
In the nineteenth district, composed of the county of Marion, a Senator in place of Jesse H. Goss, resigned.
In the twenty-second district, composed of the counties of Hillsborough and Hernando, a Senator in place of C. R. Mobley, commissioned State Attorney.
In the twenty-fourth district, composed of the counties of Manatee and Monroe, a Senator in place of Daniel Davis, deceased.
In the county of Hernando, a member of the Assembly in place of Samuel J. Pearce, commissioned County Judge.
In the county of Putnam, a member of Assembly in place of O. E. Austin, commissioned Commissioner of Immigration.
In the county of Jefferson, a member of Assembly in place of J. W. Powell, commissioned Sheriff.
In the county of Santa Rosa, a member of Assembly in place of John W. Butler, commissioned Sheriff.
In the county of Brevard, a member of Assembly, no member having been elected at last election.
It is further ordered that the Sheriffs of the several counties shall cause a copy of this notice to be published in a newspaper printed in his county, if there be a paper in the county, and if there be no paper printed in the county, they shall cause at least five copies of this notice to be posted in the most public places in the county.

[L. S.] In witness whereof, we have hereunto set our hands and affixed the Great Seal of the State of Florida, this twenty-eighth day of October, A. D. 1868.

HARRISON REED, Governor of Florida.
GEORGE J. ALDEN, Secretary of State.

SENTINEL PRINT, TALLAHASSEE, FLA.

One of the primary responsibilities during the nineteenth century was for sheriffs to oversee elections. (Courtesy of the Florida State Archives).

Chapter IV - The Hard Years of Reconstruction 1865-1877

At least one would-be sheriff brazenly addressed the governor in his own behalf. In 1871 Moses Duncan of Hamilton County wrote Reed, "I sent you a recommendation with my own request to be appointed sheriff of this county. It is a very difficult matter to find a man in this county who is not very rigid Politically against Republicanism.... If you are not opposed to make a monopoly even where it will be appreciated I will gladly accept the appointment."[14]

In 1870 Henry Rountree cautioned Reed against appointing Thomas Seeley sheriff of Hernando County. Seeley, according to Rountree, was under the influence of the Walls—father Perry E. Walls and son William W. Walls—who occupied the positions of county treasurer and head of the county commissioners. They were "the one controlling power and influence of this whole county." Further, the Walls would not "move a finger to help or save your administration." Seeley, who owed the Walls over $2,000, would be subject to their influence if appointed. Seeley's "bodily health is alone a sufficient reason why he should not be appointed to the office. He is a feeble man, not able for extra labor or exertion and very unsuitable for performing many of the duties of the Sheriff. Your excellency will please pardon me, I am deeply interested in having good, efficient, congenial minds, to unite in attending to, and promoting the administration of state & county and you will know the great benefit of such Unity." Rountree and James T. Magbee, a judge, recommended Zachariah Seward, "a good man" with the "good feelings of the coloured people and last his family connexions [sic] would influence many voters from the opposing party and be the means of rallying a number to our ranks."[15]

That was not the end of it. First, others gave Seward their support. Two men from Brooksville wrote Reed that Seward was "sober, honest, and competent." Yielding to the pressure, Reed appointed Seward, but within a year Rountree acknowledged his mistake by reporting that the sheriff "has been Insane for the last 4 weeks and has been taken to his father's house in Polk County for safe keeping. This is the second attack and his families are desirous to have him removed from office which all advise and think it best." Rountree asked Reed to appoint Benjamin Saxon as sheriff and his brother as tax collector.

93

"The Saxons are young men," he wrote, "are just the fearless kind which we need to carry out our views and principles, they are very friendly to the coloured people and great favorites with them." Rountree added, "They are Republicans and I have pleasure in recommending them."[16]

During the often severe financial times of Reconstruction, a sheriff's fiscal rewards were limited. Some either quit or declined the office for economic reasons. In 1877 William G. Mitchell resigned his post of Calhoun County sheriff. Writing from Abe Springs Bluff, Mitchell was both candid and discouraged: "I thank your Excellency for the honor done me in my appointment to the office originally but the perquisites of the office in this County are so small I can not with justice to myself and my family hold it any longer."[17] Mitchell's lamentations were legitimate. Times were hard at every level during Reconstruction. Still, some preferred the meager financial rewards of the sheriff's office over other positions. When William Francis Buckner was appointed tax assessor of Volusia County, he agreed to accept only if he was appointed sheriff as soon as the position became available. "You are aware," he wrote the secretary of state, that the office of tax assessor is "almost unremunerative, although it seems now that it requires no little skill in its execution." The offices of tax assessor, collector, and sheriff should be combined as before, said Buckner, because their pecuniary considerations were "a object to me and when united in one person the compensation is sufficient to warrant a person of ability in giving his whole time to their proper execution."[18]

In 1869 the Marion County clerk died unexpectedly, and the county sheriff sought the vacant position. As John Simpson explained to the governor, "Mr. Clontz proposes to resign the Sheriffalty [sic] in favor of Mr. John O. Matthews if he can receive the position of county clerk." Simpson thought Matthews would make an excellent sheriff because he "was a Captain in the federal army and has our entire confidence as a [R]epublican."[19] Although others supported Clontz, he had his detractors even among Republicans. One man wrote the governor that Clontz's conduct as sheriff was an "injury and a reproach to the Republican Party, and if the Democrats were at all shrewd they would make it tell heavily." Clontz had been compelled "by public sentiment" to dismiss a deputy whose "conduct was disreputable," but later restored him against party wishes. The correspondent charged that Clontz discriminated against black men, cheated them out of pay as jurors and witnesses, and had unscrupulous deputies. Such a man—

 Letter of resignation of Calhoun County Sheriff W.G. Mitchell to Governor George F. Drew. (Courtesy of the Florida State Archives).

Chapter IV - The Hard Years of Reconstruction 1865-1877

illiterate, lacking in business skills, to say nothing of integrity, should not be clerk of the court.[20]

One powerful man who knew first hand the state of affairs defended the sheriff. Circuit Judge Jesse H. Goss advised against removing Clontz from the sheriff's office, and suggested the appointment of another man as clerk. Goss insisted that changing both offices would cause too much confusion. "Mr. Clontz is a good, a very good sheriff," he wrote, adding that "He took the place amidst the perils and storms of 1868 when we had no one in this circuit to inaugurate the Court and reestablish law and order." Goss also praised sheriff George L. Barnes of Alachua County, admitting that, without him, "I could not hold a court. The whole County would be a perfect Bedlam of confusion."[21]

In the state's more isolated sections vigilante organizations composed mostly of headstrong young men took their toll on Reconstruction progress and the public peace. By 1870, for instance, regulators, as they often were called, had expelled most freedmen from Polk and Manatee counties. That year a group of citizens in Manatee County complained to Reed that Sheriff Andrew Garner had refused to pursue the killer of James Cooper, a "colored, good, quiet, and inoffensive citizen [murdered] while in his own house surrounded by his wife and little children." Cooper survived long enough to swear out an affidavit against a man named Patten. When called to account for his negligence, Garner wrote the governor that he had done all that could be expected to find the guilty party.[22]

Along with the violence came attempts to restore white control. Again using Polk and Manatee counties as examples, Conservative [Democratic party] grand juries there charged Republican sheriffs Archibald Hendry (Polk) and James D. Green (Manatee) with malfeasance. Although neither prosecution netted a conviction (charges against Hendry were dropped when he migrated to Fort Pierce, and Green was eventually acquitted), the publicity cast doubt on the men's integrity, and, by extension, harmed the general reputation of the Republican party in the two counties.[23]

Republicans furthered the interests of black suffrage and other assertions of the freedmen's rights by having northern-born and southern loyalist lawyers appointed as deputy sheriffs. The officials became the equivalent of "public defenders" for the freedmen. Conservatives despised the practice, and, on gaining strength, moved to abolish it. By January 13, 1874, Hernando County representative Samuel E. Hope had introduced an "Act to Prevent Attorneys-at-law from acting as Clerks of Sheriffs or Deputies of either."[24]

Tax collection, always a major a concern for sheriffs, posed a particularly difficult challenge in the post-war years. Economic conditions and the confusion over what laws remained in force at any given time encouraged various citizens to devise stratagems against paying taxes. Shortly after Congress passed the First Reconstruction Act in 1867, a county official from Adamsville asked guidance from state officials. Some citizens here, he declared, "think they will not have to pay state tax this year [because] we are considered by the U. S. Government to be a territory and state tax can not be collected." He continued, "I tell them that I think they are mistaken, the state revenue must be raised as usual. I would like you to drop me a few lines in order to settle the question. Some of the tax payers requested me to ask you to do so."[25]

Some residents refused payment of taxes as a form of protest. In the spring of 1867 Santa Rosa County's Sheriff A. B. Dixon recorded, "Since the passage of the 'Civil Rights Bill' [residents] refused to give in their taxes for the present year." He asked of the state comptroller, "Can you advice [sic] me what course to pursue in regard to these parties [?]"[26] In 1869 Hillsborough County's Sheriff Henry Albury sought instructions on how to deal with several proprietors of boarding and eating houses in Tampa. The owners, he explained, "refuse to pay their tax on the ground that their houses are not hotels, but boarding houses." Albury added that such persons took in both "resident and transient boarders, and make their living in no other way...." He concluded, "I can see no justice in assessing and collecting the tax from a hotel, and have these persons go free, who are ready to take any boarder that comes along."[27]

The difficult task of tax collection helped to convert the trend of consolidation of the office with that of the sheriff. The people of Hernando County, to cite an example, came to believe that each occu-

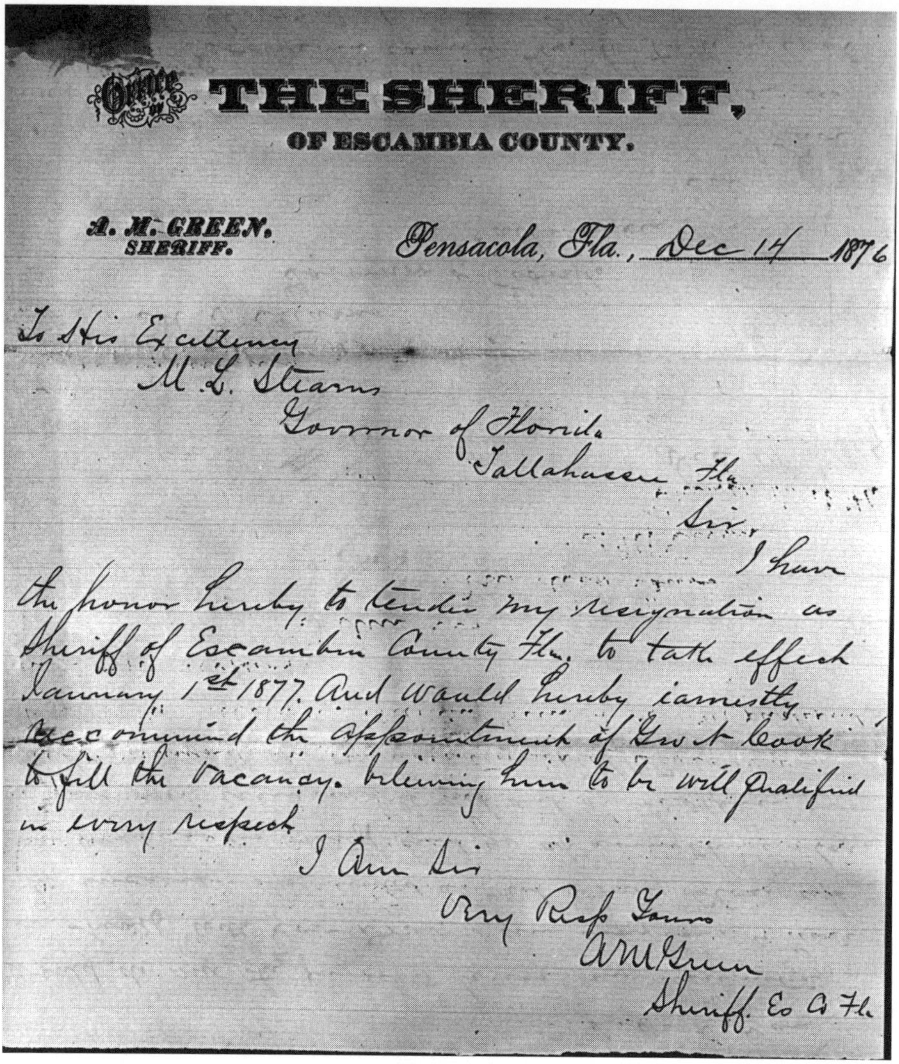

 Letter of resignation of Escambia County Sheriff A. M. Green to Gov. M. L. Stearns. (Courtesy of the Florida State Archives).

pation required a full time official. A state law of 1862 that had combined the office of tax collector and sheriff into one position was repealed in 1866. Yet, that same year economic considerations were paramount in isolated Polk County where the positions of tax collection and sheriff were consolidated.[28] The sheriff was also made ex-officio tax assessor and collector in Calhoun County.[29]

A lack of administrative skills and sometimes embarrassing illiter-

Chapter IV - The Hard Years of Reconstruction 1865-1877

acy often handicapped sheriffs during Reconstruction as they had in earlier times. The situation in Marion County offered a classic case. Sheriff Clontz proposed to exchange his position for county clerk, causing one man to write Reed that Clontz's deficiencies were acceptable in a sheriff but not in a clerk. In fact, he asserted, when Clontz became sheriff local lawyers made bets that he could not write an ordinary sentence and spell every word correctly. "I tell you [,] governor, outside of all personal and political influence or considerations [,] that he is incompetent, utterly and wholly incompetent for Clerk of such a County as Marion." He concluded. "I hope you will not accept his resignation as sheriff."[30]

With their administrative functions in disarray, many counties experienced difficulty putting the constitution of 1868 into operation. The situation resembled the confused interim between the territorial period and implementation of statehood back in 1845. A man recently appointed to a judgeship in Baker County informed Tallahassee authorities that the sheriff and clerk were gone, and the "organization of a court can not be effected without them." He noted further: "I did not see the bill organizing Co. Court until yesterday. I see that the bill makes ample provision for the pay of the clerk, sheriff, jurors &c but the judge of the court has been forgotten, he is according to the bill that I saw to give his services.... I suppose he would get his fees in probate matters under the old law, and fees as a justice of the peace, but for holding Court nothing." The cynical writer concluded, "What a magnificent arrangement. What a pity, that the members of the Legislature and all the offices, Governor &c was [sic] not placed under the same arrangement. What a splendid thing it would have been—every body, working for nothing. No taxes, No expenses, the ship of state sailing under a free breeze, all costing nothing, beautiful. But to Cap the Climax the judge must pay the state $10.00 for his commission. Is there nothing new under the Sun—Under these circumstances—I respectfully decline the appointment."[31]

Bradford County, then as now, lay south of Baker County, and there the situation, if anything, appeared bleaker. In 1871 a Bradford County judge, William W. Willis, blamed mass administration confu-

99

Chapter IV - The Hard Years of Reconstruction 1865-1877

sion on the absence of leadership in the sheriff's office. As he explained to the governor:

> We are greatly in need of a sheriff in this county, which I trust will be a sufficient apology for troubling you with a brief line. The former sheriff Robert W. Lamb after a very brief but by *no means brilliant* career some two months ago tendered his resignation which bye-the-bye, Governor, if you will pardon the remark, was the *only sensible act* of his life, & since then, as during his incumbency, we have been without a sheriff. Since then I see [by] your [Tallahassee] 'Sentinel' that Jno Howell is appointed.... Mr. Howell is no doubt 'worthy' and 'well qualified,' but he has not removed from Baker to this County, & I am credibly informed that he does not intend accepting the Sheriffalty [sic] of this county. This vacancy has already occasioned some delay in important business here & the spring term of the circuit court is fast approaching which urges still strong the necessity of the sheriff.[32]

People hostile to the new Republican order were eager both to discredit the system and to exploit its weaknesses for their own interests. If some appointees sought to enrich themselves at public expense, more were conscientious public servants. While opposition to the Republicans was based on anger at broad laws legalizing racial equality, there were complaints against individual corruption. In 1869 a man employed at the Sumter County Courthouse in Sumterville complained that the sheriff was illegally raising the rates he charged for fees. In one case the sheriff charged a three-day fee for guarding a prisoner when the prisoner was actually out on bail. Beyond that, the complainant "noticed that he made a charge against the state for feeding a Prisoner for three days, I believe; the prisoner boarded himself." He knew that the law official fraudulently charged the state for seventy-eight miles travel because "I accidentally saw the account he made out before the clerk. I believe he sent it off, he also charged five dollars for stationary [sic] and he said he purchased it at a store which is also false."[33]

Sheriffs, who were overwhelmingly Republican in political affiliation, frequently found it dangerous if not impossible to perform their duties. As historian Jerrell H. Shofner has written, "law enforcement was the most difficult problem confronting the civil administrations of Florida and the United States after 1868."[34] That was because in many Florida counties native whites were determined not to accept Republican rule. Testifying before Congress in 1871, Jonathan Gibbs, a black who had been appointed secretary of state by Reed in 1868, kept a record and revealed that 235 people were killed as a result of Reconstruction violence. Gibbs testified that substantial numbers perished not only in Jackson, Madison, and Columbia, but also in Alachua, Suwannee, Hamilton, Taylor, and Lafayette counties.[35] Although Gibbs's numbers were disputed at the time and by modern historians, they indicate the era's turbulent nature.

Violence, always a pervasive component of everyday life in Florida, was exacerbated by the Civil War and Reconstruction. During the latter period wide-scale native white disfranchisement, black voting, and black office-holding created even more fertile conditions for sustaining and accelerating a lawless legacy. The election of blacks to positions of legal equality with whites was new and resented by some of the latter. The uncertainties of the post-war period brought with them the potential for conflict. Political, economic, and social confusion continued the disruption of orderly society begun with the Civil War.

In 1866 violence between sheriffs' posses and Freedmen's Bureau officials broke out in several Florida counties such as Hernando when both exerted their authority to enforce the law.[36] Racial and political infighting, particularly the Republican and Democratic struggles during the "Jackson County War" (1869-1871), plagued the state. In Jackson County a black constable named Calvin Rogers was assassinated, and three Republican sheriffs—John W. King, Thomas West, and F. M. G. Carter—made unsuccessful efforts to keep order.[37] The Jackson County outrages were unmatched elsewhere, although there were other outbreaks of racial and political disorder. In Madison County Sheriff B. F. Tidwell, an ex-Confederate who became a Republican after the war, tried in vain to maintain peace. He estimated that from 1868 to 1881

St Augustine Florida
March 30th 1857

Honble John Beard
Comptroller of State
Tallahassee Fla

Dear Sir

Enclosed I send you Bills. You will please send me Certificate for the Amount.

Contingent Expenses of Circuit Court Spring Term 1857 as per Ext 2	$33.00
Compensation Due me as per Abstract 1 & 3	46.10
Service rendered in Circuit & Magistrates Courts & for feeding Prisoner (as per Bill)	99.89
13 Certificates on Coroners Inquest @ $1.25 each	16.25
My Bill of Cost on said Inquest	11.25
10 Witness Certificate @ $1.25 each	12.50
Conveying Prisoner to Palatka $84.48	88.35
	$297.34

Yours Respectfully

A. D. Rogero Sheriff &c

Comptroller I am patiently waiting for a Certificate for the Balance due me on my last accounts which I send you

ADR

Financial accounts of St. Johns County Sheriff A.M. Rogero sent to Florida Comptroller John Beard. (Courtesy of the Florida State Archives).

> Pensacola, Fla.
> Jany 23rd 1867.
>
> Hon Jno Beard
>   Comptroller &c
>   Tallahassee
>   Fla
>
> Having sent my accounts against the state, for the "Fall term" of the Circuit Court /66, in December last, & not hearing anything from them, I would like to know whether they have ever been received. The greater part of the money is going to other parties, & as they have become clamorous for their money, I feel anxious to know what has become of them.
>
> Very Respectfully
> Jas. B. Roberts Sheriff

Letter of Escambia County Sheriff James B. Roberts to Florida Comptroller John Beard. (Courtesy of the Florida State Archives).

over twenty persons were killed by vigilantes.[38]

Many scenes of physical combat occurred in Alachua County. "Rebel Raiders are taking advantage of circumstances and keep up much excitement in the Co.," observed a resident in August 1868. Most of the trouble was on the border of Alachua and Levy counties. "Shooting, whipping, & breaking into private residences terrifying the good citizens at midnight," the man explained, "is the order of the day."[39] W. K. Cessna of Gainesville implored the governor to order Alachua County's sheriff to form a "posse for the protection of life and property and the preservation of peace of the county." Cessna explained, "It would have a salutary effect especially if there were no distinction in the selection of parties other than that they are desirous of keeping the peace."[40]

Uncontrolled partisan behavior rocked Lafayette County. In August 1872, newly appointed Sheriff Nathan A. Harrell recorded, "things has went [sic] on so slack in this county so long & I expect I will have a hard struggal [sic] to straten [sic] up this county but if I live I will [restore order] if the other officers will do thir [sic] duty.[41] In the year previous to Harrell's appointment, law and order, already tenuous, broke down when the village of New Troy became a battleground between Republicans and Democrats. John N. Krimminger attributed the anarchy to a void in the sheriff's office. A lawman named Sears had accepted a position with the state legislature, and no other Republican (including Krimminger) in Lafayette County would accept the office. As Krimminger detailed to the governor:

> We have no officer here. One of the Republican Constables elected at the late election has died and the other declines to accept. Warrants have been issued for the arrest of rioters on the 16th of January last but no one can be found who will serve them. Can you send one here who will take the office of sheriff. If a Democrat is appointed he will not discharge his duty and [will] let the prisoners escape. They do not recognize your government.[42]

The governor eventually sent soldiers to Lafayette County to help restore order. Even so, Krimminger and several other Republicans were assassinated.[43]

In Columbia County political and racial conflict became so endemic that several sheriffs quit their positions rather than face the threat of death in the line of duty. In 1870 a gang kidnapped Robert Martin and forced him to resign as sheriff. Martin had been recommended to Reed earlier by the "colored people of Ellaville" as a "true man and one whom the K. K. K.s dread."[44] Not long afterward Ossian B. Hart, Reed's successor, turned to George G. Keen, whose family was among Columbia County's original settlers. The new lawman, out of fear for his family's safety, resigned soon after the appointment. The apprehensive Keen had replaced Warren S. Bush (Hart removed Bush because of his connection with the Ku Klux Klan). Hart's ouster of Bush and other

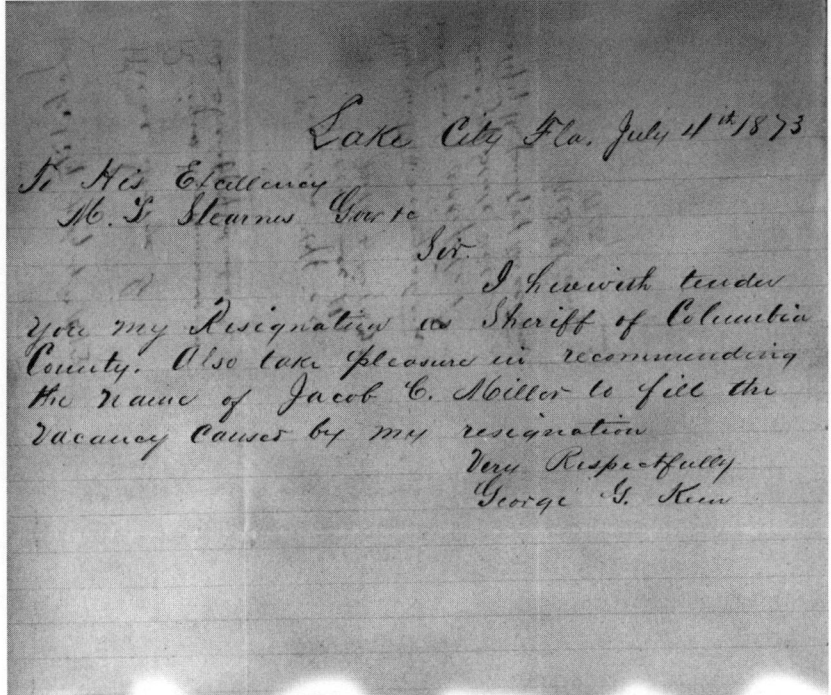

George Gillett Keen's tenure as Columbia County sheriff was brief. One of the county's original pioneers, Keen became a Republican after the Civil War. In the face of extreme violence directed against all Republicans in the county, Keen resigned only days after his appointment. (Courtesy of the Florida State Archives).

officials triggered the "Lake City Outrage" that saw the governor himself go there and help restore order.[45]

During Reconstruction a number of lawmen were either assassinated or killed while in office. In 1869 Putnam County's Sheriff William Stevens was murdered about twenty miles from Palatka.[46] In Pensacola a black constable named Robert Harrad was shot by Robert McKay, described by Escambia County's Sheriff George E. Wentbrook as a "notorious character."[47] Richard "Dick" Roach, the black deputy sheriff of Hillsborough County, was assassinated in his Tampa home. A month earlier Roach had shot and killed another black man named Duncan while making an arrest. Authorities suspected Duncan's Hernando County relatives were the murderers, but politics may also have served as the pretext.[48] Along with the unfortunate Harrad, Roach, and Calvin Rogers of Jackson County, numerous other black law enforcement officers were either elected or appointed during Reconstruction. Henry Hutchinson, a Hart appointee, served Franklin County as sheriff from 1874 to 1877.[49] During the final two years of Reconstruction Jefferson County had two black sheriffs: Lafayette Napoleon Bonaparte McCray, sometimes known as "Buck," and George W. Monroe.

Benjamin F. Collier, another black, was the chief law enforcement officer of Hamilton County from 1872 to 1874.[50] Philip L. Decourcey filled the office of Leon County sheriff from February to November 1875, when he died of pneumonia at his Tallahassee residence. "He was known as one of the most intelligent colored men in this county," acknowledged the Tallahassee *Sentinel*, "and during the last term of the circuit court he exhibited convincing evidence of his ability to perform the duties of the sheriff's office in the most acceptable manner."[51] David Montgomery, a New York-born mulatto with a talent for baseball, served as Madison County sheriff from 1868-1873. It was a time of rampant crime. In 1870 he was nearly assassinated by a group of masked men. Active in politics, Montgomery also represented Madison County in the Florida House of Representatives. In 1876 he narrowly lost a contest for lieutenant governor.[52] In Monroe, the state's southernmost county, James A. Roberts of Key West was constable from 1872 to 1874. Then, the black man held the county's most important law

Executive Department.

In the Name and under the Authority of the State of Florida.

Whereas, *David Montgomery* hath been duly appointed by the Governor, with the advice & consent of the Senate, according to the Constitution and Laws of said State to be *Sheriff of the County of Madison for four years from the ____ day of ____ A.D. 1868.*

Now, Therefore, Reposing especial trust and confidence in the loyalty, patriotism, fidelity, and prudence of the said *David Montgomery*

I, HARRISON REED,

Governor of the State of Florida, under and by virtue of the authority vested in me by the Constitution and Laws of said State, Do Hereby Commission the said *David Montgomery* to be such *Sheriff* according to the Laws and Constitution of said State for the time aforesaid, and in the name of the People of the State of Florida to have, hold, and exercise said office and all the powers appertaining thereto, and to perform the duties thereof, and to enjoy all the privileges and benefits of the same in accordance with the requirements of Law.

In Testimony Whereof, I do hereunto set my hand, and cause to be affixed the Great Seal of the State, at TALLAHASSEE, the Capital, this *Eleventh* day of *September* A. D. 18*68* and of the Independence of the United States the *98* year.

By the Governor.   Attest:

Geo. J. Alden   *Harrison Reed*
Secretary of State.   Governor of Florida.

Madison County Sheriff David Montgomery (his commission depicted here), was one of seven African-American sheriffs who served during Reconstruction. (Courtesy of the Florida State Archives).

Chapter IV - The Hard Years of Reconstruction 1865-1877

enforcement office, that of sheriff, from 1874 to 1877.[53]

Not all the disturbances involving lawmen were motivated by race or politics. The Florida that emerged from the Civil War still had vast tracts of unsettled frontier. The inhabitants of the isolated regions were a straightforward, determined, and self-reliant set of men and women. They possessed their own concepts of justice, and they were often hostile and suspicious of newcomers. Descriptions of the crackers or "plain folk," at least those penned by outsiders, were seldom complimentary. Most depictions focused on hot tempers that could explode into physical encounters. One correspondent pointed out in 1874 that Orange County possessed a large number of men who were "usually quiet, sullen, undemonstrative...inspired by that original hate which calls stranger and enemy by one name, and then jealously crops out in ways and speech, curious if not provoking." Efforts to educate and enlighten them had little effect, the man insisted. Most were dull and harmless, but "among them," the correspondent observed, "are a wild, reckless race, the remnant of wreckers; plunderers of the Indians who, refusing to work, live by such means as an over generous climate affords. No one has thought them dangerous, however, except in their immoral influences; but add whiskey, and the sullen resentment breaks out."[54]

An Orange County incident offers an illustration of how murderous cracker tempers could affect the life of the local sheriff. The victim was Nathaniel Randolph, a well-to-do migrant from Virginia. After six men, working in unison, provoked Randolph on separate occasions and were each, in their turn, thrashed by the Virginian, they regrouped and then accomplished his assassination. The killers escaped, but a posse followed them. Four of the men were captured, but two of the most deadly assailants remained at large. An onlooker explained the difficulties lawmen had in apprehending such criminals: "A prisoner's escape here is not as in settled communities. He takes to the woods [here] and leaves no trail. The only search is to beat the covers, and as the whole county is intersected by lakes, rivers, bays, hammocks, swamps, dense with lanais and rope plants, or rank with tall bamboo grass, you can understand the difficulty."[55]

Nonetheless, Sheriff Arthur Spear persisted in the hunt. He and his

 Emmanuel Fortune served briefly as town marshal of Jacksonville during Reconstruction. (Courtesy of the Canter Brown Collection).

posse captured one of the killers in a remote cabin and sent him under guard back to Orlando. Spear and the rest pressed onward. Their search for a man named Holloway, the "chief assassin," continued until the next evening when a rainstorm came up. One of the posse proclaimed: "This night will drive the wolf to shelter. We will find Holloway housed now if ever, in his friend's cabin." Surrounding the cabin, the men's vigil paid off before dawn when they captured the criminal's friend returning home. The man turned sickly white, but when the sheriff pressured him to give up the assassin, he refused. "I have told all that I will tell," he declared. "Yonder is the man, take him, but I will not betray him into the hands of the law; guilty or not guilty, do with me as you please, I can not help it." The posse pushed on, finally captured

Chapter IV - The Hard Years of Reconstruction 1865-1877

Holloway (whether in the cabin or not is uncertain), and escorted him back to Orlando for trial.[56]

In Brevard, Orange, Polk, Hernando, Hillsborough, and Manatee counties independent cattlemen clashed among themselves and those who sought to regulate them. The range wars, still ongoing at the nineteenth century's end, had their beginnings during Florida's Reconstruction years. Orlando shared the distinction with Mellonville (Sanford) as the nuclei of settlement in the peninsula's central region. Both villages were frequented by cattlemen and, as a natural course, often experienced scenes of bloodshed.

One sheriff paid with his life when, in the late 1860s, a range war in the eastern part of central Florida pitted the Barber family against men whom they accused of stealing their cattle. Moses E. Barber, who owned thousands of head of cattle in Brevard and Orange counties, accused a man named Bass of stealing some of his herd and ordered him to leave the county. Bass thereupon filed false imprisonment and assault charges against Barber and his associates. Sheriff David W. Mizell of Orange County sought to arrest the Barbers. Although the assault probably took place in Brevard County, Dempsey Cain, the sheriff there, had resigned, perhaps because he feared facing Barber and his friends. Barber and several others were indicted, but before a trial could be held in Orlando the courthouse burned down. Sheriff Mizell continued his pursuit of Barber and his men—many of them had been charged with more serious crimes. In February 1870, lawman Mizell was shot and killed while crossing a creek in Brevard County. Judge John Mizell, the sheriff's brother, organized a posse, and a full-scale range war subsequently broke out in Brevard and lower Orange counties.[57]

More deaths would follow. Needham Yates and his son John were the first to be taken into custody. Judge John Price gave an account of their capture:

> On the 2nd [March] the acting Sheriff of Orange County [John Evans] with posse arrested Needham Yates and his son John, two persons who were supposed to have murdered the sheriff of Orange County[.] [A]fter being carried some distance within

 David William Mizell, elected Orange County sheriff in 1868, was killed in the line of duty in February 1870. (Courtesy of Orange County Sheriffs Office).

fourteen miles of the Court House in passing near a scrub...,they attempted to escape and get into the scrub[,] but after going some 50 yards were fired upon and killed by the posse. There is [*sic*] some persons yet at large supposed to be implicated so far as I have heard.[58]

Several other men in the region were killed. Moses E. Barber was one of them. After being shot, Barber drowned in Orlando's Lake Conway.[59]

Such upheavals made the turnover in the Orange County sheriff's office a serious problem. By January 15, 1871, David B. Stewart was sheriff. That was the day he resigned and recommended Isaac Winegord. Reed's next two appointments, Winegord and Arthur Spear, served only six months before resigning.[60] In 1873 George W. Self, Spear's deputy, advised state authorities that "the High Sheriff of Orange County is out of the county and in Texas." He added with a certain bravado, "I have his business well in hand."[61]

On the western side of Florida, society was affected by the fluctuating rhythms of a volatile and unpredictable area that retained vestiges of the frontier. Polk, Hillsborough, and Manatee counties were the domain of cattle and the men who herded them. Canter Brown's work on the region notes that "large sections of Texas and other western states had a greater density of population than the Florida peninsula south of Orlando."[62] In the 1870s much of the violence there was random, uncalculated, and personal. Yet, a number of regional desperadoes offered a different element of crime. They were professionals, and among them were the Johnson brothers—Gus, Alonzo, and Raymond.

The Johnsons stole cattle and were captured, prosecuted, and convicted. They escaped several times, and finally disappeared for good in 1879. There were other outlaws—"Hub" Williams, the so-called "Robin Hood of South Florida," and William W. "Bill Ham" Willingham. Sheriffs Charles Slager and James R. Hay in Hillsborough County tangled with Williams. Incongruously, Williams had a talent for poetry. Charged with horse stealing, he escaped three times—from a boat, a jail, and a train. Recaptured and sentenced, Williams made his final escape as he was being taken to the penitentiary. The Tampa

Guardian reported that he "leaped head foremost out of the car window...making his escape in a dense swamp.... In the jump his head plowed the ground like a spent cannon ball."[63] Through the 1870s such men kept Polk and Hillsborough sheriffs and those in other counties from becoming bored with the administrative aspects of their jobs.

As the state and national elections of 1876 neared, Republican control of state politics was nearing its end. Florida, along with Louisiana and South Carolina, was one of three former Confederate states still "unredeemed." That is, it had not been reclaimed politically by the Democratic party. The Democrats campaigned, as had their counterparts in earlier southern elections, in the name of honest government, economy in government, and white supremacy. In the balloting the trio of states succeeded in accomplishing the final overthrow of Radical Reconstruction. The South was left to its own devices, including the handling of racial controversies, and the Northern Republican politicians shifted their interests to railroads, mines, factories, and other means of making money.

During Reconstruction Florida's sheriffs battled the critical dislocations of a lost war, as well as post-war economic, racial, social, and political tribulations. Although they owed their badges to the caprices of politics, the lawmen were more than political agents of the Republican party. If political fealty dictated their appointments, they struggled as individuals to fulfill their basic obligations of enforcing the laws, protecting Florida's citizens, and apprehending criminals. Further, they carried out the duties prescribed by state laws linking them to tax collecting, serving as election officials, performing multiple services as court officials, and many other jobs that did not require the ability to draw fast and shoot straight.

For the sheriffs the period from 1877 to the beginning of a new century in 1901 would be less critical than were the Civil War and Reconstruction eras. Still, the coming decades were transitional for Florida as the state moved toward a pre-modern status. In that time the sheriff and his office experienced the same sort of transition, and the change was not always easy, but it was significant.

Notes for Chapter IV

1. See James P. Jones and William Warren Rogers, "The Surrender of Tallahassee," *Apalachee* (1963-1967), 103-110; Jerrell H. Shofner, *Nor Is It Over Yet: Florida During the Era of Reconstruction, 1863-1873* (Gainesville, 1974), and his "Renewal and Reconstruction, 1865-1877," in Michael Gannon (Editor), *The New Florida History* (Gainesville, 1996), 249-265; John Wallace, *Carpetbag Rule in Florida: The Inside Workings of the Reconstruction of Civil Government in Florida After the Close of the Civil War* (Kennesaw, Georgia, 1959; reprint of the 1888 edition), Davis, *Civil War and Reconstruction*; Jose M. Richardson, *The Negro in the Reconstruction of Florida* (Tallahassee, 1965); J. E. Dovell, *Florida: Historic, Dramatic, Contemporary* (New York, 1952); Canter Brown Jr., *Ossian Bingley Hart: Florida's Loyalist Reconstruction Governor* (Baton Rouge, 1997), 150-297; and his *Florida's Peace River Frontier*, 176-235.
2. *FA 1865-1866*, 82-83.
3. Ibid., 27-28. For the complete act see 23-28.
4. Shofner, "Reconstruction and Renewal," 257-259; Dovell, *Florida : Historical, Dramatic, Contemporary*, 600-613.
5. For postwar population growth and development see Dovell, *Florida: Historic, Dramatic, Contemporary*, 564-569, 600-643; Brown, *Florida's Peace River Frontier*, 215-235, 255-291, 312-345; and his *Fort Meade*, 52-153; Samuel Proctor, "Prelude to the New Florida," 266-286, in Gannon, *New History of Florida*; Janet Snyder Matthews, *Edge of Wilderness*, 273-365; Jerrell H. Shofner, *A History of Brevard County* (Stuart, 1995), 82-199; James W. Covington, *The Story of Southwestern Florida* (New York, 1957), 156-189.
6. Joe M. Richardson, "The Florida Black Codes," *Florida Historical Quarterly*, XLVII (April, 1969), 365-379; Shofner, "Reconstruction and Renewal," 251-252. For the situation in the rest of the South see Theodore B. Wilson, *The Black Codes of the South* (Tuscaloosa, 1965).
7. *FA 1865*, 22, 27-28.
8. Ibid., *1865-1866*, 23-28.
9. Ibid., 118. The resolution was passed January 10, 1866.
10. *FA 1868*, 11-16. See especially 13.
11. There is a large and growing body of work on prison systems in the South and nation. See James Bacchus, "Shackles in the Sunshine," Orlando *Sentinel Star Sunday Magazine*, June 17, 1973. See issues of June 23, 30, 1983, for a continuation of the Bacchus series; Kathleen Falconer Pratt, "The Development of the Florida Prisoner System," M. A. thesis, Florida State University, 1949; especially important is N. Gordon Carper, "The Convict-Lease System in Florida, 1866-1923," Ph.D. dissertation, Florida State University, 1964, 1-8; Hilda Zimmermann, "Penal System and Penal Reforms in the South Since the Civil War, " Ph.D. disser-

tation, University of North Carolina at Chapel Hill, 1947, *passim*; George W. Cable, *The Silent South* (New York, 1885), 172, offers an important contemporary view. See also Fletcher M. Green, "Some Aspects of the Convict Lease System in the Southern States," 129, in Fletcher M. Green (Editor) *Essays in Southern History* (Chapel Hill, 1949). For two recent studies see Matthew J. Mancini, *One Dies Get Another: Convict Leasing in the American South, 1866-1928* (Columbia, South Carolina, 1996); and Alexander C. Lichtenstein, *Twice the Work of Free Labor : the Political Economy of Convict Labor in the New South* (New York, 1993).

12. Ibid., *1868*, 2, 4, 6; For the complete acts see 1-9.
13. J. E. A. Davidson to George J. Alden, August 23, 1868, Secretary of State's Correspondence, RG 151, series 1325, box 3, folder 8, FSA.
14. Moses D. Duncan to Harrison Reed, October 30, 1871, Harrison Reed Papers, 1868-1872, RG 101, series 577, box 2, folder 3, FSA.
15. Henry Rountree to Harrison Reed, March 21, 1870, June 7, 1871, and Arthur [St. Close?] and Antony May to Harrison Reed, February 16, 1870.
16. Ibid.
17. William G. Mitchell to George F. Drew, November 5, 1877, Secretary of State, Letters of Resignation and Removals from Office, RG 151, series 1326, box 1, folder 3, FSA.
18. William Francis Buckner to J. C. Gibbs, April 17, 1869, Secretary of State's Correspondence, RG 151, series 1325, box 4, folder, 4, FSA.
19. John Simpson to Harrison Reed, December 3, 1869, Harrison Reed Papers, 1868-1872, RG 101, series 577, box 2, folder 4, FSA. Additional support came from Charles V. Hillyer to Harrison Reed, December 16, 1869, ibid., and Virgil Hillyer to Harrison Reed, December 6, 1869, ibid.
20. George Burnside to Harrison Reed, December 5, 1869, ibid., box 2, folder 6, FSA.
21. Jesse H. Goss to Harrison Reed, December 6, 1869, ibid.
22. Petition of Citizens of Manatee County Relative to Conduct of Sheriff Garner, March 14, 1870, ibid., box 3, folder 9, FSA.
23. Brown, *Florida's Peace River Frontier*, 205-210.
24. Joe Knetsch, "Forging the Florida Frontier: The Life and Career of Captain Samuel E. Hope," *Sunland Tribune: Journal of the Tampa Historical Society* XX (November, 1994), 38.
25. David G. [Leigh?] to John Beard, May 20, 1867, Comptroller's Correspondence, RG 350, series 554, box 3, folder 4, FSA.
26. A. B. Dixon to John Beard, April 15, 1867, ibid, box 31, folder 4, FSA.
27. Henry Albury to Robert H. Gamble, March 11, 1869, ibid., folder 7, FSA.
28. *FA 1865-1866*, 93-94, 97.
29. Ibid., 57-58.

Chapter IV - The Hard Years of Reconstruction 1865-1877

30. Jesse H. Goss to Harrison Reed, December 6, 1869, Harrison Reed Papers, RG 101, series 577, box 2, folder 6, FSA.
31. J. E. Townsend to George J. Alden, August 18, 1868, Secretary of State's Correspondence, RG 150, series 1325, box 3, folder 8, FSA.
32. William W. Wills to Harrison Reed, March 1, 1871, Harrison Reed Papers, RG 101, series 577, box 1, folder 18, FSA. Given the virtual certainty that Howell would decline the appointment, Wills, the tax assessor, and clerk recommended Matthew L. McKinney for the job.
33. A. C. Clark to Robert H. Gamble, December 20, 1869, Comptroller's Correspondence, RG 350, series 554, box 32, folder 1, FSA.
34. Shofner, *Florida In The Era Of Reconstruction*, 225.
35. Davis, *Civil War and Reconstruction in Florida*, 582.
36. Shofner, "Reconstruction and Renewal," 252.
37. On the Jackson County War see Shofner, *Florida In The Era Of Reconstruction*, 232-234; and his "Wartime Unionists, Unreconstructed Rebels and Andrew Johnson's Amnesty Program in the Reconstructon Debacle of Jackson County, Florida," *Gulf Coast Historical Review*, IV (Spring, 1989), 167-169; Davis, *Civil War and Reconstruction in Florida*, 568, 570-579.
38. Shofner, *Florida In The Era of Reconstruction*, 288; Davis, *Civil War and Reconstruction in Florida*, 603.
39. C. H. Black to George J. Alden, August 26, 1868, Harrison Reed Papers, 1868-1872, RG 101, series 577, box 3, folder 6, FSA.
40. W. K. Cessna to Harrison Reed, September 8, 1868, Harrison Reed Papers, RG 101, series 577, box 3, folder 6, FSA.
41. Nathan A. Harrell to Harrison Reed,, August 21, 1872, ibid., box 3, folder 5, FSA.
42. John N. Krimminger to Harrison Reed, February 3, 17, 1871, ibid., FSA.
43. Shofner, *Florida In The Era Of Reconstruction*, 180, 213, 231.
44. Ibid., 228; Petition of Citizens of Columbia Co., December 19, 1869, in W. W. Moore to Harrison Reed, December 20, 1869, Harrison Reed Papers, RG 101, series 577, box 1, folder 18, FSA.
45. Shofner, *Florida In The Era Of Reconstruction*, 228; Brown, *Ossian Bingley Hart*, 283-284; George G. Keen to M. L. Stearns, July 4, 1873, Secretary of State, Letters of Resignation and Removals from Office, RG 151, series 1326, box 1, folder 4, FSA.
46. R. H. McLeod to John Beard, May 15, 1867, Comptrollers Correspondence, RG 350, series 554, box 31, folder 4, FSA.
47. George E. H. Wentbrook to George Alden, September 26, October 3, 1868, Secretary of State's Correspondence, RG 151, series 1325, box 4, folder 1, FSA; Shofner, *Florida In The Era Of Reconstruction*, 234.

48. William Wilbanks, *Forgotten Heroes Police Officers Killed In Early Florida 1840-1925* (Paducah, Kentucky, 1998), 19-20, quoting Jacksonville *Tri-Weekly Floridian*, June 27, 1874, and Savannah *Morning News*, September 1, 1874.
49. Tallahassee *Weekly Floridian*, February 24, 1874; Canter Brown, *Florida's Black Public Officials* (Tuscaloosa, 1998), 98; James M. Denham and Canter Brown, Jr. "Black Sheriffs of Post Civil War Florida," *Sheriffs Star: Journal of the Florida Sheriffs Association* 42 (September-October 1998): 12-15.
50. Brown, *Florida's Black Public Officials* 82.
51. Thomasville [Georgia] *Southern Enterprise*, May 3, 1876; Brown, *Florida's Black Public Officials*, 107.
52. Savannah *Morning News*, November 11, 1870; Tallahassee *Sentinel*, November 5, 1870; Quitman [Georgia] *Reporter*, June 22, 1876; Brown, *Florida's Black Public Officials*,112.
53. Brown, *Florida's Black Public Officials, 1867-1924*, 120.
54. "Letter from Florida," Cincinnati [Ohio] *Commercial*, January 15, 1874.
55. Ibid.
56. Ibid.
57. Jerrell H. Shofner, *A History of Brevard County* (Stuart, 1995), 74-75. John M. Eriksen, *Brevard County: A History to 1995* (Tampa, 1955), 81-82.
58. John W. Price to Harrison Reed, March 8, 1870, Harrison Reed Papers, RG 101, series 577, box 3, folder 1, FSA.
59. Shofner, *A History of Brevard County*, 74-75; Eriksen, *Revard County*, 81-82.
60. David B. Stewart to Harrison Reed, January 15, 1871, Secretary of State, Letters of Resignation and Removal from Office, RG 151, series 1326, box 1, folder 12, FSA; David B. Stewart to Harrison Reed, February 18, 1871, Harrison Reed Papers, 1868-1872, RG 10l, series 577, box 3, folder 1, FSA. When Winegord resigned the office for health reasons he recommended the appointment of William Patrick. Reed appointed Spear instead. Nevertheless, Patrick eventually replaced Spear and served four years. Isaac Winegord, John R. Mizell, and David Mizell to Harrison Reed, September 16, 1871, Secretary of State, Letters of Resignation and Removal from Office, RG 151, series 1326, box 1, folder 12, FSA; *Orange County Sheriff's Office, Orlando, Florida; 150th Anniversary History Book* (Paducah, Kentucky, 1994), 21-22.
61. George W. Self to Samuel McLin, April 29, 1873, Secretary of State's Correspondence, RG 151, series 1325, box 5, folder 1, FSA.
62. Brown, *Florida's Peace River Frontier*, 240.
63. Brown, *Jewish Pioneers of the Tampa Bay Frontier* (Tampa, 1998), 44, quoting Tampa *Guardian*. See also Brown, *Florida's Peace River Frontier*, 240.

CHAPTER V

CLOSING THE NINETEENTH AND INTO THE TWENTIETH CENTURY, 1877-1900

In the nineteenth-century's last decades, the office of sheriff became elective again. After 1877 Florida's sheriffs would serve exclusively under Democratic governors until the 1916 election of the colorful Independent-Prohibitionist Governor Sidney J. Catts. Their status would be defined not only by new laws but by the new constitution of 1885. The state experienced population growth, new counties were created, and railroads added a spectacular boost by connecting Florida's burgeoning towns and cities. As those changes occurred, sheriffs became less isolated and less provincial. They needed closer contact with one another, and that need produced a statewide organization of lawmen in the 1890s. The sheriff's responsibilities increased as he coped with the traditional job-related dangers, performed his prescribed duties, and found himself challenged by a rapidly changing world.

With newly elected Democrat George F. Drew in the governor's office by early 1877 and the 1868 constitution still in force, most Republican county officials expected to be ousted. As Edward Williamson, the historian of Florida's Gilded Age, has noted, "Needing only the formality of a friendly Senate, Drew possessed the authority to dismiss almost every Republican on the state payroll and to appoint an entire new slate of state and county officials."[1] Drew largely took the advice of county organizations when making appointments. Most incumbent sheriffs (and other appointed Republican officials) were soon replaced. Within days after Drew's inauguration on January 2, 1878, four sheriffs resigned: A. M. Green of Escambia; J. S. Driggs of

Francis Fleming served as governor of Florida, 1889-1893. (Courtesy of the Florida State Archives).

Duval; John H. Sutton of Taylor; and John Hall of Bradford. Norton Sapp of Lafayette County turned in his badge in October. Surviving records indicated that new sheriffs (all Democrats) were appointed in every county except Brevard, Franklin, Hamilton, Liberty, Santa Rosa, and Volusia.[2]

Florida's late nineteenth-century governors—George F. Drew, William D. Bloxham (twice), Edward A. Perry, Francis P. Fleming, and Henry L. Mitchell—were no less occupied in enforcing laws than their predecessors. Local authorities, especially county sheriffs, regularly communicated with governors on many issues. Sheriffs engaged in time-consuming correspondence with the chief executives on critical matters such as recapturing criminals fleeing to other states. That was because only the governor could authorize the issuance of requisitions and rewards. Requisitions were necessary for the repatriation of criminals, and if culprits remained at large, rewards were vital inducements for their capture.

In April 1894, for example, an Escambia County deputy sheriff wrote Governor Henry L. Mitchell for a requisition to apprehend a man who shot "one of our best police men off his horse and left him for dead" three years earlier. The deputy suggested that Mitchell save time by sending the "Requisition direct to Jackson, Mississippi." He added, "Don't let anyone know that I have wrote [*sic*] you.... For the D— newspaper reporters may hear of it. And publish it to the world." According to him the reporters "do a man more harm than good. So please keep it a secret. And send the requisition immediately."[3]

In 1899 a similar case involved an appeal from Holmes County Sheriff Daniel J. Paul requesting William D. Bloxham to make out a requisition and a reward for William Dorsey wanted for the murder of Joshua Creel. A proclamation and reward for Dorsey had been issued in 1888 when the killing occurred, but since then Dorsey had remained at large. Sheriff Paul (spelling and grammar were not his specialties, although compassion and a sense of justice were) had learned "On good authority" that the fugitive was residing in Texas. He explained that there was little chance of arresting him there unless the governor reactivated the reward. Creel, Paul declared, "was a good man [who] was murdered in the presence of his wife. She was left with a family of 5 or 6 Children and a very Pore wamman finantially. I have bin trying to locate the aledged Ever since I have bin in office and this is my first sight, and I am anxious for his capture."[4]

Well before the imminent constitutional process began, the legislature, at the redeemer Governor Drew's insistence, had addressed the convict lease system. It provided a profitable way to manage the state's growing prison population. The revised and expanded system was a major overhaul, and affected how the sheriffs dealt with prisoners and the future of Florida's lawmen. What Drew suggested continued the

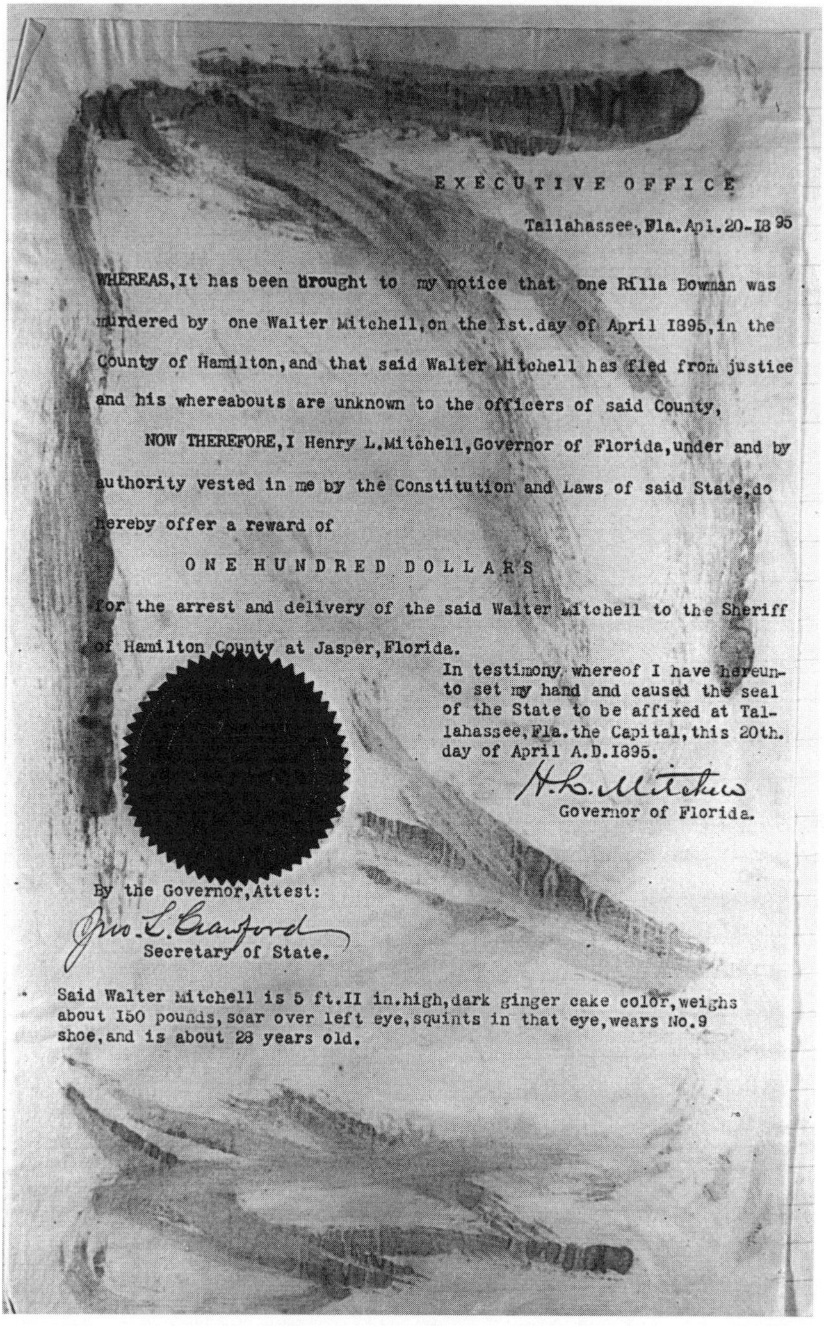

EXECUTIVE OFFICE

Tallahassee, Fla. Apl. 20-1895

WHEREAS, It has been brought to my notice that one Rilla Bowman was murdered by one Walter Mitchell, on the 1st. day of April 1895, in the County of Hamilton, and that said Walter Mitchell has fled from justice and his whereabouts are unknown to the officers of said County,

NOW THEREFORE, I Henry L. Mitchell, Governor of Florida, under and by authority vested in me by the Constitution and Laws of said State, do hereby offer a reward of

ONE HUNDRED DOLLARS

for the arrest and delivery of the said Walter Mitchell to the Sheriff of Hamilton County at Jasper, Florida.

In testimony whereof I have hereunto set my hand and caused the seal of the State to be affixed at Tallahassee, Fla. the Capital, this 20th. day of April A.D. 1895.

H. L. Mitchell
Governor of Florida.

By the Governor, Attest:

Jno. L. Crawford
Secretary of State.

Said Walter Mitchell is 5 ft. II in. high, dark ginger cake color, weighs about 150 pounds, scar over left eye, squints in that eye, wears No. 9 shoe, and is about 28 years old.

Proclamation of Governor Henry L. Mitchell for the arrest of a fugitive from Hamilton County. (Courtesy of the Florida State Archives).

Chapter V - Closing the Nineteenth and Into The Twentieth Century, 1877-1900

policy inaugurated by the Republicans: Florida would lease its convicts to private employers who would work them, take care of the prisoners, and pay an annual fee to the state. With both a state and county system in place, sheriffs participated increasingly in the mechanics of leasing. Prisoners would be used by the state's mines, railroads, turpentine camps, and in farm work. The entire process was open to obvious abuses and became a growing scandal. Florida was the last state to adopt convict leasing, and it was, next to Alabama, the last to abandon it. That did not occur until 1923.

During his gubernatorial campaign in 1877 Drew pledged to cut taxes and conduct state business in an inexpensive way. True to its fiscal pledges, Drew's administration slashed education and other state services sharply. It was not surprising that the old Chattahoochee arsenal came under the governor's survey. The facility had served both as home to the insane and as a state prison since 1869, but had become a costly, ill-kept eyesore. Because Drew had owned a large lumber and sawmill in Ellaville on the Suwannee River he saw ways that convicts could be used in such enterprises. Early in Drew's tenure a house committee endorsed the governor's proposal "that convicts be leased upon the most advantageous terms obtainable." Laws passed establishing the convict lease system and setting aside the Chattahoochee facility exclusively for the insane. Florida followed the southern pattern of leasing its convicts to private contractors willing to house and feed them and pay the state.[5] Before Drew's election about seventy convicts were already toiling near Lake Eustis on a railroad project. Those at the Chattahoochee institution were leased to Green Chaires, a Leon County cotton planter. The lessees housed the prisoners for two years, and the state paid a token amount of their upkeep.[6] Chaires's first report to the governor revealed dangerous working conditions. It was a foretaste of a system that constituted one of the darkest chapters in Florida's history.[7] Leased convicts were utilized in timber and turpentine camps until 1923 when both the state and county systems were abolished. Prisoners also cut canals, built railroads, graded roads, and mined phosphate.

After 1877 Florida lawmen were closely concerned with how developments in state law and a proposed new constitution would affect them. The Democrats were determined to solidify their regained supremacy over the state's political life. Party leaders chose in 1885 to write a constitution stripping various appointive powers from the governor. Beyond that, there was a consensus among Bourbon Democrats to prohibit the governor from succeeding himself in office and to abolish the position of lieutenant governor. The governor could be and was further weakened by making the six-man cabinet elective rather than appointive. Ultimately, the Bourbons succeeded in accomplishing their fundamental goal: shifting real political power in Florida to the counties and county leaders and to the state Democratic party's administrative hierarchy.

The constitutional convention met in the capitol building at Tallahassee on June 9, 1885. Various committees were appointed to work out the several articles and report them to the whole convention for approval, disapproval, or amendments. The Committee on County, Township and City Organization (county committee) was concerned with the sheriff and other county officers.[8] The initial draft of Article VIII, Section Five by the county committee made the sheriff, the five-man county commission, constables, clerk of the circuit court, county tax assessor, tax collector, treasurer, superintendent of public instruction, five-member board of public instruction, and county surveyor subject to popular election for four-year terms. Committee decisions were debated, but except for having county commissioners appointed by the governor, the sheriffs and other officials kept their popularly elected status. Some county officials had their tenures changed, but the sheriff's remained at four years.[9]

While the new constitution's Article VIII dealt with the sheriff's popular election and term of office, Article XVI, the Miscellaneous Provisions part of the document, concerned where the occupants would establish their offices. According to Section Four all county officials would maintain their offices and keep their official books and records at the county seat. Even so, "the Clerk and Sheriff shall either reside or have a sworn deputy within two miles of the county seat."[10] The reasons for making those exceptions were not explained. Floridians ratified the constitution in the fall of 1886, and, although much amended,

Chapter V - Closing the Nineteenth and Into The Twentieth Century, 1877-1900

the document would stand as Florida's basic instrument of government until it was revised in 1968.

The new constitution meant changes for the state's black population, and it meant the sheriff, especially in performing his election responsibilities, would play an important role. The constitution of 1885 did not specifically disenfranchise blacks, but it made possible the enactment of a poll tax. That was subsequently done by an act of 1889, and the result was the elimination of many black voters—and poor whites as well. That same year the "Eight Box Ballot Law" complicated voting procedures to the point that illiterate voters frequently had their ballots voided. Tensions ran high at polling places, and the sheriff and his deputies had to keep order.

Even if state laws passed in 1889 were largely intended to exclude African Americans from the ballot box, the statutes were not universally applied for several years. In 1888 the citizens of Monroe County elected Charles F. DuPont, a black, sheriff. Born in 1861 in Tampa, DuPont migrated to Key West after the Civil War, became a carpenter and Republican activist, and in 1889 was inaugurated as Florida's first popularly elected black sheriff. DuPont's four years in office were tumultuous. On one occasion he saved the lives of several prisoners in his custody, refusing to turn them over to a lynch mob.[11] His election in 1888 did not indicate, at least locally, a popular demand for disenfranchising legislation.

DuPont was popular with blacks and whites in Key West. In 1890 the Monroe County Grand Jury publicly commended him and his deputies for their "Gentlemanly and Courteous" behavior.[12] Still, there was prejudice against DuPont and his deputies, all but one of them African Americans. In DuPont's first summer as sheriff one of his black deputies named James A. Fleming was charged with swearing at a prominent cigar manufacturer's wife. Fleming was angry because the white woman refused to accompany him to the courthouse to settle a tax matter. Mrs. Louisa Marrero feigned illness, appealed to the circuit judge, and swore out a formal complaint against Fleming. Several of the manufacturer's employees corroborated her story, and a number of other citizens wrote the governor expressing their sympathy for

Monroe County Sheriff Charles F. DuPont, 1989-1893, was the last African American to serve as sheriff until the late twentieth century. (Courtesy of the Florida State Archives).

Marrero. Even so, her case against Fleming unraveled when circuit judge G. A. Hanson wrote the governor that after "quietly investigat[ing] the matter" he was:

> satisfied that she was more in fault than the officer....You know as well as I could tell you, how I feel about colored officers taking white people in custody, (But in this case there is no difference in color) and I have advised this officer kindly but firmly, that he must be polite, and courteous to all; and from close personal observation, and from general reputation, I am compelled to say to your Excellency that there is not in the circuit, a more efficient, painstaking, and politic officer, than Charles F. DuPont, Sheriff, and Deputy Fleming. They have never to my knowledge, in the least degree, shown favor, or partiality, to their color or any person with whom they have business. This much is due them, and I can not say less.[13]

As late as 1882 much of the Florida peninsula remained a frontier. Clear evidence of the lingering wilderness was seen in an act of that year authorizing county commissioners to pay $5 for every wolf, bear, and panther and $3 for every wildcat that was killed.[14] Various railroad corporations were extending and consolidating old lines and establishing new ones, but horsepower, in its literal sense, was basic to the economy. Horses (and mules) were to Florida's frontier what cars (and trucks) were to its twentieth century landscape. The historic problems caused by horse thieves still remained after 1885. A state law of 1866 provided a wide range of possible punishment for such felons: death by hanging, imprisonment, fine, or fine and imprisonment. The statute was repealed in 1885 and replaced by a less stringent measure that made horse thieves liable to a fine of $500 or two years in the state penitentiary.[15] Nor did persons in certain sections practice a high level of social etiquette. One authority has written of High Springs, an Alachua County phosphate boomtown in 1896, that it "resembled a western mining town on its pay days. Drunken miners roamed its streets, engaged in gun fights, and terrorized the town inhabitants."[16]

Conditions were even more frontier-like in Florida's lower peninsula. In 1887 the Florida legislature created six new counties: DeSoto, Lee, and Osceola in the south and Citrus, Pasco, and Lake in the central portion. The establishment of county government did not automatically advance the cause of civilization. That was obvious in south Florida where cattle culture, recent phosphate strikes, and frontier individualism combined to make violence a common occurrence. Conditions were better but less than ideal in older counties.

In November 1881, the editor of the Bartow *Informant* complained that his own county (Polk) needed a more efficient administration. Roads were "deplorable;" there was not a "good bridge in the county." Even worse, though Polk County had been created twenty years earlier, it still lacked a suitable jail. Because the citizens refused to pay taxes to support the housing of criminals, misdemeanors went unpunished. "The officers must parole all persons arrested for small offenses, as the pay of guards is too great to keep them in custody. Men may fight, get drunk, and act disorderly, and go 'scot-free' to the disgust of all good people because there is no place to lock them up." Moreover, "our old half-finished, unpainted courthouse is an eyesore to the visiting stranger and makes a bad impression." Another necessity was the appointment of a county attorney who "could serve as an advisor to county officers, so as to give proper forms and procedures of prosecuting wrong doers, as well as collecting fines, fees and delinquent accounts."[17]

Amid the disarray local citizens often took matters into their own hands. Efforts to prosecute local bully George W. Morgan who was accused of assassinating a respected Polk countian, were unsuccessful. Finally, Morgan himself was wounded by unknown assailants as he hunted cattle on the Peace River. When notified of the attack Polk County Sheriff C. C. Gresham formed a posse and pursued the suspects to no effect. Morgan managed to survive, only to be killed in his own home approximately ten days later. Although a newspaper did not defend Morgan's killing, it asserted that he was "quarrelsome and a terror to nearly everyone of his neighbors. He had threatened the lives of many of our best citizens and was the source of many an agonizing heart-chill to some of our best ladies." Morgan, the journal continued, was such a "terror to the community as to be termed a desperado."[18]

The adjective "primitive" cannot be excluded from words describing Florida in the late nineteenth-century years. Apprehending horse thieves, controlling rowdiness—it was all part of a lawman's work. Whatever their faults, Florida's sheriffs, deputies, and marshals were never accused of being overpaid or of having easy jobs.

Although much of the peninsula's southern portion resembled the "Old West," economic forces were already at work to attract large numbers of permanent and part-time residents. They sought prosperity and better lives. The years between the state's "redemption" and the turn of the century were ones of growth and development. The Bourbon administrations of Drew and Bloxham encouraged the inflow of northern capital investment through a deft combination of low taxes and liberal land grant policies. The short-term benefits of these polices had long-term costs for the state and its citizens, but few people realized them at the time.

In 1881 Governor Bloxham contracted with Philadelphia tool manufacturer Hamilton Disston for the sale of four million acres of "overflowed" land for the paltry sum of twenty-five cents an acre. Disston's plan was to use the latest technology to drain the uninhabitable region surrounding Lake Okeechobee and open it for settlement and agriculture. Disston died before his dream became reality. Yet, his efforts resulted in substantial migration and economic activity in, until then, practically uninhabited portions of the state. The phosphate boom brought large numbers south, as did the timber, citrus, and tourism industries. The latter was made possible when railroad barons Henry Plant and Henry Flagler extended lines to Tampa and Punta Gorda (1887) and to Miami (1896).

The state did not continue merely as home to native-born Americans. By the 1880s Key West had become one of the largest cigar-manufacturing centers in the United States. By 1886 labor unrest and local conditions caused much of the cigar-producing establishment to move to Tampa. Cigar manufacturer Vincente Ybor established one of America's most flourishing ethnic communities. Recent immigrants from Cuba, Spain, Italy, and Germany came to Ybor City and rolled some of the world's finest cigars. In law enforcement, as in other matters, cultures sometimes fused and sometimes clashed with the prevailing white Protestant establishment.[19]

Sheriffs coped with violence whether it was in Florida's emerging counties or elsewhere, and given their daily proximity to conflicting personal interests, sometimes lawmen battled one another. Individual differences do not respect people, time, place, or position. That human condition—individual differences—precipitated an intriguing Florida episode and an even more unusual conclusion in Columbia and Suwannee counties. In 1880 Gottschalf "Gus" Potsdamer, a prominent Jewish citizen of Lake City (Columbia County), was the town marshal. Somehow, young Potsdamer developed an unspecified but ongoing disagreement with the equally young Columbia County Sheriff John C. Henry (elected in the late 1870s). On January 27, 1880, Sheriff Henry encountered Potsdamer, probably by accident, in Lake City. One thing led to another and eventually to a fistfight that got out of control. Supposedly, Henry used the butt of his handgun to beat Potsdamer over the head. Retaliating, Potsdamer pulled his own pistol and shot Henry to death. In the trial that followed Potsdamer was found guilty by a Columbia County jury. The jury's recommendation of mercy saved him from hanging, but he was convicted of murder and sentenced to life in prison.[20]

Following his conviction Potsdamer was sent by train to Live Oak, seat of government for Suwannee County, and delivered to J. C. Powell, captain of the convict camp known as Sing Sing. The camp was located four miles from the county seat on the aptly named Padlock Road. In his book *The American Siberia* (1891), Powell, who never underestimated his own importance or bravery, recounted how the people in Live Oak speculated that Potsdamer would be rescued before he reached Sing Sing. On the other hand, a number of Jewish friends had accompanied the convicted man, and they were present to see that no lynching took place before Potsdamer was incarcerated. According to Powell, he told the fearful Columbia County sheriff and state's attorney, who were in charge of Potsdamer, as well as the prisoner's friends, that there was no need for a posse. He, Powell, would safely deliver his man to Sing Sing. Powell had the convicted felon's chains removed, and, unaided, safely marched him from Live Oak to the prison camp.[21]

The prisoner's friends had not forgotten him. They sought legal redress, and thirty days later Potsdamer was released while his case was appealed. To his chagrin, the prisoner soon heard the news: the Florida Supreme Court had upheld his conviction. Refusing to accept the verdict, his supporters redoubled their efforts, flooding the governor's office with appeals. Finally persuaded, Governor Edward A. Perry pardoned Potsdamer. He was set free (the fight was adjudged a "mutual" conflict). After his release Potsdamer returned to Lake City but later moved to Live Oak. There he became well liked, and, ironically, ran for sheriff of Suwannee County in 1889. He was elected and held office for three terms, 1889-1893 and 1913-1914. He was Florida's only example of a man who served as sheriff after having killed another sheriff. According to Powell, Potsdamer was never bitter about his own experience in the convict camp.[22]

As noted above, in the period after the new constitution was adopted, the sheriff was popularly elected as in antebellum times. He was forced to become a politician as well as a lawman, especially in an election year. In the new era a sheriff's role was defined by old laws and laws that were refinements of previous legislation. Every two years the lawman was further charged with enforcing new statutes emanating from Tallahassee. As Florida moved toward modern times the lawman's job became more demanding. Like other county officers, the sheriff had to give bond. It fluctuated from county to county, and setting the exact amount was up to the commissioners in any county. In 1887 a law required that the sheriff's bond be not less than $2,000 and not more than $10,000. A separate statute established the bonds of constables and justices of the peace at $500.[23]

The sheriff presented his fees for mileage in criminal cases to the county commissioners.[24] The old fee system was retained and steadily extended. If nothing else, the amounts of the fees were signs of the times, reflecting the state's economy. By 1893 a sheriff collected fees for executing various writs, calling juries, and, as always, for mileage.

The routine of incarcerating a prisoner was both a physical and a bureaucratic exercise. The sheriff collected fifty cents for committing a prisoner to jail under process. He also got ten cents a mile for conveying a prisoner to jail or for removing one. Each recommitment order netted him twenty-five cents, as did the release of a prisoner. The sheriff's fee for executing a writ of habeas corpus was one dollar. For hanging a prisoner he was paid twenty-five dollars and no more than fifteen dollars for erecting the gallows. The fee list seemed limitless, although in total amount it was not large. Besides prisoners, when a sheriff had to keep horses, mules, and other livestock under various processes of law he collected fifty cents per head per day.[25] The amount covered his costs of feeding and caring for the stock. By 1897 when Dade County had a stock law, the local sheriff was paid twenty-five cents a day as impounder and fifty cents a day for maintaining the animals.[26]

Toward the end of the century sheriffs received forty cents a day per prisoner for feeding ten or less inmates. If the number exceeded ten the fee was thirty cents. If a prisoner was from another place, the sheriff had to present his bill to the commissioners of the prisoner's home county.[27] An important law passed in 1895 that established a fine and forfeiture fund in each county. It regulated the payment of criminal costs and authorized a special tax to make the payments. Additionally, the act provided for the feeding of prisoners and the hiring of convicts. Besides continuing his duty of supplying food to the prisoners, the sheriff had to furnish a list of their names and the length of their imprisonment. Obligations for payment continued to be separated on an in-county and out-of-county basis.[28]

The county's chief law enforcement officer never relinquished his responsibilities as an election official. Legislation passed in 1887 required him, on receiving notice from the secretary of state for an election, to have at least five announcements of the contest put in the county newspaper. If there was no paper he was to post the copies in the county's most public places.[29] The general assembly's session in 1889 required the sheriff to deputize a man to be present at each polling place in Florida during an election. The deputy was to see to it "that there is no interruption of good order," and if necessary to summon a posse. No

Chapter V - Closing the Nineteenth and Into The Twentieth Century, 1877-1900

doubt the deputy's diligence was increased by the provision that failure to perform his duty was a misdemeanor and made him liable for a fine of $500 or six months in the county prison, or both.[30]

By 1900 some Floridians became part of a national phenomenon known as the "Progressive Movement." It was a reform crusade whose adherents wanted to restore justice, equity, and democracy to all areas of American life—social, political, and economic. The movement lasted until about 1920 and achieved some significant results. A number of Floridians adopted the reform of restructuring the state's political machinery. With good reason, they demanded the substitution of the "direct primary" for the old system of party caucuses and conventions in nominating candidates for public office. In Florida the political part of the Progressive Movement became a revolt against the county officials and Democratic leaders who had been empowered by the constitution of 1885. In some areas local leaders were flagrant in their excesses and came to form what were pejoratively called "courthouse rings." Individual lawmen might fall short of expectations, but there was no organized or massive public outcry against sheriffs. In fact, their jurisdiction was extended to new laws pertaining to politics. Florida passed a primary law in 1897. Since the primary was an election, the sheriff was required to guarantee good order at the ballot box, just as he was already doing in general elections.[31]

The Progressive period in Florida was one of mixed results. Yet, it had an important influence on the state. Previous political opposition to the Bourbon Democrats had taken the form of Independent, Greenback, and Populist parties, but their efforts had failed. The Democrats withstood the challenges primarily because they posed as the party of white supremacy, proclaiming only they preserved that principle. The rival parties were denounced as divisive elements that threatened to make possible a return to the perceived corruption of Republicanism and Reconstruction. Even so, there were mounting cries for reform.

Ironically, Florida's primary law was originally intended as a reform, but it had the opposite results. In any state that had a two party system the candidates nominated in the Democratic and

Republican primaries faced each other in the fall general elections. Since Florida, like other southern states, had no effective Republican opposition, the Democratic party's nominees were automatically assured of winning the general election. Ultimately, what had been intended as a progressive reform would be aborted and put to strange uses in the twentieth century.

The constitution of 1885 was followed by new circumstances that affected Florida's sheriffs. One uniquely Florida development concerned sponges. The commercial sponging industry, while limited, became important, and in 1889 the legislature designated the area between Pensacola and Cape Florida as its Sponge Fishing Grounds. Unauthorized spongers were prohibited from having access to the zone, and the sheriff and other arresting officers could seize the trespassers' diving gear.[32]

The overdue realization that Florida's fishing and wildlife needed protection involved the sheriff as a matter of course. Individual laws protecting certain Florida rivers and estuaries appeared as early as the 1880s. When sheriffs failed to exert their authority to the satisfaction of local citizens and at-risk business owners, complaints to Tallahassee sometimes resulted. On March 6, 1888, Palatka merchant W. B. Cross complained to Governor Perry that a man named Vanderpool was taking shad on the sand bars of lakes Dexter and Harney with an illegal seine net. The Volusia County sheriff, although notified, had refused to enforce the law, causing Cross to write, "we beg to appeal to your protection that immediate steps be taken in this matter to prevent the abuse and destroying [of] the shad business on the St. Johns River." When questioned, Sheriff G. P. Healy responded that he had tried to enforce the restrictions, but nothing could be done without the cooperation of county officers along the St. Johns. The lawman had nothing but contempt for Cross, claiming that the merchant's complaints stemmed not from any goal of protecting the river but because he was a fisherman and less expert in breaking the law than Vanderpool. "Mr. Cross," the sheriff charged, "would not hesitate for a moment to entirely denude the St. Johns of eatable fish for a hundred dollars of ready money, and the anxiety that he shows for the enforcement of the law is the outcome

Chapter V - Closing the Nineteenth and Into The Twentieth Century, 1877-1900

of his desire for a monopoly of law breaking on the River. I have no objection to Mr. Cross's seeing this letter."[33]

By the 1890s America's rapid industrialization brought with it a host of new crimes and with them ever-increasing challenges for Florida lawmen. Expanded opportunities for sophisticated criminal activity created a greater need for identifying and apprehending those who used the nation's railroad systems to escape. With no federal law enforcement arm yet in place, victimized private enterprises such as railroads, banks, and others relied on private agencies. The Pinkerton National Detective Agency was the prototype. The "Pinkertons" identified, informed on, and offered rewards for the capture of criminals who fled to other states. The agency had offices in major cities across the country.[34] Beginning in the 1880s county sheriffs' offices in Florida began receiving bulletins, posters, and handbills from out of state sheriffs' offices, big city police departments, railroad and banking companies, and national detective agencies such as the Pinkertons. They offered rewards for an astonishing variety of lawbreakers and missing persons.

During the 1890s the Leon County Sheriff's Office, like its Florida counterparts, received public and private notices for fugitives. They were received from at least twenty-seven states, but most came from neighboring southern states, particularly Georgia (136) and Alabama (31). Many Georgia fugitives fled from the numerous labor camps operated by that state's penitentiary system. A number of Alabamians were leased convicts who had escaped from the Tennessee Coal and Iron Railroad Company's Pratt Mines prison near Birmingham. The notices were intended for interstate distribution, although sheriffs from other states specifically wrote Florida sheriffs when they thought escapees were headed their way.

In 1898 a sheriff in Aiken, South Carolina, wrote Leon County Sheriff John A. Pearce alerting him to two white men accused of murder and likely to escape to Florida. Frank Bowden had killed a black woman he was living with in North Georgia and put her in the bottom of a well. Bowden was able to escape, the sheriff speculated, with the help of his uncle who was the county sheriff. Charley Walton, the other fugitive, had lived in Aiken three years before being identified as a man wanted for murder in North Carolina and Tennessee.[35] Four years earlier a Crenshaw County, Alabama, sheriff warned Sheriff Pearce about Sam Skipper "who is said to be in Florida crossing the line at Geneva." Skipper was described as a tall, lanky man with a "narrow, sharp face, long hooked nose—fair—blue eyes light hair...chews and spits much—loves whiskey & women and will be found about low places—especially in the country."[36]

Florida sheriffs also corresponded with one another in the pursuit of fugitives. In 1893 Columbia County's W. N. Cone wrote Marion County Sheriff B. Du Pre Hodge, offering his assistance in capturing one Jenkins, a murder suspect who had escaped to Georgia. As Cone explained to Hodge, his interest was more personal than professional because Jenkins had murdered his brother, an Ocala policeman.[37]

Living and working conditions in county jails and chain gangs were major concerns of the public and the county commissioners. Serious complaints had to be investigated. In May 1892, Francis P. Fleming received a series of letters from Charles E. Wellborn, a prisoner who protested to the governor that he was wrongly convicted of larceny. Wellborn added that he was being brutally treated in the Duval County jail. Inmates, according to him, subsisted on sour, stale cornbread and dirty goat meat. He complained that Patrick Fallen, the jailer, had ignored his medical needs and had repeatedly locked him in the "death sentence dungeon." Moreover, Wellborn had been put on the county chain gang, although he received better treatment there than in jail.[38]

Governor Fleming ordered county solicitor R. M. Call to investigate. He did, and reported that none of Wellborn's allegations were true. Call was backed up by jailer Fallen and W. E. Scull, a deputy. Fallen noted, "Wellborn was a very troublesome prisoner but I always felt sorry for him because I thought he came from a good family and perhaps had a good mother. I often sent him things to eat from my table.... In charity to Wellborn I think he is light in the head; he never made any complaint to me while in jail but often said that he was well treated."[39] The question remains one of whether Wellborn's charges against the authorities were true. No historical documents exist to determine the issue. That he had a case seems probable.

Florida governors received numerous complaints and charges against sheriffs. Sometimes officials from neighboring counties quarreled over jurisdiction and asked the governor to resolve their disputes. One serious complaint involved a combination of incompetence and criminal wrongdoing in Hamilton County. Sheriff S. S. Sharp had a reputation for drunkenness and on one occasion, according to a body of local citizens, had brutally whipped a man in the Jasper public square for no reason. Matters reached a crisis in 1892 when nine prisoners escaped from the county jail. A number of Jasper citizens, including a local attorney, wrote Fleming stating that the sheriff was "entirely responsible for the escape of prisoners.... Things are going hellwards here..., and if we don't get rid of Sharp and get another man...no telling where we will soon land." The attorney added that on a previous occasion Sharp had failed to apprehend a man accused of setting fire to a store in Jasper to collect insurance money, despite having a warrant for his arrest.[40]

Governor Fleming ordered Circuit Judge John F. White to investigate, and a number of affidavits were taken. On being questioned Sharp's deputy was forced to admit that he could "not exonerate" the sheriff "entirely from drinking more or less," but added, "I do certify" that strong drink had never prevented Sharp from performing his duties. The statement was hardly a ringing endorsement, but the most serious charge concerned a murder case pending in the Hamilton County Court. It began two years earlier when a friend of the sheriff's named Mathis was charged with murder. Sharp failed to arrest the accused, facilitated his escape to Texas, and corresponded with the fugitive, warning him of efforts to capture him. Nevertheless, Mathis subsequently returned to Florida, and despite Sharp's failure to act was taken into custody. With the trial set to begin, judge White asked Fleming to suspend Sharp and appoint another man in the short time remaining before the next election. He did not expect Sharp to run again. The governor agreed and selected another person to serve out the remaining six months of the sheriff's term.[41]

Governor Fleming removed another sheriff (John W. Johnston of

Hernando County) for falsifying his accounts for feeding and housing county prisoners.[42] In 1895 similar investigations against Columbia County's W. N. Cone uncovered numerous instances of fee overcharges for travel and other duties. Sheriff Cone was further charged with mismanaging the jail and failing to provide adequately for county prisoners. The charges were dropped once numerous officials, including the chairman of the county commission, came to Cone's defense. The sheriff completed the remaining years of his term and was elected again in 1901.[43]

When eight prisoners escaped from Arcadia jail many citizens blamed DeSoto County Sheriff Owen Dishong. As a local attorney explained to Governor Bloxham, the situation "most certainly demands Executive Investigation." The escape was the second in two weeks, and a local attorney declared, "there is no doubt we have a good jail, one that with moderately good attention will hold any man, and if half that is told me is true then no doubt can exist about it being carelessness." He concluded, "it is certain that some of our foulest murders have been done because of the fact that the public has no faith in our sheriff."[44] Because of the charges a three-month investigation was launched. Dishong responded to no avail that the attacks against him were politically motivated.[45] Finally, upon the county commission's assertion that the sheriff was negligent, Bloxham suspended him until the next meeting of the state senate. Indignant, the lawman immediately resigned, and Bloxham appointed Dishong's predecessor to finish his term.[46]

Florida's county jails remained vulnerable to escapes. Throughout the 1880s and 1890s sheriffs published and distributed numerous notices for the arrest of escaped prisoners. On March 25, 1896, T. K. Spencer, Hillsborough County's sheriff, offered a $200 reward for the arrest of Steve Stanley who was wanted for the murder of Jesse Clower at the Port of Tampa. Stanley was a "very dark brown negro" with a "large gurgle in the throat and rough looking face [,] has a soft voice, is slow in movement, and leans forward when standing. Has also three or four buckshot marks on [his] left breast close to nipple."[47] Most of the "at large" flyers contained vivid descriptions similar to that of Stanley. On October 25, 1905, Sheriff Henry Gordon of Marion County issued a

Chapter V - Closing the Nineteenth and Into The Twentieth Century, 1877-1900

proclamation and reward for the arrest of five men who escaped from his jail in Ocala. Among those who departed was a forty-five-year-old "noted banjo picker" named Bill Canty. The fugitive had gunshot wounds in the "rump" and "right groin."[48] In 1897 Sheriff A. J. McClellan of Calhoun County offered a substantial reward and payment of all legal fees to anyone capturing one Harrison who was under a murder sentence. The fugitive had escaped from the Ocala jail.[49]

According to a notice from Citrus County's Sheriff A. T. Priest four fugitives had escaped from his Inverness jail in April 1898. Of the four, three were wanted for murder. Will Wallace, whose crime was unspecified, might be found working phosphate or gambling. Murder suspect Jack Randall projected a "rather pleasant appearance," but had "several scars and marks about the face and head [and] has had syphilis; runs pump and small engines; and is a gambler and blind tiger man [seller of illegal alcoholic beverages]." The most wanted was Primas Mitchell, alias Jim Jones, who killed a man near Crystal River and had already served five years in the penitentiary for another crime. Mitchell's occupation, declared the sheriff, "is turpentine work, and [he] is a good hand. Goes well armed, had on when last seen two pistols, one 6 inch blue steel in a scabbard around his waist, and the other was a 4 inch barrel S. & W.; he carried a pistol at work." Though a native of Archer, Mitchell was last seen in Jackson County.[50]

A somber reminder of the precarious nature of being a lawman always came when a sheriff died in the line of duty. In 1890 Sheriff Henry W. Epperson of Bradford County was killed by Frank Foster, but the murderer broke out of jail in Starke less than a week before he was scheduled to hang. The Bradford County commission offered a $200 reward for the felon.[51] Whether Foster was ever captured is not known, but Epperson was one of three Bradford County sheriffs to be killed in five years. In 1885 the slain man's own father, George W. Epperson, had been fatally wounded while making an arrest in Valdosta, Georgia. Then in May 1891, Starke's City Marshal David Levy Alvarez, who was acting as Bradford County sheriff, was killed when he tried to arrest Harmon Murray, the black leader of the notorious "north Florida gang." Two weeks previous to Alvarez's murder, Murray had also killed

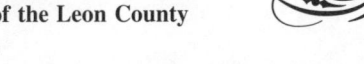

Thomas K. Spencer served as Hillsborough County sheriff, 1893-1901. (Courtesy of the Hillsborough County Sheriffs Office).

Hillsborough County Sheriff T.K. Spencer's proclamation for a fugitive.(Courtesy of the Leon County Sheriffs Office).

Levin Armwood served as Hillsborough County deputy sheriff around the turn of the century. (Courtesy of the Armwood Family Collection, University of South Florida).

Nassau county sheriff's deputy Joseph W. Robinson. Later in 1891 Murray was slain by a friend who then claimed the $1,500 reward.[52]

Bad luck for sheriffs continued in 1891. In Suwannee County "a most horrible and cold-blooded murder was committed" when S. M. Carson, Sheriff Gus Potsdamer's deputy, tried to arrest a black man named Burden on a warrant issued in Madison County. Judge John F. White wrote the governor, explaining that the "people of this county

$50 REWARD

Delivered to me in........................ for Mack Sirmons, alias Henry Sirmons, alias Henry Miller. Color, coal black; age, 23 to 24 years; height, 5 feet 8 to 10 inches; large eyes, white of eyes shows well; little pop-eyed; wide mouth; flat nose; some of upper front teeth may be decayed a little, one or two may be broken off or out; smooth face when he left here one year ago; supposed to weigh 160 to 170 pounds, but all guess work; shot in small of back or hip with small shot, on left side; may find shot under the skin now, and at times limps with the wounds when he left here; it is said that some of the shot or a ball passed through his body and lodged in his groins. He is a banjo picker, turpentine hand and saw mill hand, and works about in the country at farm work. Born near Valdosta, Ga. Has worked around Lake City and Tallahassee, and in Hamilton County, Florida. Usually goes poorly dressed, and left here wearing a wide rim hat. Has lived with Mousiri Banks, of Thomasville, Ga., for two years. The woman's mother lives in Boston, Ga. I give you this information to help you identify Sirmons. He is wanted here for making an assault on a respectable white lady.

I enclose you circulars so you may furnish your deputies and work your county out. Please do all in your power to help me catch this scoundrel. I have requisition ready on your State. When last heard of was in Henry County, Alabama. Ellen Williams, a mulatto woman, about 30 years old, who is now in Alabama somewhere, knows this man. She was raised (I think) arround Troy, Alabama. If you get any information and it is too far for you to go, please write me at once.

J. W. HAWKINS,
Sheriff Suwannee County, Florida.

Proclamation for the arrest of Mack Sirmans, wanted by Suwannee County Sheriff J. W. Hawkins. (Courtesy of Florida Sheriffs Association).

Chapter V - Closing the Nineteenth and Into The Twentieth Century, 1877-1900

are very much aroused and excited and are desirous that some extraordinary inducement be used to cause the capture of this desperate Negro." Months later in Levy County a black man was killed in a fight at Otter Creek. Several area men, hoping to collect a reward, first claimed that the dead man was Harmon Murray. When the identification proved to be inaccurate, the men declared that the dead man was Burden. Hearing of the incident, Sheriff Potsdamer investigated and concluded that the dead man was neither Murray nor Burden. Consequently, Potsdamer warned Governor Fleming not to authorize the payment of the reward. Burden, the lawman insisted, "[is] not dead, but is still at large and I have positive evidence.... Aside from the interest I officially feel in this case I am exceedingly anxious to have Burton [Burden] got as he killed my friend and faithful deputy."[53]

The last decades of the nineteenth century saw the sheriffs make fewer appeals to the legislature for compensatory relief they believed was their due. Still, there were some who did. Most of their appeals were routine, such as those that occurred in Leon County in 1881 and in Calhoun County in 1895. In Leon Sheriff Alex Moseley, under orders from the circuit judge, housed and fed two men indicted for murder. The men were from Calhoun County, and because their prolonged stay in jail was from October 25, 1880, to May 9, 1881, Moseley's bill was for $162.62. When the money was not forthcoming the sheriff took his case to the legislature. That body agreed and ordered the state treasurer to pay in full. As previously discussed, toward the end of Reconstruction sheriffs were assigned roles as timber agents and charged with arresting persons who trespassed on public lands and cut timber illegally. In 1895 Caley Holley, sheriff and ex-officio timber agent of Calhoun County, presented the commissioners a bill of $78.44 for expenses incurred in arresting men stealing timber off public lands. When the county commissioners declined Holley made a successful appeal to the legislature. In 1888 a more extraordinary event occurred in Taylor County. In an argument involving two county citizens, John D. Cox and Lucius Henderson, Cox was killed. Henderson was accused of murder and locked up to await trial. In the interim Henderson was murdered while in the county jail by unknown persons. Besides not

141

Chapter V - Closing the Nineteenth and Into The Twentieth Century, 1877-1900

saying much about local security, the event caused problems. Sheriff George W. Carlton of Taylor County and his counterpart, S. A. Paramore of Madison County, along with the clerk of the court, two lawyers, a physician, and nine witnesses, were involved in pre-trial activities. Yet, there was no trial, no verdict of guilty or not guilty, and county authorities balked at paying anything. Finally, in 1895, the by then former sheriffs Carlton and Paramore and others brought the matter before the general assembly. All of the claimants were awarded small amounts of money. Carlton was paid $94.36, and Paramore received $13.90.[54]

With the inhumanity of its convict lease system and with its treatment of prisoners, especially blacks, Florida had an imperfect penal system. Still, there were examples of changing views and informed attitudes. For instance, in 1891 a legislative statute declared that a person convicted in municipal court and forced to work the streets "shall not be confined either with ball or chain at such work."[55] As the state moved toward assuming a responsibility in economic and social issues, the sheriff frequently was assigned a part.

In 1889 Florida's lawmakers established a much needed State Board of Health. In medical emergencies the State Health Officer was empowered to place a region under quarantine. In such an event the local sheriff and constable were put under the Health Officer's direction to help enforce the measure. Another act followed in 1895 and assigned sheriffs and constables to the Health Officer when there was a threat of rabies.[56]

Prize fighting was popular in the United States, and the fighters, especially those in the heavyweight division, were national heroes. Pugilism's unsavory aspects—the brutality, the betting it attracted, the criminal character of many persons associated with the sport—caused a negative reaction among the public. Lawmakers in various states responded with restrictive laws. Even so, the sport had many fans.

In Tallahassee the legislature of 1895 passed an act prohibiting prize fighting in the state. The law made it a felony for a person to engage in a fight, with or without gloves, involving money for admission, or for any betting to take place. Those found guilty were subject to a fine of from $2,500 to $5,000, or five years' imprisonment, or both. The law applied equally to any "second, stake holder, counselor, or adviser." Not surprisingly, the law declared, "It shall be the duty of the sheriff or his deputies, in any county, where there is cause to believe that such an encounter or contest is about to occur, to enter any house or enclosure or any other place and arrest without warrant, any party or parties engaged, or about to engage in such contest."[57] Enacting a statute was one thing but enforcing it was another. A segment of the public wanted to see the bouts, and promoters went to great lengths, all of them illegal, to answer the demand. Florida's sheriffs were just as determined to enforce the law. A subsequent chapter recounts how the sheriff of Duval County, the assertively named Napoleon Bonaparte Broward, participated in trying to prevent a heavyweight championship fight. In large part, Broward used the public notice he gained to launch an important political career.

Less spectacularly, sheriffs were drawn into enforcing other new acts. Because Florida and the South were increasingly dependent upon commercial fertilizer to increase crop yields, the demand for the product and its sale and manufacture offered opportunities for abuse. Large numbers of spurious brands flooded the market, many of them containing no information about the substances contained within the bags. A law of 1895 ordered sheriffs to seize and sell all imported fertilizers that were not labeled.[58] The law was not restrictive enough because some brands that printed the chemical and mineral elements on their bags contained false information.

In the Florida judicial system the sheriff continued his various duties as a key official of the courts. His services were expanded as old courts required new responsibilities of him and new courts were established. A law of 1895 amended older statutes and assigned sheriffs (or constables) as the executive officers in justice of the peace courts. Their duties included serving process. They also were made the executive officers in county courts.[59]

The Progressive Movement had the widely publicized goal of regulating the railroads. Because of flagrant abuses by the owners of the lines—high and discriminatory freight rates, rebates, political machinations and collusion, poor service—public opinion supported curbing their power. There were various levels of regulation—local, state, and federal (in Washington the Interstate Commerce commission was created in 1887). There had been a number of laws passed in Florida since 1866 pertaining to railroads, the constitution dealt briefly with the carriers, and in 1887 an ineffective railroad commission was established. The commission was abolished in the early 1890s but recreated permanently in 1897. A Florida law of 1897 taxed the railroads and set time limits for payment. If the taxes were not paid by the appointed time, the comptroller was to issue a warrant for the sheriff to serve. He then collected the taxes and forwarded them to the comptroller. The fines were ultimately distributed to aid the public schools. For his efforts the sheriff was allowed his "usual fee."[60]

The legislature passed a major act in the spring of 1897 regulating railroad schedules and setting tariffs on freight, as well as on express, sleeping, and passenger cars. The secretary of the State Railroad Commission could order county commissioners to issue a subpoena notice, or other process. In the chain of command they would in turn direct the sheriff to serve the documents. As he did for his participation in collecting railroad taxes, the lawman collected a fee.[61]

Funds for public education in Florida were inadequate compared to that of states outside the South. Even so, the education sections of the constitution of 1885 were better than reformers expected. A segregated school system was made a part of the constitution, but the state's appropriation for education was more generous than Bourbon Democrats would have liked. By 1897 there was the beginning of the realization that juvenile crime was linked to education and that incarceration of young offenders with hardened criminals offered no short or long-range solutions. In response, the lawmakers enacted a measure that year authorizing the governor, attorney general, and commissioner of agriculture to buy from 50 acres to 320 acres of land for a reform school. They were not to pay over $5 an acre. There were, as always, the minutia of implementing laws, and sheriffs were enlisted to transport the offenders to the school.[62]

As the twentieth century approached, Florida sheriffs found themselves busy with their jobs and their private lives. Their responsibilities had increased, and they faced reelection every four years. Because an individual sheriff operated mainly in his own county, his jurisdiction was geographically circumscribed. Still, he interacted with sheriffs in other counties and often in other states. For one reason or another, formal and informal visits to Tallahassee were sometimes required. He was called on to transport prisoners outside his county, and in many ways his job required him to be more than an isolated official concerned only with local affairs. Many of his activities and problems were shared by his contemporaries. Although there was a commonalty among sheriffs, they had no statewide organization. There was little exchange of mutual interests. The deficiency had not gone unnoticed, but it was not until the early spring of 1893 that an attempt was made to rectify it.

Sheriff A. U. Hilleary, who was elected sheriff of Alachua County in 1892, was the catalyst for the formation of The Florida Sheriffs' Mutual Benefit Association. Apparently, Hilleary conferred with some other sheriffs, and the word was sent out to their colleagues who responded favorably to the idea. On Thursday morning March 23, 1893, representatives from thirty-five counties (some of them represented by proxy) gathered in Jacksonville to form their organization. In the opinion of the Jacksonville *Florida Times-Union*, "a finer body of men never assembled in the city." As the host, Duval County's Sheriff Napoleon B. Broward made arrangements for his colleagues to meet in the hall of Montedore Lodge, Knights of Pythias.[63]

The morning session was occupied with effecting a permanent organization and drafting a constitution. The brief document declared that the organization was to be made up of Florida's sheriffs, and that its purpose was to provide united action among the members in assisting each other to perform their duties. In the event any member was killed while engaged in the performance of official duties, the association set up a relief plan. The members pledged to contribute $50 each for the benefit of his widow or other family representative. The lawmen's document decreed that there would be annual gatherings, and the president could call special sessions. Officers and a five-man exec-

Chapter V - Closing the Nineteenth and Into The Twentieth Century, 1877-1900

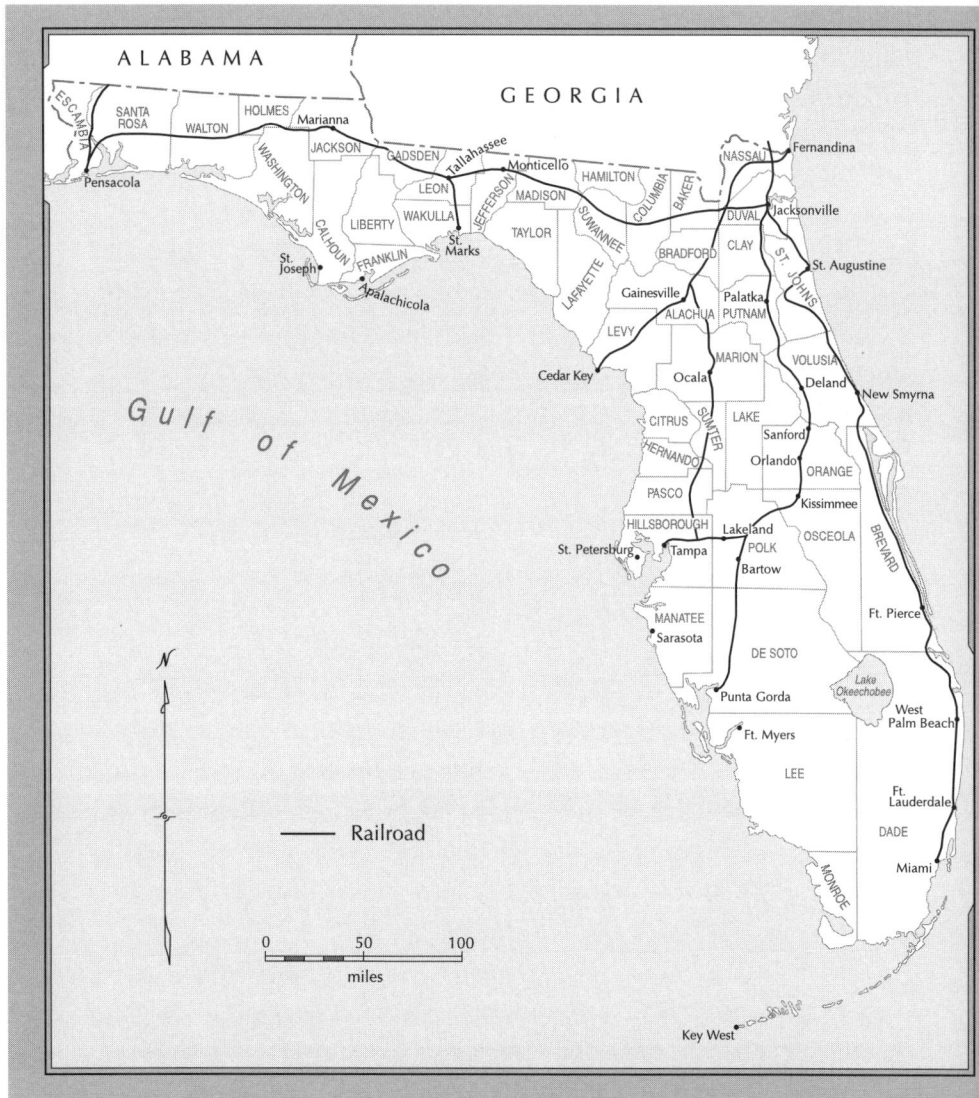

Florida as it entered the twentieth century.

utive committee would be chosen annually (the first officers were: president, A. U. Hilleary; vice president, B. W. Chester of Gadsden County, and treasurer, N. B. Broward).[64]

Hilleary played a prominent role in establishing the Sheriff's Association, and by becoming its first president gave every indication that he expected to remain in law enforcement. Yet, for unknown reasons he resigned as sheriff of Alachua County in 1895. He was succeeded by H. M. Tillis who had widespread support. All of the many letters written to Governor Henry L. Mitchell urging the appointment of Tillis mentioned that Hilleary was resigning. None criticized the outgoing sheriff (most did not praise him, but that was not their intent), and none hinted at why he was stepping down. One Tillis supporter spoke of Hilleary as "our present and worthy sheriff." It is possible that Hilleary got tired of the petty harassment of the office and decided not to continue. In the spring of 1894 a constituent, one with a dubious reputation, issued a series of unsubstantiated charges against him.[65] The retiring sheriff may well have envisioned more success with fewer vexations in the business world that he entered. Whatever his reasons, Hilleary deserves credit as the founder of what became the present-day Florida Sheriffs' Association. Helping lawmen confront the twentieth century, the organization worked to further their interests.

Chapter V - Closing the Nineteenth and Into The Twentieth Century, 1877-1900

Notes for Chapter V

1. Edwin C. Williamson, *Florida Politics in the Gilded Age, 1877-1893* (Gainesville, 1976), 25-26.
2. Resignations from Office, RG 156, series 260, vol. 1, FSA; Roll of County Sheriffs provided to authors by the Florida Sheriffs Association. From 1877-1887 only one sheriff, Thomas Osteen of Taylor County, lost his office for wrongdoing. He was removed by Governor William D. Bloxham in February 1883, Removals from Public Office, 1869-1888, RG 151, series 261, vol. 3 FSA. See also *Florida Senate Journal 1877*, 26, for the names of office holders removed from office by Drew in 1877.
3. J. W. Tyler to Henry L. Mitchell, April 28, 1894, Henry L. Mitchell Papers, 1893-1897, RG 101, series 581, box 22, FSA.
4. Daniel J. Paul to William D. Bloxham, November 9, 18, December 2, 1889. Paul's predecessor had also written to Tallahassee asking if the reward for Dorsey was still in force. See W. M. Bowen to Henry L. Mitchell, August 12, 1896, all in ibid.
5. Jeffrey A. Drobney, *Lumbermen and Log Sawyers: Life, Labor, and Culture in the North Florida Timber Industry, 1830-1930* (Macon, 1997), 153-154; Williamson, *Florida Politics in the Gilded Age*, 28-29.
6. Williamson, *Florida Politics in the Gilded Age*, 28-30.
7. Green Chaires, "Report for October 1, 1878," George F. Drew Papers, 1877-1881, RG 101, Ser. 577, box 5, folder 1, FSA.
8. *Journal of the Proceedings of the Constitutional Convention of the State of Florida...1885* (Tallahassee, 1885), 9. Hereafter cited as *Constitutional Convention, 1885*. Committee members were: R. A. Monsalvatage, W. H. Hausman, W. N. Sheats, F. B. Genovar, F. J. Lutterloh, Henry C. Hicks, Philip Walter, and W. B. Carr, ibid., 9.
9. Ibid., 169, 320, 486-487.
10. Ibid. The *Constitutional Convention Journal* conveniently contains at the end of the proceedings a copy of the completed constitution of 1885.
11. Denham and Brown "Black Sheriffs of Post-Civil War Florida," 15; Canter Brown Jr., *Florida's Black Public Officials, 1867-1924* (Tuscaloosa, 1998), 86; Jacksonville *Florida Times-Union*, June 16, 189.
12. Monroe County Grand Jury Presentment, March 27, 1889, Francis P. Fleming Papers, 1889-1893, RG 101, series 580, box 10, folder 6, FSA.
13. G. A. Hanson to Francis P. Fleming, January 9, 1890, Francis P. Fleming Papers, 1889-1893, RG 101, series 580, box 8, folder 7, FSA.
14. *FA 1882*, 144-145.
15. Ibid., 2 The same law made robbery of a person a death penalty felony. See also ibid., *1885*, 63.

16. John B. Pickard, *Florida's Eden An Illustrated History of Alachua County* (Gainesville, 1994), 44.
17. Bartow *Informant*, November 19, 1881.
18. Ibid., May 13, 27, 1882.
19. See Edward A. Fernald and Elizabeth D. Purdum, *Atlas of Florida* (Gainesville, 1992), 100-109; Samuel Proctor, "Prelude to the New Florida, 1877-1919," 266-286, in Gannon, *New History of Florida* ; Brown, *Florida's Peace River Frontier*, 255-345; Joe Knetsch, "Hamilton Disston and the Development of Florida," *Sunland Tribune: Journal of the Tampa Historical Society*, XXIV (1998), 5-20.
20. J. C. Powell, *The American Siberia* (Philadelphia, 1891), 125-129; Wilbanks, *Forgotten Heroes*, 20-21.
21. Powell, *American Siberia*, 126.
22. Ibid., 126-129.
23. *FA 1887*, 93; ibid., 94.
24. Ibid., 46-49.
25. Ibid., *1889*, 31-33. To the extent that a constable was involved, he was also compensated.
26. Ibid., *1897*, 191.
27. Ibid., *1895*, 172.
28. Ibid., 43-47. Sheriffs also collected fees for serving as defendants in matters of administration and trusts, as well as seventy-five cents for each approval of criminal bonds. See ibid., 172, 167.
29. Ibid., *1887*, 54-56.
30. Ibid., *1889*, 103.
31. Ibid., *1897*, 62-64. For the movement's regional impact see Dewey Grantham, *Southern Progressivism: The Reconciliation of Progress and Tradition* (Knoxville, 1983).
32. Ibid., *1889*, 152-153.
33. W. A. Cross to Edward A. Perry, March 6, 1888, and G. P. Healy to Edward A. Perry, March 13, 1888, Edward A. Perry Papers, 1885-1889, RG 101, series 577, box 6, folder 1, FSA.
34. See Frank Morn, *"The Eye That Never Sleeps" A History of the Pinkerton National Detective Agency* (Bloomington, Indiana, 1982); and James D. Horan, *The Pinkertons: The Detective Agency That Made History* (New York, 1967).
35. Unidentified lawman from Aiken, South Carolina, to John A. Pearce, July 14, 1898, Ledger of Wanted Notices, Leon County Sheriffs Office, 192. Hereafter cited as Ledger.
36. Sheriff of Crenshaw County, Alabama, to John A. Pearce, July 28, 1894, ibid., 207.
37. W. N. Cone to B. Du Pre Hodge, July 1, 1893, Henry L. Mitchell Papers, 1893-1897, RG 101, series 581, box 22, FSA.

Chapter V - Closing the Nineteenth and Into The Twentieth Century, 1877-1900

38. Charles E. Wellborn to Francis P. Fleming, May 2, 7, 10, 1892, Francis P. Fleming Papers, 1889-1893, RG 101, series 580, box 10, folder 4, FSA.
39. R. M. Call to Francis Fleming, May 25, 1892; Affidavit of W. E. Scull, May 16, 1892; affidavit of Patrick Fallen, May 17, 1892, ibid, FSA.
40. L. E. Roberson levied charges against Sharp and inclosed a petition with twenty-three signatures requesting Fleming's removal of the sheriff. L. E. Roberson to Francis Fleming, May 31, July 14, 19, 1892, Francis P. Fleming Papers, 1889-1893, RG 101, series 580, box 8, folder 5, FSA.
41. John F. White to Francis Fleming, July 20, 1892, and another letter ibid. to ibid., with no date, Francis P. Fleming Papers, 1889-1893, RG 101, series 580, box 10, folder 4, FSA; affidavit of E. C. Horne, June 13, 1892, ibid., box 8, folder 5; Proclamation of Francis P. Fleming, August 17, 18, 1892, FSA.
42. Proclamation of Francis P. Fleming, March 4, 1892, Francis P. Fleming Papers, 1888-1893, RG 101, series 580, box 8, folder 6, FSA.
43. Charges Against W. N. Cone, Sheriff of Columbia County, September 5, 1895 and Response, October 1, 1895, Henry L. Mitchell Papers, 1893-1897, RG 101, series 581, box 10, folder 6, FSA.
44. Oscar Stanford to William D. Bloxham, May 28, 1898, William D. Bloxham Papers, 1897-1901, RG 101, series 578, box 10, folder 3, FSA.
45. Owen H. Dishong to William D. Bloxham, June 15, 1898, ibid.
46. Ibid., August 18, 1898, and Report DeSoto County Commissioners, June 9, 1898, and Owen Dishong to William D. Bloxham, August 13, 1898, ibid.
47. Ledger, 152.
48. Ibid, 168.
49. Ibid., 185.
50. Ibid., 190.
51. Ibid., 134.
52. Billy Jaynes Chandler, "Harmon Murray: Black Desperado in Late Nineteenth Century Florida," *Florida Historical Quarterly*, LXXIII (October, 1994), 184-199; Robert S. Schuyler to Francis P. Fleming, May 20, 1891, and G. L. Baltzell to Francis Pl. Fleming, May 22, 1891, Francis P. Fleming Papers, 1889-1893, RG 101, series 580, box 19, folder 1 and box 18, folder 4, FSA.
53. John F. White to Francis P. Fleming, May 9, 1891, and G. Potsdamer to Francis P. Fleming, February 6, December 19, 1892, ibid, box 19, folder 4 and box 18, folder 4, FSA.
54. *FA 1881*, 196-197; ibid., *1895*, 205, 206-207.
55. Ibid., *1891*, 56.
56. Ibid., *1889*, 1-7; ibid., *1895*, 117-118.
57. Ibid., *1895*, 163.
58. Ibid., 131-132. For overviews of southern agriculture and the problems of farmers see Gilbert C. Fite, *Cotton Fields No More Southern Agriculture, 1865-1980*

(Lexington, 1984), and Stephen DeCanio, *Agriculture in the Postbellum South: The Economics of Production and Supply* (Cambridge, 1974).
59. *FA 1895*, 131-132, 150-151. If neither the sheriff nor the constable could serve, a justice of the peace or the county judge could appoint interested parties to substitute for them.
60. Ibid., *1897*, 12. For the entire act see 1-12. At least the sheriffs were spared having to deal with the controversial political aspects of the railroad commission. See Durward Long, "Florida's First Railroad Commission, 1887-1891," Part I, *Florida Historical Quarterly*, XLII (October, 1963), 103-124. For Part II see ibid. (January, 1964), 248-257. See also Tracy E. Danese, "Railroads, Farmers, and Senatorial Politics: The Florida Railroad Commission in the 1890s," *Florida Historical Quarterly*, LXXV (Fall, 1996), 146-166.
61. *FA 1897*, 82-94.
62. Ibid., 107-110. The sheriffs received fees for their services.
63. Jacksonville *Florida Times-Union*, March 24, 1893. In 1995 Bob Smith, volunteer historian for the Volusia County sheriff's office found the notice of the Jacksonville meeting. Thanks to him and Robert L. Vogel Jr., Sheriff Director of Public Safety for Volusia County, for making this information available. For Hilleary's bond and oath, filed December 27, 1892, see RG 151, series 1284, State and County Directories, 1845-1961, vol. 8, FSA.
64. Ibid. Present at the meeting were: A. U. Hilleary, Gainesville, F. B. Spencer, Tampa, J. D. Kurtz, DeLand; N. B. Broward, Jacksonville; J. W. Hagan, Palatka; W. N. Cone, Lake City; S. W. Chester, Gadsden County; C. J. Perry, St. Augustine; F. C. Bathes, Arcadia; Al R. Brown, Brooksville; J. W. Hawkins, Live Oak; W. F. Higginbotham, Fernandina; A. M. Kuleard, Gainesville; and B. J. Odell, Dade City.
65. See a series of letters involving Hilleary, his defenders, governor's officials, and his sole accuser in Henry L. Mitchell Papers, 1893-1897, series 581, Box 10, folder 2, FSA.

CHAPTER VI

THE KU KLUX KLAN AND THE ENDEMIC PROBLEM OF VIOLENCE

efore continuing the chronological story of Florida sheriffs into the 1900s, it is logical to shift the narrative focus to two major problems that affected Floridians and southerners, and particularly sheriffs in both centuries. The issues are the Ku Klux Klan, a significant expression of violence, and the general subject of unlawful mob action (even more dangerous and unpredictable), and more specifically, lynching. Aspects of both issues have been covered in earlier chapters, but this discussion puts them in greater and unified perspective. The Klan was significant in numerous ways, and the Invisible Empire wherever and whenever it appears is always identified with the noun "violence." The word is the signature of the hooded order. On a condensed scale, an examination of the secret organization during Reconstruction, the regulator and vigilante groups that replaced it in the later nineteenth and early twentieth centuries, and the revival of the Klan after 1916 provides an overarching line to the subject of violence in Florida.

The Ku Klux Klan

No monograph details the story of the Klan in Florida, and a complete study is outside the scope of this work. Even so, the state's sheriffs had to confront the Klan's activities, and some sheriffs were members of the order themselves. Jerrell H. Shofner, the modern interpreter of Reconstruction in Florida, and William W. Davis, author of the state's first scholarly book on the subject (1913), differ widely in their approaches. Still, both agree that Florida's Ku Klux Klan was smaller and less well organized than those of other southern states. It was never statewide or centralized. According to Davis, it was "a loose confederation of county clubs, the group in each county being a complete unit itself and independent of that in any other county."[1] Both historians point out the KKK existed in Florida, was paramilitary, and used violence, including murder, to attain its primary goals: controlling blacks, intimidating black and white Republicans, and "redeeming" the state from what klansmen considered Yankee Republican oppression.[2]

Florida had kindred groups to the Klan, especially the Young Men's Democratic Club, which was a regulator group that originated in Leon County, and spread across other Black Belt counties in northern Florida. The constitution of the Young Men's Democratic Club in Leon County became a model that was copied by similarly named clubs in surrounding counties.[3]

Joe M. Richardson, who studied Florida's black population during Reconstruction, notes that the state had regulator groups before and after the Civil War and before the state constitution of 1868 enfranchised the former bondsmen.[4] The leading authority on the Ku Klux Klan in the South during Reconstruction, Allen W. Trelease, has stated that the Invisible Empire began as a social fraternity in Pulaski, Tennessee, in 1866, but was soon transformed into a terrorist group dedicated to preserving white supremacy. The Klan worked relentlessly for the return to power of the Democratic party. Embittered by defeat and the political control of outsiders, many native whites opposed Klan methods but approved of its objectives. Trelease argued that wherever the Klan conspiracy prevailed, "the traditional system of local justice was undermined and subverted."[5]

Some Florida sheriffs faced the dilemma of controlling an organization whose ends they undoubtedly sanctioned. Still, there were Republican sheriffs and other lawmen who were killed by klansmen. The peak years of Klan activity in Florida were 1868 to 1871, although it briefly revived, especially during the political campaign of 1876. The decline came in the 1870s when the federal government passed legislation providing for the arrest and prosecution of Klan members, and

Chapter VI - The Ku Klux Klan and the Endemic Problem of Violence

United States troops were sent in. Many white southerners realized that extra-legal machinations resulted in greater intervention from Washington. Other white Floridians became ashamed of the order's excesses and resigned their membership. The national government lessened what Klan advocates believed was the need for their organization when it began withdrawing from the South's internal affairs, and Democratic control and white rule were reestablished.

The end of the Ku Klux Klan in Florida did not mean an end of vigilante justice. After the 1870s violence in Florida remained mainly local, but was even less well organized than during Reconstruction. Men and women of both races became victims of the extra-legal, self-defined, self-administered system of white justice. The small scale but organized and orchestrated terror in the post-Reconstruction decades centered on economics, race, and morality (prostitution, illegal traffic in liquor, and the like). The white men who formed these vigilante or regulator groups were also known in other southern states as "whitecappers."[6] These Florida regulators were sometimes masked and organized as clubs, sometimes not. Even if they were permanent or quasi-permanent, they were local. The vigilantes usually functioned to meet a temporary need, and often had community approval. Severe arbiters of morality, they were less violent and less politically and racially oriented than the Ku Klux Klan had been. Even so, they were inspired by the Klan's example, and sometimes their activities resulted in murder even when that was not the original intention.

The term "white caps," "white cappers," and "white capping" were not commonly used in Florida, but sometimes they were. In 1894 a white man named Smith, who had been in New Smyrna for little more than a week, blatantly opened a brothel in the downtown section. He was visited one night by twenty or more white cappers. They bodily carried him two hundred yards from the house and horsewhipped him with a hundred or more lashes. Smith was then released and told to run. The men then returned to the house of ill repute and ordered the "inmates" to leave town the next day or face serious consequences. Not long afterwards Smith was seen on the outskirts of town in "a very bad [physical] condition." Soon, the same self-appointed custodians of public morality contacted a certain man who operated a "blind tiger" (a place where illegal liquor was sold). He had been running the blind tiger in New Smyrna for some time, but that ended when the owner discovered a card tacked over the door of his establishment. It read: "J. D. Allen—You have until Wednesday, March 21, to discontinue your lawless business, or you will be dealt with without mercy. TWENTY WHITE CAPS."[7]

The same year, 1894, Peacock & Company, a large manufacturer of turpentine, suffered delays and financial losses because white cappers whipped a number of the firm's workers. For the company, located in the pine woods of Suwannee County near Ellaville, the result was widespread fear among its laborers. A number of them quit their jobs, and others considered leaving. As the white cap outrages continued, so did rumors of more and more victims. The whole area was thrown into uncertainty and confusion because no one knew the cause of the whippings.[8] Other regulator gangs, usually without specific names, operated all over the state. They were particularly active in small towns and rural areas.

The Ku Klux Klan's return to the South before 1920 was accompanied by its spread and acceptance in other parts of the United States. The southern Klan still operated behind its Reconstruction shibboleths of white supremacy and black inferiority, but, as in the rest of the country, it now opposed non-Anglo-Saxon foreigners, religious groups (especially Catholics and Jews), members of labor unions, anti-prohibitionists, radicals, communists, socialists, and anarchists. Like the Klan of Reconstruction the modern version became deeply involved in politics, and was unabashedly xenophobic and nativistic, proudly standing for what klansmen called one-hundred percent Americanism. In 1923 the Reverend A. S. Shuler of Jacksonville spoke to a large crowd of Tallahassee men and women on "True Americanism And The Truth About The Ku Klux Klan."

Following Florida's tradition of uncoordinated violence, the Klan of the twenties, thirties, and forties was not a large statewide organization. The foremost authority on the Klan in Florida for the period has written that it was "a myriad of growing, active individual Klaverns."[9]

Florida was ripe for the Klan's return. The state was beset by anti-Catholicism, as promoted in state publications and in Tom Watson's *Jeffersonian Magazine*. The former Georgia Populist leader's influence was also evidenced in the rise to power of Florida's prohibitionist Governor Sidney J. Catts (1917-1921). The Klan made a spectacular impression in Florida in December 1922, with a huge parade in Jacksonville. Membership spread rapidly across the state, and the order had a pattern of violence from the start.[10]

The Klan concentrated on politics and worked to keep blacks from the polls. Nowhere was its influence more evident than in Volusia County. The largest Klavern was Stonewall Jackson No 1 of Jacksonville, followed by John B. Gordon No 24 of Miami and Olustee No 30 of St. Petersburg. As the hooded order's popularity increased the state became honeycombed with chapters. Acceptance and endorsement were evident everywhere. County fairs in Duval and Levy counties had Klan days. The unnatural union of Klans and Bibles illustrated ties with city churches and even greater rapport with rural congregations. Members of the secret order wanted Bible reading required in public schools. Bidding for teacher support, it strongly favored increased funding for schools. Local Klaverns attended church services en masse, and made donations and presentations of food and money. In the state capital members of Tallahassee Klavern No 80 had men and women members. Dressed in full regalia, they visited Trinity Methodist Church in 1923 and commended the startled minister on his good work. Members repeated the performance in 1927 by attending evening services at the First Baptist Church. When one evangelist held a meeting in the capital in 1928 the Klan displayed its Protestant ecumenicalism by making an appearance. Throughout the 1920s the Tallahassee *Democrat* published articles on Klan activities.

In St. Petersburg there were contributions to the YMCA, and, as the Klan grew, many towns had their own meeting halls. Klan lecturers were everywhere. In Jacksonville a mammoth statewide Klanvocation was held in 1923 to mark the inauguration of Florida as a self-governing realm in the Invisible Empire. The KKK was not regarded as an organization with a sense of humor, but perhaps some of its members were so blessed. It is not known that Tallahassee's Faultless Cleaners were bidding for Klan business in 1927, but the owner's newspaper advertisement read, "We Klean Klothes Klean." The order posed as the friend of the poor, sponsoring uncountable fish frys and barbecues. Stressing ties with the Klan of Reconstruction, modern members regularly participated in cleaning Confederate monuments and the grounds surrounding them. Often, when a klansman died, the order conducted the funeral, usually erecting a fiery cross in a ritual called the "ceremonies of the night vigil."

The Klan regarded itself as the peerless custodian of law and order. It moved righteously against slot machines, and denounced harness and dog racing as well as other forms of gambling. Its membership demanded punishment for crimes, especially those alleging interracial rape or attempted rape.[11] Various stories in the Tallahassee *Democrat* during December 1926 had nothing to do with the Christmas spirit. They centered on a black man accused of "attacking" a white woman in Leon County. His escape set off a search by law enforcement officials. The day after the supposed crime, the local order inserted an advertisement in the *Democrat*. A reward of $100 was offered for information on the black. Any person with pertinent knowledge was urged to "communicate by letter to Leon County [Post Office Box] 888 or the sheriff of Leon County. KKK by order of the E.C.T.F." The next day Klan members upped the reward to $250, and a like amount was offered by the county commissioners. On the third day following the incident, two local Loyal Order of Moose members added $100, bringing the reward to $600. A close search of documents does not indicate that the fugitive was ever caught.

All such activities could not hide the Klan's violent side, its killings, whippings, floggings, tarring and feathering. Tampa was a center for that kind of retribution.[12] The Klan credo saw virtue, not evil, in whipping men who mistreated their families. In 1926 James W. Martin, reacting to sixty-three floggings in Putnam County and acting on his authority as governor, called Palatka's mayor and the county sheriff to Tallahassee. Discussing the problem with them, Martin threatened to remove the sheriff if the attacks continued. Klan

Chapter VI - The Ku Klux Klan and the Endemic Problem of Violence

directed violence was felt by bootleggers and operators of bawdy houses. There was limited revulsion at Klan tactics among whites, although scattered opposition came from a few newspapers, some ministers, and politicians.[13]

A brutal Klan incident occurred in 1914 in Gainesville, site of the University of Florida. A young native of Jacksonville, Father John Francis Conoley, came to Gainesville as pastor of St. Patrick's church which had a small membership. Father Conoley was controversial because in 1917 he had written an article sharply critical of how Protestants treated Catholics in Florida. Conoley soon became a close friend of Albert A. Murphree, president of the University of Florida. A devout member of the Southern Baptist church, Murphree prided himself as being a man of religious tolerance. Conoley received permission from his bishop to establish a Catholic student center, and Murphree gave his consent. Crane Hall, a Catholic chapel and dormitory, opened in 1923. At the president's invitation the young priest organized a student dramatic club that was popular on campus, and, accompanied by Conoley, toured the state giving performances. The well-liked priest spoke around town. In a brief talk to the local Kiwanis club, he praised the value of the university to Gainesville and the state, urging the businessmen present to give part-time jobs to college students.

The local paper praised the speech, but it infuriated anti-Catholic members of Alachua Klan No 46. Its members soon distributed a leaflet around town denouncing the Catholic church and demanding the priest's dismissal from the dramatic club. All recognition of him by the university was to cease. The Gainesville *Sun* assumed a neutral position, but the Pensacola *News* printed the leaflet and sided with Conoley. Other publications backed the criticism, but President Murphree praised the priest and defended the university in a letter to the state Board of Control. Pressure on the president and the board mounted as criticism escalated. Finally, the Board of Control passed a rule against all Catholic clergy at state colleges. Unsubstantiated charges castigated Conoley and led to his dismissal from the drama group. All references to him in the student newspaper ended. Finally, the priest was kidnapped in February 1924 by three klansmen. He was severely beaten, taken to the Catholic church in Palatka, and supposedly castrated. Physically and emotionally depleted, Conoley left Gainesville, and spent two years in a monastery before becoming a priest in the diocese of Portland, Maine. He later wrote, "I have learned, long since, how terrible the criticism of so-called 'good' people can be!" Retiring in 1956, Father Conoley remained in Maine and died there in 1960.[14]

The Klan was so anti-Al Smith in the presidential campaign of 1928 that some Miami officials, including the Dade county sheriff, resigned. Although Florida had been a Democratic bastion since Reconstruction, the contest between Republican Herbert Hoover and Democrat Al Smith was a dramatic study in contrasts. Many voters abandoned their party loyalty temporarily, and former dedicated Democrats helped carry Florida and the nation for the Republicans. The Klan took the side of the Republicans in favoring drys over wets, conservatives over liberals, rural values over city values, Anglo-Saxon principles over those of minorities and aliens, and the Protestant faith over that of Roman Catholics and Jews. The campaign was particularly complex in Florida because in the 1920s so many people had moved to the state. There was great diversity of opinion. The Klan fought hard against Smith, although the order itself was not responsible for Florida's Republican majority. The historian Jack Doherty wrote, "Floridians did not vote for Herbert Hoover, they voted against Alfred Smith. Florida did not go Republican, it went anti-Smith." Doherty and most scholars contend that prohibition and religion were the campaign's telling issues in Florida.[15]

The KKK lost face and membership in the late twenties because its tactics created an adverse popular reaction. The exposure of embarrassing and compromising activities by its leaders further hurt the Klan's cause. Although the KKK lost power, it was never repudiated in Florida. The Invisible Empire kept its structure in the 1930s and 1940s, and became revitalized across the South during the 1950s as a reaction to the Civil Rights movement.

Chapter VI - The Ku Klux Klan and the Endemic Problem of Violence

Violence

After Reconstruction ended in 1877, Floridians generally accepted the decisions of their court system, and, once convictions were obtained, the resulting punishments. Sheriffs were involved at every level—the pursuit, capture, and incarceration of the accused; as witnesses and court officers during trials; and, sometimes, as the persons who carried out the sentences, especially in capital cases. Although an elaborate legal system existed, some southerners and Floridians often went outside the legal process and resorted to lynch law. The vast majority of lynchings resulted when white mobs killed blacks. Historian David Nasaw holds that lynching was "the ultimate crime against humanity, a crime that in its unspeakable violence and its casual, at times almost celebratory disregard for law and order" was, as others have also declared, a disgrace to the United States.[16]

Extra-legal killings in the state were both spontaneous and calculated, directed against an individual or individuals, and, in the cases of Ocoee (1920) and Rosewood (1923) became race riots that included entire communities. Ocoee, located in Orange County, was the site of a pitched battle on election day in 1920. Attempting to assert their right to vote, blacks marched to the polls, but were physically assaulted. Several were killed, some had their property damaged and burned, and many were forced to leave the area.[17] During the bitter cold first week in January 1923, a white woman in Levy County accused a black man of raping her, although later evidence cast heavy doubt on the allegation. The manhunt for the accused black man by posses and mobs (it was difficult to tell which was which) ended in a combination lynching and race riot that saw at least two whites and six blacks killed. The small, all-black town of Rosewood was burned. Robert Elias Walker, popularly known as "Bob," sheriff of Levy County, informed the governor that state troops were not needed. Perhaps Walker thought he had the situation contained, but the riot went on for almost a week. The sheriff drew heavy criticism. He resigned shortly afterwards. Ironically, the accused man, an escapee from a nearby convict camp, was never caught.[18] Later, following the Rosewood Compensation Act of 1994, the Florida legislature awarded monetary damages to certain blacks and their family members who suffered property loses in the affair.[19]

Sheriffs were bound by laws and by the state constitution to see that prisoners accused of serious crimes were safely incarcerated until they stood trial. How effectively Florida's lawmen fulfilled their obligations or perhaps even colluded with lynchers invites speculation and sometimes yields definitive answers. Individual incidents have to be dealt with separately. Each had its own setting, cast of characters, and circumstances. Even so, a particular lynching can be traced and examined, and there are some overriding themes that apply and help explain the lawless phenomenon.

Southern violence reached its peak late in the nineteenth and early twentieth centuries. After that there was a sharp drop in the number of lynchings. Between 1900 and 1917 approximately ninety black men and women were lynched in Florida. In 1920 eight people lost their lives to mobs, although the figure declined to one in 1930. A number of reasons have been forwarded to explain southern violence: geography and climate, as well as ethnic, cultural, social, economic, and political factors. Other explanations include class conflicts, religious fundamentalism (some church-going southerners took literally the Old Testament's admonition of "an eye for an eye and a tooth for a tooth"), the Celtic descendant's heritage of personal vengeance, frontier and rural life that taught individualism and self-reliance, and lifetime familiarity with weapons. Lynching, which is vigilante terrorism, has been the deadliest form of mob violence. Rape or attempted rape are the most frequently noted causes of lynching and are the incidents with the greatest longevity.[20]

Most lynching deaths in Florida and the South resulted from white racism directed against black males. Blacks have made up eighty-four percent of all lynch mob victims. Over ninety-five percent of those who died were males. Citing racism as the motive for lynchings is too simplistic because racial violence has many facets. Without question, much racial violence has been political. The Ku Klux Klan (see above) represented organized violence. During Reconstruction the Klan or else Klan-like local groups attempted to intimidate voters, overthrow Republican rule, and place Democrats in power. In the 1880s white

161

mobs murdered blacks to achieve political ends. The decades preceding the Populist revolt in the 1890s and the Populist period itself witnessed Democrats practicing racial violence, including murder, to prevent blacks and whites from voting for third party and independent candidates. Lynching has the connotation of racial violence. It is the extra-legal taking of a person's life by mob action. It is criminal murder effected by force and without resort to constitutional channels of legal procedure. That broad construct includes laws and lawyers, trials and witnesses, judges and juries. Jails and prisons have been built, and Florida, like other states, has capital punishment as a deterrent to murder. Even so, too often there was a tolerance of lynching among southern whites. Making a strong point, one historian has concluded that in the period from 1889 to 1918 the most frequent causes of lynching "were neither state nor regional—they were local." He contends, "Local conditions were the determining factors, and though actions taken may have reflected a perception of what was occurring outside the immediate area, that perception was shaped by local concerns."[21] Individual sheriffs had to face the local causes. Florida's sheriffs in the last half of the nineteenth and the first decades of the twentieth centuries coped with an alarming statistic: based on population percentage, their state led the nation in the number of lynchings.[22] Surviving records, especially Florida's newspapers and the governors' papers, offer guides to the successes and failures of sheriffs in both centuries.

There was a continuity of violence from the nineteenth to the twentieth century. In the decades after Reconstruction ended there were occasions when sheriffs confronted mobs determined to administer immediate justice—their own highly personalized version of that concept. Sheriffs often risked their jobs and their lives to protect persons accused of crime. Except for the foresight and bravery of Julius C. Anderson in 1892, two notorious criminals named Futch and Floyd, also known as the "train robbers," would have been lynched. After a daring robbery, the fugitives were tracked down by the sheriff of Orange County. Anderson and his posse captured the men in some woods near Sanford (Seminole County). In the ensuing gunfire two of the fugitives were killed and two escaped, but Floyd and Futch were

 Julius Caeser Anderson served as Orange County sheriff, 1885-1901. (Courtesy of the Orange County Sheriffs Office).

captured. Preparing to take the desperados back to the Orlando jail, Sheriff Anderson anticipated being attacked by angry citizens. As he explained to governor Francis Fleming, "I shall do everything in my power to prevent any Mob Law or lynching." Anderson had the foresight to draft a defensive plan with state authorities, and two companies of state troops were made available had the sheriff needed them. Fortunately, he did not.[23]

A much more volatile situation in 1892 was faced by Sheriff Napoleon B. Broward in Jacksonville. A black man and a white man engaged in a waterfront brawl that resulted in the death of the white. A belligerent crowd of whites gathered with the idea of lynching the prisoner, but a large number of blacks formed a protective front at the jail. They were equally determined that the black would stand trial. The situation was tense, and the crowds grew more restless over three days and nights. Broward consulted with the governor, and several companies of state troops were sent in to protect the prisoner and to prevent the blacks and whites from engaging in a riot. The sheriff talked to both sides and skillfully placated all factions. The crisis was followed by newspapers across the state and nation. The excitement finally died down, and Broward received much credit for averting a catastrophe. His biographer declared the sheriff's "tact, levelheadedness, and sense of fairness contributed largely to the protection of his prisoner...."[24]

A different situation elicited a different response in 1881. It is unlikely that Hernando County's Sheriff J. B. Mickler did anything to save the life of the man who invaded his home and killed his three sons. According to a newspaper account, the culprit, a black named Sidney King, was "working out' a fine for burglary" with the sheriff, but suddenly left the job, entered the sheriff's house, and began plundering it. When King was discovered by Mickler's three sons, he shot two and cut the other's throat. As the newspaper ungrammatically but tersely reported, when the sheriff returned home the man "took flight and fled. He was pursued and captured by the indignant citizens and hung."[25]

Sheriffs in both centuries discovered that unless significant numbers of citizens assisted them they could do little to protect their prisoners against an unruly and determined mob. A highly publicized case at

Tampa in 1882 illustrates the point. A drifter sexually assaulted the daughter of a well-to-do citizen. After fleeing, he was captured by Hillsborough County's sheriff D. Isaac Craft, and lodged in jail. Later that evening the sheriff lost control of his prisoner when a mob led by local attorney Joseph B. Wall and a number of other community leaders descended on Craft's house and forced him to surrender the jail keys. Wall's leadership in the subsequent lynching was controversial because he was a brigadier general in the state militia and U. S. Attorney. In the heated aftermath of the tragedy all agreed that Sheriff Craft had been powerless to stop the lynching.[26]

In 1886 R. P. Kilpatrick, the sheriff of Polk County, faced the same problem that overcame Sheriff Craft. In May two brothers named Mann killed two Bartow policemen and fled. The sheriff organized a posse which captured the men. Brought back to town, the culprits were marched through the streets toward the jail. Soon shouts were heard demanding that the killers be hanged at once. The local newspaper reported that the sheriff and his men "moved steadily and firmly through the crowd, faced by their neighbors and best friends, and threatened on every hand and facing now and then a pistol, a Winchester rifle or a double barreled shot gun, never wavered for a moment, but pressed right on to jail, where the prisoners were locked up and a strong guard of well armed men [was] detailed to guard the jail."[27] As the crowd increased and its cries mounted to a crescendo, the desperate sheriff told its members to remember that the prisoners were in custody. He warned them he would resist with force any attempt to seize and lynch them. Ignoring Kilpatrick, the crowd grew angrier and more unrestrained as the evening wore on. Finally, a crowd of over two hundred men rushed the jail, seized the sheriff from behind, and took him from the scene. Now, with no lawful authority present, the crowd broke into the jail and dragged the prisoners away. Then the lynch mob accomplished its mission.[28]

In the twentieth century William S. Jennings, governor from 1901 to 1905, made strenuous efforts to enforce the law throughout his term. After a man named Williams was lynched in Putnam County in 1903 Jennings offered a $500 reward for the arrest and conviction of

 William Sherman Jennings served as governor of Florida, 1901-1905. (Courtesy of the Florida State Archives).

those responsible. An angry chief executive explained to the local sheriff, R. C. Howell, "This is a reflection upon the State, and every effort should be made by the officials to bring the guilty parties to the bar of justice, and I shall ask your active cooperation in this work."[29]

In 1920 a lynching in Sumter County was narrowly averted when

Chapter VI - The Ku Klux Klan and the Endemic Problem of Violence

two black men (one of whom was accused of shooting the sheriff) escaped from jail. The felons entered the sheriff's private residence, struck down his wife, seized a rifle, and killed deputy sheriff Lee Graham.[30] Eventually capturing one of the culprits (Henry Wilson), J. H. Lane placed his prisoner in the Tampa jail instead of returning him to Sumterville. Later the sheriff explained to Jennings, to have done otherwise meant a certain lynching. The governor wired his congratulations and ordered Judge W. S. Bullock at Ocala, seat of government for neighboring Marion County, to call a special term of court in Sumterville.[31] Despite demands in Putnam County for Lane's removal, the lawman remained in office. With the aid of a judge and the sheriff of Marion County, Lane returned Wilson to Sumterville. Lane's attorney vigorously defended the sheriff's actions. In less than fifteen minutes the jury returned a verdict of guilty, and the judge imposed a death sentence. As Wilson was brought out of the courthouse the crowd surged forward, attempting to seize him. By a determined effort law officers and some civilians saved the black man from being lynched.[32] Had the sheriff not kept Wilson in Tampa the black would probably have been killed, and had Lane and others not resisted the crowd outside the courthouse, the condemned man surely would have been.

Judge Bullock appeased the crowd by promising them a public hanging, and Lane erected a high stockade where the execution took place. The governor's death warrant was delivered by J. C. Koonce, a Sumterville attorney. Koonce reported to the governor that despite certain fears, the crowd

> behaved very well indeed. Before the prisoner was brought from jail I made a short address to the people and urged upon them the importance of their good behavior and they complied with all my requests willingly so that every thing has passed off satisfactorily. Your prompt action in this matter has saved our county from disgrace...the law [did] everything possible to vindicate the crime and punish the criminal, and I feel greatly relieved.[33]

A number of people wrote the governor on behalf of Lane praising

167

the sheriff as an honorable and energetic man of integrity. Jennings responded by setting aside some petitions asking for his removal, and allowed the lawman to remain in office.

When a lynching occurred near Inverness in 1906, former sheriff and the sitting governor Napoleon Bonaparte Broward suspended Citrus County Sheriff George Carter and launched an investigation. Carter's friends appealed to the governor contending there was nothing he could have done to avert the incident. "I believe I can safely say to you," wrote one supporter of the sheriff, "that had Carter...and a dozen other determined men been present and doing all in their power they could not have prevented the lynching. I am satisfied beyond the possibility of a doubt that 19 voters out of 20 in this county would sign a petition for the reinstatement of Carter." Further authenticating the sheriff's reputation, the correspondent stated that one Methodist minister was holding "services to empty benches" because he "took a active part against Mr. Carter." Broward's investigation yielded no significant evidence of Carter's misconduct, and the governor reinstated him.[34]

A contrast in individual sheriffs was vividly seen in incidents that occurred in Palm Beach County in 1923 and in Hendry County in 1926. When Henry Simmons, a black man, was hanged and shot by a mob in 1923, Sheriff Robert C. Baker (see below for more on Baker) attempted to apprehend the guilty parties. Baker even offered a personal reward of $100 for information leading to their arrest. In May 1926, Hendry County's shameful moment came when Henry Patterson, a black construction worker, was lynched in broad daylight by prominent men of LaBelle, the county seat. Sheriff Dan L. McLaughlin was conveniently out of town when the black was caught. A white woman had seen Patterson approaching, and started screaming. Patterson fled, but a mob of forty to sixty residents, many of them leading citizens, pursued and caught him. Judge Herbert A. Rider, the county prosecutor, watched events unfold, but could not prevent them. The black man was tortured, mutilated, dragged by a car, hanged, and shot. There were many witnesses. At Rider's insistence, seventeen men were arrested and put in jail on murder charges. McLaughlin defended the men's actions. Even so, the sheriff appointed a special guard, and a unit of state troops came in for six days. The National Association for the Advancement of Colored People (NAACP) and other groups contributed money to help the investigation. Ultimately, the hurricane of 1926 disrupted everything, witnesses vanished, and the grand jury failed to return a true bill. Still, the grand jury recommended the removal of McLaughlin from office, but as the governor and final arbiter, Martin refused. For a while Rider and his family were ostracized, but in time he came to be admired for following his conscience without regard to personal safety or ambition.[35]

A lynching in Gadsden County during the early 1930s demonstrated how difficult it was for authorities either to prevent lynchings or to prosecute them. Sheriff G. Scott Gregory, one citizen wrote Governor Doyle Carlton, "has the reputation of being a capable officer sufficiently conscientious," and yet, "he is as unable to investigate those mobists [*sic*] as he was to prevent the lynching. He would be assassinated if he disclosed the identity of any member of that mob. They would kill your Excellency," the man added, "should you go to Gadsden County and put your hand on one of the mob without having the militia by your side. No civil power in Florida can successfully investigate those lynchers." In the recent past, the despairing correspondent continued, two white men were lynched "by the ancestor of the present mob. At that time an investigation was unthinkable. It is not far from that now.... There is in Gadsden County a mob dynasty of more than forty years existence who carefully train their posterity in lynching programs and have given the county a nasty reputation. There are many good citizens in the county too but what are they against the mob tanked up with moonshine whiskey?"[36]

A number of black Floridians were lynched because they were accused of assaulting or killing sheriffs or other lawmen. Frequently, accused men arrested on such charges were taken out of cells and killed. A lynching was easier to accomplish and more difficult to investigate when the accused could be taken from authorities earlier, preferably while they were taking him to jail. That happened in 1926 when a black man named Davis, accused of killing a deputy sheriff in Pasco County, was lynched as he was being transported from Ocala to

Chapter VI - The Ku Klux Klan and the Endemic Problem of Violence

Brooksville.[37] If a sheriff or arresting officer was involved, proving violence was doubly difficult because the deadly clichè, "shot while attempting to escape," was difficult to disprove.

People in the state's capital were shocked in 1909 when a black turpentine worker named Mick Morris was lynched after he shot and killed Leon County sheriff William W. Langston. The young lawman's death occurred as Morris was resisting arrest while Langston attempted to serve him with a warrant from Georgia. A massive manhunt involving several posses finally tracked Morris down across the state line in Thomas County, Georgia. The fugitive was returned to Leon County where Albert W. Gilchrist, the governor, ordered Morris lodged in the Duval County jail for safekeeping. Gilchrist worked feverishly to secure an immediate trial for him. Despite Morris's conviction and death sentence, a mob of angry men overpowered the guard late one evening (five days before his scheduled hanging) and lynched him in the jail yard. There were never any arrests, even though mob members made no attempt to conceal their identities, and there were numerous witnesses.[38]

In 1926 an example of a sheriff's quick thinking saved an accused black man from being hanged. One February night a white man named H. C. Cross (a native of Albany, Georgia) was in Gainesville, and, the story went, somehow brushed up against Arthur Johnson, a black man, on a city street. Allegedly, Johnson took exception and killed Cross. Fearing mob retribution, authorities took him forty-six miles east to Palatka, Putnam County's seat of government, for safekeeping. Sheriff P. M. Hagan, who lived upstairs in the county jail with his wife and daughter Gertrude, received the prisoner. Word of Johnson's whereabouts became known, and early one March morning at about 1:45 cars pulled up to the jail and stopped. Thirteen unmasked men got out, walked up to the combination residence-jail, and began knocking on the door. Sheriff Hagan came downstairs, and as he turned the knob, the intruders poked pistols in his face. Striking the nearest attacker over the head with his pistol, Hagan jumped back inside, quickly slamming the door. Immediately, shooting started—eighteen shots were fired into the building. By this time Hagan's wife had come downstairs. One of the bullets hit the sheriff in his left hand, and another came within six inches of Mrs. Hagan. Upstairs, young Gertrude looked out of the upstairs window, only to be greeted by a bullet that struck within a foot of her. Shortly, the men retreated to their cars and sped away, but not before Hagan retaliated. The sheriff pursued the assailants into the street firing his shotgun three times at them. Not much time elapsed before the accused man was taken to the more secure jail in Jacksonville.[39]

Within a day warrants were sworn out for thirteen men charging them with assault to commit murder and firing into an occupied dwelling. Sheriff Hagan called Gainesville where he received cooperation from Alachua County's sheriff, and arrests followed for a number of men. Most of them were employees of the State Road Department's maintenance camp nearby. They were brought to Palatka and identified by Hagan and his deputy. Hagan had recognized them on the night of the attack, and he remembered how they looked. Each of the white men was put under a $15,000 bond, and because none of them could raise the amount, they spent their time waiting arraignment in the Putnam County jail. The prisoners were not allowed to have visitors. At the preliminary hearing the county judge found no evidence against four of them, but the other nine were bound over to the grand jury at their next term of circuit court.[40] The Jacksonville *Florida Times-Union* praised the sheriff's departments of Putnam and Alachua counties, and declared that Sheriff Hagan "will be honored by all law abiding men throughout the country, for...his devotion to duty and his dauntless bravery...."[41]

In 1937, after their apprehension by a Tallahassee city policeman at a burglary scene, two black youths severely stabbed him. The young men fled but were later captured and jailed. Not long afterwards they were kidnapped from their cells, taken to a distant location, and shot. Since the kidnapping occurred at the lightly guarded Tallahassee jail, Leon County's Sheriff Frank Stoutamire came under suspicion (for more on Stoutamire see Chapter X). Governor Fred Cone considered suspending the lawman, but a number of Tallahassee officials sprang to his defense. "I have been officially associated with Mr. Stoutamire for more than ten years," wrote a circuit judge. "I can assure you," the judge noted, "that he is one of the best most efficient and straightest sheriffs in the state of Florida." Despite the involvement of federal authorities, the investigation was soon concluded with no charges being brought.[42]

Because sheriffs and deputies were intimately related to their communities by blood and political and economic relationships, a lawman's own interest or his family's connection might be tied to the safety or lack of it for his prisoner. Inevitably, the sheriff might be implicated as a willing accomplice if a prisoner in his protective custody was lynched. A typical example, even though it occurred in an era when lynchings were unusual, came in 1945. That year a sharecropper named Jesse Payne was lynched while in the custody of Madison County's sheriff Lonnie T. Davis.

Payne was charged with raping the daughter of Davis's brother-in-law, a man named Goodman. Further investigation revealed the charges may have been made against Payne by his landlord in an attempt to steal the tenant's crop. The personal and economic interests of Davis and Goodman were intertwined to the point that many suspected the sheriff's collusion in the crime. Because Payne's lynching was the only one in the entire nation that year state and national media brought intense scrutiny to bear. Governor Millard Caldwell ordered an immediate investigation, and the governor's special agent found substantial evidence of Davis's negligence. The investigator complained to the governor about the lack of cooperation or determination by local whites to bring charges against Davis. He wrote the governor, "Regardless of whatever evidence anyone would be able to secure about the lynching or the Sheriff's negligence, no Grand Jury you might be able to get [here] would indict or make any presentments."[43] Without the aid of willing witnesses there was little chance of extending the sheriff's negligence to criminal culpability. Ultimately, the chief executive concluded that "Payne's death 'resulted from the stupid inefficiency of the sheriff and not from his abetting or participation.'" Although as sheriff Davis had "proven his unfitness for office, he was, nevertheless, the choice of the people of Madison County...." Caldwell concluded, "Stupidity and ineptitude are not sufficient grounds for removal of an elected official by the Governor."[44]

Florida's most publicized lynching up to that time was that of Claude Neal at Marianna (Jackson County) in 1934. The black man was accused of raping and murdering a young white girl. W. F. "Flake" Chambliss, sheriff of Jackson County, arrested Neal on the same day he discovered the girl's body. News of the girl's grisly murder spread rapidly. The sheriff himself predicted to a friend, "All Hell is going to break loose around here."[45] Expecting violence against the suspect, Chambliss jailed Neal in nearby Washington County. Later that evening the suspect was whisked away to the Bay County jail in Panama City. The next day a group of furious whites descended on the sheriff's home. The men demanded to know where Neal was. The unpopular sheriff barely managed to escape their wrath. Despite his efforts to hide Neal's whereabouts, the mob eventually found out that the assumed culprit was incarcerated in Panama City. A lawless group of inflamed men descended on the jail there, but missed their victim by half-an-hour. He had been removed by boat to Fort Walton Beach and then to Pensacola by car.[46]

Thinking his own jail unsafe, Escambia County Sheriff Herbert E. Gandy decided to put Neal in a jail across the border in Brewton, Alabama. While there Neal confessed to the crime. Eventually the whites learned of his whereabouts, seized him, and took their victim back to Florida. He was held in custody several days before being brutally lynched. Critics have charged Governor David Sholtz and law enforcement officials, including Chambliss, with not doing enough to rescue Neal from the unrestrained mob. Called to account, the sheriff countered that he had deputized thirty-two men and twelve special officers and ordered them to stop the vigilantes. The sheriff's attention had been diverted from the Neal crisis when one of his deputies was shot in the back and killed while helping law officers transport captured bank robbers to jail. As the historian of the affair, James McGovern, has noted, "It is doubtful that Sheriff Chambliss could have prevented the lynching...." Although the sheriff was a "generous and considerate man and fearless when administering the law to the likes of bank robbers—he felt ineffective in the face of the lynch mob."[47]

Chapter VI - The Ku Klux Klan and the Endemic Problem of Violence

Notes for Chapter VI

1. Davis, *Civil War and Reconstruction in Florida*, 562.
2. Shofner, *Florida in the Era of Reconstruction*, 225-242; Davis, *Civil War and Reconstruction in Florida*, 554-558.
3. For a copy of the constitution see *Testimony Taken By The Joint Select Committee To Inquire Into The Condition Of Affairs In The Late Insurrectionary States. Florida* (Washington, 1872), 157-158.
4. Richardson, *The Negro In Reconstruction Florida*, 16 For his discussion of the Klan and lawlessness in Florida see 161-176.
5. Allan W. Trelease, *White Terror: the Ku Klux Kan Conspiracy and Southern Reconstruction*. (New York, 1971), xii. Trelease deals succinctly with Florida. See his chapters fourteen and nineteen. Also on the Klan see Nancy MacLean, *Behind the Mask of Chivalry: The Making of the Second Ku Klux Klan* (New York, 1994); John Higham, *Strangers in the Land: Patterns of American Nativism, 1860-1925* (New York, 1985), 285-99.
6. William D. Holmes has made careful studies of whitecapping in several southern states. For example, see his "Whitecapping in Georgia: Carroll and Houston Counties, 1893," *Georgia Historical Quarterly*, LXIV (Winter, 1980), 388-404.
7. Jacksonville *Florida Times-Union*, May 7, 1894.
8. Ibid., May 5, 1894.
9. David Chalmers, "The Ku Klux Klan In The Sunshine State: The 1920s," *Florida Historical Quarterly*, XLII (January, 1964), 200-215.
10. Ibid., 210.
11. Ibid., *passim*.
12. For vivid and well documented studies see Robert P. Ingalls, *Urban Vigilantes in the New South: Tampa, 1882-1936* (Knoxville, 1988), and Jeffrey S. Adler, "Black Violence in the New South Patterns of Conflict in Late-Nineteenth-Century Tampa," 207-239, in David R. Colburn and Jane L. Landers, *The African American Heritage of Florida* (Gainesville, 1995).
13. Chalmers, "Ku Klux Klan In the Sunshine State," 214-215.
14. See Stephen R. Prescott, "White Roses and Crosses: Father John Conoley, the Ku Klux Klan and the University of Florida," *Florida Historical Quarterly*, I, LXXI (July, 1992), 18-40; see also Leland Hawes, "Brutal Tale Emerges of Priest's Castration in the '20s," Tampa *Tribune*, August 2, 1992.
15. Herbert Jackson Doherty, Jr., "Florida and the President Election of 1928," *Florida Historical Quarterly*, XXVI (October, 1947), 186. For the complete article see 174-186.
16. See David Nasaw's review of David Margolick's *Strange Fruit Billie Holiday, Café Society, and an Early Cry for Civil Rights* (Philadelphia, 2000) in New York *Times* Book Review, May 21, 2000, 38. For the prevalence of violence in Florida see

Denham, *A Rogue's Paradise*, 59-66, 205-208; Brown, *Florida's Peace River Frontier.*

17. Less Dabbs, Jr., "A Report on the Circumstances and Events of the Race Riot on 2 November 1920 in Ocoee, Florida," Unpublished Master's thesis, Stetson University, 1969; Maxine Jones, "The African-American Experience in Twentieth-Century Florida," 374, in Gannon, *New Florida History.* See also St. Petersburg *Times*, October 31, 1998, quoting article by Roger Thurow in New York *Wall Street Journal*, and Higham, *Strangers in the Land*, 149-157.

18. See Maxine Jones, Larry E. Rivers, David R. Colburn, R. Thomas Dye, and William W. Rogers, "A Documented History of the Incident Which Occurred at Rosewood, Florida, in January 1923." Completed on assignment from the state, this 93-page document was submitted to the Florida Board of Regents on December 23, 1993. See also Michael D'Orso, *Like Judgment Day the Ruin and Redemption of a Town Called Rosewood* (New York, 1996).

19. Jones, "African-American Experience," 370. For the entire chapter see 373-390.

20. See A. Cash Koeniger, "Climate and Southern Distinctiveness," *Journal of Southern History*, LIV (February, 1988), 21-44; Harvey H. Jackson, "The Middle-Class Democracy Victorious: The Mitcham War of Clarke County, Alabama, 1893," *Journal of Southern History*, XVII (August, 1991), 453-478; John Shelton Reed, "Below the Smith and Wesson Line: Southern Violence," in *One South: An Ethnic Approach to Regional Culture* (Baton Rouge, 1982), 139-153; and his "To Live–and Die in Dixie: A Contribution to the Study of Violence," *Political Science Quarterly*, XXXVI (September, 1971), 429-443; H. C. Brearley, "The Pattern of Violence," in *Culture in the South*, W. T. Couch (Editor) (Chapel Hill, 1935). Also on lynching and Southern violence see Bertram Wyatt-Brown, *Southern Honor: Ethics and Behavior in the Old South* (New York, 1982); Wilber J. Cash, *The Mind of the South* (New York, 1941); Edward L. Ayers, *Vengeance and Justice: Crime and Punishment in the 19th Century American South* (New York, 1984); Sheldon Hackney, "Southern Violence," *American Historical Review*, LXXIV (February, 1969), 906-925. Excellent recent studies are W. Fitzhugh Brundage, *Lynching in the New South: Georgia and Virginia, 1880-1930* (Urbana, 1993); idem., *Under Sentence of Death: Lynching in the South* (Chapel Hill, 1997); Stewart E. Tolney and E. M. Beck, *A Festival of Violence: An Analysis of Southern Lynchings, 1882-1930* (Urbana, 1992); Orlando Patterson, *Rituals of Blood: Consequences of Slavery in Two American Centuries.* (Washington, 1998), 169-232.

21. Jackson, "Mitcham War," 456. See also Mary Louise Ellis, "Surrender to Violence: Mob Justice in Southwest Georgia, July 1899," Master's Thesis, Florida State University, 1988, and her "A Lynching Averted: The Ordeal of John Miller," *Georgia Historical Quarterly* LXX (Summer, 1986), 306-316. See also by Ellis, "'Rain Down Fire:' The Lynching Of Sam Hose," Ph.D. Dissertation, Florida State University, 1992.

22. *Thirteenth Census, 1910*, II, 306, 315; National Association for the Advancement of Colored People, *Thirty Years of Lynching in the United States, 1889-1918* (New York, 1969 (Reprint)), 53-56; Monroe N. Work (Editor), *The Negro Year Book: An Annual Encyclopedia of the Negro, 1931-1932* (Tuskegee, 1931), 293. See also Walter White, *Rope and Faggot: A Biography of Judge Lynch* (New York, 1929).
23. J. C. Anderson to Francis Fleming, May 26, 1892, and N. D., and J. D. Beggs to Francis Fleming, May 23, 1892, Francis P. Fleming Papers, 1889-1893, RG 101, series 580, box 11, folder 3, FSA.
24. Proctor, *Napoleon Bonaparte Broward*, 71.
25. Bartow *Informant*, July 7, August 25, 1881.
26. Robert P. Ingalls, "General Joseph B. Wall and Lynch Law in Tampa," *Florida Historical Quarterly*, LXVIII (July, 1984), 51-70.
27. Bartow *Polk County Informant*, May 17, 1886.
28. Ibid.
29. William Jennings to R. C. Howell, October 26, 1903, Jennings Papers, 1901-1905, RG 101, series 596, box 9, folder 3, FSA.
30. William F. Himes to W. S. Jennings, February 22, 1902, ibid, box 9, folder 5, FSA.
31. J. H. Lane to W. S. Jennings, March 25, 1902, W. S. Jennings to J. H. Lane, March 25, 1902, and W. S. Bullock to W. S. Jennings, March 25, 1902, ibid.
32. William F. Himes to W. S. Jennings, April 2, 1902, ibid.
33. J. C. B. Koonce to W. S. Jennings, April 5, 1902, ibid.
34. Allan Rodgers to N. B. Broward, March 23, 1907, and Proclamation of N. B. Broward, May 10, 1907, Broward Papers, 1905-1909, RG 101, series 664, box 4, folder 1, FSA.
35. Jerrell H. Shofner, "Judge Herbert Rider and the Lynching at LaBelle," *Florida Historical Quarterly*, LIX (January, 1981), 292-306.
36. James Hazleton to Doyle Carlton, N. D., Carlton Papers, 1929-1933, RG 102, series 204, box 32, folder 1, FSA.
37. Maxine Jones, "'Without Compromise or Fear': Florida's African American Female Activists," *Florida Historical Quarterly*, LXXVII (Spring, 1999), 478.
38. Ric Kabat and William Warren Rogers, "Mob Violence in Tallahassee, Florida, 1909,"in Greenberg et. al., *Florida's Heritage of Diversity*, 111-122.
39. Lakeland *Star-Telegram*, March 3, 1923; Gainesville *Daily Sun*, March 3, 4, 1923.
40. Lakeland *Star-Telegram*, March 5, 10, 1923.
41. Gainesville *Daily Sun*, March 5, 1923, quoting Jacksonville *Florida Times-Union*.
42. Quoted in Howard, "Vigilante Justice and National Reaction: The 1937 Tallahassee Double Lynching," *Florida Historical Quarterly*, LXVII (July, 1988), 38. See also his *Lynching: Extralegal Violence in Florida During the 1930s* (Selinsgrove, Pennsylvania, 1995).
43. Confidential Report, W. H. Gasque to Millard F. Caldwell, November 7, 1945. See also Governor Caldwell's News Release, November 8, 1945, quoted in Jack E.

Davis, "Whitewash in Florida: The Lynching of Jesse James Payne," *Florida Historical Quarterly*, LXVIII (January, 1990), 284-285.
44. Ibid., For Davis's entire article see 277-298.
45. W. F. Chambliss quoted in James R. McGovern, *Anatomy of a Lynching: the Killing of Claude Neal* (Baton Rouge, 1982).
46. Ibid, 42-66, 69-70, 75-76.
47. Ibid., 75-76. See Chapter Five, "The Local Reaction," 95-114.

CHAPTER VII

THE FIRST TWO DECADES OF THE TWENTIETH CENTURY

As they left the nineteenth century behind, Florida's sheriffs saw their authority and duties increase to fit the demands of a modern age. Early on the sheriffs were affected by a number of acts that benefited their calling, and the Sheriffs Association, founded in 1893, was in the process of evolving into a body that benefited sheriffs as individuals and gave them a collective influence they had previously lacked.

Among the acts that governed their actions, sheriffs were authorized by the legislature to approve the bonds of persons committed to them by magistrates and to fix their fees. More importantly to the lawmen, that same year they—along with deputies, constables, and police officers—were permitted to carry weapons (concealed or otherwise) without giving bond.[1]

Much of the lawman's world was "inside-the-county courthouse." There he filed multiple records and filled out seemingly endless documents. Those sheriffs without bookkeeping skills often failed to enter the proper mileage statements for conveying prisoners. Others, understandably, neglected to keep up with the ever-changing fee system. Sometimes their uncertainties, oversights, and fears of probable censure kept them from seeking legitimate compensation. A special statute of 1903 brought relief by permitting county commissioners to award sheriffs their adjusted fees retroactively as earned pay.[2] In the same session the state recognized the sheriff's relationship with the state militia or national guard. An act directed service authorities to pay sheriffs for executing military processes and mandates, including writs and warrants, to enforce the power of military courts.[3] Further evidence of the diverse assignments sheriffs handled came in 1905 when a statutory provision directed that their fees in lunacy hearings equal those they received in criminal cases.[4]

Within the broad subject of fees lawmakers had long recognized the state's obligation to compensate sheriffs who left Florida to bring back accused felons. A bill was introduced and passed in 1905 that paid lawmen five cents a mile for the distance they traveled and for their expenses while on assignment.[5] Florida's sheriffs were grateful that the legislature had responded favorably to their needs. Their situation was due in part to the activities of their state association, not the least being the group's lobbying activities in Tallahassee. Even so, the organization went through a laborious, though ultimately successful, period of acquiring a voice that commanded attention.

From its establishment in 1893 to the early 1920s the statewide body went through phases of growth and decline, but the association did not disband. While the records of all its meetings have not been found, it is probable they were held annually. Down to 1920 the organization represented the lawmen and attempted to influence the state legislature. Beyond that, it was a valuable social and professional society for the members. The conventions were usually held in March because the legislature met in April, although only every other year. The annual meeting became a time when the sheriffs could plot strategy, exchange ideas, hold sessions dealing with the problems of crime, and partake of the host city's hospitality. The sheriff of the county hosting the meeting was usually in charge of arrangements. Through World War II Jacksonville was the favorite locale for state meetings.

Typical of early sessions was the one held in 1897. The sheriffs convened what was theoretically their fifth annual meeting in the Knights of Pythias Hall in Ocala. Attendance was low. Sickness offered one reason, plus many counties were holding their spring term of court and sheriffs had to be in attendance.[6] The delegates elected Marion County's sheriff R. Dupree Hodge as president, and for vice president they selected N. B. Broward of Duval County. The members resolved to

Chapter VII - The First Two Decades of the Twentieth Century

ask the state to establish a uniform system of writs and papers for general use and a uniform scale of costs and charges. They also discussed the desirability of establishing a journal devoted to Florida's sheriffs but took no action.[7]

Besides dealing with lofty philosophical themes, the sheriffs concerned themselves with every day challenges and difficulties. In 1897 Florida had an expanding network of railroads, certainly an economic boon, but one that created difficulties. A small but real problem was "beating on trains," a phrase that has long since passed into oblivion. Beating on trains occurred when an individual illegally jumped on a train, rode it for a short distance, and jumped off while the cars were still in motion. Train beating was done because it involved daring and provided thrills. It was also a dangerous undertaking, resulting in many accidents. Association members asked the legislature to make train beating a misdemeanor punishable by a fine. Train conductors would be authorized to arrest violators and turn them over to local county authorities.[8]

Feeding prisoners was a chronic problem for sheriffs. Because special problems were raised when the number of prisoners was small, the lawmen asked for a law allocating forty cents a day per person when they numbered less than ten and thirty cents a day when they were more than ten. The chair appointed a special committee to address the matter and a general committee to make suggestions. The goal was to effect changes in existing laws and promote remedial acts. Before adjournment, the convention voted to meet again on July 1, and hear a report from the special legislative committee. The July meeting took place in Jacksonville's criminal courtroom on Market Street. Only fifteen lawmen were present (the summer heat did little to attract wide attendance), although an additional twenty-seven sheriffs were represented by proxy. Unfortunately, the proceedings were withheld from the public.[9]

Action by the sheriffs in their 1901 convention, held once again in Jacksonville's criminal courtroom, indicated that the association did not consider itself operating as a permanent, efficient entity. The Jacksonville *Florida Times-Union* referred to the group as the "Sheriffs and Police Officers' Organization." U. C. Herndon, sheriff of Baker County, was described as the president and chairman. W. T. Scully, secretary, and P. H. Nugent, assistant secretary, were the only other officers mentioned. Sheriffs were present from fifteen counties, as well as the sheriff and a deputy sheriff from Madison and Bradford counties. The sheriff of Suwannee County brought along the marshal of Live Oak, the county seat. Constables were present from Duval and Volusia counties, as well as the marshal of Fort Brooke (an independent section of Tampa), and a proxy for Alachua County's sheriff. The meeting quickly got down to business. A legislative committee was appointed to draft resolutions and a bill for the lawmakers in Tallahassee. Another committee was directed to confer statewide with newspapers and persuade them to print full descriptions of escaped prisoners. A finance committee was appointed, following general discussion, to consider how any county's fine and forfeiture fund should be handled and dispersed, as well as concerns over how county commissioners should deal with fee bills and who should be allowed to carry weapons.[10]

> **REWARD.**
>
> One Hundred and Fifty Dollars, ($150.00) will be paid for the arrest, and delivery to the Sheriff of Hamilton county, Florida, of one **James Hoard**, wanted for shooting Robert Alderman at Jennings, Fla., on the afternoon of the 19th of last June, and $150.00 more on his conviction.
>
> **DESCRIPTION.** About 5 feet 6 or 7 inches high, age about 26 years, weight about 140 pounds, wears No. 6 or 7 shoe, medium black, round face, large eyes, showing white of eyes more than the average negro. Voice coarse, quick spoken, quick movement, small moustache, thick upper lip, large, sound, white teeth, holds his head down when he is talking. Mr. Robert Alderman is a highly respected white citizen.
>
> Thos. B. Johns,
> Sheriff, Hamilton County, Fla.
>
> Jasper, Fla., July 26th, 1902.

Handbills, like this one issued by Hamilton County sheriff Thomas B. Johns for fugitive James Hoard circulated during the several decades before and after the turn of the twentieth century. (Courtesy of the Leon County Sheriffs Office).

Chapter VII - The First Two Decades of the Twentieth Century

Receiving notification that the sheriff of Lafayette County, W. B. Mathis, had been killed three weeks earlier while pursuing a fugitive, the members took up a collection for his wife and children. Additional funds that came in later were also forwarded to Mrs. Mathis whose husband had been sheriff for only a month. The tragedy hinted that 1901 would be an unlucky one for Florida lawmen. In June Jefferson County Deputy Sheriff William H. Dawkins was shot and killed. Then in October Frank Adams, deputy sheriff of Monroe County, met his death by gunfire. Dawkins became the sixth known black enforcement officer to lose his life in the line of duty.[11]

The statistics overrode any question as to whether sheriffs and their deputies were subject to danger. It was an ongoing fact. As it was, no one objected in 1933 when the legislature authorized county commissioners to pay a deputy's salary up to $1,500 for wages lost and expenses incurred due to an on-the-job accident.[12]

The legislative committee reported during the evening session. Delegates to the 1901 convention approved the committee's request for a law regulating the carrying of pistols and other weapons. As far back as 1885 a law made it a misdemeanor to carry concealed arms of any kind, or any dirk, or pistol, or any weapon except a common pocket knife. A statute concerning the owning and carrying of repeating rifles already existed. The committee favored laws that established an official publication listing employees in sheriffs' offices to facilitate statewide communication in investigating crimes; empowered sheriffs to arrest felons with or without a warrant on Sunday; required county commissioners to pay sheriffs, their deputies, and constables promptly each month; made sheriffs executive officers for county judges' courts; required state witnesses to be paid for mileage the same as witnesses in county judges and justices of the peace courts; and mandated payment of the witnesses on a day-to-day basis. The sheriffs' convention, committee members declared, were "of vast benefit, and we are satisfied that the continuance of these gatherings cannot fail to result in great good to the members individually, and to the betterment of the public service in which they are engaged." In complete agreement, the delegates resolved to make their organization permanent and stated that its

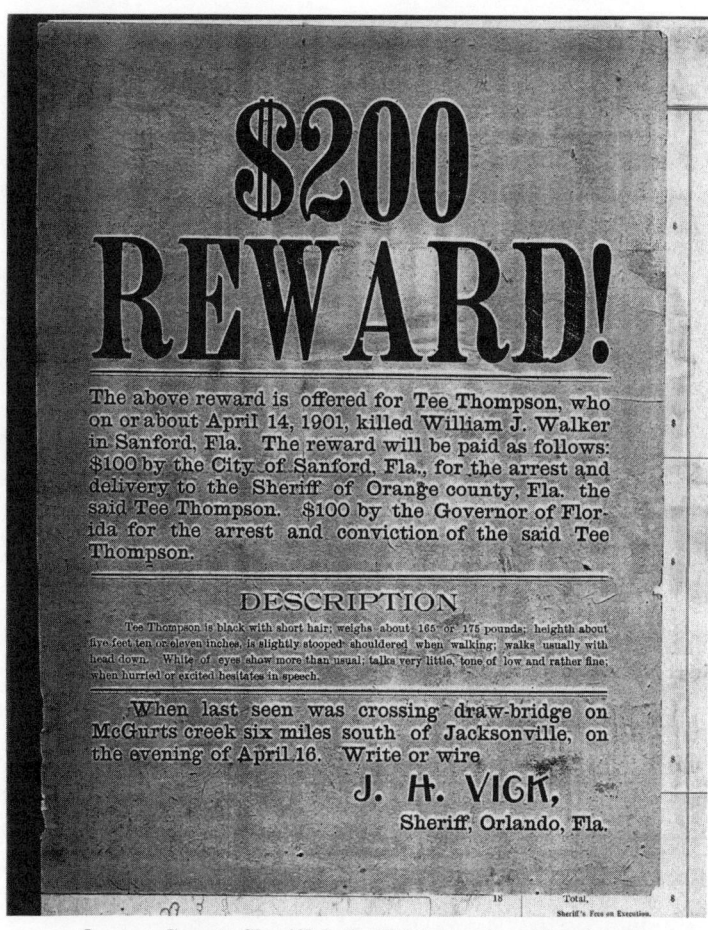

Orange County Sheriff J. H. Vick's proclamation for the arrest of fugitive Tee Thompson. (Courtesy of the Orange County Sheriffs Office).

purpose was to provide the greatest service to both the sheriffs and the public. The members voted to meet annually at Jacksonville and to hold special meetings if needed. Finally, the convention accepted the finance committee's recommendation to set annual dues at $6 for each sheriff and chief of police and $1 for deputies and marshals.[13]

The new spirit of cooperative action proved heady and prompted the sheriffs to hold a special session at Jacksonville in July 1901. The finance committee wanted a newspaper committee established to determine the cost of having newspapers print monthly descriptions of escaped and captured felons. Sheriffs would then know whom to look for and when to stop looking. Obviously, their society was modernizing and upgrading its organization and goals. Graphic evidence of progressive impulses could be seen in one of their resolutions, one that proved controversial. As Florida entered the new century the convict lease system—though under attack—remained in operation at the state and county levels. In the various counties supervision rested under the sheriffs' control.[14] The sheriffs' statement declared, "Resolved, That this convention condemn the leasing of county convicts, and recommend the placing of convicts on county roads." As discussed in Chapter V, convict leasing with all its cruelties and injustices was a way for the state and counties to make money from their prisoners. Equally important, convict leasing enabled the state and counties not to lose money in maintaining their lawbreakers. Beyond that, of course, the system was an important source of revenue for planters, phosphate mine owners, and proprietors of forests (especially the turpentine interests). The resolution prompted lively debate and "a great deal of opposition." Opponents claimed the proposal would create serious antagonism between sheriffs and county commissioners. The delicate balances and rhythms of county government would be threatened, they said. The resolution was dropped, and the members left the issue "with the Legislature to handle as they thought best." Still, in proposing the abolition of convict leasing, the sheriffs were two decades ahead of their time, and they had raised and debated a question of significant economic, political, and racial consequences.[15]

The leasing debate continued. By 1912 Governor Park Trammell emphatically had declared his opposition to its abuses. In his first address to the legislature Trammell called for the immediate "discontinuance of the lease system."[16] The governor and other officials were borrowing pages from the sheriffs' notebook. Final abolition of the state's convict lease system was signed into law by Trammell's successor Sidney J. Catts in 1919. County leasing of convicts continued in turpentine camps, agricultural operations, and other private concerns until 1923 when the legislature banned the practice. Public outrage in Florida and throughout the country forced the action after a young white man

 **Park Trammell served as governor of Florida, 1913-1917. (Courtesy of the Florida State Archives).**

was arrested in Leon County for vagrancy, convicted, and leased to a turpentine company. While working out his time (he had been unable to pay his fine) he was viciously beaten to death. Afterwards, most counties used convict labor to build and maintain roads. Some counties leased their convicts to other counties.[17]

Interest in convict leasing numbered among many areas of policy in which the sheriffs collectively concerned themselves as their sophisti-

Photo above - Florida convicts working in early stages of road construction.
Photo below - Florida prisoners engaged in road building following the end of convict leasing in 1923. (Courtesy of the Florida State Archives).

Prisoners working in the turpentine industry. This labor was part of Florida's notorious convict lease system that began after the Civil War and did not end until 1923. This picture appears to date from the nineteen teens to the early nineteen twenties. (Courtesy of the Florida State Archives).

A Florida convict "rolling cage" used as a mobile prison to transport prisoners from one work site to another. (Courtesy of the Florida State Archives).

> **$125 Reward for John Brown!**
>
> $100 by the State; $25 by the Sheriff.
>
> DESCRIPTION——Color, black; age about 33; weight about 160; height about 5 ft. 10 in.; one upper front tooth out; slightly bow-legged; smiles when he talks. Brown has some education and devotes much time to reading newspapers. He is wanted for assault with intent to murder. Was employed as turpentine hand.
>
> R. C. HOWELL,
> Sheriff Putnam County.
>
> Palatka, Florida.

The advent of the convict lease system added to sheriffs' responsibilities. Putnam County sheriff R.C. Howell's proclamation for an escaped turpentine worker wanted for murder is a case in point. (Courtesy of the Leon County Sheriffs Office).

cation in influencing legislators quickly matured. In 1903, for instance, Florida's lawmen gathered in convention in the chambers of Duval's county judge. Attracted to the familiar site at Jacksonville were sheriffs from seventeen counties and marshals from Kissimmee (Osceola County), and Fort Brooke (Hillsborough county). John Price of Duval County was elected president and J. W. Hawkins of Suwannee County was picked for second in command. The sheriffs had a definite agenda, but were so determined to have it enacted they declined to inform reporters the names of bills they favored and those they opposed. Certain members were chosen to go to Tallahassee and lobby personally with the legislators. The society was determined to get certain laws altered, even if slightly, to make them more applicable and workable for sheriffs out in the counties. What looked good on paper, they had long since discovered, did not always work in practice. The members finished their work in one day and departed. The brief meeting illustrated the nature of their profession—they could not afford to stay away from their work for long.[18]

Chapter VII - The First Two Decades of the Twentieth Century

Jacksonville, as usual, was the site for the 1905 convention. The sheriffs convened in the Duval County Courthouse at the county judge's office. It was April Fool's day, and the first session was at night. The most important item for discussion was the need to reform the always controversial fee system. Because only ten counties were represented (the host county of Duval was not one of them; there was an honorary member for an unnamed city and county) the turnout was small. Despite the paucity of attendance the local paper noted those present as being "certainly in earnest in their efforts to have reforms." Nevertheless, it was clear the association was threatening to become moribund. The odd hour of beginning at night was illustrative of a less than determined sense of priorities. The meeting had been scheduled to begin in the afternoon, but it was canceled so that the rural sheriffs could see Jacksonville's baseball team play a game.[19] Although not referred to as president, Lewis Washington "Uncle Wash" Fennell, veteran sheriff, colorful politician, and famed outdoorsman of Alachua County, was selected "chairman" of the meeting. Actually, he was the association's president.[20] At their 1905 convention the sheriffs agreed to help each other in the apprehension of criminals. A committee of five was appointed to go to Tallahassee and help persuade the solons to change Florida's fee system. They agreed that the existing system's defects were "glaring and numerous." The committee was authorized to employ an attorney to help them draft a fee bill. A copy would be sent to each sheriff who could make suggestions, return them to the committee, and, if possible, they would be included in the bill proposed to the legislature. Each sheriff was urged to become an individual lobbyist and help persuade his local representatives to work for the measure.[21]

Between 1905 and 1912 the association reached a plateau of pro forma existence that did not alter until 1913 when it began to regain some of its verve and power. In the host city, the Jacksonville *Florida Times-Union* gave the convention page one coverage. The session began when members from twenty-one counties elected W. H. Dowling, sheriff of Duval County, as president. He succeeded Robert A. Jackson, Hillsborough County's sheriff. Jackson was one of a long line of colorful and controversial lawmen from that county. Sheriff

189

Chapter VII - The First Two Decades of the Twentieth Century

$650 REWARD.

Gainesville, Fla., August 20th, 1902.

For the capture of Manny Price, alias Manny Austin, who murdered W. F. Bronson, Supt. Buttgenbach & Co's mine near Newberry, on August/6th, 1902.

Description.—Black, short and thick set, weight about 140 pounds, height about 5 feet 5 inches, good teeth—very prominent, upper jaw extending considerably beyond lower jaw; has a high pitched voice and is always smiling. Was wearing white cloth No. 8 shoes. Has scar on right arm between elbow and wrist, has old bullet wound in big toe. Age 23.

Buttgenbach & Co. offer $500 and the Governor $150 reward.

L. W. FENNELL,
Sheriff Alachua County, Fla.

Alachua County sheriff L.W. Fennell's proclamation for the arrest of a fugitive. (Courtesy of the Leon County Sheriffs Office).

Robert A. Jackson served as sheriff of Hillsborough County, 1905-1908, was suspended briefly but was re-elected again in 1909, serving until 1913. (Courtesy of the Hillsborough County Sheriffs Association).

 Lewis Washington Fennell served as Alachua County sheriff, 1890-1893 and 1897-1909. (Courtesy of the Florida State Archives).

from 1901-1908, he was suspended in 1908, reelected the same year, and served until 1912. Alachua County's Sheriff, P. G. Ramsey, was chosen as vice president. Both Dowling and Ramsey had emerged as recognized leaders in the association. The lawmakers considered issues such as reimbursement rates for boarding prisoners and raises for bailiffs and guards,[22] but on a broader level, they rededicated them-

Chapter VII - The First Two Decades of the Twentieth Century

selves to their responsibility of catching criminals, particularly murderers. Implementing the goal meant securing legislation that permitted county commissioners to employ special detectives when the occasion demanded it. As matters stood, some county commissioners claimed that such hiring was unlawful. The need for undercover operatives was especially acute in enforcing liquor laws in dry counties, where, at best, it was an "uphill struggle." The members agreed to meet at Tallahassee in April, just as the legislature began its session. In the meantime, they determined to lobby their representatives individually. When secretary-treasurer J. P. S. Houston, sheriff of Leon County, reminded old and new members to pay their dues there was a "rainstorm of greenbacks." The 1913 convention was a success, one where a "hearty handshaking among all and a sort of zeal pervade the atmosphere...." It ended on an up beat with president Dowling entertaining the members with a closing banquet at the Hotel Seminole.[23]

The subsequent Tallahassee gathering illustrated how the sheriffs could work together to achieve their goals. As planned, lawmen met on the opening day of the legislative session. Making their presence felt was difficult because there was so much going on in the capital city. Besides the usual excitement of having the lawmakers in town, many citizens were riveted to a three-day—Thursday through Saturday—series of baseball games between the University of Florida and Auburn University (then known as Alabama Polytechnic Institute). There was so much interest in what was called "the most interesting baseball contest ever pulled off in this city" that stores closed and business was entirely suspended. A special train filled with fans was run from Gainesville. Perhaps it was not entirely a coincidence that Leon County's Sheriff J. P. S. Houston and his deputy sheriff raided "The Leon County Temperance Club." The club manager was a white man with an unsavory reputation for liquor dealing. According to a front-page story in the local *Democrat*, The Temperance Club was "a very malodorous resort, in a very ill-favored section of the city...." The lawmen confiscated six barrels of beer and a number of cases of whiskey. For the *Democrat* there was ample evidence "that the place is anything but a temperance club, and the number of hangers-on found there did

 1913 Florida Sheriffs Association meeting.
(Courtesy of the Florida Sheriffs Association).

not have the countenances of patrons of the water wagon." Legislators who read the paper at least knew that the sheriffs were active, and they may have been equally convinced by another front-page account of the sheriffs being in town with a set of bills they wanted passed.[24]

As planned and advertised, sheriffs from nine counties caucused at the Leon County Courthouse, and, led by president Dowling and secretary-treasurer Houston, selected a legislative committee. They further agreed to hire an attorney to help draft the measures discussed in February. A key issue involved a pending "sheriff's salary" bill. The association recorded its opposition. The sheriffs either accepted the fee system as better, or the proposed bill lacked acceptable specifics.[25] The sheriffs' negative reaction helped explain why the bill failed to pass.

Chapter VII - The First Two Decades of the Twentieth Century

As discussed earlier, the first thirteen years of the new century saw the sheriffs association hold on and make progress. In those years and beyond the individual sheriff dealt with events as they occurred. The new century saw an increase in the number of Floridians and an accompanying larger number of criminals. Nor did the dangers lawmen faced decline even though technologically their weapons' sophistication and efficiency improved. Automobiles and new techniques of communication aided greatly; records keeping was improved; fingerprinting, photography, and other scientific modes of detection and prevention were constantly advanced. Cooperation and communication among sheriffs and with other lawmen became common (the work of the state association proved valuable); paved roads, automobiles, and increasingly, aircraft facilitated law enforcement. Even so, many of the modern advancements were equally available to people who ignored legal restraints. The character flaws in certain persons, however acquired or developed, that propelled them to crime showed no respect for the era in which they were committed. Crimes were carried out in periods of high prosperity and of bleak poverty. During the great Depression, the Palm Beach *Times* remarked: "Record breaking hard times of 1931 apparently stimulated rather than slackened the activities of those who operate outside the law. The moonshiners went on moonshining. Those who gain a living by theft and robbery and other violence went right on practicing their shady professions."[26] The age old battle of lawmen versus criminals simply moved to a new level in the twentieth century. At the same time administrative aspects of the sheriff's job never ceased to grow.

At least one sheriff used his fame as a lawman to win the governorship. A previous chapter noted that Napoleon Bonaparte Broward used his prominence as a sheriff to good effect in his campaign for governor in 1904. How he gained that renown entitles Broward to special attention. Some Florida sheriffs held other political posts before and after their tenures as lawmen. The positions were usually at the city or county level, but sometimes they were elected to the state legislature. As the exception, Broward served as Florida's nineteenth governor from 1905 to 1909. Born on a Duval County farm in 1857, he lost both

Napoleon Bonaparte Broward, of Jacksonville, served as Duval County sheriff, 1888-1894 and 1897-1900, before his election as governor in 1905. (Courtesy of the Florida State Archives).

parents when he was twelve. His varied career included work in a log camp, as a farm hand, steamboat roustabout, seaman, fisherman in Newfoundland, river pilot and steamboat owner on the St. Johns River, wood yard operator, phosphate developer, and arms runner to Cuban revolutionaries.[27]

Chapter VII - The First Two Decades of the Twentieth Century

Public outcry against an incumbent Duval County sheriff (his ineptness permitted a prisoner to escape) caused Governor Edward A. Perry to remove him from office. At the local Democratic county executive committee's urging, the governor appointed Broward sheriff in February. Without favor to man or position, the vigorous Broward not only closed down Jacksonville's gambling houses, he made arrests that resulted in convictions. The sheriff's local popularity soared as he became a figure of statewide reputation. Later, in 1888, Broward was renominated and won. In a bitter contest his faction (the "Straightouts") defeated their opponents (the "Antis"), swept other political offices, and took control of Jacksonville and the county. It seemed fitting that in national elections Grover Cleveland, the winning Democratic candidate in 1884 and 1892, was a former sheriff, having been elected to that office in Erie County, New York, in 1869.

Reflecting the times, one major issue of concern involved the new sheriff and prize fighting. Some Jacksonville sports enthusiasts and businessmen formed the Duval Athletic Club, and announced its sponsorship of a heavyweight boxing contest in January 1894. The opponents would be the American champion, James J. "Gentleman Jim" Corbett, and the foreign challenger, Charles Mitchell of England. Sheriff Broward; Duncan U. Fletcher, Jacksonville's mayor and future U. S. Senator; and Henry L. Mitchell, the sitting governor, strongly opposed the fight. A state law forbade such contests. Backing Broward, the governor dispatched four companies of state troops to Jacksonville to aid in keeping the peace. Newspapers in Florida and across the country followed events with daily stories. Twisting the limits of justice, the Athletic Club secured from the circuit judge a permanent injunction against Broward forbidding his interference with the fight. A large crowd of local fans and outsiders packed the old fair grounds to watch Corbett knock Mitchell out in the third round and retain his world title. After the fight Broward's men served the boxers with warrants ordering them to appear in court. They posted bond, and in a later trial the jury found Corbett not guilty. The case against Mitchell was dropped. Although the fight took place, Broward's efforts to prevent it and his uncompromising stand both legally and philosophically, increased his popularity.

196

A sheriff's concern for uncompromising stands could land him in trouble, as Broward soon learned. In the elections of 1894 Jacksonville endured bitter factional contests between the "Straightouts" and the "Antis." Broward suspected that fraud would mar the balloting, and, acting on what he considered his duty, exceeded his constitutional authority by stationing deputies at the polls. For that, Francis P. Fleming removed him from office. The governor replaced him with his political enemy Fleming Bowden. In the elections the "Antis" won, but were denounced by a flood of local and statewide protests against their tactics. The Jacksonville *Florida Times-Union* and many voters stuck by Broward making him a political martyr. His reputation enhanced, Broward emerged as the enemy of corruption, dishonesty, and fraud. His faction nominated him for sheriff again in 1896. Broward's vindication was his narrow victory over Bowden. Talk soon followed that the sheriff should occupy the governor's chair, and in the election of 1904 he ran and won. Broward became a progressive reform governor who established a board of control for higher education and led the campaign to drain the Everglades. He lost a race for the U. S. Senate in 1908 but won the nomination two years later. The former lawman died in 1910 before assuming office. His important career as a political leader in Florida began with his years as sheriff, an office that brought him to the public's attention.[28]

A county's ever changing system of fines for law violators provided a large part of a sheriff's income. Florida had a common system of fines, but each county was unique. County officials established the various offenses and set the amount violators paid. The sheriff, often a county's single most powerful governmental official, undoubtedly had input into framing the ordinances. The sheriff and his deputies were the men who made the arrests, and the sheriff often kept his own fine book that listed the offenses, the offenders, and the amount they were fined.

Sheriff George B. Baker, chief law enforcement officer of Palm Beach County from its founding in 1909 and until his death in 1920, was such a man. During that period he kept a carefully documented "Fine Book" that details some of the crimes with which a sheriff had to deal. The amount was usually small, ranging from $10 to $25, although

Chapter VII - The First Two Decades of the Twentieth Century

for the time, the amount was considered sufficiently punitive by the county and excessively punitive by those who paid the fines. A random sampling between 1914 and 1917 revealed people who were fined for using obscene language (many violators), fornication, gambling (many violators), drunkenness (almost uncountable violators), and various gun charges such as carrying a concealed weapon, carrying a pistol without a license, and reckless display of a dangerous weapon. People were fined for other reasons: peddling, aggravated assault, illegal branding, trespassing, larceny, vagrancy, and forgery. Fines were levied on citizens for disturbing religious ceremonies and, in one case, "imputing a want of chastity to a female," a violation that dated back to 1885. The most common fines were for fishing without a license (related to this was the setting of gill nets) and hunting without a license. People paid fines for violating railroad laws—they clung to the outside of cars in motion and raced trains to crossings. Sheriff Baker became so weary from writing "illegal sale of liquor" in his fine book that he began scrawling the word "booze" to save time and energy. Before 1917 he had cause to fine only one person for selling cocaine. The major drug problem that developed later in the century and extended into the twenty-first century could not have been imagined.[29]

Although benefiting from their share of money produced by fines, all Florida sheriffs remained basically dependent upon the state's fee system. It was an intricate web that spread with each passing year. Feeding prisoners was an ongoing necessity, and strict accounting was maintained. One act in 1915 required sheriffs and tax collectors "to pay promptly" all monies that they had collected to the proper officials. Otherwise, they faced loss of commissions and removal from office.[30] A new statute in 1919, so detailed that it occupied six pages in the *Laws of Florida*, established a revised fee system for Florida sheriffs.[31]

Florida's counties, and thus its sheriffs, were directly affected by the constitution of 1885. Article VIII of the constitution pertained to "Counties and Cities." Of its eight sections, seven dealt with counties. Section 6 provided for the election of a sheriff and other county officers. Counties were recognized as being local entities for local purposes, but both counties and cities were regarded as creatures of the state without inherent powers of their own. All powers were granted by the legislature. As already seen, the document of 1885 was the instrument of government that Florida operated under until the constitution was revised in 1968. The constitution provided for general laws that applied across the state and were to be uniform in their operation. The constitution also made provision for local and special laws. Local laws applied to particular subdivisions or portions of the state or to particular places of classified localities. Special laws related to particular persons or things or other particular objects of a class.

Article III, Section 20 of the 1885 document enumerated a number of cases in which local or special acts could not be enacted, including in some cases sheriffs and other constitutional officers. When a law was needed as a local or special act but was forbidden, it could be passed as a general law, but only with prior notice of its passage and approval of its passage by a referendum. Such a process, applied without deviation, was often impractical, inconvenient, expensive, and time-consuming. Some expedient was needed, and "population laws" evolved as the answer to the Florida sheriffs' dilemma. Population laws became the most commonly used form of classification, substituting for special or local laws for various reasons, although the primary one was to avoid holding popular referendums. As opposed to having a local statute designating a particular county by name, a population law applied to all counties within a narrow and specific population based on the most recent census figures. Thus, a fiction was created that implied broader applicability than a single county. In fact, the truth of mathematics limited the law to a single county, or at best to only a few. That such laws were of dubious legality was true, although the practice continued until the constitution of 1968 provided for self-government for the counties.[32] The practice strongly affected Florida sheriffs and their administrative operations.

The proliferation of automobiles and the building of highways influenced Florida and its sheriffs profoundly, directly tying population to law enforcement. Cars had become important enough in Florida by 1905 that a law was passed requiring each owner and operator of a motor vehicle to file a brief description, including the vehicle's horse power and make, with the secretary of state. After paying a filing fee of $2, the owner or operator was issued a certificate of registration. The act contained other details. Each vehicle had to have a "suitable bell, horn or whistle to be used as a signal," and have on the back a tag with a set of Arabic numerals at least three inches high and two inches wide. Among the act's other provisions the operator was required to keep the vehicle under control and not to exceed a speed of four miles an hour at sharp curves, bridges, fills, intersections, crossings, or other roads. The driver was to give way when approaching pedestrians, horses, or draft animals being ridden, led, or driven.[33]

No doubt many sheriffs believed that sooner or later their offices would be called upon to play a part in regulating machines with so much potential for good and yet were so inherently dangerous. Those lawmen harboring such thoughts were correct, and it was sooner rather than later. During the same session, 1905, that the legislators passed the tag registration law they also approved a measure regulating racing. Anyone sponsoring an auto race had to notify the local sheriff at least ten days in advance. The sheriff was to require such precautions as "shall be reasonably necessary for the safeguarding of the public and the protection of persons from injury while any such race is in progress." At least thirty minutes before any race the sheriff, who could appoint all the deputies he needed, was to clear the track of all non-participating persons, animals, and vehicles. Those who ignored the warnings were subject to arrest, removal from the grounds, and fines of $50. For performing these duties the sheriff and his deputies each received $2 a day.[34]

What became an avalanche of automobile registrations began as a small slide. In 1905 only 296 Floridians owned cars. By 1911 the registration law was changed. Owners had to pay an annual license fee to the county tax collector where they lived. The amount was based on the car's horsepower, charging $5 for cars with less than ten horsepower and increasing to $50 for those with 71 horsepower and over. The money collected was allocated to road and bridge funds in each county. The number of Floridians who owned automobiles had increased to 2,820 by 1916, although the demand was in its embryonic stage. Still,

SHERIFF'S OFFICE

Live Oak, Florida, February 7th, 1914
Automobile stolen last night from Dr. J. M. Price, Ford Roadster, 1912 model. Green Cross with P in center on Radiator. Top is ripped and holes in it. Goodyear and Portage tires on front wheels and Goodyear and Fisk tires on rear wheels. Factory number 102101. Please arrest party or parties with above machine and wire me. Will pay liberal reward.
Hillsborough County License Tag 609.

G. POTSDAMER, SHERIFF,
Suwannee County, Florida.

The twentieth century brought with it new types of crimes as witnessed by this proclamation for the arrest of a car thief issued by Suwannee County Sheriff Gus Potsdamer. Automobiles added a new dimension to crime after 1910. (Courtesy of the Florida Sheriffs Association).

Floridians could choose from a long list of cars still familiar to many—Ford, Cadillac, Buick, Oldsmobile, Dodge—some still vaguely recognizable—Hudson, Studebaker, Packard, W[illys] Overland—some less well known but still remembered—Pierce-Arrow, Hupmobile, Stanley-Steamer, Maxwell—and some known only to car enthusiasts and a few specialized historians—Regal, Peerless, Saxon, Premier, Meta, Argo—to name only a few.[35]

Because there was so much going on in Florida and because so much of it involved the sheriffs, the members of the statewide group worked to upgrade their association. As seen earlier, W. H. Dowling of Duval County had been elected president in 1913. The vigorous sheriff was reelected in 1914, and at the Ocala meeting in 1915 the delegates chose him as their leader for the third time. Three vice presidents were selected, and J. P. S. Houston succeeded himself as secretary-treasurer. The meeting was held in the circuit court's chambers in the courthouse. There was an unusually large number of letters and telegrams received from sheriffs explaining their absence. Even so, sheriffs from twenty-four counties and the police chief of St. Petersburg were present. The revival of interest so evident in 1913 had apparently been short-lived. President Dowling's address asked the association to make itself a permanent organization. The delegates agreed, and Dowling appointed a six-man committee to draft a constitution and by-laws. State Senator Ion L. Farris of Jacksonville helped draw up the document, and Lee Lovering of the National Sheriffs Association provided additional aid. The constitution, as presented later in the convention, gave the lawmakers a new name: the Florida State Sheriffs Association. Sheriffs and their chief deputies were eligible for membership. Their deputies and police chiefs could become honorary members. There would be a president, three vice presidents, and a secretary-treasurer. The new instrument provided for several permanent committees and for the Florida organization to send a delegate to the national association's annual meetings.[36]

The organization proved willing to deal with issues that transcended their own interests. Sheriff G. Scott Gregory of Gadsden County introduced a significant resolution that was unanimously passed by the Ocala convention. His proposal asked the pending legislative session to abandon the practice of hanging for capital offenses and substitute electrocution instead. Delegates asked also for a less controversial law increasing the allowance for boarding jurors who were placed under a bailiff and not permitted separate apartments during certain trials. In addition, the sheriffs returned to their familiar request for the state to do something about boarding prisoners. They pointed out that Georgia and Alabama allowed more money than Florida for feeding prisoners, and wanted their state to be brought into the regional average by conforming with the cost of living. Sheriff J. P. Galloway of Marion County took the delegates on a tour of nearby Silver Springs and Silver River. On the way back to town Galloway showed them Marion County's model prison farm. That evening members were given a farewell dinner at the Harrington Hall hotel.[37]

The last years of the twentieth-century's second decade saw the sheriffs keep their organization, although World War I tended to dominate domestic as well as foreign affairs. It seems probable that the society expanded because in April 1919, members from all of Florida's fifty-two counties came to Jacksonville for the annual meeting. P. G.

Ramsey, Alachua County's sheriff, presided as president.[38] A major discussion topic was an age-old criminal activity that had achieved recent prominence: the "moonshine problem." Details of how the sheriffs planned to deal effectively with the illegal sale of liquors and other matters went unreported in the press. Even so, adjournment was reached with the understanding that the members would reassemble at Tallahassee on April 8, when the legislature was in session. A special committee was appointed to lobby the lawmakers, especially on the need to revise the state's fee system. It had been in force for years, and if it remained, as seemed probable, the sheriffs wanted a general revision upward. A committee made up of W. H. Lyle of Suwannee County, William Jones of St. Lucie County, and I. W. Hudson of Pasco County was appointed to prepare a fee bill for legislative consideration.[39] The law that passed in 1919 revising the fee system reflected, at least in part, the association's wishes. Sheriffs were still dependent on fees for their salaries, but the amount designated in various categories differed in counties of forty thousand or less from that of counties whose populations exceeded forty thousand.[40]

The Florida State Sheriffs Association soon dropped the world "State" from its name and became the Florida Sheriffs Association, but continued its involvement in issues of statewide concern. Florida officials were concerned with the liquor question. It is a complicated story.[41] Some scholars have seen prohibition as a positive crusade, one that encompassed the Progressive era's social reforms, while others have viewed it as a negative movement designed to enact social control imposed by a minority on the majority (the lower ranks of society). The broad outlines of the Florida story provide a context for what the state's lawmen faced at the practical level. From 1885 to 1920 the Florida supreme court used a loose construction of the state's liquor laws, accepting an extension of state police power, but when it became a national issue, the court moved toward protecting state sovereignty as a shield against what the judges saw as a federal erosion of constitutional rights. In brief, the judicial branch of authority supported state laws that limited property rights, regulated drinking, and, finally, banned statewide liquor sales. Advocates of controlled liquor consumption had powerful arguments: the moral force of Christian evangelicalism and a broad humanitarian concern for social justice. A number of whites believed that prohibition provided needed controls over the inferior black race. Other opponents pointed out that liquor was immoral, expensive, led to crime, caused poverty, and was a big factor in breaking up family life.

As the nineteenth century closed, the temperance campaign went well for Florida's prohibitionists or "drys," automatically creating a huge work load for the state's sheriffs and their deputies. A law in 1883 that was upheld by the courts required any person or firm wishing to sell spiritous beverages in a county to apply to the county board of commissioners for permission. The request had to be accompanied by a petition and meet other conditions.[42] Then in 1885 Section XIX of the new Florida constitution made legal liquor sales a matter of local option. If one-fourth of the registered voters in a county wished to vote a dry county wet, or a wet county dry, they could petition for a popular referendum. A majority vote decided the question. The petition could not occur more than once every two years. Backing up the constitution, a law of 1887 made the sale of intoxicating beverages in a dry county a misdemeanor. Persons found guilty of breaking the law were subject to six months in jail, or a $500 fine, or both. All bars and saloons had to close at six p.m. on the day before an election and were to remain closed until six in the evening on election day.[43] Local option, if passed, operated as a prohibition rather than as a mere restriction and removed from the county commissioners exclusive liquor licensing power. Between 1901 and 1907 the Florida legislature passed several laws complementing local option ordinances. In cases coming before the state supreme court the principle of local option prevailed.

The modern national prohibition movement began in 1907 when Georgia adopted statewide prohibition and was followed by South Carolina and Alabama. Florida failed to get statewide prohibition enacted in 1907, but by 1908 thirty-four of the state's forty-seven counties were dry by local option. Florida's opponents of liquor were relentless. The Women's Christian Temperance Union and the Anti-Saloon League joined forces and together with other drys forced the passage of several

 T. J. McKewon served as Calhoun County sheriff, 1913-1917. (Courtesy of the Florida State Archives).

laws aimed at drinking. Although failing to get a statewide prohibition amendment before the voters, the opponents of intoxicating beverages obtained a law in 1913 forbidding open saloons and permitting social drinking only in private clubs that were taxed. The measure was upheld by the state supreme court. Liquor dealers fought back. They claimed the liquor laws violated the state constitution's Article XIX (local option) as well as the document's Declaration of Rights by violating property rights. Their efforts failed, and in November 1918, the Florida senate, by joint resolution, amended Article XIX by doing away with local option and making the sale of intoxicating beverages "forever prohibited in the State of Florida." Governor Sidney J. Catts, who had been elected in 1919 as the candidate of the Prohibition Party, signed an emergency law that made the state dry for the rest of the year. When the amendment was submitted to the people every county returned a majority vote favoring statewide prohibition.[44]

Meanwhile, on December 18, 1917, Congress adopted and submitted to the states the Eighteenth Amendment that established nationwide prohibition. It was declared ratified on January 19, 1919, and went into operation on January 16, 1920. The National Prohibition Enforcement Act, better known as the Volstead Act, passed in October 1919, and was the amendment's enabling act. For thirteen years Florida and the country would experience the "noble experiment." Professor John J. Guthrie, Jr., the authority on prohibition in Florida, has written that "national prohibition enforcement fell disproportionately upon persons who ranked near the bottom of Florida society."[45] Enforcement grew increasingly difficult and the mood of the country changed. In April 1933, Congress revised the Volstead Act and "near beer" became legal under federal law. That May chief executive David Sholtz signed laws legalizing near beer and light wine in Florida. Nationally, the Eighteenth Amendment was repealed in December 1933. Nevertheless, Florida's constitutional ban, its "bone dry," amendment against the sale of intoxicating beverages remained in effect until November 6, 1934. On that date the state's voters decided by a two to one majority to repeal it. Even then, some counties remained dry. The state had gone full cycle—from local option in 1885 back again to local option in 1935.[46]

Along the way, Florida's sheriffs had been hard pressed. In both urban and rural areas the enforcement of local, state, and national liquor laws, as well as state and national constitutional amendments prohibiting the sale of alcoholic beverages, had continuously engaged Florida's sheriffs. After 1935 the lawmen's responsibilities for violations of various liquor laws were less demanding, but they were still there. Not until the advent of illegal drugs as a national criminal, social, and health problem would sheriffs face a more challenging adversary.

Notes for Chapter VII

1. *FA 1901*, I, 54, 56-57.
2. Ibid., *1903*, I, 125
3. Ibid., 164. For the entire act see 148-173.
4. Ibid., *1905*, I, 148.
5. Ibid., 84.
6. Jacksonville *Florida Times-Union*, March 27, 1897.
7. Ibid., March 26-27, 1897.
8. Ibid.
9. Ibid. See also issues of July 1-2, 1897.
10. Ibid., March 15, 1901.
11. Ibid., See also Wilbanks, *Forgotten Heroes*, 69-76.
12. *FA 1933*, I, 676.
13. See ibid., *1885*, I, 61-62, for the earlier act. See also Jacksonville *Florida Times-Union*, March 15, 1906.
14. See Chapter V and endnote 5 in that chapter. See also Mark N. Goodnow, "Turpentine Impressions of the Convicts' Camp of Florida," *Internationalist Socialist Review*, XVI (June, 1915), 724-733; Robert Lauriault, "'Can't to Can't': the North Florida Turpentine Camp, 1900-1950," *Florida Historical Quarterly*, LXVIII (January, 1989), 724-733; N. Gordon Carper, "Martin Tabert: Martyr of an Era," *Florida Historical Quarterly* LII (October, 1973), 115-131; and Miller Karnes, "Florida's Convict Lease System, 1865-1923," Unpublished Master's thesis, Florida State University, 1993.

207

15. Jacksonville *Florida Times-Union*, July 6, 1901.
16. *Message of Park Trammell, Governor of Florida to the Legislative Regular Session* (Tallahassee, 1913), 11-12.
17. See Flynt, *Cracker Messiah: Sidney J. Catts of Florida*, (Baton Rouge, 1977), 238; and Carper, "Martin Tabert," *passim*.
18. Jacksonville *Florida Times-Union*, March 21, 1903.
19. Ibid., April 1, 1905.
20. Spillane, "Alachua County Sheriffs," manuscript, 84.
21. Jacksonville *Florida Times-Unio*, April 1, 1905.
22. Ibid., February 25, 1913.
23. Ibid
24. Tallahassee *Daily Democrat*, April 10, 1913.
25. Ibid. See also Jacksonville *Florida Times-Union*, April 1, 1913.
26. Palm Beach *Times*, January 4, 1932.
27. For Broward's career see Samuel Proctor, *Napoleon Bonaparte Broward Florida's Fighting Democrat* (Gainesville, 1950).
28. Ibid., 39-4 See also Allen Morris and Joan Perry Morris, *The Florida Handbook 1999-2000* (Tallahassee, 1999), 291.
29. For the act of 1885 see *FA 1885*, I, 73; Fine Book of sheriff George B. Baker, on file at the Palm Beach Historical Society, Palm Beach, Florida.
30. *FA 1915*, I, 272-273.
31. Ibid., *1919*, I, 119-122.
32. See Steven L. Sparkman, "The History and Status of Local Government Powers in Florida," *University of Florida Law Review*, XXV (1972-1973), 271-307.
33. *FA 1905*, I, 119-122.
34. Ibid., 122-125.
35. "Register of Automobiles, 1905-1917," 2 vols., I. The Register has two parts, 1905-1913 and 1913-1917, and is on file at FSA; *Report of the Florida Secretary of State 1905-1906; FA 1911*, 176-178 and 5, 233; see also *Biennial Report of The Secretary of State of the State of Florida 1915-1916*, Pt. 3, Automobiles, 3-126.
36. Jacksonville *Florida Times-Union*, March 18, 1915.
37. Ibid.
38. Ibid., March 3-4, 1919.
39. Ibid.
40. *FA 1919*, I, 226-231.
41. See Frank Alduino, "Prohibition in Tampa," *Tampa Bay History*, IX (Spring-Summer, 1987), 17-28; Patricia Buchanan, "Miami's Bootleg Boom," *Tequesta*, XXX (1970), 13-31; Richard Cofer, "Bootleggers in the Backwoods: Prohibition in the Depression of Hernando County," *Tampa Bay History*, I (Spring-Summer, 1979), 17-33; Jack E. Davis, "The Spirits of St. Petersburg: The Struggle for Local Prohibition," *Tampa Bay History*, X(Spring, 1988), 19-33; Paul S. George,

"Bootleggers, Prohibitionists, and Police: The Temperance Movement in Miami, 1896-1920," *Tequesta*, XXXIX (1979), 3-41; Edward M. Hughes, "Florida Preachers and the Election of 1928," *Florida Historical Quarterly*, LXVII (October, 1988), 136-146; Ric Kabat, "Everybody Votes for Gilchrist: The Florida Gubernatorial Campaign of 1908," *Florida Historical Quarterly*, LXVII (October, 1988), 184-202. From the long list of books on prohibition in the United States see Andrew Sinclair, *Prohibition: The Era of Excess* (New York and London, 1975), and W. J. Rorabaugh, *The Alcoholic Republic* (New York, 1979).

42. Ibid., *1883*, I, 43-44.
43. Ibid., *1887*, I, 52-66.
44. See John G. Guthrie, Jr., *Keepers of the Spirits The Judicial Response to Prohibition Enforcement in Florida, 1885-1935* (Westport, Connecticut, and London, 1998); and his "The Florida Supreme Court and the Intoxicating Liquor Laws: From Local Option to National Prohibition, 1885-1920," *Georgia Journal of Southern Legal History*, II (Spring-Summer, 1993), 99-137.
45. John A. Guthrie, Jr., "Hard Times, Hard Liquor, And Hard Luck: Selective Enforcement Of Prohibition In North Florida," *Florida Historical Quarterly*, LXXI (April, 1994), 436. For the entire article see 435-452.
46. John A. Guthrie, Jr., "Rekindling the Spirits: From National Prohibition to Local Option in Florida, 1928-1935," *Florida Historical Quarterly*, LXXIV (Summer, 1995), 23-39.

CHAPTER VIII

BOB BAKER AND THE ASHLEY GANG

n the 1920s the Florida Sheriffs Association rose to a level of permanent influence and prominence in Florida. Robert C. "Bob" Baker was the man most responsible for the advance. He realized the importance of organization, of collective action as necessary to achieve goals that benefited sheriffs as a group and as individuals. As sheriff of Palm Beach County, Baker contributed in important ways to the growth of scientific and technological advances in law enforcement. He championed the "modernization" and effective utilization of new techniques in criminal investigation. More flamboyantly, Baker made headlines for his role in breaking up the notorious Ashley gang. The outlaws plagued the counties of Florida's lower east coast, an area known as the Gold Coast, in the twentieth-century's second two decades. Like many Florida and southern sheriffs, Baker came to his job in large part because of family background. In common with other Florida sheriffs who held office for several terms and gained public attention, he made enemies as well as friends. His actions, personally and professionally, were not always above criticism. Despite inevitable human flaws, Baker, on the whole, was an excellent lawman and one of Florida's most significant sheriffs in the twentieth century.

Bob's father, George B. Baker, a native of Bellville in Hamilton County, Florida, was born in 1854. He married Julia P. McClendon in 1884, a union that would produce eight children: Robert C. "Bob," Leola, Eva, Estelle, George, Jr., L. R. "Jake," Edwin, and Henry. The

 Robert C. Baker served as sheriff of Palm Beach County, 1920-1933. (Courtesy of the Florida State Archives).

Chapter VIII - Bob Baker and The Ashley Gang

senior Baker came to West Palm Beach, then in Dade County, in 1901. His first job was as an employee of Henry M. Flagler's Florida East Coast Railroad. Interested in civic affairs and politics, George became mayor, alderman, and a member of the Dade County Board of Commissioners. When the legislature created Palm Beach County out of Dade in 1909, Governor Albert W. Gilchrist appointed him sheriff of the new county. One of his first acts was to appoint his son Bob as a deputy.[1] George Baker was a popular and effective sheriff, winning against opposition in the Palm Beach countywide election in 1912 and in every subsequent election until his death in 1920. He prevailed over his opponents, but had to overcome the opposition of the Palm Beach *Tropical Sun* and individuals who accused him of allowing the Beach Club, well known for its gambling activities, to operate and of accepting contributions from donors of questionable reputations.[2] After a series of accusations and explanations between the sheriff and the governor, the chief executive removed Baker from office. Even so, spirited demands for a reversal by many citizens of Palm Beach County led to Baker's quick reinstatement.[3]

In March 1920 the sixty-six-year-old lawman, whose health had been bad for several months, died. Governor Catts appointed Baker's son and deputy to replace him.[4] When first appointed deputy, Bob, born July 12, 1888, at Ocala, was a handsome, brown-haired, young man. An excellent athlete, he was considered one of the county's best baseball players, and he maintained a lifetime interest in the sport. In 1921 Bob and a friend became managers of the local semi-professional team when it encountered financial difficulties. He was disappointed shortly afterward when Cary A. Hardee, the governor, wrote him a letter calling his attention to a state statute banning Sunday baseball. Baker resigned as manager, but kept up his interest, and received special recognition by West Palm Beach Lodge No 1352 in 1927 for his promotion of the lodge's nine.[5]

Shortly after becoming deputy, Baker was forced to curtail his participation in sports and other activities. By the physical standards normally expected of a sheriff, he should not have held the position. In 1910 the twenty-three-year-old law officer was sent to arrest Wash

Cary A. Hardee served as governor of Florida, 1921-1925. (Courtesy of the Florida State Archives).

Pope, a black man. On confronting him, Baker ordered Pope to drop the double-barreled shotgun he was holding, but, ignoring the command, the man fired a blast that almost severed Baker's right leg. After Pope was finally subdued the deputy was taken to the rear of a nearby drugstore. There a doctor amputated his leg above the knee, managing to save the deputy's life. Sheriff Baker, realizing that Pope would not be safe from a mob in Palm Beach County, had him transferred quickly to Dade County for imprisonment. Pope later served twenty years in prison. In time young Baker recovered, was fitted with an artificial leg, and continued as a deputy.[6] In 1912 Bob married Anna E. Chandler. The marriage produced three children, all girls, but ended in an unpleasant divorce in 1926. In 1928 he married E. Kathryn Moore.[7]

Following his appointment in 1920, Baker served out his father's unexpired term. In January 1921, he sought reelection in the popular canvass and won. He was equally successful in subsequent elections in 1924, 1928, and 1932, once defeating three opponents in the primary.[8] Sometime during his administration Baker appointed Henry, one of his brothers, as his deputy. Like his father, Bob faced challenges and accusations. In 1923 Bob and four co-defendants were indicted by a federal grand jury for conspiracy to violate the national prohibition laws and to bribe a federal agent. Governor Hardee, who had appointed Baker to office, suspended him as sheriff because it appeared that he was guilty of malfeasance and misfeasance in office. When they were tried by a jury in the United States District Court, all were acquitted, and Baker was reinstated as sheriff.[9] In 1926 Baker was confined to bed for two months suffering from a heart ailment. He was sent to Johns Hopkins Hospital in Baltimore for a time, but returned to West Palm Beach and resumed his duties.[10] Despite having only one leg, Baker became widely known as a modern sheriff. He established one of the state's more effective fingerprint departments and adopted the latest techniques in fighting crime. Jovial and plain spoken, Baker carried on the good relations with the Seminole Indians that had been established by his father. The Indians made him a member of their tribe. Few Florida sheriffs were as active or well affiliated with so many clubs and organizations. He was a member of the Elks club, the Kiwanis club (he sang in the Kiwanis quartet), the Knights of Pythias, the Woodmen of the World, and the Florida State Game and Fish Protective Association. Most important for the future of the Florida Sheriffs Association, Baker was active in the American Sheriffs' and Peace Officers' Association,

Palm Beach County Sheriffs Office, 1924, from left to right: Julian Warren Landholtes (I.D. man), Henry Baker (deputy), Red Lawrence (motorcycle man), Frank H. Packwood (deputy), Ruth (secretary), Sheriff R.C. "Bob" Baker, W.H. "Hi" Lawrence (chief deputy), J.F. "Ned" Hardwick, Jr. (deputy), Elmer Padgett (deputy), Tom Riggs (jailor), H.B. "Barney" Savage (deputy). (Courtesy of Martin County Sheriff "Bob" Crowder).

International; the International Association for Identification; and the International Sheriffs' Peace Officers' Association.[11]

As sheriff, Baker and other lawmen in Florida and across America faced the formidable task of enforcing national prohibition. In 1917 Congress passed a joint resolution providing for the Eighteenth Amendment. It was submitted to the states for ratification, and early in 1919 the necessary thirty-six states had ratified. The constitutional change went into effect on January 16, 1919, and as noted, Congress passed the National Prohibition Enforcement Act (better known as the Volstead Act) to implement the amendment. As recounted earlier, Florida had proceeded from local option laws to "bone dry" statewide prohibition, and now there was a federal amendment to support the previous legislation. It would be fourteen years before repeal came with the adoption of the Twenty-First Amendment on December 5, 1933. Controlling illegal traffic in whiskey and other alcoholic beverages became a major job for Bob Baker in Palm Beach County.[12]

Before becoming aware of Baker's large role in the Florida Sheriffs Association, many people in Florida and throughout the South read about his war with the Ashley gang. Baker shared the fame with other law officials, especially with J. R. Merritt, sheriff of St. Lucie County, created in 1905, and located north of Palm Beach County. Ft. Pierce became the seat of government. Yet, it was George and Bob Baker who hounded Ashley and his followers for years, and it was Bob who was responsible for ending his career of crime.

Among other things, John Ashley and his followers were accused of bootlegging, attempted train robbery, bank heists, jail breaking, piracy on the high seas, looting of the harbor at West End, Grand Bahamas (the British government also wanted them for that transgression), attempted murder, and murder. Ashley's later notoriety was not indicated by his youth. Born on March 19, 1888, John was only a few months older than Bob Baker. The two met as young men when they were both picking and hauling tomatoes at Pompano in what is now Broward County. John fished and hunted, making a living as a trapper and trader in the Everglades. He often did business with the Seminoles who accepted him because of their close relationship with his brother Bill. Once John Ashley wound up in jail for being "drunk and disorderly" and the reckless display of firearms. He was released on bond. The future outlaw would never had been released had law officers known he had just committed a murder. The homicide led to the next encounter between Baker and Ashley. That occurred when Baker was a deputy sheriff and Ashley was in the West Palm Beach jail charged with killing a Seminole Indian named De Soto Tiger, stealing his otter hides, and selling them in Miami.

John was the antithesis of Bob. Ashley was the son of Pa and Ma Ashley, quintessential crackers who were born during the Civil War. In 1904 Julius Warren Ashley, usually known as Joe or Pa, and his wife,

Palm Beach County Deputy Sheriff H.B. "Barney" Savage after a manhunt in 1924. (Courtesy of Mickey F. Mann, Jr., chief deputy, Martin County Sheriffs Office).

Lugenia Clay Ashley (died in 1946), always known as Ma, moved with their children—there were five boys and four girls—to Palm Beach County from Rockingham, a small community near Fort Myers in Lee County, Florida. Engaged at Rockingham in the hog and cattle business, the family acquired a bad reputation. The Ashleys first moved to Pompano, from there to West Palm Beach, and then to northern Palm Beach County near Stuart. They settled at Fruita, a small community in the 12,000-acre Gomez tract, a Spanish land grant dating to 1815. Gomez is near the northern part of Hobe Sound. Pa Ashley went to work for Flagler's railroad as a woodchopper. John would later form a gang composed of his father as an occasional participant and his brothers, except for William S., better known as Bill, the only male sibling who sometimes broke the law but was not a habitual criminal. From time to time there were other gang members—relatives, friends, neighbors, and assorted criminals whom John met in and out of jail. Again and again the gang would find refuge in the large and complicated stretches of the 'Glades, the name applied to the Everglades around Lake Okeechobee.

An unusual woman with an unusual name, Laura Upthegrove, became a key member of the Ashley gang. Newspapers gave her the sobriquet "Queen of the Everglades." Member of a respected Lake Okeechobee family, she was an attractive, intelligent woman of amazonian physical strength and size, who often wore a .38 pistol strapped to her waist. Laura was John's mistress, and exercised a large influence over the gang, serving as an information courier, helping to plan robberies, and participating in its bootlegging activities. There was no doubt that John and Laura were in love. He never married, but Laura had been married twice and had four children, two by each of her husbands.[13]

After killing De Soto Tiger, a Seminole Indian of good reputation and family, Ashley became a fugitive. When a reward was offered for his capture, he left the state. Still, he missed his family and Florida. He returned in 1914. By a prearranged negotiation, he met with Sheriff Baker at Gomez and gave himself up. The first trial for De Soto Tiger's murder, held in the Palm Beach County court in July 1914, was declared a mistrial. At the second trial the state secured a change of venue to Dade County. When the murder case was transferred to Miami, Ashley, knowing his chances for acquittal in Miami were slim, escaped from the custody of Deputy Bob Baker, fled the Palm Beach County jail yard, and hid out in the Everglades. About this time he made the acquaintance of several men who would become members of his gang: John Clarence Middleton, Kid Lowe, and Roy Y. Matthews.

Once at large, Ashley was content to lay low. In 1915 John, his father, and eleven-year-old Hanford Mobley, who idolized his Uncle John, tried but failed to rob the Palm Beach Limited, a Florida East Coast Railroad train. As time passed and Mobley matured, he improved his professional skills, and the outlaws would sometimes be known as the Ashley-Mobley gang. Within a week John, his brother Bob, and Kid Lowe robbed the bank at Stuart (seat of government of present day Martin County, created in 1915) of $44,500. They succeeded in getting the money and in escaping in a stolen car, but then trouble began. Kid Lowe, disappointed because the take was not larger, either deliberately or inadvertently shot Ashley. The bullet pierced his right eye and part of his face. Infection set in, and Ashley was forced to seek medical relief. Bob Ashley and Kid Lowe escaped, but the Bakers and other law enforcement officers captured John. The prisoner was operated on in West Palm Beach where a doctor put in what became his trademark, a glass eye. Sometimes the outlaw wore a black patch over his eye socket.

In March Ashley was brought before a Miami court to face jury trial a second time on the homicide charge. While in prison Ashley attempted an escape by digging a twelve-foot tunnel under the floor, avoiding detection by working at night, getting rid of the dirt by flushing it away, and covering the hole during the day with a rug. Jail authorities discovered his efforts, leaving Ashley nothing to show for his digging except the exercise. Before John attempted his internal means of escape, his brother Bob tried to execute an external jail delivery. Bob came to Miami armed with revolvers and a rifle and a poorly conceived plan of rescue based mainly on emotion. In a bloody and foolhardy one-man assault he killed the jailer and deputy sheriff, Wilbur W. Hendrickson, and John Rihehart Riblet, a Miami police officer, only to be shot to death by the dying Riblet after a wild car chase. Despite the disruptive events, in April 1915, the circuit court jury found John guilty of murder and sentenced him to be hanged. In a bizarre twist of justice, the Florida Supreme Court reversed the circuit court's decision. The murder case was *nol-prossed,* and Ashley was returned to Palm Beach County to stand trial for the bank robbery at Stuart. He pled guilty and was sentenced to seventeen-and-one-half years in Raiford prison. Arriving at the prison in 1916, Ashley became a model prisoner. In 1918 he was assigned to a road work camp in the Panhandle county of Okaloosa. He remained only a few months before escaping to the protective 'Glades. His reputation as a model prisoner had proved short-lived.

In the next few tumultuous years Ashley and his followers were participants in a remarkable series of events. With national and state prohibition in effect, many east coast Floridians, respectable and otherwise, made fortunes illegally importing liquor. The Gold Coast counties were centers of the trade.[14] Other Floridians profited from making and selling moonshine whiskey. John, his father, brothers, and gang members successfully engaged in rumrunning to the Bahamas, a labor they enjoyed, and one they improved on by hijacking the liquor of other rumrunners. In addition, the Ashleys operated three large liquor stills in north Palm Beach County, smuggling their moonshine in stolen cars. Whiskey was portable but heavy, and the Ashley gang rented mules and wagons to haul the heavy cargoes from the stills to the paved roads. From there it was loaded in stolen cars and delivered. Auto thefts increased in startling numbers, the natural result of the booming liquor business.

Besides the Bakers, the outlaws earned the wrath of sheriffs in neighboring counties, including Dan Hardie, L. W. Moran, and Louis Allen of Dade County. J. R. Merritt, sheriff of St. Lucie County, coped with bootleggers and car thieves, often the same persons, and built a deserved reputation as a tough, no-nonsense sheriff. After its creation in 1915, Broward County and Ft. Lauderdale took their places legally on the Florida map as a county and county seat. As before, the county continued to be an area of the Ashleys' activities. When Bob Baker's father died in 1920, the newly appointed sheriff continued his work, including the relentless campaign to capture John Ashley. Each adversary was handicapped—Baker with one leg and Ashley with one eye—even so, in the 1920s Baker's singled-minded pursuit developed into an intensely personal struggle, an on-going contest by two men exercising move and countermove.

The history of the struggle between the wets and drys in Florida and the legal triumph of the drys has been reviewed earlier. The prohibitionists were only theoretical victors because the wets flourished despite laws forbidding their operations. Because no southern state struggled with the prohibition era more than Florida, the setting in which the Ashley gang operated needs explanation. Since the peninsula was close to the Bahamas and the Caribbean islands and had an exten-

Sheriff Dan Hardie served as Dade County sheriff, 1909-1917. He successfully confronted the Rice and the Ashley Gang and all manner of frontier disorder in the first two decades of the twentieth century. Re-elected in 1933 on a cleanup campaign, Hardie was suspended by Governor Scholtz for "lack of sound judgment and mental instability." (Donald Thompson and Al Goodman, History of the Metro-Dade Police Department).

sive coastline indented with numerous bays and inlets, it became the locale for large-scale "rumrunning" and liquor smuggling. Camouflaged seagoing craft (barges and speedy "Bimini boats," built in south Florida's boatyards) were joined by airplanes to bring in liquor from the Grand Bahamas and Bimini's major ports. Floridians consumed their share of the imported beverages, but most of it was destined for northern cities. Florida was a way station for illegal liquor. The state got limited help from British officials who did little to prevent their colonials from participating in the profitable trade. Not until 1924 did Great Britain sign an Anglo-American Rumrunning Convention and finally a treaty. The U. S. negotiated similar treaties with other nations. The treaties were less effective than increased congressional appropriations for the coast guard, better information gathering about foreign vessels, and improved coordination among Coast Guard, Bureau of Prohibition, and Bureau of Customs personnel. More effective enforcement occurred in the North than in Florida, where, besides its difficult-to-patrol geography, there was widespread apathy.[15]

The Bureau of Prohibition's Frank Buckley conducted a Prohibition Survey of Florida. He discovered that the state simply did not want to lose the revenue from liquor and tourists. Buckley wrote, "Numerous sheriffs, mayors, and other public officials...espouse the cause of prohibition and believe in vigorous enforcement thereof—at least during the drowsy summer months when the tourist army has departed."[16] What the Florida courts lacked in vigorous prosecution of cases, they made up for in the sheer number of trials. All that did was

Chapter VIII - Bob Baker and The Ashley Gang

frustrate federal, state, and county officials, including sheriffs. The result was congested dockets and overworked courts. The main counties for rumrunning were Dade, Duval, Hillsborough, and Palm Beach. At one point government attorneys in Florida actually tried to dodge prohibition cases. Ultimately, the Twenty-First Amendment in 1933 repealed prohibition.[17] Within the state the manufacture and sale of moonshine whiskey and other alcoholic beverages provided another layer of enforcement difficulties. Even so, sheriffs and other law officials tried to enforce the law. The misfortunes of the Ashley gang were proof that they could be successful.

The Ashleys' lucrative liquor business began to collapse. In July 1920, Pa and Bill Ashley were arrested at Sebring (Highlands County) for bootlegging. Uncharacteristically careless, John was captured in July 1921, at Wauchula (Hardee County) while making a liquor delivery. The courts sent the felon to Raiford prison. That same year two of John's brothers, Ed and Frank, were drowned in a storm during a liquor run to the island of Bimini. The gang carried on under Hanford Mobley, the previously mentioned son of Wesley and Mary Mobley, until John's kinsman revisited the Stuart bank in September 1923. Heavily veiled and wearing a dress in an attempt to fool bank guards and pursuers, Mobley was joined by John Clarence Middleton and Roy Y. Matthews (also known as Roy Y. Young). The latter was the "outside man." Matthews escaped by train to Jacksonville, but was later captured at Griffin, Georgia, where he confessed to helping in the second Stuart bank robbery. Sheriff Baker traced Mobley and Middleton to Plant City (Hillsborough County) where they were captured and brought to the West Palm Beach jail, as was Matthews. Hearing of a possible jail delivery, Baker had the felons transferred to the lockup at Ft. Lauderdale. It was to no avail because Mobley and Matthews escaped a few weeks later, although Middleton refused to break out and was sent to Raiford.

Incarcerated at Raiford under a ten-year sentence, Middleton made friends with fellow inmate Ray "Shorty" Lynn, a young Floridian who had previously deserted from the army and whose wife had left him. The two men soon conspired with Ashley to break out. The three escaped and once again engaged in the profitable vocation of making and selling illegal alcoholic beverages. The Ashley gang had informants everywhere and supposedly had "bought" some deputies and police officers, much to the anguish of other lawmen in Florida's lower east coast counties. What remained of the reunited Ashley gang raided the Pompano Bank (Broward County) on September 12, 1924. They garnered $23,000 before sending Baker a bullet and a message explaining that the gift was in case the sheriff ever "gets out to the 'Glades.'" Sending bullets to his enemies was a trademark of Ashley's.

The latest insult infuriated Bob. "The bunch of desperadoes cost me many thousands of dollars and many restless nights," he declared later, "but after they sent me the message with the bullet I was determined to get them." Baker borrowed rifles and ammunition from the local National Guard unit, deputized numerous citizens, and sent a large posse to a camp and moonshine still two miles south of the Ashley homestead. Because Baker's physical handicap prevented him from posse duty, he sent his cousin Fred Baker to lead the attack. Fred's fifty men were well equipped with small arms, rifles, and a machine gun. Setting out for the area around Fruita, the posse penetrated three miles of high sawgrass and dense swamp jungle to reach Ashley's camp and still, located on high hammock ground. Arriving quietly and early on January 29, 1924, the men surprised the gang members asleep in tents. Quickly, the attackers began firing. The startled gang members returned fire ineffectively. Pa Ashley was killed. Five bullets cut the sixty-five-year-old Ashley patriarch down as he was hastily putting on his shoes. Deputy Baker was shot and killed, his assailant being either Albert Miller or John Ashley. Miller escaped, but was wounded and captured a day later. Laura suffered buckshot wounds in the knee and was also captured. The wily Ashley, Middleton, and Lynn who suffered minor wounds, managed to escape. Fred Baker's death caused an angry crowd to burn Joe Ashley and Hanford Mobley's homes, as well as Albert Miller's small grocery. All of the Ashley family members and kin who could be located were taken into custody. The action delayed the claiming of Joe Ashley's body because the relatives not arrested were hiding in the woods.

Chapter VIII - Bob Baker and The Ashley Gang

In the next weeks Baker intensified the manhunt. Sometimes gang members were spotted. Shots were exchanged, but the fugitives managed to escape. One successful area robbery was blamed on Mobley, but pressure from Sheriff Baker grew so great the gang had to break up. Brooding over the disaster at the whiskey still and saddened by his father's death, John decided to assemble his closest confederates and drive up the Dixie Highway en route to Jacksonville. Supposedly, their final destination would be California. The felons—John Ashley, John Clarence Middleton, Ray Lynn, and Hanford Mobley—stole a Ford touring car to make the trip. The sheriff somehow learned Ashley's exact plans. One printed account claims he was tipped off by a disgruntled brother-in-law. Another contends the informer was Laura Upthegrove, who either was upset about not being included or did not want Ashley to undertake the trip (various area residents have told the authors they believe Laura was Baker's source).

A violent climax awaited the travelers. Sheriff Baker said later, "I knew they had relations all along [the] highway to Ft. Pierce, and for that reason I decided to attempt the capture at the Sebastian River bridge 28 miles north of Ft. Pierce." The sheriff sent some of his men—chief deputy H. L. Stubbs, deputies Elmer Padgett, J. B. "Len" Thomas, and Stuart's town marshal O. B. Padgett—to inform J. R. Merritt of Ashley's plans. Reaching Ft. Pierce around five in the afternoon, they conferred with the sheriff, and Merritt offered to lead them. As he described the meeting, they agreed to let him direct the capture. Merritt added C. E. Wiggins, his chief deputy, and J. M. Smith, Ft. Pierce's chief of police. The gang left the Gomez and Fruita area on Saturday afternoon, October 31. Mobley drove. Middleford sat beside him, while Ashley and Lynn were in the back. The men were heavily armed. Ashley carried a high-powered rifle and two pistols. Lynn boasted a rifle and one pistol. Mobley held two pistols, and Middleton relied on a single pistol. The car contained several hundred rounds of ammunition, a small supply of food, and some clothing. Although the outlaws' car was sighted not far north of Stuart, Mobley eluded pursuit. Further north in St. Lucie County lawman Merritt put his plan, a deadly ambush, into effect.

The law officers drove north, past Vero Beach, past the small town of Sebastian, and stopped two miles north of there at a wooden bridge that spanned the Sebastian River inlet. The bridge was located at the bottom of a hill. They drove their cars across the bridge into Brevard County and parked them in the woods near the highway. Walking back across the bridge to the south end in St. Lucie County, they stretched a heavy chain across the structure and hung a red lantern in the middle. Next, they concealed themselves behind some mangrove trees alongside the road. There they waited.

It would not take long. At 10:45 headlights came into view, but the approaching car proved to be that of two young men, Ted Miller and T. O. Davis. The area men were curious, but had no choice other than to stop at the chain. In just a matter of minutes Ashley's car drove up and halted. Sensing no danger, the occupants wondered why the automobile in front of them was not moving. Miller and his companion became scared witnesses to what would be lifetime memories. The lawmen came out of the woods and surrounded the gang's vehicle. Ashley reached for his rifle, but Merritt and Wiggins got the drop on him and took the gun. After Smith secured Lynn's rifle, the fugitives were made to get out with their hands up and walk around in front of the Ford where the lights shone on them. Leaving orders for the four men to be searched, Merritt took Miller's car across the bridge to retrieve his own vehicle which contained several pairs of handcuffs. He returned shortly, and was in the process of sorting out cuffs and keys when Ashley gave a signal. At that point, reportedly the outlaws reached for their pistols. The opposing groups were ten or fifteen feet apart. For some reason the gang members had still not been searched. Before the outlaws could fire, a lethal fusillade cut them down. As Merritt remembered, "When the smoke cleared away all four of the desperadoes lay on the ground dead." No law officer was injured.

Miller and Davis drove into Sebastian to spread the news about the incident at the bridge. There was an instantaneous reaction, and there would emerge a controversy that has never been resolved. The bodies of Ashley, Mobley, Middleton, and Lynn were taken into Ft. Pierce in the Ford they had stolen. The corpses were laid out in front of undertaker W. I. Fee's funeral home, a combination mortuary and hardware store. All day Sunday curious crowds converged on Ft. Pierce, anxious to obtain more details and view the bodies. Although the bodies had been on display outside the funeral home, family members made a request that was granted: once the dead men were taken inside would-be spectators were prevented from entering the building. Details of how the Ashley gang members met their deaths were strongly debated. In the first of two inquests Miller and Davis testified they had seen the outlaws in handcuffs. In the second, heard by a different coroner's jury, the deputies testified that Ashley and his men had attempted to escape. The judge ruled the killings justifiable homicide. In her book, *Florida's Ashley Gang* (1966), author and St. Lucie County native Ada Coats Williams reveals that one of the officers present at the ambush told her the prisoners were in handcuffs when a sudden movement by Ashley caused a deputy to fire. Startled by the event, the other deputies began shooting. Later, the Ashley and Upthegrove families would view the deaths at the Sebastian River inlet bridge as an execution. They believed their families' reputations had been demeaned and the truth distorted. Descendants of sheriffs Baker and Merritt and their deputies related a different interpretation of the night's events.

Even the post mortem ceremonies stirred interest. After the inquests Ashley and Mobley's bodies were shipped to the outlaw leader's mother in Gomez, strangely enough by way of West Palm Beach. Middleton's brother Jack, a heavyweight boxer, had the slain man's body expressed to Jacksonville where their mother lived. Lynn, whose body was unclaimed, was to have been buried by St. Lucie County. Instead, his body was requested by the Ashleys and buried in their family cemetery at Gomez.[18] The burial of the gang members drew a large crowd of mourners, including Bill, the Ashley brother who was in jail for possession of illegal whiskey. Sheriff Baker released him so that he could attend the funeral. Ma Ashley wanted a Christian funeral, but because the family had no religious affiliation such an internment was not feasible. Instead, at the request of Laura Upthegrove personnel from the Salvation Army conducted the graveside ceremonies.

The graves of John H. Ashley, Ray Lynn, and Handford Mobley. (Courtesy of Martin County Sheriff Robert "Bob" Crowder).

The grief of family and friends was understandable, but their sorrow was not shared by the state at large. The Jacksonville *Florida Times Union* editorialized on November 5, 1924, "the extinction of the Ashley gang by the summary means employed...will call forth no sympathy, but, rather there will be freer breathing because these outlaws no more will strike terror into the hearts of innocent people, no more will molest, rob and murder, as was their practice." The paper added, "Too much credit cannot be given the [law officers'] display of vigilance and bravery." A day later the Gainesville *Daily Sun* declared: "Like all lawless characters, the Ashley gang of highwaymen have finally gotten what was coming to them. They have long been a terror to the east coast of Florida but they have gone out of business."[19]

Ultimately, other sometime members of the gang were captured or were killed in shootouts with law officials. Some of the money the gang accrued from various bootlegging dealings and bank robberies was recovered, but there was no accounting for most of it. Laura, grieving over John's loss, moved about for the next three years living variously at West Palm Beach, Jacksonville, and finally in Palm Beach County at the family homestead on the eastern shore of Lake Okeechobee south of

Chapter VIII - Bob Baker and The Ashley Gang

Canal Point. Although never charged with a serious crime, she spent the years in and out of jail because of liquor violations. At the family homestead she dispensed the beverages out of a combination gas station and store. In the first week of August 1927, Laura, her mother, a customer, and several other people were at home. Laura and the patron became involved in an argument over a liquor transaction. The dispute led to violence, and when Laura seized a gun, the customer fled. Her mother took the weapon, but, in her anger, Laura rushed upstairs where she grasped a bottle of Lysol and drank it. The disinfectant took quick effect. Within twenty minutes the sad and turbulent life of John Ashley's mistress was over. Laura Upthegrove, who previously had made several attempts to commit suicide, was buried at Canal Point. Her funeral was conducted by a Methodist minister.[20] Ma Ashley died in 1946. Bill Ashley, the most law-abiding of the brothers, worked on the construction of Henry Flagler's Breakers hotel in Palm Beach. Performing other jobs, he also operated a hunters' lodge near Jupiter in Palm Beach County where he served as a guide for sportsmen. He died a natural death in 1940.

How did Baker know the criminals' plans and that they would cross Sebastian Inlet close to midnight? The question was often put to him in later years, but the sheriff's only reply was an enigmatic statement, "I had to know." Both Baker and Merritt, whose stories conflicted somewhat, were considered heroes. Even so, Merritt, who was elected sheriff shortly after the killings (to that point he had been acting sheriff), was defeated in his attempt to be reelected. Although rejected as a lawman, Merritt was repeatedly elected to the board of county commissioners. Ridding the area of the Ashley gang removed any doubt that Baker had the situation under control in Palm Beach County. Now a heralded figure of statewide importance, he would use that status to good effect in his work helping to re-energize and reorganize the Florida Sheriffs Association. Although crime continued in Palm Beach County as it did elsewhere, the Ashley gang was no more. Well before the twentieth century ended, the irreconcilable enemies Baker and Ashley became icons who shared a place not only in history but in folklore and legend as well.

Notes for Chapter VIII

1. Baker Family Papers, Palm Beach County Historical Society, West Palm Beach. See obituary clipping in Palm Beach *Post*, March 13, 1930. Hereafter cited as Baker Family Papers, with appropriate references.
2. Baker Family Papers, see Palm Beach *Tropical Sun* clippings, February 20, 27, 1912, and Palm Beach *Post*, February 15, 1916.
3. See a series of letters between the governor and Baker in February 1913, March 1915, and April 1915, in Park Trammell Papers, 1913-1917, RG 101, series 613, box 3, folder 8, FSA.
4. For a noncritical and unsigned biographical sketch of Bob Baker see *Florida Sheriffs Yearbook 1929-1930*, 3-5.
5. Baker Family Papers, see Palm Beach *Post* clipping, July 19, 1921; the letter from Hardee was also noted in the *Post*. See also Palm Beach *Times*, clipping September 22, 1928.
6. Ibid., see Palm Beach *Times*, October 31, 1920 clipping, and Palm Beach *Times*, February 23, 1933.
7. Baker Family Papers, see Transcript of Record in Case of Anna Ethene Baker Appellant vs. Robert Clarence Baker Complainant, 4 vols.
8. Ibid., see Palm Beach *Times*, May 4, 1925, February 3, 1928, clippings, see also Palm Beach *Post*, June 6, 1928.
9. Jacksonville *Florida Times-Union*, March 23, 1923; Baker Family Papers, see Palm Beach *Post*, February 8, 1924, clipping. See also Lakeland *Star-Telegram*, March 23, 1923.
10. Baker Family Papers, see Palm Beach *Times*, November 28, 1926, clipping.
11. Ibid., see unidentified West Palm Beach newspaper, 1928, clipping.
12. See the works of John J. Guthrie, Jr., previously cited in Chapter VII. See also Frank Alduino, "The Noble Experiment in Tampa: A Study in Prohibition in Urban America," Unpublished doctoral dissertation, Florida State University, 1989.
13. For biographical information on Laura Upthegrove see Palm Beach *Times*, August 8, 1927; Palm Beach *Post,* August 7, 1927.
14. James A. Carter, "Florida And Rumrunning During National Prohibition," Master's thesis, Florida State University, 1965.
15. James A. Carter, "Florida And Rumrunning During National Prohibition," *Florida Historical Quarterly*, XLVIII (June, 1960), 47-56. Material cited here is covered in greater depth in the author's thesis cited in footnote 14.
16. Cited in ibid., 54.
17. Ibid., 54-56.
18. The authors are grateful to Robert L. Crowder, sheriff of Martin County, for a list of persons buried in the Ashley family cemetery.

19. For contemporary sources see Miami *Herald*, November 2-4, 1924; Miami *Daily News*, November 3, 1924; Jacksonville *Florida Times-Union*, November 2, 1914; Gainesville *Daily Sun*, November 2, 6, 1924; and St. Petersburg *Times*, November 2, 3, 1924; Atlanta *Constitution*, November 3, 1924; coverage by New York *Times*, November 2, 1924, was largely accurate; *Florida Sheriffs Association Yearbook 1929-1930*, 5. For a succinct overview of the Ashleys and their times see Chapter XVI, "The Ashley Gang," 204-216, of Alfred Jackson Hanna and Kathryn Abbey Hanna, *Lake Okeechobee Wellspring Of The Everglades* (Indianapolis and New York, 1949). For newspaper articles see Gene Burnett, "The Ashley-Gang-Scourge of Florida," *Florida Trend*, XIX (August, 1976), 76-78; Joe Crankshaw, "Florida's Jesse James Rode the Crest of a 13-Year Crime Wave," St. Petersburg *Times* , "Sunday Magazine," May 26, 1963, and Scott Hovanyetz, "Outlaws of the Treasure Coast," Fort Pierce *Tribune*, March 30, 1997. C. Stuart Hix, *The Notorious Ashley Gang A Saga of the King and Queen of the Everglades* (Stuart, Florida, 1928) was the first book written about the Ashley gang. It is a non-objective work written by an amateur historian who dedicated it to Sheriff Bob Baker. The style is sprightly, and the author knew personally most of the principals. The best book on the subject is Ada Coats Williams, *Florida's Ashley Gang* (Port Salerno, Florida, 1996). Brief but based on careful research conducted over a number of years, the work is a reliable source. James Carlos Blake, *Red Grass River A Legend* (New York, 1998) is an entertaining work of fiction. Blake uses actual names and adheres generally to the historical record. In 1969 a movie based on the Ashley gang was filmed on location in Stuart. Entitled "Big John and Little Laura," it was not a box-office success. Colonel M. F. Mann, Jr., of the Martin County Sheriff's Office kindly helped the authors locate materials, and Ada Coats Williams provided important information about the Baker-Ashley years in two telephone interviews, February 9, 11, 2000.
20. Palm Beach *Post*, August 8, 1927; Palm Beach *Times*, August 7-9, 1927. Laura had property in Palm Beach and Okeechobee counties, and left an estate of some value. Her brother was also an outlaw, although not a member of the Ashley gang. Sheriff Baker related a story that demonstrated Laura's tenacity and fighting spirit. The sheriff had stated that one day he would wear Ashley's glass eye as a watch fob. After the affair at the Sebastian River bridge one of the deputies retrieved Ashley's artificial eye and brought it to Baker. Laura heard of the incident and wrote the lawman a letter demanding the eye and threatening to kill him if he did not. As Baker put it, he dutifully returned the eye.

CHAPTER IX

BOOM TIMES AND THE GREAT DEPRESSION

As Florida's population grew dramatically in the 1920s Palm Beach County's Bob Baker and other lawmen realized that the Florida Sheriffs Association (FSA) needed to rebuild and increase its membership. Since its founding in 1893 the organization had undergone periods of rise and decline, but had always managed to survive. In the post-World War I decade Baker, cooperating with some determined lawmen, brought the association to a lasting place of power and influence.

With his record of joining organizations it is not surprising that Baker was an active FSA member. Curiously, his father had shown little interest in the organization. Bob Baker's problems in 1923 have been described in Chapter Eight. He was indicted and suspended from office. At least once he visited personally with Cary A. Hardee in Tallahassee to explain to the governor events from his perspective. Understandably, the Palm Beach County sheriff did not attend the FSA meeting that March in Jacksonville. Nevertheless, his presence was felt. His fellow sheriffs passed a resolution and forwarded it to Hardee expressing their full confidence in Baker. They asked the chief executive to consider carefully "all the evidence laid before him, bearing in mind the host of enemies any sheriff makes in attempting an impartial enforcement of the law.[1]

By the 1920s Florida's sheriffs were deeply involved in carrying out the existing prohibition laws and additional enforcement legislation that came from the legislature. Prohibition gave the sheriffs a powerful

E. Scott Gregory, sheriff of Gadsden County, 1909-1933, was president of the Florida Sheriffs Association in 1923, and helped persuade the state legislature to switch from hanging to the electric chair as the state's method of punishing capital crimes. Courtesy of the Gregory family.

motive to work together. At best only twenty-eight sheriffs attended the 1923 FSA meeting. E. Scott Gregory, president and sheriff of Gadsden County, and the delegates concentrated on ways to succeed in their struggle to stifle the flow of illegal liquor. The lawmen asked for a statute permitting officers to search a car suspected of carrying liquor even if they had no warrant. The sheriffs complained about the bootleggers' scheme of transporting their cargo in some one else's vehicle. If caught, they pled that the car belonged to another owner, and it was not confiscated. FSA members also favored a measure allowing the seizure of any automobile caught transporting whiskey. The sheriffs, who controlled the county traffic officers, were concerned about another plan brewing in the legislature. Tampa Police Chief F. M. Williams, backed by members of the statewide Florida League of Municipalities, was pushing a state police bill. Coming out strongly against the measure, the sheriffs argued that it would be prohibitively expensive. Such a

233

force would also diminish the sheriff's authority. To forward its own agenda the association voted to have a person present at the upcoming legislative session. Additionally, a committee comprised of Gregory and four other sheriffs was appointed to promote the FSA's program to the lawmakers at Tallahassee.[2]

Other matters commanded the delegates' attention. In 1915 the FSA had called for the state to change its means of inflicting capital punishment from hanging to the electric chair. Considered a more efficient and humane system, electrocution by the state was a long-lasting issue. Now, in 1923 the FSA passed another formal resolution favoring the new system. Widespread public support existed for such a law, and one passed that year. The FSA's endorsement gave added impetus and authority to the popular outcry, undoubtedly speeding the bill's passage. The new law declared that on or after January 1, 1924, "death by hanging as a means of punishment for crime in Florida is hereby abolished and electrocution, or death by electricity substituted therefor." The electric chair, which became known as "Old Sparky," was devised by Ralph Green, Sr., a Jacksonville physician, and was built at Cook's Cabinet Shop in Jacksonville. On October 7, 1924, Frank Johnson, a black man of Duval County who had confessed to a murder charge, became the first person to be electrocuted by the state.[3]

As mentioned before, the FSA opposed establishing a state police force. Instead, it supported the county traffic patrol system begun in 1921. A population law, the act provided for a new law enforcement official: the county traffic officer (CTO). The statute was applicable in counties having a population of more than 80,000 and less than 100,000. Hillsborough, which contained Tampa and ranked second in the state after Duval, was the only county that fit the designation. Using the population laws system made passage as simple as enacting a local statute. Appointed by the governor, the CTO served a one-year term. He was selected on the recommendation of the county commissioners who also paid his annual salary of $1,800. The money came from the local fine and forfeiture fund. A county traffic officer's duties were to patrol the roads and enforce traffic laws and regulations. He possessed the same arrest powers as sheriffs and constables. The chief CTO was to

The last hanging in Levy County took place on September 30, 1902. (Courtesy of Florida State Archives).

Electric chair at the Raiford Prison 1936. (Courtesy of Florida State Archives).

"Old Sparky" is the nickname for Florida's electric chair that was first used in 1923. In January, 2000, the state chose lethal injection as its primary method of execution. Today, under Florida law, defendants can choose either. If the defendant fails to make a conscious choice, the state defaults to lethal injection. (Courtesy of Florida State Archives).

Chapter IX - Boom Times and The Great Depression

appoint from one to three deputies who were also nominated by the county commissioners.[4]

Similarly, the 1921 legislature had acted to place the county traffic officer more under the supervision of Dade County's sheriff. It provided that two persons, known as the Motorcycle Squad, were to be appointed by the sheriff as deputy sheriffs. The officers had the broad duty of patrolling the roads, enforcing traffic laws, protecting citrus crops from being stolen, and arresting violators of the state's prohibition laws. They were paid out of the county's fine and forfeiture fund. The two acts, applying to Hillsborough and Dade counties, set the precedent of using population as the basis for CTO laws. More significantly, the laws created the forerunners of the Florida Highway Patrol, which was not established until 1939.[5]

These two local statutes set precedents for future legislative actions. Dade County's county traffic officer law was amended in 1923 to raise salaries and make other minor adjustments.[6] New population laws pertaining to CTOs in other counties became common, and the sheriff's role was usually enlarged in the supplementary legislation. Additional CTO statutes reflected the state's population increase by natural birth and, more important, by people moving into the state from all over the country. The creation of twenty new counties in the first twenty-five years of the twentieth century was indicative of a rapidly growing state. The final four were established in 1925: Martin, Indian River, Gulf, and, last, Gilchrist on December 4. A few newcomers came by planes, more arrived by railroads, but most utilized automobiles. The influx caused a dramatic increase in the number of cars and other vehicles using the state's roads and national highways.

A 1927 law made a significant change. All future county traffic officers were to be appointed as deputies acting under the sheriffs of various counties. Appointed by the sheriffs, they were still called county traffic officers. Their annual salaries provided $50 a month as expense money, and they could accept no other employment.[7] Even so, a population law of 1929 had the governor appoint the county officers in counties with populations of 9,643 to 9,650 and 17,020 to 17,050 persons.[8] The population laws were too numerous and similar to warrant individual discus-

Hillsborough County traffic officers, circa 1920s. (Courtesy of the Hillsborough County Sheriffs Office).

sion, but what they accomplished for county traffic officers was to increase their number (one was added for each additional ten thousand people) and salaries; provide them with expense money; place them under the sheriffs' control; prescribe for them distinctive badges and uniforms (done to instill them with pride and to familiarize the public with the officers); permit their salaries to come from the general county fund as well as from the fine and forfeiture fund; give them the same arrest powers as the sheriffs; and prohibit them from accepting any other employment.[9] A number of Florida's future sheriffs began their careers as county traffic officers. Many Floridians, although they accepted the CTO system, believed that Florida should establish a state highway patrol. The idea was gaining in popularity throughout the country, and the issue came to the fore in the 1930s.

With so many different specifics, population laws enacted between the world wars were also used to help reduce dependency on fees by the

Chapter IX - Boom Times and The Great Depression

sheriffs. Under that aegis a number of counties did away with the fee arrangement altogether, replacing it with a salary system. Even so, population laws could also be used to establish a fee system in a county, as one did in 1937 for Flagler County.[10] Seemingly, the reliance on fees had the system's proponents and opponents forever at loggerheads. The question would not go away. The complicated fee law of 1919 remained in place until 1925 when, mercifully, another measure cut the 1919 act's provisions by half. The fee system still lived, though not particularly well, in 1933 when a law established a new list of charges-for-service for sheriffs, constables, and clerks of circuit courts.[11] Set salaries were also applied to other county officers besides sheriffs.

Through the early 1920s Baker rose as a leader in the FSA and was elected president in 1926. He was reelected when the association met in 1927 at the small town of Okeechobee. He took the lead in persuading the members to pass a resolution favoring a state bureau of criminal identification. Such an agency would act as a clearing house for information on criminals. No less a person than Governor John W. Martin, traveling by car and train, came down from Tallahassee to address the meeting. Former Governor Park Trammell (1913-1917) who was a sitting United States Senator, explained to the delegates nearby drainage activities. Those attending were entertained by Okeechobee's first county fair, a rodeo, a fiddling contest, and an old-fashioned breakdown dance. A group of Seminoles who had come with Chief Billy Bowlegs from their Big Cypress Reservation to hear Martin, staged a war dance. Unfortunately, the governor knew nothing about the Seminole language. Sheriff Baker, who understood a few words, acted as an interpreter and earned Martin's gratitude. The governor got more expert language assistance from Frank L. Tipping from Fort Myers (sheriff of Lee County) when he addressed drainage problems and the issue of parimutuel betting.[12] The next year, the association's annual conclave was held at the Hotel George Washington in Jacksonville in March. Duval County Sheriff W. H. Dowling, a leader in the FSA, was the host. The incumbent president, Bob Baker, won a third term without a dissenting vote. Baker had become such a force that the Palm Beach *Times* erroneously claimed he was instrumental in the organization's founding. The paper was correct in asserting he had "probably done more to carry along [its] purposes than any other officer of the state," and exaggerated only slightly by adding, "Under [the association's] practices the fullest cooperation is given by each county executive to the sheriff of every other county in the apprehension of fleeing criminals and the standards of [the office] throughout the state has taken a higher plane than existed before."[13]

Sheriff W. H. Lyle of Suwannee County, emerging as an association leader, was elected first vice president at the 1928 meeting. The FSA had expanded so much in the 1920s that each county in Florida now was represented at the annual convention by either a sheriff or a chief deputy sheriff. As usual, the Jacksonville delegates heard speeches from local and state civic leaders and politicians. Beyond the oratory and the pleasures of conviviality, the lawmen held serious sessions. One was devoted to law enforcement methods and ended with a resolution favoring a statewide uniform system of subpoenas. Deceased sheriffs were recognized, especially such men as Perry Hall of Flagler County who was killed a few months earlier while making an arrest.[14] Within three years, and at Baker's urging, the society would position itself to offer more than sympathy in times of personal crisis. In 1931 Sheriff N. Pearson of Lafayette County was murdered in the line of duty. Left a widow with several children and no adequate means of support, his wife faced a financial crisis. Baker suggested that the FSA contribute $500 to a fund established for her by Governor Doyle E. Carlton. "I am sorry that during his life...Sheriff Pearson never joined our Association," Baker explained to the chief executive, "[because] by paying his dues and taking advantage of the insurance which the Association arranged for recently [his family would have benefitted]." Still, Baker continued, "this fact would bear no weight with me in helping his widow and orphans, and it will be a pleasure for me to assist them in any way I possibly can."[15]

The membership accepted the invitation of Sheriff Cleve Niles of Monroe County to hold their 1929 convention at Key West and to name it the Sheriffs' Overseas Highway Convention (it would be 1938 before U. S. Highway 1 was completed to the city). The gathering was an

239

important one. Convening in March, the sheriffs found Key West a place of unique geographical and historical setting. They spent more time than usual in sightseeing. Baker was reelected, making it his fourth time to hold the position. His presumptive successor, Live Oak's W. H. Lyle was reelected as first vice president. The FSA operated under the constitution and by-laws adopted in 1915. Periodic amendments probably had been made, but it was near past time for a new governing instrument, one tailored to serve a modern Florida. President Baker was given major credit for writing an updated constitution, although undoubtedly he had help. The convention adopted it, but the document was not made public until the 1930 meeting in Gainesville. Its printed form was made available to members and the public in the *Florida Sheriffs Association Year Book (1929-1930)*. The need for such a publication had been talked about for decades. The yearbook, also the result of Baker's work, became an important document of record and an attractive presentation of the FSA's activities. Revenue from many advertisers helped defray the costs of publication.[16]

Baker's influence in the FSA persisted well after the end of the 1920s. Because Baker had taken ill the FSA's 1930 meeting, scheduled to begin March 19, at Gainesville's Hotel Thomas, was postponed until March 24-25. Meeting at a university town was unique for the lawmen. Still, Alachua County had furnished the association's first president, Sheriff A. U. Hilleary, back in 1893, and the county's lawmen had always been active in the state body. The host sheriff and secretary of the association, R. J. "Bob" Wells, delivered the welcoming address, and Live Oak's president-elect Lyle made an appropriate response. Sixty delegates heard the speeches, and both were broadcast over WRUF, a station operated by the University of Florida. The live broadcasts were a first for the association. Later, Baker made his official address and stepped down as president. The lectures and discussions centered on modern police methods. Leisure time, unlike that spent observing historic landmarks, aquamarine waters, and glistening beaches at Key West, was occupied by a visit to the state prison farm at Raiford. Still, not all was business. The delegates enjoyed a dance given in their honor on the Spanish patio of Hotel Thomas.[17]

 Doyle E. Carlton served as governor of Florida, 1929-1933. (Courtesy of the Florida State Archives).

Chapter IX - Boom Times and The Great Depression

The sheriffs were pleased with the handsome, profusely illustrated yearbook that was distributed among them. The constitution and by-laws, as printed in the yearbook, were neither complicated nor overly long. Article I verified the body's formation. Article II established eligibility rules: sheriffs, chief deputy sheriffs, chiefs of police, and railroad company special agents in Florida could join. In additional to the active members, provision was made in the by-laws for honorary members. Article III declared the FSA's object: bringing together the members "for a more mutual acquaintance, for interchange of thought, the apprehension of criminals, and such other purposes as the majority may from time to time designate." Article VI gave the membership power to enact by-laws to administer its affairs. The organization was authorized by Article V to create offices and elect officers (their number and title to be fixed in the by-laws). The association was empowered by Article VII to discipline its members with either temporary suspensions or expulsions for violating its rules and "for conduct unbecoming an officer and a gentleman." Article VIII permitted constitutional amendments by a two-thirds vote. Emphasizing the FSA's permanence, Article IX declared, "The Association can not be disbanded as long as there are ten members in good standing who are desirous of continuing the same." Extensive and subject to change, the by-laws established annual dues, set the times for yearly meetings, and permitted special meetings if needed. Soon, extra meetings, usually devoted to one special subject, were called. As outlined in the constitution, the by-laws set meeting times and provided for officers (a president, first vice president, second vice president, secretary, treasurer, and attorney, publications, and so on). That the sheriffs made a good impression in Gainesville was seen in an editorial from the local *Daily Sun*:

> To look in on the sessions...at the Hotel Thomas, will bring a surprise to those with old-fashioned ideas that sheriffs are a desperate looking lot of men, armed to the teeth, ferocious and capable of biting an iron crow-bar in two with their teeth. The sheriffs...are in appearance not one whit different from any of the gentlemen who have preceded them as delegates to other conventions. If anything are a bit more gentle and

unassuming...they are evidently men of action when action is necessary and are here for the sole purpose of considering such matters as will continue to make Florida a place of security and where citizens of all lands can pursue their lives in peace and without molestation.[18]

Like other Floridians, sheriffs had to cope personally with the Great Depression, and carry out their public duties under laws tailored to fit the needs of the decade. In the first year of the 1930s Sheriff W. B. Cahoon's Duval County office worked 4,185 criminal cases. The increased sophistication of criminal activity forced the sheriff and other

Sheriff W. B. Cahoon served as sheriff of Duval County, 1929-1931. Here he poses in front of confiscated illegal alcoholic beverages. (Courtesy of Florida State Archives).

Florida lawmen to adopt means to combat the menace, no easy task when public funds were scarce. Despite the limitations, Cahoon reported, "through rigid economy and good business methods, we have succeeded in making the Sheriff's office a financial asset instead of a liability."[19] Use of population acts increased in the 1930s because they helped combat the hard times. Here was a way to lower expenses by cutting salaries and making them more uniform. In 1937 legislation affecting heavily populated counties provided that pay for county officers, including sheriffs, would be determined by the net income of their offices up to $7,000, and no official was to make over $7,000.[20] At the same session legislators passed a population law that applied only to deputy sheriffs, and made their salaries contingent upon the county commissioners' sense of justice. In counties of 22,000 to 23,300 persons, deputies' pay was to be "reasonable and proper."[21] Broadly speaking, the population laws relating to law enforcement created county traffic officers, established specific salaries for sheriffs in certain counties, set limits that sheriffs' salaries were not to exceed the income generated by their officers (but left open the possibility of paying them less), provided the sheriff with additional money for his deputy and jailer, and gave extra pay for sheriffs to feed prisoners and attend meetings of the county commissioners. One population measure in 1937 set the bond limits for officials in counties having over 150,000 people. The sheriff's bond was not to be below $10,000 or more than $25,000.[22]

Through the first four decades of the twentieth century Florida's sheriffs carried out their traditional duties, while responding to new conditions. Sometimes additional types of officers were needed, offering competition to the sheriff's traditional authority. For example, in 1925 Orange County's State Attorney for the Seventeenth Judicial Circuit and the Solicitor for the Criminal Court of Record were given unusual powers by a special act. Either was authorized to hire a detective or detectives. Each detective was to be paid by the Orange County Commissioners at a salary not to exceed $4,000 a year.[23] The pragmatic act illustrated that specific needs in a county could be addressed when they became apparent. In 1929, for instance, laws repealed the post of deputy constable in Dade County, and, for counties of from 110,000 to 115,000 people, established a fee schedule for bailiffs ($7.50 a day) and guaranteed deputy sheriffs $2.50 a day for testifying.[24]

A sheriff could predict but he could never fully know what his duties would require of him. Asked what his job had to do with wells, the typical lawman would have replied not much. Yet, in 1935 certain owners of lessees of free flowing and artesian wells in Seminole and Sarasota counties abused their rights. Two new laws declared that a person, persons, or company in charge of a free flowing well—whether it discharged water, oil, gas, or other natural products—had to have mechanical controls such as pumps and gauges to regulate the flow. Likewise, a bored artesian well had to have similar devices to control any damaging discharges. The legislature made it a misdemeanor subject to fine and imprisonment for persons who violated the requirements. Sheriffs in the two counties were designated to carry out the act, and, while probably unversed in hydraulic engineering, they proved competent as inspectors and enforced compliance.[25]

In the 1930s the Florida Sheriffs Association became more active than ever. At their Sarasota meeting in March 1931, delegates from thirty-eight counties reelected W. H. Lyle as president. The sheriffs dealt with a large number of deaths among their members. They voted to pay $500 to the widow of Sheriff G. D. Clark of Calhoun County. He had been killed while performing his duty. The members voted a small amount to sheriffs Thad Bell of Walton County and W. A. Keen of Sarasota County who were severely injured while enforcing the law. Resolutions expressing regret were passed in honor of sheriffs J. P. Steele of Okaloosa County and P. M. Hagan of Putnam County who died during the past year.[26]

An interesting experiment emerged from the Sarasota meeting. One delegate, anxious to utilize radio in upholding law and order, suggested a statewide program that would feature crime news. Shortly after the convention ended, radio station WRUF at the University of Florida began broadcasting criminal activities within the state. How many sheriffs' offices used the facility is unknown. As the system operated, crime news was telegraphed to Alachua County's Sheriff R. J.

245

Wells, who was also secretary of the FSA, from across the state. The reports were then broadcast through a remote control arrangement in Wells's office at 8:55 in the morning, 1:45 in the afternoon, and eight o'clock at night. W. B. Cahoon of Duval County, to name one sheriff, installed a set in his Jacksonville office to receive the daily reports. The service was available to all Florida law enforcement officers, and was considered particularly valuable for reporting stolen automobiles.[27] By 1935 the experiment had ended, but its results caused the FSA to recommend state funding for short wave radio stations and interstate communication to improve crime control. According to the association's proposal, patrol stations, under the control of the county sheriff affected, would be established on highways leading into Florida with officers on duty who were equipped with short wave radio sets. Beyond that, the sheriffs wanted three state controlled short wave "crime" radio stations in Florida. One would be at Gainesville, the second at Tallahassee, and the third at a city to be selected later.[28]

The FSA met at Ocala on March 15, 1932. More than fifty sheriffs attended according to the local chamber of commerce. Sheriff Cahoon invited the lawmen to hold their next annual meeting at Jacksonville, by far the sheriffs' most frequently used convention city.[29] Undeterred, three other locales—Tallahassee, Key West, and for the first time, a city of a foreign nation, Havana, Cuba—extended invitations. Key West was selected. W. H. Lyle was elected president for the third consecutive time, and Columbia County Sheriff W. B. Douglas was chosen first vice president again.[30] From Ocala the sheriffs sent resolutions of sympathy and reassurance to Charles A. Lindberg and his wife Ann. The family was offered the "whole-hearted co-operation of every sheriff's office in Florida to do anything in their power to help find the baby and apprehend the kidnapers." The nation closely followed the story of the aviation hero and his wife's ordeal from its beginning in March 1931, with the kidnapping of their son, Charles A. Lindbergh, Jr., to the discovery of the dead child, the arrest, trial, and conviction of Bruno R. Hauptmann, and to his electrocution in Trenton, New Jersey, in April 1936.[31]

For reasons not entirely clear the 1933 gathering met at Tampa

Florida Sheriffs' Association Convention, Sarasota, Florida, March 17, 1931. (Courtesy of the Florida Sheriffs' Association).

rather than Key West. Sadly, before the convention began Sheriff Baker died at his home at West Palm Beach on Thursday morning, February 23. Baker had chronic high blood pressure and had suffered a heart attack five years earlier. In recent years his health had been thought to be good. Physicians ascribed his death to a cerebral hemorrhage. At the time Baker was busily engaged in a campaign against a wave of burglaries at the homes of Palm Beach's wealthy winter visitors. According to a Jacksonville paper, the sheriff "died with his boots off and left Florida shocked at [the] loss of one of its most renowned peace officers."[32] The news stunned and saddened many Palm Beach countians. Across the county flags flew at half mast. Many public and private meetings were canceled. An honor guard presided over his body which lay in state at the local funeral parlor. Numerous citizens came to view his remains, and two thousand people attended the funeral. Delegates to the FSA's annual convention had a medallion struck in Baker's honor and presented it to his mother.[33]

In the wake of Baker's passing, the 1933 Tampa convention was highly politicized and well attended by sheriffs, deputy sheriffs, and delegates who were not sheriffs. The non-sheriffs included single detectives, special agents, and police from the Atlantic Coast Line, Florida East Coast Railway, and four such men from the Seaboard Air Line Railway. Selecting a new president resulted in a spirited contest between Lyle and Hillsborough County's Sheriff Will G. Spencer. The first vote was a tie, resulting in a runoff that was won by Lyle. Spencer was chosen as the first vice president.[34]

The delegates' main issue was the familiar one of fees. The recently adjourned legislature had passed a new county fee law that cut the income of sheriffs by about sixty percent. The action was not vindictive. It was taken to help relieve the state's financial stress that accompanied the Great Depression. Even so, it affected FSA members and other county officials dependent on fees. Alarmed FSA members formed a committee made up of president Lyle and sheriffs Rex Sweat of Duval and S. E. Stone of Volusia counties to get in touch with the State Association of Clerks of Circuit Court (circuit clerks were also adversely affected) to work for a revision of the law. If necessary the committee was authorized to attack the measure with

William C. "Will" Spencer, of Tampa, served as Hillsborough County sheriff during three nonconsecutive terms, 1913-1917, 1921-1925, and 1933-1935. (Courtesy of the Hillsborough County Sheriffs Office).

court action. Further, the convention appointed five sheriffs to serve as a legislative committee.

The delegates gave careful attention to State Senator W. C. Hodges of Tallahassee, a politician sympathetic to the association, who told them Governor Sholtz would probably call a special session of the legislature. Hodges urged the sheriffs who complained because the new fee bill reduced mileage compensation from 12.5 cents to 6 cents to organize a strong lobby and fight for fair fees at the special session. As the senator bluntly put it, "cutting the [present fee] is the height of foolishness." He added that, speaking from his long legislative experience:

> You have got to protect yourselves. You are just out of luck in these times if you do not. A legislative session is an open season on sheriffs. If I were you boys I would perfect this organization, the Florida Sheriffs [A]ssociation. It can be the salvation of sheriffs in this state. Get together and get a hole in the wall

at Tallahassee. And I don't mean that any place else will do, at West Palm Beach, or Tampa, or Miami. Have it somewhere in Tallahassee, where you can talk matters over with someone who is friendly to you.... Unless you are strong and able to explain your needs you will come up shy.... If you people had an organized lobby, not in the usual sense, in the last session, to explain about this mileage matter I think there would have been few votes against a fair fee."

Concluding his strong remarks, Hodges declared that politics had dominated the session. The result was bad legislation, including the county salary bill. "The office of sheriff," he said, "is one of the most important in any county, if not the most important. He is the peace officer.... To say that he should not get compensation high enough to hold a responsible man is a travesty on common sense. And I don't think that under the constitution they can fix a salary for a sheriff. He is entitled to fees. You might get a lawyer to look into that for you."[35]

In the eyes of his fellow sheriffs, Sheriff Lyle's success as their president was self evident, but a change in leadership was in the offering. When FSA members gathered at Homosassa Springs, April 24-25, 1934, there was no contest over who their president would be. The delegates adopted a resolution of high commendation for Lyle. The four-term president was replaced by the controversial Will C. Spencer who had no opposition. As committed as ever, Lyle had left Live Oak in time to be among the first to arrive. Unfortunately, Lyle died in 1935. Frank Stoutamire of Leon County, Charles Dean of Citrus County, Rex Sweat of Duval County, and J. E. Stone of Volusia County were the other elected officers.

The delegates heard talks by Attorney General Cary D. Landis, Adjutant General Vivian Collins (representing Governor David Sholtz), Asher Frank, head of the State Safety League, and Ward L. F. Chapman of Raiford State Prison. Resolutions on the deaths of two sheriffs—Lamar Sledge, slain Jefferson County officer, and F. M. Lipscomb of Taylor County—were adopted. Miami was chosen as the next convention site. The usual types of entertainment, the traditional banquet and a dance, provided breaks from the business sessions.[36]

By 1935 the association began having two statewide gatherings a year. The semi-annual meeting was known as the mid-winter meeting if held in January, or the spring meeting if held in March. The annual meeting shifted from March to June, but some years there were exceptions to this arrangement. In March 1935, delegates registered at the Miami Biltmore, elegant and quasi-Moorish in design.[37] A revealing look at how the FSA operated in the 1930s can be seen by a detailed analysis of the 1935 convention. David Sholtz, who occupied the governor's chair in Tallahassee from 1933 to 1937, was busy putting in motion his statewide Little New Deal to complement Franklin D. Roosevelt's massive federal New Deal. The sheriffs were occupied either directly or indirectly with agencies at both levels, and, all the while, fulfilled their local responsibilities.

Outgoing FSA president Will Spencer presided temporarily at the 1935 meeting. Then incoming president Rex Sweat, one of the association's more important members, took the gavel. By this time the annual convention sometimes lasted three days. Continuing the time-tested format, the delegates heard abundant oratory by invited guests, mostly prominent politicians. They listened to Florida state senate president W. C. Hodges, future governor (1937-1941) Frederick Cone and railroad commissioner Jerry W. Carter, already becoming known as Florida's "Mr. Democrat," several cabinet members, and, as always, a number of lawyers. Letters from several sheriffs explaining that illness had caused their absences were read. There was a special letter from J. Edgar Hoover, director of the Federal Bureau of Investigation.

At the opening session delegates were invited by Fernando H. Cato, representing the Royal Palm Hotel in Havana, to end their convention with a visit to Cuba. Cato assured members that a recent revolt had been settled. He was supported by the Chief of the Cuban Constitutional Army who explained that the military had the situation well in hand. By acclamation the convention accepted the invitation. Even though the trip would be a modest excursion, it was still an international venture that involved the governor's permission. A number of sheriffs simultaneously absent from Florida at the same time was a circumstance that had to be considered. A query was sent to Governor Sholtz who promptly wired his permission, wishing them bon voyage. Their brief visit was later made by plane, and was accomplished without incident by at least eighteen sheriffs. Once the Cuban visit was decided on, the delegates attended to other business, including the establishment of a committee headed by the FSA president, to lobby the state legislature. At the suggestion of President Spencer the members voted to back a law providing reimbursement to sheriffs for expenses incurred in unsuccessful searches for criminals. The members took the afternoon off to go to the races at Miami's Tropical Park where the management honored their visit by naming the fifth race, a test for three-year-old fillies, the Florida State Sheriffs Association Purse.[38]

In his remarks to the convention President Sweat urged greater cooperation between Florida's law enforcement officials and federal authorities, especially in the extradition of prisoners. He argued for an upgrading of standards for sheriffs because employing "higher type officers, men equipped mentally to meet clever criminals on an equal basis" was necessary. In the future "certain branches of law enforcement will insist upon the employment of none but highly educated men in the service...."Undoubtedly, "these officers will be looked up to and respected as are professional men today. Crime is costing too much money today not to awaken our citizens to a realization of the benefits to be derived from more efficient departments of crime detection and prevention." Sweat stressed education as a major solution to the rising problem of traffic fatalities. "Until we recognize the fact that the motor vehicle is a deadly weapon in the hands of the wrong person—is as deadly as a machine gun," he declared, "little or no progress will be made toward the prevention of these unnecessary deaths."[39]

The sheriffs learned how Dade County used a cooperative effort to fight crime. Miami's special place in Florida and the nation made it a city that attracted law breakers. Al Capone and other notorious national underworld mobsters found Miami an ideal locale to combine vacations with business.[40] To meet the challenge Dade County's Sheriff, D. C. Coleman, cooperated with the chiefs of police in Miami, Miami Beach, Hialeah, Coral Gables, Homestead, and other county municipalities to monitor the powerful crime lords in "America's playground," especially during the winter season. During those months experienced detectives from across the country were hired to work with local lawmen. While remaining anonymous and staying in the background they identified certain out-of-state criminals. Acting on their tips, Coleman and his men, popularly known as the "flying squadron," took action when it was needed to deter crime. The sheriff also instituted a "morning lineup" that aided crime prevention. As the sheriff said, it put "the fear of God in the criminal because every officer in the territory can readily recognize him after the lineup."[41]

As they left Miami, some sheriffs from the more rural counties may well have pondered whether the country was actually undergoing a crippling economic depression. They had basked on beaches, gone swimming in the hotel pool as well as the Atlantic Ocean, enjoyed the race tracks and dog tracks, eaten lavish meals, consumed exotic beverages, and been housed in a luxury hotel. Returning home, they soon faced reality again and discovered that, yes, the Great Depression was real, bleak, and abroad in the land.[42]

The sheriffs voted to meet at Orlando in 1936. Headquarters for the March conclave was the large Angebilt Hotel which billed itself as "Orlando's Only Strictly Fire-Proof Hotel." When Rex Sweat declined reelection; the progressive Dade County Sheriff, D. C. Coleman was chosen president. That year in 1937 the association instituted a new practice by agreeing to offer a scholarship to the University of Florida. The student would be selected by the institution's athletic department, although it was not clear whether the person chosen would be an athlete.[43] In 1937 the convention site shifted to Clearwater where E. G. Cunningham of Pinellas County served as host sheriff. Walter R. Clark of Broward County succeeded D. C. Coleman as president. Lawmen from forty counties listened to an array of speakers who included the state attorney general, Jerry Carter and a colleague on the railroad commission, the commissioner of agriculture, four state senators, two state representatives, the state comptroller, and Secretary of State Robert Gray.[44]

The delegates endorsed the state drivers' license bill as recommended by Asher Frank, director of the Florida Safety Council, and a proposed State Traffic Patrol with the sheriff of each county in charge of the local patrolmen.[45] Since the system of county traffic officers already existed and was largely controlled by the sheriffs, the new proposal may have been an attempt to forestall the establishment of a highway patrol system not under the sheriffs' hegemony. From the sheriffs' perspective, the highway patrol concept had the potential of becoming a state police arrangement, something they continued to oppose as an even greater threat to their autonomy.

As important as the FSA was for developing policy strategy, and as significant as the annual and semi-annual meetings were, the individual Florida sheriff always faced formidable challenges in his home county. Not the least was his administrative role with myriad documents—serving, recording, and preserving them—all within the guidelines of detailed legislative acts. Beyond that, he was a county official who by constitutional, state, and local law interacted closely and daily with judicial and county officials. Further, he had the endless and unpredictable task of enforcing the law and protecting the public. Finally, as a constitutional officer subject to popular election, he was automatically a politician. He could not afford to alienate the electorate, nor could he curry favor by neglecting an impartial performance of his duty. If these conditions were not enough, the sheriff's position was also highly visible, making him the target of criticism both justified and unjustified. It was not necessary to wait for the next four-year election cycle to disrupt his tenure. The governor had the constitutional right to suspend and possibly remove him from office. The court's verdict could decide if a governor's actions were justified, and the state senate had to vote its approval, but the right of suspension lay with the chief executive.[46] The prerogative was exercised from time to time by various governors. Usually, but not always, the governor had an advantage over the sheriff. Some Florida sheriffs, like other persons in public and private life, were corrupt. Some escaped detection, some were caught and removed from office. The position itself and what it entailed made the sheriff a powerful man and put temptations in front of him. If a sheriff chose, as some did, to use his position in a criminal way, the opportunity was always there. A number of them took advantage of the situation. Various sheriffs, politicians, and others questioned the right of suspension, but the number of suspensions clearly indicated the need for constitutional safeguards.

Some sheriffs who clashed with governors were successful. The examples of Palm Beach County's Bakers, father and son, who were suspended only to be reinstated have been noted. In the 1930s Hillsborough County's Will Spencer, previously mentioned as a president of the FSA, fought his suspension by Governor Sholtz. He announced to the FSA's 1937 convention that the governor had declared him incompetent and suspended him, but stated emphatically that he would fight the charges.[47] Throughout the early twentieth century gambling and illegal liquor sales flourished in Florida. As examples, Tampa and the rural areas of Hillsborough County were centers of criminal activity, and it was not uncommon for law officials to be implicated. Crackdowns ebbed and flowed, but the situation frequently threatened to get out of hand. Brutality and racial prejudice were integral parts of the corruption that tainted the reputations of some law officials in Florida.

As a result of Hillsborough County's political and social composition a succession of sheriffs struggled to cope with the problems of gambling and bootlegging, or sometimes became self-profiting participants in criminal activities. A number of sheriffs, judges, solicitors, and state attorneys were indicted, suspended, or removed. All the while, Will Spencer's family enjoyed local prominence. Ancestors had helped to pioneer the area in the early 1850s. His grandfather served as sheriff from 1858 to the Civil War, and his father was sheriff from 1893 to 1901. Will Spencer, elected county sheriff in 1912, was defeated in 1916, reelected in 1920, defeated in 1924, and reelected in 1932. Then allegations of improper conduct caught up with the sheriff, and Governor Sholtz suspended him on October 10, 1935.

According to the accusations Spencer was guilty of various offenses that included having close connections with gamblers and bootleggers, negligence in performing his duties, taking protection money, permitting lax jail security, and personal drunkenness and gambling.[48]

255

Based on a grand jury's secret report some, but not a majority of the jurors, thought Spencer should be removed. As it turned out, the sheriff was not tried. There was little to do other than reinstate him, and that was done on May 28, 1937. Following the constitutional mandate, the legislature voted Spencer over $7,000 for the time he was suspended, and the 1939 session awarded him over $2,000 in additional compensation.[49] While Spencer was exonerated and, on a broader scale, he demonstrated that it was possible for a sheriff to prevail over a governor, the episode and its various ramifications revealed that criminal corruption could pervade and tarnish the very officials supposed to uphold the law.

In 1938 more than fifty sheriffs gathered at the Mayflower hotel in Jacksonville. Green Cove Spring's John P. Hall, sheriff of Clay County, was elected president. By this time the FSA also elected a board of directors who were usually senior members of the association. There were key committees—education, legislative, safety and traffic, and fish and streams—whose reports and suggestions facilitated the proceedings. Apparently for the first time, the FSA elected a chaplain, the Reverend Sam Durrance of Wauchula, and chose Warren E. Van Loon of Miami (not a sheriff) as field secretary. Florida sheriffs experienced another first in 1938. After Sheriff Claude Simmons of Okeechobee County died of pneumonia, Governor Cone had appointed Simmons's wife, Eugenia, to replace him. The widow became the state's first woman sheriff. She never wore a badge or carried a gun and did not seek reelection. She would serve seven months with the assistance of her late husband's brother, Cossie, who had been a deputy and succeeded her as sheriff at the next election. Unfortunately, the press of duties kept her from attending the 1938 FSA meeting.

In the same year, Celia Adkinson, the widow of Sheriff Adkinson of Walton County, became sheriff when her husband was fatally shot. Appointed by Governor Cone, she served out her husband's term and did not seek reelection.

The three-day gathering featured more oratory than any FSA convention in history. Events such as a marksmanship contest and a seminar at the Jacksonville police headquarters had to be canceled because

Eugenia Simmons, of Okeechobee County, was appointed sheriff by Governor Fred Cone in 1938, following the death of her husband. She was Florida's first woman sheriff. (Courtesy of the Florida State Archives).

After the fatal shooting of her husband, Sheriff Adkinson of Walton County, Celia Adkinson was appointed sheriff in 1938. She was Florida's second woman sheriff. (Courtesy of the Florida State Archives).

there was not enough time to fit them in.[50] Rex Sweat—accomplished sheriff, student of government, and practitioner of *realpolitik*—was without peer as a host sheriff. He arranged for the visitors a shrimp pilau supper at his country home, greyhound competition (the featured race was billed as the Sheriffs' handicap) as guests of the Jacksonsville Kennel Club, an outdoor barbecue luncheon at a leading local restaurant, and another luncheon at the Roosevelt hotel. There they heard brief remarks from Colin English, State Superintendent of Public Instruction; a state senator; the ubiquitous Jerry Carter; others connected with the railroad commission; a former sheriff and early FSA member from Columbia County; a member of Governor Cone's personal staff; and the assistant state auditor.[51]

Charles Francis Coe, a noted writer, aspiring politician, and student of criminology was the master of ceremonies at the annual banquet which featured Fred P. Cone as the principal speaker. It was probably the first time since 1927 when John W. Martin was the guest at the Okeechobee convention that a governor had made a formal address to the sheriffs. Governor Cone spoke admiringly of the sheriffs' importance during 150 years of Florida history. He discussed an issue that concerned the lawmen: the possible establishment of a highway patrol. "As long as I am governor the sheriffs will continue to be the leading officers of the counties," he said. Cone added, "There may or may not be a road patrol in Florida—some say we need one and others say we do not—but if there is a road patrol it will be under the jurisdiction of the sheriffs." Concluding, he declared, "The sheriffs [have] done a good job and I will stand behind them."[52] Like the governor, an honored guest and a friend of the sheriffs, Senator Claude Pepper appraised the governor in his diary, "He is a grand fellow...an old cracker with the cunning of an Indian and a heart of gold."[53]

No less than fourteen other speakers were called on. Fortunately, they honored the rule of brevity. From Washington came J. J. McGuire, administrative assistant to FBI director J. Edgar Hoover. McGuire urged sheriffs to help fight crime by supporting youth guidance programs. The "G-Man" expressed his department's thanks to local lawmen for their cooperation, and hit hard at the parole system in many states where "mal-administration was one of the greatest obstacles in the way of effective law enforcement." The lawmen greeted their old friend Rivers Buford, Associate Justice of the Florida Supreme Court, a veteran of twelve years on the court, and a candidate for reelection. Judge Buford had met many sheriffs during his experience as state's attorney for the Marianna Circuit and as the state's attorney general.[54]

On the convention's last day the Florida Sheriffs Association was chartered as a legal non-profit corporation. Circuit Judge A. D. McNeill approved a ninety-nine-year charter that limited the association's indebtedness to $25,000 and its real estate holdings to $50,000. The charter stipulated that the FSA's membership consisted of sixty-three of Florida's sixty-seven counties.[55] The 1938 convention gave a strong impression of the FSA as an active group that served the state's sheriffs well.

Responding to strong pressure, the 1939 session of the Florida legislature initiated steps to establish a highway patrol. The move did not have the support of Governor Cone. Some years earlier Governor Dave Sholtz had established a short-lived state patrol as part of the Florida Highway Department. Cone personalized his opposition with a facetious remark in his inaugural address: "I am proud of the patrol that rides up and down the State and looks after the filling stations, but, my friends, it should have been authorized by the Legislature and not created by the State Road Department." The folksy governor got applause when he declared his determination to uphold the laws and singled out his favorite agency of law enforcement: "You sheriffs, when you deal with bandits and criminals, don't be too particular how you handle them, for the governor will be back of you."[56] Once in office Cone abolished the Sholtz agency, and in 1937 bills establishing the state patrol failed in the legislature. Even so, it was clear some kind of measure was going to be passed, and informed estimates predicted a beginning highway patrol force of one hundred men equipped with motorcycles, automobiles, radios, and other modern devices.

Meeting at Homosassa Springs in 1939 the sheriffs had other ideas. Led by President W. T. Coleman of Sumter County, they drafted their own road patrol bill, but declined to leak any of its details to the press.

259

Chapter IX - Boom Times and The Great Depression

Rex Sweat, who headed the Duval County road patrol, was credited with writing the sheriffs' bill which resembled the old county traffic officers arrangement. Together with his lawyer, Edward Hemphill of Jacksonville, Sweat fashioned the measure. The sheriffs did not secure passage of their primary bill, although the legislature created county traffic officers for counties of 85,000 to 165,000 people and assigned the sheriff a primary role in the law's operation.[57] They failed to obtain a major statewide law because several legislators had announced their intention to introduce bills creating a separate highway patrol. Their new system would be based on merit in employment and promotion, and the patrol would be financed by an automobile drivers' license fee. The patrol would not operate under the sheriffs, and some of its powers would be at their expense. Thus, the major new law regarding highway safety was lengthy and complicated. It passed June 12, 1939, and created the State Department of Public Safety, an agency that was destined to wield a powerful and continuing influence in the state.

Bills were introduced in the House of Representatives, but they all had two main parts: one created the Division of the Florida Highway Patrol and the other created the Division of State Motor Vehicle Drivers Licenses. The department was put under the control and administration of an executive board composed of the governor and chairman of the State Road Department. Headquarters was established at Tallahassee, and the board employed a Director of the Florida Highway Patrol at $4,000 a year. Patrol officers were to earn an annual salary of $1,500. They were assigned military ranks—director, captain, lieutenant, sergeant, and patrol officers.[58]

Initiated in the House, the bills were referred to the Committee on Motor Vehicles and Carriers. Unanimously rejecting them in their original form, the committee combined the various bills into a House Substitute which finally passed by a vote of eighty-four to five. Over in the senate there was strong support for the bill. The Senate added five amendments, but defeated attempts to add two more changes. The final senate vote was a powerful endorsement: thirty-two to three. The House accepted three of the amendments, and, with both chambers in agreement, the bill passed and was sent to the governor. Most county

Florida Sheriffs Association meeting at Homosassa Springs. April 24-25, 1934

traffic officer bills had become law without the chief executive's signature, and following the pattern, Cone declined to sign the Public Safety measure.[59] Perhaps he sensed that despite his personal opposition the bill had popular support, and rather than issue a politically damaging veto, he let it become law. Floridians referred to the agency as the "Highway Patrol" and to its personnel as "State Troopers." Even so, the establishment of the Department of Public Safety and the Highway Patrol as a division within it did not mean the end of the county traffic officers.

In 1940 America had reached a watershed, although not many Americans realized it. They had come to the end of a decade and the beginning of the end to the Great Depression. It was the end of an era of peace for the United States, and it was the prelude to involvement in a world war. Two great international expositions, the New York and the San Francisco World's Fairs, offered spectacular promises for mankind's progress, promises that would have to be deferred. On the international front war ravaged Asia and Europe, while in the United States President Roosevelt had begun a belated push toward an armaments program. In the midst of such momentous events individual Americans, including Floridians, were involved with their everyday concerns. In the nation, no matter how commanding or extreme conditions were elsewhere, nothing could eclipse the importance of politics at every level, and 1940 was an election year. Most voting Floridians were Democrats, but even Republicans, knowing full well that victory would not be theirs, got caught up in the excitement that accompanied the various contests for public office.

Notes for Chapter IX

1. Jacksonville *Florida Times-Union*, March 22, 1923.
2. Ibid., Tampa *Tribune*, March 23, 1923.
3. *FA 1923*, I, 175; for the entire act see 175-177. See also Bill Foley, "Sparky's Still In Business," Jacksonville *Florida Times-Union*, April 20, 1977. For Johnson's electrocution see ibid, October 8, 1924.
4. *FA 1921*, I, 338-340.
5. The first act passed as a General Law on June 22, 1921, but the Special Law of that year passed without the governor's signature and has no day and month of passage. Both acts contained the basic principle of population laws.
6. *FA 1923*, I, 378.
7. Ibid., *1927*, 547-548.
8. See ibid., *1929*, I, 697-699.
9. Ibid., *1923*, I, 378; *1925*, I, 276-277, 1093-1095; *1919*, I, 697-699, 1095; *1933*, I, 855-857; *1939*, I, 7-9, 908.
10. Ibid., *1937*, I, 906-907.
11. Ibid., *1925*, I, 112-115; I, *1933*, 254-258.
12. Palm Beach *Post*, March 19, 1927, clipping in Baker Papers; clipping from an unnamed newspaper, March 18, 1927, ibid. See also Jacksonville *Florida Times-Union*, March 16-18, 1927, and Tampa *Tribune*, March 18-19, 23, 1927.
13. Palm Beach *Times*, March 18, 1928. See ibid., May 1928, clippings in Baker Papers; see Palm Beach *Post*, undated clipping, all in Baker Papers. See also Jacksonville *Florida Times-Union*, March 15, 1928.
14. Jacksonville *Times-Union*, March 15, 17, 1928.
15. R. C. Baker to Governor Doyle Carlton, October 30, 1929, Doyle E. Carlton Papers, 1929-1933, RG 102, series 204, box 49, folder 7, FSA; *Florida Sheriffs Association Year Book 1929-1930*, 2.
16. Jacksonville *Florida Times-Union*, March 15, 17, 1928.
17. Ibid., March 24-25, 27, 30, 1930; Gainesville *Daily Sun*, March 24-25, 1930.
18. Gainesville *Daily Sun*, March 25, 1930.
19. Second Annual Report of the Duval County Sheriffs Department, January 1, 1930, to December 31, 1931, Doyle E. Carlton Papers, 1929-1933, RG 102, series 204, box 24, folder 13, FSA.
20. *FA 1937*, I, 267-268. For another example see ibid., *1935*, I, 281-283.
21. Ibid., *1937*, I, 81-82.
22. Ibid., 93-94.
23. Ibid., *1925*, I, 115-116.
24. Ibid., *1929*, I, 549, 975.
25. Ibid., *1935*, I, 68-71, 71-74.
26. Jacksonville *Florida Times-Union*, March 7, 1931.

Chapter IX - Boom Times and The Great Depression

27. Ibid., March 17, 1932.
28. Miami *Herald*, March 28, 1935.
29. Jacksonville *Florida Times-Union*, March 15, 1932.
30. Ibid., March 17, 1932.
31. Ibid. For the kidnapping see A. Scott Berg, *Lindberg* (New York, 1998), 237-352.
32. Jacksonville *Florida Times-Union*, February 23, 1933; see also Miami *Daily News*, February 23, 1933.
33. Palm Beach *Times* February 24, 1933; Palm Beach *Post*, February 24-26, 1933; Tampa *Tribune*, June 15, 1933.
34. Tampa *Tribune*, March 15, 1933; Jacksonville *Florida Times-Union*, June 15, 1933.
35. Tampa *Tribune*, June 15, 1933. For more on circuit courts see William Warren Rogers and Canter Brown, Jr., *Florida's Clerks of the Circuit Court Their History and Experiences* (Tallahassee, 1996). See especially 93-98.
36. Miami *Daily News*, March 21, 1935; Miami *Herald*, March 25-26, 1935; Jacksonville *Florida Times-Union*, April 24-25, 1934.
37. Miami *Daily News*, March 26, 1935.
38. *Florida Sheriffs Association Year Book 1935-36*, no pagination.
39. Ibid.
40. Stephen C. Bosquet, "The Gangster in Our Midst: Al Capone in South Florida, 1930-1947," *Florida Historical Quarterly*, LXXVI (Winter, 1998), 297-309. There are several biographies of Capone, but see Laurence Bergreen, *Capone: The Man and the Era* (New York, 1944).
41. *Florida Sheriff's Association Year Book 1935-1936*, no pagination.
42. See Miami *Herald*, March 28, 1935.
43. Jacksonville *Florida Times-Union*, March 6, 1936.
44. Ibid., March 17-18, 1937.
45. Ibid. The driver's license bill was passed in 1939 as part of the larger statute that created the Florida Department of Public Safety.
46. Article IV, Section 15, of the Florida constitution of 1885 declared that elected and appointed officers not liable to impeachment could be suspended from office by the governor for malfeasance or misfeasance, neglect of duty while in office, the commission of any felony, drunkenness, or incompetence. The governor was to communicate his action to the person accused and to the senate at its next session. The senate's consent was required. A suspension continued until the senate's adjournment or the officer was removed. The governor could reinstate the suspended person if the charges proved untrue. Should the senate refuse to remove a person or fail to take action before it adjourned the suspended officer was reinstated. If reinstated, the officer was to receive back pay for any time lost while under suspension. The suspension or removal did not clear the person affected from the possibility of being tried separately on the charges.
47. Jacksonville *Florida Times-Union*, March 18, 1937.

48. These and other charges against Spencer can be found in Governor David Sholtz Papers, 1933-1937, RG 102, series 278, box 58, folder 2, FSA.
49. *FA 1937*, I, 831-832; ibid., *1939*, I, 275.
50. Jacksonville *Florida Times-Union*, March 28, April 1, 1938. For the appointment of Eugenia Simmons see also Morris, *Florida Handbook 1999-2000*, 624. See also Jacksonville *Journal*, March 30, 1938; Tampa *Morning Tribune*, March 31, October 2, 1938 ; and Fort Myers *News-Press*, March 31, 1938.
51. Jacksonville *Florida Times-Union*, March 29, 1938.
52. Ibid., March 31, 1938.
53. "Claude Pepper Diary," March 25, 1938, 25. The diary as well as a vast number of Pepper papers are housed with the Claude D. Pepper Collection at Florida State University, Tallahassee.
54. Jacksonville *Florida Times-Union*, March 29-30, 1938.
55. Ibid., April 1, 1938.
56. The governor did not use prepared notes in his inaugural address, and different newspapers had slightly different versions of what he said. The quotes here are from the Tallahassee *Democrat*, January 5, 1937. Following tradition, the inauguration took place on Tuesday afternoon January 5. A large crowd was on hand despite the overcast day and was enthusiastic in support of the homespun governor.
57. *FA, 1939*, I, 1012-1014.
58. Ibid., 1276-1297.
59. For the legislative process see *Florida House Journal 1939*, 59, 700-701, 775, 928-929, 943, 1,546, 1,757, 1,772; *Florida Senate Journal 1939*, 603, 613, 648, 835, 888-889.

CHAPTER X

WARTIME FLORIDA, 1941-1945

In 1940 Floridians joined their fellow Americans in wanting the country to stay out of war, but international events forced many to believe that United States involvement was inevitable. Floridians would play a major role in the global conflict that followed, as its citizens manned the home front and furnished military personnel for the armed forces. The state's population grew so rapidly that accommodating the influx created major problems. Florida's sheriffs took an active part in helping the state adjust and maintain its equilibrium in a time of tension and uncertainty. Numerous sheriffs would lay aside their badges and exchange their peacekeepers uniforms for those of military personnel.

In the first year of the tumultuous decade Florida's politicians courted the sheriffs at their annual convention in Tampa. Before, the meetings had attracted office holders and those seeking office but never so many or with such fervor as in 1940. The Sheriff's Association had become so powerful that women, no less than men, made their presence felt at a FSA gathering. The Tampa *Morning Tribune* accurately gauged the situation in an editorial:

> A program of both entertainment and business has been planned, with a big barbecue tonight at the Tampa police pistol range and the annual banquet tomorrow night highlighting the entertainment events. As an added feature in this election year, the Association has invited candidates for Governor and other state offices

Florida had sixty-seven counties when it entered the post-World War II era.

to appear and outline their programs. That should make the convention doubly interesting both for the Sheriffs and Tampans.

At the outset the FSA made clear that its members welcomed the aspiring candidates but would not issue any endorsements.

Attendance alone portended a successful meeting—some three hundred persons, including sheriffs, both active and inactive, their wives, and other delegates arrived at the Tampa Terrace hotel, convention headquarters. Soon, the host sheriff, J. R. "Jerry" McLeod of Hillsborough County, took those arriving early to visit the Plant City strawberry festival. Later, the delegates were guests of the manager of the Sulphur Springs dog track.[1]

So many politicians attended that they were separated into speaking groups. As expected, all praised the lawmen as defenders of the state and bulwarks of democracy and themselves as admirers who, if elected, would promote without stint those who wore the star. The first group were the contenders for governor: Spessard Holland of Bartow, who was the ultimate winner; B. P. Paty of West Palm Beach, who wound up fourth in a field of eleven; and Francis P. Whitehair of DeLand, who finished second before losing to Holland in the runoff primary. Holland claimed close professional and personal relationships with numerous sheriffs over a long period. Paty advocated curbing the governor's power to suspend elected officials—an authority past governors had regularly exercised on sheriffs. Paty believed "it is better to leave the power in the hands of the people to use at the ballot box than to put it in the hands of one man." Whitehair echoed Paty's theme by declaring, "I will never remove or worry you for the political expediency of some one or group of men. Instead of being 'sheriff in chief' of Florida, I shall be your friend, co-operate with you by minding my own official business."[2]

Three out of the six candidates for United States Senator were present—Charles Francis Coe, Governor Cone, and Jerry Carter—and they formed another speaking unit. Charles O. Andrews, the incumbent, who would be reelected, was not present because of what was described as pressing business in Washington. He was represented by

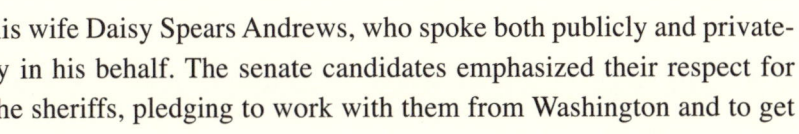

Spessard Holland of Bartow, served as governor of Florida, 1941-1945. (Courtesy of the Florida State Archives).

his wife Daisy Spears Andrews, who spoke both publicly and privately in his behalf. The senate candidates emphasized their respect for the sheriffs, pledging to work with them from Washington and to get maximum support there. They all declared their opposition to any

Chapter X - Wartime Florida, 1941-1945

centralized control from the capital that would turn the sheriffs into rubber stamps.

Besides Daisy Andrews, other women with political agendas were at the Tampa convention. In 1936 Florida women had cast fifty-two percent of the state's total vote in the presidential election, and at Tampa their presence was manifest as never before. Hortense K. Wells, a talented and energetic person, had served as a Democratic National Committeewoman since 1932, and in 1934 was Florida's first woman candidate for the U. S. Senate. She contemplated another run for the Washington senate seat, but changed her mind. Instead, Wells was reelected National Committeewomen and served until 1940. Other women who addressed the convention were: Louise McGregor, head of the Democratic women's unit in Florida; Georgia Robles Conger, member of the state Democratic committee; Mrs. J. D. Alderman, member of the state milk board; and Nell Alford, Mrs. Enid Broward Hardee, and Polly Rose, all candidates to succeed Hortense Wells as national committeewoman.[3]

There seemed to be no end to the political speeches at the 1940 convention. Candidates for attorney general, state treasurer, and for delegate seats to the National Democratic Convention had their say. So did other dignitaries who were not seeking election: the state prison superintendent, a federal district attorney, and various members of the governor's cabinet. With so many politicians the center of attention at Tampa, one sheriff was himself graphic proof of how political winds could blow a person away. J. R. McLeod of Hillsborough County had been elected president of the state organization only to be defeated in the local sheriff's race. Outgoing president W. T. Coleman of Bushnell (Sumter County) explained that a new president would be elected in January when McLeod's term expired.[4]

In 1941 many Americans were convinced that the nation's involvement in war was imminent, but the Japanese attack at the Pearl Harbor naval base in Hawaii on December 7, caught the nation off-guard. The surprise attack devastated the U. S. military complex there, taking a heavy toll of men, ships, planes, and ground installations. In a dramatic speech President Franklin D. Roosevelt reacted by asking for and getting a declaration of war from Congress. War with the other Axis powers, Germany and Italy, followed, and within days the country was involved in a worldwide conflict. World War II abruptly changed the lives of every American. Florida furnished over 254,000 men and women to the armed forces, and well in excess of two million military personnel were trained in the state. Florida's civilian population was transformed. Yet, at the same time that their focus and circumstances were changing, life on the home front, as Floridians had known it and knew it, went on.

Sheriffs found themselves confronting familiar and new circumstances at the same time, even as they, with the fee system conundrum as a good example, found themselves caught in a dilemma that seemingly would not go away. The Great Depression had nurtured the economic advantages of having a salary system for sheriffs and other county officers. Population laws had been the instruments to accomplish uniformity in some counties, but the old fee system remained. An act passed in 1941 repealed the laws of 1919 and 1929 pertaining to fees for sheriffs, but what it did was to modify and perpetuate the old system.[5] In Liberty County a sheriff was paid $6,000 annually, and got an extra $500 from the county fine and forfeiture fund. He received separate pay for feeding prisoners and travel outside of Florida. Only one of many county systems, Liberty's was fairly typical. Across the state the same sort of basic system applied to salaries for deputy sheriffs and constables.[6] State legislation affecting fees was usually linked to both sheriffs and constables; the latter officials continued as important county officers.[7]

Early in March 1941, the sheriffs gathered at Bradenton where John P. Hall of Clay County was recognized as their new president. He took office at the annual meeting in June at Daytona Beach. At Bradenton the sheriffs followed the established patterns of renewing old friendships, meeting new sheriffs, hearing speeches from leading Floridians, and attending sessions dealing with current problems and their legislative agenda. The gravity of the times was such that no one considered it unusual when Frank Hammack of the Miami FBI office urged the sheriffs to investigate every report of espionage and furnish

271

the FBI with all available information on people named in such complaints. As always, the delegates enjoyed the social arrangements, and in 1941 they were treated to a tour of the Ringling Circus headquarters at nearby Sarasota, as well as an old fashioned barbecue at the Bradenton Country Club.[8]

The same year the somber mood prevailed at the annual FSA convention in June at Daytona Beach. Around sixty delegates attended the three-day meeting that featured a bomb demonstration in a wooded section near town. Because of their secretive nature, some of the FSA's sessions, including the bomb demonstration, were closed to the general public. It was conducted by R. G. Danner, FBI agent in charge of Florida, who was assisted by two FBI experts. Lieutenant General Albert H. Blanding, retired chief of home defense in Florida, spoke about the need for civil authorities and military agencies to cooperate. Blanding emphasized the importance of preventing mass hysteria among civilians in times of extreme emergencies. Lawmen could help, he said, by building up civilian confidence in the armed forces' ability to protect the country. He urged law officers to study various methods of sabotage and how to combat them. According to the general, they should be constantly alert to protecting actual and potential targets. Although some sessions were closed, sheriff Ed Stone and his deputy Walter Campbell of Volusia County allowed public access to their other events. The sheriffs closed their meeting with a social event, a fish fry on the beach, followed by a dance at Club Pier Casino.[9] The sheriffs reelected Hall as president, and chose two vice presidents, a secretary, a treasurer, and the board of trustees. When the lawmen adjourned they did not know that at their spring meeting at Lakeland and the annual meeting at Pensacola in June the United States would be at war.[10]

On the eve of World War II Florida had both the county traffic officers and the Department of Public Safety and the Highway Patrol as a division within it. In 1941 few counties could match Hillsborough's modern system of county traffic officers. A new population law for the densely peopled county (between 100,000 and 200,000 residents) provided for a chief TCO ($3,000 annual salary), a deputy county traffic officer, and two other deputies. Previous legislation giving the county commissioners appointive power was now assigned to the sheriff. The chief law officer appointed the CTOs to terms contingent with his own. They were commissioned as deputy sheriffs. Each CTO furnished his own car, but was paid $5 a month to maintain it, and the sheriff was allowed county money to purchase gas and oil. The county furnished the traffic officers two-way radios and paid them $100 for uniforms and badges.[11] Neighboring Pinellas County had a similar arrangement, although the appointive power was different, pay was less, and each county traffic officer had to post a $2,000 bond. In addition, Pinellas County officers were to be "one or more discreet persons" who knew about traffic.[12]

Despite the continued existence of county traffic officers, the Highway Patrol was coming into its own. It had an immediate and constructive impact on Florida. Initial shortcomings were corrected when an extensive revision was made in 1941 in the Highway Safety Act of the previous session.[13] Throughout the war the Highway Patrol would maintain its mission, and its permanence was underwritten by various laws. Important legislation passed in 1945 regarding the pay of its personnel, while another statute established a pension system for the patrol.[14] The County Traffic Officers and the Deputy CTOs remained a presence in some counties, but wartime legislation affecting them in 1943 and 1945 applied only to large counties. In every instance, the sheriff's authority over them, including their pay which came from a county's fine and forfeiture fund, was extended.[15]

In March 1942 World War II was in its early stages, and the conflict was going badly for the United States and the Allies. Some of the FSA's winter sessions at Pensacola were private. R. G. Danner, Florida's main FBI man, was again on hand. As early as 1939 President Roosevelt had called on the FBI to take over the handling of all investigation problems arising under the National Defense Program. The president also asked the heads of all law enforcement agencies to cooperate with the FBI. Agent Danner reminded the sheriffs of their responsibility for the state's internal security. The lawmen assisted with the operation of blackouts (designated periods when all lights in one or more areas, usually a town or city, were extinguished as a precaution against attacks by enemy planes). The sheriffs helped coordinate such activities throughout the war, and had training in the procedures to be followed should an actual attack occur. The delegates elected Charles S. Dean, sheriff of Citrus County, as their president. Dean was one of the core FSA members—men such as J. P. Ramsey, Baker, Lyle, Dowling, Sweat, Coleman of Dade County, and Stoutamire—who through the years had provided leadership for their fellow sheriffs and had given the association continuity and vitality.[16]

A determined atmosphere prevailed at Lakeland's annual meeting in 1942. Wartime law enforcement problems were the main topics at the various sessions. The familiar face of the FBI's R. G. Danner was seen and his voice heard in a speech. The sheriffs were praised by Secretary of State R. A. Gray for their work in Florida's civilian defense program and told, "You will be called upon to render still greater service if the war comes close to us." Ralph Davis, Holland's executive secretary, expressed the governor's appreciation for their defense work. Specifically, Davis praised the sheriffs' quick action in getting rid of gambling along the East Coast and urged them to remain alert for establishments that used slot machines (a violation of state law) to attract customers.[17]

L. Grady Burton of Wauchula, state attorney for the Tenth Judicial Circuit, warned the sheriffs about the evils of "jook joints" or "juke joints." He was speaking mainly about white establishments, although the word had an African derivation and had been coined years before by blacks. A jook was a no-frills nightspot that always had a record machine or music box. The generic name for such machines came from their ubiquitous presence in juke joints that had begun in the black community. Gaudily lighted, the coin machines cost five cents a record to operate and usually played from early openings to late closings. The establishments varied from place to place but all had in common an unmistakable ambiance that sprang from a rustic setting, dim lighting, a small dance floor, a bar and an eclectic assortment of chairs and small tables, music dominated by country songs (in the segregated South black jukes specialized in "gut bucket" blues), soft drinks, although beer was king (sometimes stronger alcoholic beverages were obtainable, or, secured in a brown bag, could be brought in by patrons who paid for set ups). The food defied classification, or, more likely, potato chips, peanuts, pickled eggs and pigs' feet (extracted from large glass containers containing an unsavory liquid) were the only food available. The unsanitary restrooms, as often as not, could only be reached by going outside and around the back. Any night when at least one fight did not occur was exceptional. They were enormously popular places of refuge for both races, for civilians and especially for lonesome servicemen far from home.[18]

Although Burton was deadly serious, his remarks must have added a note of levity to the meeting. Considering things in perspective, the establishments and their alleged evils did not take high priority on the citizens' problems list. Opinion was divided and many considered them a positive good. Jooks would continue to exist despite the tire and gasoline shortages, the state attorney said. He insisted, "A confirmed jooker is going to get there somehow." Burton wanted the legislature to authorize courts to revoke licenses in places where juke joints were considered nuisances. His logic was that fear of losing their beer and liquor licenses would cause the owners to remedy the evil.[19]

Arcadia and Ocala were the convention sites for 1943. It was with poetic justice that the mid-winter meeting in January saw L. R. "Jack" Baker, son of the legendary Sheriff Bob Baker of Palm Beach County, elected president. Later that year Baker presided over the annual June gathering at Ocala. Sheriff J. P. Ramsey of Alachua was elected first vice president. Ramsey's father, Perry Gilbert Ramsey, a native Georgian and veteran Democratic politician, was a past president of the FSA, and beginning in 1908, had served three terms as sheriff of Alachua County. Other officers and directors were elected, including Rex Sweat as a director.[20]

At Ocala the delegates heard A. P. Kitchen, FBI special agent from Miami, and State Attorney J. W. Hunter of the Fifth Circuit. Congressman R. A. "Lex" Green of Starke used the occasion to hint at a bid for governor in 1944. He followed up later, making the runoff primary in a field of six, only to lose to Millard Caldwell. Green assured the sheriffs that he would not interfere with local government. Claude

275

Pepper's was easily the most recognizable face among the speakers. The U. S. senator speculated on a peacetime world. He said, "I don't want to have to see the peace officers of our local government called upon to put down insurrection against constituted authority spring from the failure of the Government to see its duty now and prepare to meet the post-war problems of our people. I'd much rather our Government face the issues of today and lay plans for meeting the demands of the post-war economy."[21]

By the 1940s Florida's expansion beyond its status as a regional state was reflected in the activities of some FSA members. Two past presidents, D. C. Coleman of Miami and Rex Sweat of Jacksonville, who were members of the FSA's board of directors, were also active in the National Sheriffs' Association. In 1943 the two sheriffs participated in an executive conference of that body in Washington. The meeting reviewed national law enforcement problems. According to Coleman, "we [discussed] just about everything there is in national police work." Two major areas of interest were the handling of juvenile delinquents and drafting measures for universal fingerprinting.[22]

The war years were pivotal for Floridians.[23] Because the United States mainland was not invaded by enemy troops, its role in the conflict had a duality. There was the intensity of being a military participant accompanied by a strange "wartime" existence in a "peacetime" setting. Various Florida laws applied to the sheriffs' routine activities. Three laws in 1941 adjusted their role in levying writs and requiring bonds from courts, required them and county clerks to adjust procedures in the operation of fine and forfeiture funds, and authorized law enforcers to sell confiscated liquors to the highest bidders.[24] Evidence of improved crime fighting techniques was seen in 1943 when sheriffs were authorized to fingerprint any person charged with or convicted of breaking the law. The sheriff was to send a copy of the prints to the Federal Bureau of Identification.[25]

If there were no air raids, no armies marching, and no adversarial forces shooting cannons at one another, there was still abundant evidence that the United States was at war, and nowhere more than in Florida. German submarines took a heavy toll of Allied ships off

Florida's Atlantic and Gulf coasts. The state emerged as a major area for training soldiers, sailors, and airmen. Security of military installations became a priority. The security concerns were applied especially to "industries" that might be targets of sabotage. As defined by the legislature an industry was any person, firm, or corporation engaged in the war effort. A wartime act of 1943 authorized industries to employ guards to protect their property. The men were selected by the sheriff of the county where the industry was located. The guards could be the sheriff's regular deputies or special deputies bonded and under his control. Any particular industry was required to pay the expenses to the sheriff who then paid the guards.[26]

Sheriff Alex D. Littlefield of Volusia County hosted the mid-winter convention of 1944 at Daytona Beach. Gordon Morehead of Ocala, sheriff of Marion County, was elected president. Since 1944 was a presidential election year, the May Democratic primary was a major item of discussion. On the national level Roosevelt would defeat Governor Thomas E. Dewey of New York, winning the office for a fourth term. As usual, FBI personnel participated in the FSA's program. A. P. Kitchen, agent in charge of the Miami office, was a featured speaker. So was Charles Hahn, secretary of the National Sheriff's Association. His presence was an indication of the ties between the FSA and the national body. The lawmen held sessions on wartime law enforcement problems and the state's campaign against venereal disease.[27]

Because of the numerous military bases in Florida and the unprecedented expansion of war-related industries, there had been a burst of population growth. The entire state was in transition, and wartime conduct in morals and manners declined. Not surprisingly, sexually active men and women created a "problem." Accordingly, the state had experienced disturbing rates of prostitution and "VD." Military authorities around bases and cities cooperated with police and sheriffs in controlling a worsening situation. In 1943 the legislature passed a statewide quarantine law. It converted four Civilian Conservation Corps (CCC) camps at Miami, Ocala, Wakulla, and Jacksonville into VD hospitals. The legislation authorized police, sheriffs, and their deputies to enroll all persons who tested positive for venereal disease into compulsory

Chapter X - Wartime Florida, 1941-1945

treatment programs. When sheriffs were involved in taking people to the camps they were paid the same mileage fees as for criminal cases. Two other related laws were passed in 1943. One provided funds for the construction near Avon Park of a state hospital for the care of people infected with venereal diseases. Another measure required any person rejected for military service because of VD to report to the nearest state-owned venereal disease clinic and submit to treatment or offer proof of continuing medical care by a physician.[28]

World War II meant an end to the bleak years of the Great Depression. The state's population endured personal sacrifices and loses, and sheriffs adjusted their duties to meet the exigencies of war. Certain segments of the economy suffered, but overall the state boomed. Employment by men and women was high. There was an overall reduction in civilian traffic on Florida's highways and roads during the war, and the conflict effectively slowed the state' all-important tourist industry (major resort cities turned their hotels over to the armed services) but did not end it. Road building, much of it associated with defense installations and funded by the federal government, increased. By 1945 the State Road Department maintained eight thousand miles of highway.[29] As a part of the war effort there was a national speed limit of 45 miles an hour. The manufacture of cars for civilian use was halted with the 1941 models and not resumed until after the end of the war. In December 1941, tires were the first of a long list of goods and products to be rationed. The rubber shortage was solved by rationing and by the development of synthetic rubber, although controls on tire sales were not removed until December 1945. Gas was rationed with occupation or profession determining how much gas male and female automobile owners were eligible to purchase. Owners of vehicles were required to put decals of distinct coloring and alphabetic designation on their windshields. The decals indicated the owners' classification. Car owners were also issued coupon books containing gas stamps which were surrendered to filling station operators when they purchased gas.

Citizens were subject to federal, state, and local controls geared to help win the war. Price ceilings and rent controls were imposed by the

278

Office of Price Administration (OPA), and Americans accepted having their lives regulated by "point rationing" from various coupon books containing stamps for sugar, coffee, meat, fats and oils, butter, cheese, processed food, and shoes. Rationing was not lifted for a number of products until late 1945, and was continued for sugar until 1947. There was some grumbling, and black marketing was not unknown, but most Americans were patriotic and obeyed the laws because they believed them necessary to defeat the Axis powers.[30]

The mid-winter assembling of the FSA in 1945 was a preordained success because, although the war went grimly on in the European and Asian theaters, it seemed clear that the goals of Victory in Europe (VE-Day) and Victory in Japan (VJ-Day) were inevitable, though no one knew when. The FSA's meeting place—the Roosevelt hotel, Jacksonville, and its host, Rex Sweat—left little doubt of a productive and pleasurable assembly. Hugh Culbreath, sheriff of Hillsborough County, was elected president. On the first day sheriffs heard speeches by Congressman Emory H. Price of the Second Florida District, FBI agent R. G. Danner, state senator John E. Mathews of Jacksonville, and Representative-elect Fletcher Morgan of Duval County. Rivers Buford, immediate past Chief Justice of the Florida Supreme Court, was one of the second day's speakers. Buford was a longtime advocate of the sheriffs and an honorary member of the FSA. He told the sheriffs, "It is the little things that get most law enforcement officers into trouble, and my advice to you is to avoid the little mistakes. If you do your duty as your conscience tells you to do it, you won't have to apologize to anyone." Buford's speech went beyond the typical convention cliches because he related numerous anecdotes from his days as a state's attorney in West Florida.

As their new president, the delegates elected veteran sheriff and member of the FSA (he had often served as treasurer) Frank Stoutamire of Leon County. The lawman had begun his sheriff's career in 1923, and, though able, had critics. He was installed as the FSA's president at the annual meeting in Tampa in late June. Stoutamire first entered the field of protecting the public as a deputy sheriff serving warrants on horseback. When appointed sheriff he held the post of Tallahassee city commissioner. For the next thirty years, with one exception, he was opposed in every reelection race. Overcoming his opposition, Stoutamire won each contest in the first primary, never facing a runoff. The veteran lawman finally retired in 1953 only to accept an appointment as Tallahassee's police chief. When he stepped down in 1968 Stoutamire had served fifty years in law enforcement. Before concluding the mid-winter meeting the members elected two at-large members of the board of directors and one for each of the state's congressional districts.[31]

Before the FSA's Tampa meeting in 1945, President Roosevelt, who had been back in the White House only a few months, died on April 12, and was succeeded by his vice president Harry S. Truman. The former U. S. Senator from Missouri had not been kept fully informed on wartime strategies. Nonetheless, Truman was an intelligent, forthright individual who became a decisive president. Accomplishing the stated goal of "unconditional surrender," Americans celebrated VE-Day on May 5, although the conflict with Japan continued.

The annual FSA gathering was quieter than usual, partly because there was a special session of the legislature, and several scheduled speakers were forced to cancel their appearances. Even so, there were plenty of orators. The delegates who registered at the Tampa Terrace hotel convention headquarters numbered about a hundred and represented most of the state's counties. Outgoing president Hugh Culbreath and various committee chairmen had an array of judges, state's attorneys, FBI representatives, the state auditor, and a former American Legion commander as speakers. An important discussion was held that outlined the essentials in preparing a case for court, obtaining evidence, and courtroom procedure in presenting evidence.[32]

Before World War II ended in 1945 the legislature passed laws reestablishing and redefining the Florida sheriff's duties. The chief lawman was to appoint his deputies, whose actions were the sheriff's responsibility. Each deputy had to give a $1,000 bond. The man who wore the most authoritative star was assigned eleven major responsibilities, but they primarily repeated his historic duties. He continued to appoint special deputies for elections, execute the process of various courts and boards of county commissioners, handle writs, warrants, and other papers, attend terms of various courts, be present at certain meetings, conserve the peace, and suppress riots. Probably without enthusiasm, the sheriffs continued their nineteenth century duties of serving as ex-officio timber agents in their counties. The duties of a timber agent were spelled out in lengthy detail. In case they had overlooked something, the lawmakers added a final obligation. The sheriff was to "perform other such duties as imposed by law."[33] During the summer of 1945 the new and devastating weapon of warfare, the painstakingly developed atomic bomb, was dropped on two key Japanese cities, forcing the country to surrender. News that the Empire of Japan had capitulated spread, resulting in tumultuous VJ-Day celebrations in America on August 14. Across the peninsula, according to a student of the period, "Collectively in perhaps the most joyous celebration in state history, Floridians erupted in planned and spontaneous parades and demonstrations."[34] Florida emerged from World War II with an affluent population anxious to spend accumulated savings. Thousands of people had been introduced to the state as a result of being stationed there as military personnel. They and their families liked what they saw, and decided to remain or to return later. They were the vanguard of a great surge of people who moved to Florida after 1945.

With their state on the verge of unprecedented growth the sheriffs knew that the expansions created new benefits and new difficulties. In the twenty-five years since 1920 Florida and the nation had gone through the boom times and the Jazz Age of the 1920s, suffered through the economic crisis of the thirties and the Great Depression, and been a successful partner of the Allies in the military crisis of World War II. In that quarter of a century the Florida sheriffs had adopted modern methods of dealing with crime. They had increased their standards and seen the Florida Sheriffs Association rise to a place of influence. The state's lawmen stood ready for the postwar world. No one, least of all the sheriffs themselves, doubted that they would be busy.

Notes for Chapter X

1. Tampa *Morning Tribune,* March 6, 1940.
2. For Holland and Paty's views see ibid., March 8, 1940; for those of Whitehair see ibid., March 4, 1940.
3. Ibid., March 7, 1940.
4. Jacksonville *Florida Times-Union,* June 13, 1940.
5. *FA 1941,* I, 2,496-2,488.
6. Ibid., 1,410-1,41 See also ibid., 2,641-2,642, 745, 2,747-2,748.
7. Ibid., *1945,* I, 113-115, 133-134.
8. Jacksonville *Florida Times-Union,* March 5-6, 1941.
9. Ibid., June 10-11, 1941.
10. Ibid., June 12, 1941.
11. *FA 1941,* I, 2,632-2,634.
12. Ibid., 1,384-1,387.
13. Ibid., *1940,* I, 753-755.
14. Ibid., *1945,* I, 894-895, 882-892.
15. Ibid., *1943,* I, 430, 95-96; *1945,* I, 91-92.
16. Jacksonville *Florida Times-Union,* March 26-27. See also *Florida Sheriffs Association Magazine & Directory 1942,* 45. This was the title of the sheriffs' yearbook for that year.
17. Jacksonville *Florida Times Union,* June 9-10, 1942.
18. The significance of jook joints has been well studied by Madeliene Hirsiger Carr in her "Jook Joints in Northern Florida," Unpublished master's thesis, Florida State University, 1998.
19. Jacksonville *Florida Times-Union,* June 6, 1942.
20. Spillane, Alachua County manuscript, 86; Jacksonville *Florida Times-Union,* January 14, June 8, 1943.
21. Jacksonville *Florida Times-Union,* June 14, 1943.
22. Ibid., October 10, 20, 1943.
23. Gary Mormino, "World War II," 323-343, in Gannon (Editor), *New History of Florida*; Tracy Jean Revels, "World War II–Era Florida: Changes in the 1940s," 137-150, in Greenberg and others, *Florida's Heritage of Diversity.*
24. *Florida Acts 1943,* I, 804-805, 747-748, 755-756.
25. Ibid., 801.
26. Ibid., *1943,* I, 252-253.
27. Jacksonville *Florida Times-Union,* January 8, 12, 14, 1944.
28. *FA 1943,* I, 536-538, 215-316, 43-44. See also Mormino "World War II," 338-339. Records of the annual FSA meeting in 1944 have not been located.
29. Charlton W. Tebeau, *A History of Florida* (Miami, 1971), 415.

30. Among several studies of the American home front during wartime see John Morton Blum, *V Was For Victory Politics nd American Culture During World War II* (New York and London, 1976), and Richard Polenberg (Editor), *America At War The Home Front, 1941-1945* (Englewood Cliffs, New Jersey, 1968).
31. Jacksonville *Florida Times-Union*, January 9, 11, 1945. See also *Florida Highways*, XIII (February, 1945), 16-17, 30-3 For Stoutamire's career see Tallahassee *Democrat*, August 9, 1968; August 13, 1973.
32. Tampa *Morning Tribune*, June 13, 1945; Jacksonville *Florida Times-Union*, June 11, 1945.
33. *FA 1945*, I, 606-610.
34. Mormino, "World War II, 340.

APPENDIX

Roster of Florida Sheriffs

The following is a list of Florida's sheriffs 1821-2000. From 1821 to 1829 when the office became elective, governors appointed sheriffs with the advice and consent of the legislative council. Sheriffs elected from that time until 1845 are hard to document. Records of elections, commissions, resignations, and removals are available in the Florida State Archives but are often incomplete and contradictory. Newspapers and correspondence to Florida governors, secretaries of state, and other state authorities shed some light, but conflicting sources sometimes add to the confusion. During Florida's Civil War and Reconstruction years the problem of precisely identifying sheriffs becomes even more difficult. The authors found that some counties had no records at all for the Reconstruction years. This was so largely because of the political turmoil following the Civil War. The Constitution of 1868 granted governors the authority to appoint sheriffs and other important county officials. Until the state was "redeemed" in 1876, this meant that Republicans and some African Americans were appointed to the office. The turbulent, often violent, nature of local politics wreaked havoc on civil government, resulting in the destruction of records. In 1877 order was restored in the form of one party (Democratic) rule under the rubric of White Supremacy. Nearly a decade later the Constitution of 1885 made the office once again elective. From the late nineteenth century into the twentieth century fewer problems exist in record keeping. Even so, investigations of wrongdoing in numerous county sheriffs' offices by Florida governors often resulted in suspensions and temporary interim appointments.

Given the numerous previously stated difficulties the following list contains some errors, but it represents the best efforts the authors can make given the incomplete and sometimes contradictory nature of the sources. This compilation lists the years the sheriffs served.

ALACHUA COUNTY

1827	Simeon Dell
1832	John B. Tiner
1840-41	Thomas Barron
1842-43	John McNeill
1844-45	Isaac Blanton
1845-47	Thomas C. Ellis
1847-48	William Gibbons
1848	Thomas C. Ellis
1848-49	A. E. Geiger
1849-55	Charles L. Wilson
1855-57	George B. Ellis
1857-65	S. W. Burnett
1865-67	John C. Crosby
1868-72	George L. Barnes
1872-73	D.W.L. Barton
1873	John W. Howell
1873-77	L. A. Barnes
1877-80	Samuel Tucker
1880	A. J. Weeks
1881-83	John W. Turner
1883-86	S. C. Tucker
1886	A. J. Collins
1886-90	Samuel Hamlin Wienges
1890	S. C. Tucker
1890-93	Lewis Washington Fennell
1893-95	A. U. Hilleary
1895-97	H. M. Tillis
1897-09	Lewis Washington Fennell
1909-25	Perry Gilbert Ramsey
1925-29	Charles Pinkoson
1929-33	R. J. Wells
1933-45	J. P. Ramsey
1945-49	Fred Hollomon
1949-55	Frank M. Sexton
1955-76	Joe M. Crevasse, Jr.
1977-92	L. J. "Lu" Hindery
1992	Stephen Oelrich

BAKER COUNTY

1859-61	Roland Thomas
1861-67	James M. Burnsed
1868-69	Thomas Leddy
1869-74	John H. Howell
1875	William Green
1876	A. A. Allen
1877	N. C. Herndon
1879	Ben S. Roberts
1880	John C. Williams
1881-84	N. E. Handon
1885-88	J. W. Van Buskirk
1889-91	C. F. Pons
1891-93	J. W. Gargains
1893-97	C. F. Pons
1897-98	J. F. W. Driggers
1898-1905	U. C. Herndon
1905-11	J. Powers
1911-17	L. M. Dyal
1917	J. H. Brown
1918	J. R. Corbett
1918	G. M. Rhoden
1919	A. J. Sweat
1920-21	L. F. Sweat
1921	D. V. Selph
1921-22	J. A. Rowe
1922	Joe Jones
1922-37	Joe Jones, Jr.
1937-41	S. R. Green
1941-42	J. E. Combs
1942-57	Asa Coleman, Jr.
1957-65	Ed Yarborough
1965-66	Carl H. Rochester
1966-73	Paul T. Thrift
1973-74	Joe Newmans
1974	Gary Fraser
1974-92	Joe Newmans
1993-97	Murray Richardson
1997	Joey B. Dobson

BAY COUNTY

1913-14	W. A. Brown
1914-15	C. E. Scott
1915-17	F. M. Nelson
1917-25	C. S. Russ
1925-37	O. E. Hobbs
1937-45	John Scott
1945-49	C. C. Rushing
1949-53	A. F. Thomas
1953-61	M. J. Daffin
1961-63	Charlie Abbot
1963-71	M. J. Daffin
1971-80	Tullis D. Easterling
1981-87	Lavelle Pitts
1987	Frank Doolittle
1987-1988	William Lewis
1988-89	LaVelle Pitts
1989	Guy Tunnell

BRADFORD COUNTY

1859-60	Roland Thomas
1861-62	R. W. Jones
1862-65	S. T. Watkins
1865-68	Roland Thomas
1868	Francis M. Weeks
1869	Simeon Roberts
1870	Robert W. Lamb
1871-72	Mathew L. McKinney
1873-74	Roland Thomas
1874-75	C. L. Shepard
1875-77	John Hall
1877-85	W. W. Tumblin
1885	George W. Epperson
1886-88	Henry W. Epperson
1889-90	E. W. Epperson
1890-91	David L. Alvarez
1891-93	P. S. Crews
1893-97	E. E. Johns

1897-1901	S. B. Denmark
1901-05	E. E. Johns
1905-07	J. A. Bennett
1907-12	J. W. Langford
1912-17	S. B. Denmark
1917-36	W. J. Epperson
1936-49	A. O. Andreu
1948-72	P. D. Reddish
1973-88	Dolph Reddish
1989-93	Kenneth Etheridge
1993	Bob Milner

BREVARD COUNTY

1855-57	James A. Armour
1845-47	Mills O. Burnham
1847-50	F.M.K. Millison
1850-55	C.L. Brayton
1857-63	William B. Davis
1863-65	T. M. McDaniel
1865-67	Jackson Clifflon
1868-71	Dempsey Cain
1871	John Q. Stewart
1875	Charles Bass
1877-79	Abner J. Wright
1879-83	W. F. Richards
1883-86	M.E. English
1883-97	James E. Bowman
1897-1917	J. P. Brown
1917-20	Minor B. Jones
1921-29	L. W. Doolittle
1929-37	Roy Roberts
1938-57	H. T. (Bill) Williams
1957-62	J. W. Dunn
1962-63	Ralph Clark
1963-76	Leigh S. Wilson
1977-78	Rollin W. Zimmerman
1978-79	David U. Strawn
1979-80	Collin W. "Jake" Miller

1980-81	Rollin W. Zimmerman
1981-97	Collin W. "Jake" Zimmerman
1997	Philip B. Williams

BROWARD COUNTY

1915-25	A. W. Turner
1925-27	Paul C. Bryan
1927-31	A. W. Turner
1931-39	W. R. Clark
1939-40	Edward Lee
1941-51	W. R. Clark
1951-57	Amos H. Hall
1957-61	Justice A. Lloyd
1961-68	Allen B. Michell
1968	Tom Walker
1969-79	Edward J. Stack
1979-82	Robert Butterworth
1983-85	George Brescher
1985-1993	Nick Navarro
1993-1997	Ron Cochran
1997-present	Ken Jenne

CALHOUN COUNTY

1832	Gerry Pattason
1839	Francis A. Ross
1840-42	Thomas Green
1843-43	Alexander McAlpine
1845-47	Issac Jackson
1847-51	Elias Branch
1852-55	Thomas J. Land
1855-59	James B. Stone
1859-61	James Stanfield
1862-63	Tyrus L. Hausford
1863-67	Jackson N. Richards
1868-1871	James W. Yearty
1871-75	James Stanfield
1875	J. B. Armstrong

1877	W. G. Mitchell
1877-79	John M. Bush
1881-89	J. T. Stone
1889-97	Caleb Joshua Holley
1897-1905	A. J. McClellan
1905-13	J. L. Alexander
1913-17	T. J. McKeown
1917-30	C. D. Clark
1930	E. A. McClellan
1930-32	R. J. Flanders
1932-33	L. T. Taylor
1933-37	R. L. Flanders
1937-41	J. K. Musgrove
1941-53	J. C. Tucker
1953-56	George C. Guilford
1957-77	W. C. Reeder
1977-2000	W. G. "Buddy" Smith
2001	David Tatum

CHARLOTTE COUNTY

1921-41	J. H. Lipscomb
1941-57	Arthur F. Quednau
1957-65	Travis Parnell
1965-66	Richard A. Stickley
1966-66	John Shannon
1966-67	David Deegan
1967-77	John P. Bent
1977-80	Alan L. LeBeau
1981-85	Glen E. Sapp
1985	J.M."Buddy" Phillips
1985-86	John McDougall
1986-88	Glen E. Sapp
1989-2000	Richard Worch
2001	Bill Clement

CITRUS COUNTY

1888-97	James C. Priest
1897-1905	A. T. Priest
1905-06	George R. Carter

1906-07	E. Port Graham		**COLLIER COUNTY**	
1907-17	George R. Carter			
1917-29	B. O. Bowden		1923-28	W. R. Maynard
1929-45	Charles S. Dean		1928-53	L. J. Thorp
1945-53	Frank Morris		1953-57	Roy O. Atkins
1953-80	Burton R. Quinn		1957-75	E. A. Doug Hendry
1981-96	Charles S. Dean, Sr.		1975-88	Aubrey Rogers
1996-97	Terry LaCasse		1989	Don Hunter
1997	Jeffrey J. Dawsy			

CLAY COUNTY

COLUMBIA COUNTY

1859-63	Elam J. Daniels		1840-42	N. M. Moody
1863-65	Joshua B. O'Hern		1843	John W. Love
1866-67	William J. Wilson		1844	Charles Fitchett
1868-70	John W. Sullivan		1845-48	Thomas B. Fitzpatrick
1870-73	Henry Bradford		1848	Asa A. Stewart
1874-77	Thomas Roberts		1849-53	Arthur J. T. Wright
1877-85	James W. Dewitt		1854	Reuben Hogans
1885	Clairborne Wright		1855-61	Thomas M. Mickler
1885-89	Christian Black		1861-64	Nathaniel Jameson
1889-94	Josephus A. Peeler		1864-67	Thomas M. Mickler
1894	J. M. Beery		1867	John D. Moncrief
1894-95	George W. Hanford, Jr.		1868-70	Benjamin F. McFarland
1895-1900	James Weeks		1870	Robert C. Martin
1900-05	William F. Peeler		1870-71	Warren S. Bush
1905-06	Charles Wilson		1873	George G. Keen
1906	K. C. Canova		1873-74	A. A. Hoyte
1906-11	James Weeks		1875-77	J. W. Tompkins
1911	Lewis T. Ivey		1877-81	John C. Henry
1911-13	Theodore Shelton "Shelt" Cherry		1881-85	J. W. Perry
1913-17	J. H. King		1885-89	C. P. Farnell
1917-18	J. Slater Smith		1889-93	J. A. Bethea
1918-29	Elam J. Weeks		1893-97	W. N. Cone
1929-65	John Preston Hall, Sr.		1897-1901	William M. Hancock
1965-89	O. Jennings Murrhee, Jr.		1901-05	W. N. Cone
			1905-09	D. W. Purvis
			1908	J. W. Nance
1989-93	C. Dalton Bray		1910-13	W. E. Dennard
1993	Scott Lancaster		1913-21	J. W. Perry

1921-33	W. B. Douglas	1945-50	Jimmy Sullivan
1933-45	Walter Davis	1950-51	Thomas J. Kelly
1945-67	Ralph P. Witt, Sr.	1951-52	Jimmy Sullivan
1967-69	Floyd Crawford	1952-53	J. B. Henderson
1969-74	Harry J. Spradley	1953-62	Thomas J. Kelly
1974-79	J. Glenn Bailey	1962-63	Talmadge A. Buchanan
1981-84	Steve W. Spradley		
1984	J.M."Buddy" Phillips	1963-64	Jessie Barkett
1984	Ray Dyal	1964-66	Talmadge A. Buchanan
1985-97	Tom Tramel		
1997	Frank Owens	1964	Robert L. Floyd
		1965	George E. Leppig
		1966	Talmadge A. Buchanan

DADE COUNTY

1840-44	Lemuel Otis	1966	Leonard M. NcNutt
1844	Joseph Bethel	1967	George E. Leppig
1844-46	Charles Gyles	1966-79	E. Wilson Purdy
1846-47	Edwin Quimby	1979-87	Bobby L. Jones
1869	O. Amor	1987-97	Fred Taylor
1870-74	Francis Infinger	1997	Carlos Alvarez
1874	Benjamin Coachman		
1874-75	William J. Smith	**DESOTO COUNTY**	
1875	William M. Mettair		
1875	Robert J. Rhodes	1887-93	O. H. Dishong
1875-77	W. S. Smith	1893-95	F. C. Bethea
1877-83	John F. Peacock	1895-97	Andrew L. Pearce
1883-90	William M. Mattaur	1897-98	Owen H. Dishong
1890-91	John F. Highsmith	1898-1900	Andrew L. Pearce
1891-93	F. W. Church	1901-05	L. E. Fielder
1893-94	William T. Wilkins	1905-13	A. C. Freeman
1894-95	L. L. Dodge	1913-21	John Leslie Dishong
1895-1901	R. J. Chillingworth	1921-37	J. L. Hampton
1901-09	John Frohock	1937-45	J. E. Albritton
1909-17	Dan Hardie	1945-50	T. M. Anderson
1917-21	D. W. Moran	1950-65	Lloyd R. Holton
1921-25	Louis A. Allen	1965-66	Inez Holton
1925-29	Henry R. Chase	1966-80	Frank E. Cline
1929-32	M. P. Lehman	1981-84	R. A. "Bob" Thomas
1932-33	G. A. Windham	1985-92	Joe Varnadore
1933	Dan Hardie	1993-2000	Vernon Keen
1933-45	D. C. Coleman	2001	Johnny Fugate

DIXIE COUNTY

1921-26	S. C. Chavous
1926	J. S. Bodiford
1926-28	S. C. Chavous
1928-29	E. F. Fisher
1929-33	W. M. Mills
1933-45	F. L. Anderson
1945-49	J. L. Baggett
1949-50	D. H. Hatcher
1950-57	L. E. Hatcher
1957-76	Al Parker
1977-89	Glen Dyals
1989-93	Sammy Woodall
1993-97	Larry Edmonds
1997-2000	Dewey Hatcher
2001	Sammy Woodall

DUVAL COUNTY

1822	James Dell
1824-27	Daniel C. Hart
1833-41	Albert G. Phillips
1842-44	Jacob Gutterson
1844-45	Harrison B. Blanchard
1845-47	Thomas Ledwith
1847-48	William G. Saunders
1848-49	Thomas Ledwith
1849-51	John G. Smith
1851-53	George H. Smith
1853-59	Uriah Bowden
1859-61	Paul D. Canova
1861-65	Uriah Bowden
1865	D. P. Smith
1865-67	M. Bowden
1868-69	John J. Holland
1869	Daniel C. Rodman
1869-70	S. N. Williams
1871-75	William M. Ledwith
1873-75	J. H. Durkee
1876-78	John S. Driggs
1878-83	Uriah Bowden
1884-87	H. D. Holland
1888-94	N. B. Broward
1895-96	R. Fleming Bowden
1897-1900	N. B. Broward
1901-04	John Price
1905	P. W. Bloxham
1905	W. B. Pickett
1906	M. A. Brown
1907-12	R. Fleming Bowden
1913-21	W. H. Dowling
1916	H. H. Lewis
1922-23	R. E. Merritt
1924-28	W. H. Dowling
1929-31	W. B. Cahoon
1932-57	Rex Sweat
1958	Al Cahill
1958-86	Dale Carson
1986-95	Jim McMillan
1995	Nathaniel (Nat) Glover

ESCAMBIA COUNTY

1827-28	Charles Mifflin
1828	Henry Wilson
1829	Adam Gordon
1830	Florencio Commyns
1840	Peter Woodbine
1842-45	Ebenezer Doff
1846	Mortimar Bright
1846-47	Angus Nicholson
1847-51	Antoine J. Collins
1851-52	Francis de la Rue
1852-54	Francis Maura
1854-57	Joseph C. Crosby
1858-59	William M. R. Jordan
1859-65	Daniel Williams

Appendix

1865-68	James B. Roberts	1965-80	P. A. Edmonson
1868-70	George E. Wentworth	1981-83	Daniel H. Bennett
1870	Henry C. Campbell	1983	J. M."Buddy" Phillips
1870	E. R. Payne	1983-2000	Robert McCarthy
1870-73	George S. Wells	2001	James L. Manfre
1874	J. N. Coombs		
1875-77	A. M. Green	**FRANKLIN COUNTY**	
1877-85	W. H. Hutchinson		
1885-93	Joseph Wilkins	1831	N. Baker
1893-1903	George E. Smith	1841	Henry Williams
1903-13	James C. Van Pelt	1843-44	Charles Shepard
1913-17	A. C. Ellis	1845-49	John Lucas
1917-19.	C. Van Pelt	1849-51	Benjamin Lucas
1919-21	Hurdis Whitaker	1851-59	Clinton Thigpin
1921-22	A. Cary Ellis	1859-62	Henry K. Simmons
1923-32	Mose S. Penton	1863-65	John F. Benezet
1933-40	H. E. Gandy	1865-67	A. W. Hunter
1941-44	Howard Mayes	1868-69	Henry Grady
1945-56	R. L. Kendrick	1869	Robert Kerickmeyer
1957-61	Emmett Shelby	1874	W. H. Quaile
1961-70	William E. Davis	1874-77	Henry Hutchinson*
1970-80	Royal Untreiner	1877	Edward T. Raney
1981-88	Joseph Vincent "Vince" Seely	1878-83	John Teabold
		1883-85	S. A. Floyd
1989-93	Charlie Johnson	1885-87	J. J. Berry
1993-2000	Jim Lowman	1886	W. C. Pickett
2001	Ron McNesby	1887-89	W. O. Kew
		1889-93	E. M. Montgomery
FLAGLER COUNTY		1893-1904	William H. Neel
		1904-17	A. B. Gibson
1917-25	E. W. Johnston	1917-19	J. H. Hose
1925-27	Perry Hall	1918	J. T. Bragdon
1927-28	W. J. Williams	1919-22	D. S. Hose
1928-33	J. H. McKnight	1923-37	W. J. Lovett
1933-37	H. R. Whitaker	1937-40	C. L. Robbins
1937-41	E. W. Johnston	1940-45	W. J. Lovett
1941-53	Henry Wells	1945-53	Stanford Bragdon
1953-58	T. K. "Buddy" McKnight	1953-69	Herbert O. Marshall
		1969-89	Jack Taylor, Jr.
1957-65	Homer William Brooks	1993-97	Warren Roddenberry
		1997	Bruce Varnes

291

GADSDEN COUNTY

1827	Robert Forbes
1840-43	Roderick Shaw
1844	William H. McMillan
1845-50	Benjamin C. West
1849-54	Samuel B. Love
1855-62	James M. Smith
1865-68	J. P. Jordan
1868	John P. Jordan
1869	Charles P. Williams
1870	John P. Jordan
1874-77	R. S. Tucker
1877-81	J. C. DuPont
1881-93	Thomas Mitchell
1893-1900	S. W. Chester
1900-02	S. F. Edwards
1902-09	W. S. McCall
1909-33	G. Scott Gregory
1933-41	W. M. Inman
1941-44	M. P. Luten
1944-68	Otho W. Edwards
1969-71	Robert L. Martin
1971-71	James Mitchell
1971	William A. Woodham

GILCHRIST COUNTY

1925-31	A. D. Fields
1931-33	D. W. Deen, Sr.
1933-41	R. E. Davis
1941	D. W. Deen, Jr.
1941-53	D. H. Browning, Sr.
1953-56	R. E. Davis, Jr.
1956	Mark Read
1956-67	Clyde Williams
1967-75	Charlie Parrish
1977-88	Roy J. Rodgers

1989-96	Jim Floyd
1996	David Turner

GLADES COUNTY

1921-27	Frank Richards
1928-49	J. J. Wiggins
1949-56	C. S. Pressley
1956	Mrs. C. S. Pressley
1957-80	Roy Lundy
1981-83	William "Billy" Arnold
1983	J.M."Buddy" Phillips
1983-88	Russell Henderson
1989-92	Charles Schramm
1993-96	Barry Walbourn
1997	Jim Rider

GULF COUNTY

1925-26	Oscar J. McDaniel
1926-37	J. E. Pridgeon
1937-72	Byrd E. Parker
1972-76	Raymond Lawrence
1977-84	K. E. "Ken" Murphy
1985-93	Al Harrison
1994-95	James Coates
1995-97	Frank McKeithen

HAMILTON COUNTY

1828	Shaddrack Sutton
1840-44	John G. Smith
1845-46	Milton J. Bryant
1846-47	Josiah T. Baisden
1847-49	John G. Smith
1849-51	William J. J. Duncan
1853-57	James N. Hendry

1857-59	Larkin B. McTyier	**HENDRY COUNTY**	
1859-65	Alexander Bell		
1868-70	Duval Selph	1923-29	D. L. McLaughlin
1870	Thomas N. Bell	1930	R. H. Hancock
1871	M. L. Duncan	1931-41	H. L. Delaney
1872-74	Benjamin F. Collier*	1941-61	Bill Maddox
1874-78	John H. Lee	1961-80	Earl S. Dyess, Sr.
1879	M. L. Duncan	1981-84	Robert T. Durkis
1879-80	C. C. Parker	1985-92	Earl S. Dyess, Jr.
1881-85	Sampson Altman	1992-97	Thomas Wayne "Tommy" Vaughan
1885-89	Sampson Tavell		
1889	N. O. Waldron	1997-2000	Ronnie Lee
1889-92	S. S. Sharp	2001	Steve Worley
1892-93	A. M. Knowles		
1893-1900	T. A. Polhill	**HERNANDO COUNTY**	
1900-13	Thomas B. Johns		
1913-29	A. F. Hancock	1845-47	James M. Bates
1929-31	W. R. Hunter	1847	N. M. Moody
1931-37	J. H. Hunter	1853-60	Charles J. McMinn
1937-41	A. F. Hancock	1860-62	Thomas W. Law
1941-49	Eddie McGhin	1862-63	T. B. Law
1949-53	Brock Allen	1863-66	John L. Peterson
1953-57	George Royals	1866-67	E. A. Hill
1957-88	Charlie Rhoden	1868	Samuel Pearce
1989	Harrell Reid	1868	W. M. Smith
		1870	Zachariah Seward
HARDEE COUNTY		1871-76	Benjamin Saxon
		1877-79	D. L. Heddick
1921-25	John Poucher	1879-85	J. B. Mickler
1925-38	Chester S. Dishong	1885-88	J. A. Jennings
1938-39	L. G. Sanders	1888-90	J. W. Johnson
1939-44	W. B. Whidden	1890-91	M. R. Bums
1944-53	E. Ollie Roberts	1891-92	Johnston W. Johnston
1953-65	E. Odell Carlton	1892-99	M. R. Bums
1965-81	Newton H. Murdock	1899-1901	A. M. White
1981-93	Doyle W. Bryan	1901-21	W. E. Law
1993-97	Rickey G. Dick	1921-33	W. D. Cobb
1997	J. Loran Cogburn	1933-46	N. F. Law

1945	S. L. Lowman		1874-77	J. R. Hay
1946-49	N. F. Law		1877-85	D. 1. Craft
1949-71	S. L. Lowman		1885-93	J. P. Martin
1973-84	Melvin Kelley		1893-1901	T. K. Spencer
1985-2000	Tom Mylander		1901-05	W. T. Lesley
2001	Rich Nugent		1905-07	R. A. Jackson
			1908-09	E. D. Hobbs

HIGHLANDS COUNTY

			1909-13	R. A. Jackson
			1913-17	W. C. Spencer
1929-37	W. M. Griffin		1917-21	A. J. White
1923-27	R. H. Hancock		1921-25	W. C. Spencer
1927-29	J. M. Hancock		1925-28	L. M. Hiers
1929-32	O. E. Wolf		1928	L. M. Hatton, Jr.
1933-41	Doyle Schumacher		1929-33	R. T. Joughin
1941-45	E. G. Long		1933-35	W. C. Spencer
1945-49	Doyle Schumacher		1935-41	J. R. McLeod
1949-69	Broward Coker		1941-50	Hugh Culbreath
1969-70	Joe D. Keene		1950	Elbert Moore
1970-76	O. L. Raulerson, Jr.		1951-53	Hugh Culbreath
1977-88	Joe Sheppard		1953-65	Ed Blackburn
1989	Howard Godwin		1965-78	Malcolm E. Beard
			1978-93	Walter C. Heinrich
			1993	Cal Henderson

HILLSBOROUGH COUNTY

HOLMES COUNTY

1834	William S. Junior			
1839-43	R. V. Buffurn			
1845-47	John Parker		1848-49	James E. Turner
1845	David Boney		1849-51	Ethelred Hewett
1845-47	John Parker		1851-54	Robert R. Golden
1847-50	John J. Hooker		1855-57	John A. Vaughan
1849-52	Benjamin J. Hagler		1857-64	Daniel J. Brownell
1852-56	Edward T. Kendrick		1859-65	John A. Vaughan
1855-58	Henry Parker		1865-67	Thomas Pittman
1858-65	William S. Spencer		1868-73	Daniel J. Brownell
1865-67	John T. Lesley		1870-72	John Neel
1868-71	Henry Albury		1877-81	H. E. Hickman
1871	F. T. Gould		1881-85	F. M. Ellis
1871-72	Charles Slager		1885-93	W. M. Brown

1893-94	H. E. Hickman	**JACKSON COUNTY**	
1894-96	W. M. Brown		
1897-1905	Daniel J. Paul	1823-26	William M. Loftin
1905-13	H. E. Hickman	1827-32	William S. Mooring
1913-17	J. Z. Mayo	1833-40	Thomas M. White
1917	J. H. Mattox	1840-47	Samuel Stephens
1917-18	J. S. Andrews	1847-49	John T. Myrick
1918-28	T. W. Johnson	1849-51	Samuel Stephens
1929	J. W. Chance	1851-59	James Griffin
1928-33	W. B. Driver	1859-63	Henry O. Bassett
1933-41	L. F. Brown	1862-63	Benjamin F. Parker
1941-45	W. B. Driver	1863-64	W. H. Kimball
1945-49	J. R. Brown	1864-65	W. J. Robinson
1949-53	J. R. Chance	1865-67	W. H. Kimball
1953-58	H. L. Stevenson	1868-69	John S. King
1957-69	Cletus Andrews	1869	Thomas H. West
1969-72	Harvie J. Belser	1871-72	F. M. G. Carter
1973-77	Wilburn E. Raley	1874-77	James A. Finlayson
1977-79	W. C. Jones	1877	Robert J. Pitman
1981-85	Drew Galloway	1877-80	R. J. Pitman
1985-88	Thomas Strickland	1880	A. Merritt
1989-97	John Braxton	1881-93	Andrew Scott
1997	Dennis Lee	1893-1905	J. A. Finlayson
		1905-13	H. H. Lewis
INDIAN RIVER COUNTY		1913-17	H. A. Bowles
		1917-33	A. J. Lewis
1925-29	J. W. Knight	1933-37	W. F. "Flake" Chambliss
1928-29	J. H. Sutherland		
1929-34	C. S. Rice	1937-41	W. L. Watford
1933-45	William Frick	1941-49	Barkley Gause
1945-54	Leonard B. O'Steen	1949-54	Ernest F. Barnes
1954-79	Sam T. Joyce	1954	Mrs. Ernest F. Barnes
1981-93	R. T. "Tim" Dobeck	1955-60	Roy Robertson
1993-2000	Gary C. Wheeler	1961-71	Barkley Gause
2001	Roy Raymond	1973-76	Ronald Craven
		1977-80	Charles H. Applewhite
		1981	John P. McDaniel

JEFFERSON COUNTY

1827-29	Asa Townsend
1830	Solomon E. Mathers
1842-45	William R. Taylor
1845-47	Smith Simpkins
1847-51	James R. Tucker
1851-53	Daniel T. Lingo
1853-55	Joel Walker
1855-57	William H. Andrews
1857-59	B. W. Edwards
1859-61	William H. Ellis
1861-63	Valentine Clem
1863-64	Joseph O. Taylor
1864	Joseph H. Taylor
1864-65	Joseph T. Budd
1865-67	W. H. Ellis
1867	D. L. Oakley
1868-69	J. W. Powell
1869-72	J. W. Johnson
1872	Sturgis B. Baldwin
1873-76	L. B. Baldwin
1876	Lafayette Napoleon McCray*
1877	George W. Monroe*
1877-81	William Z. Bailey
1881-83	T. B. Simpkins
1883-86	D. B. Bird
1889-1900	T. B. Simpkins
1900-05	R. L. Kilpatrick
1905-13	D. B. Bird
1913-17	R. L. Kilpatrick
1917-33	G. C. Allman
1933-34	Lamar W. Sledge
1934-45	A. S. Grant
1945-49	J. R. Cooksey, Jr.
1949-50	Minnie J. Cooksey
1950-52	C. O. Allen
1953-56	Jesse H. Lovett, Sr.
1956	Mrs. Jesse H. Lovett, Sr.
1956-67	J. B. Thomas
1966	Lavelle Pitts
1967-70	Don R. Watson
1971-84	James H. Scott
1984	Ken Fortune

LAFAYETTE COUNTY

1857-59	William Edwards
1859-60	G. W. Lyons
1860-65	James J. Ward
1865	S. W. Grant
1865	J. H. Sutton
1868	William D. Sears
1871	John Whitfield
1872	Nathan Harrell
1874	Willian D. Sears
1875-77	Newton Sapp
1878	Seth Stevens
1879-81	J.J.Johnson
1881-83	T. J. Walker
1883-85	J.J.Johnson
1885	John Hatcher
1889-89	C. J. Weathersbee
1889-93	W. B. Martin
1893-1901	J. J. Mouring
1901	W. B. Mathis
1901	J. A. Hinton
1902-13	Chandler Land
1913-17	J. D. Johnson
1917-29	W. E. Murray
1929-31	N. Pearson
1931-37	T. J. Pearson
1937-45	J. C. Sessions
1945-46	W. J. Winburn

1946-60	J. W. Pridgeon	1933-41	Bob King
1960-69	Marvin E. Witt	1941-45	Fred Roberts
1970-71	J. W. Pridgeon	1945-49	Floyd Ellis
1971-80	Stanley Cannon	1949-72	Flanders G. Thompson
1981-88	Bobby McCray		
1989-93	William Townsend	1973-88	Frank N. Wanicka
1993	Dwayne Walker	1989-2000	John McDougall
		2001	Rod Shoap

LAKE COUNTY

LEON COUNTY

1887-97	John P. Galloway		
1897-1905	J. W. Northrup	1825	William Cameron
1905-08	Henry E. Murhee	1827	Romeo Lewis
1908	Martin Wadsworth	1842-45	James Barry
1908	1 W. Hunter	1845-51	Alfred A. Fisher
1908-09	Balton A. Cassady	1851-57	Haley T. Blocker
1909-13	H. E. Murrhee	1857-67	Richard Saunders
1913-20	Thad C. Smyth	1868	John Taylor
1920-21	J. L. Hux	1868	Alvin M. Munger
1921-33	Balton A. Cassady	1874	E. C. Weeks
1933-37	W. B. Gibson	1874	S. L. Tibbetts
1937-44	Balton A. Cassady	1875	P. L. DeCoursey*
1944-45	Emil Yde	1875-77	J. N. Stokes
1945-72	Willis V. McCall	1877-79	Henry Brenreuter
1972	Frank F. Meech	1879-85	Alexander Mosley
1972-77	Guy C. Bliss	1885-1903	John A. Pearce
1977-81	Malcolm V. McCall	1903-07	Charles Hopkins
1981-89	Noel E. Griffin	1907-09	W. M. Langston
1989	George Knupp, Jr.	1909-21	J. P. S. Houston
		1929-38	J. R. Jones
		1923-53	Frank Stoutamire
		1953-68	W.P. "Bill" Joyce

LEE COUNTY

1887-1901	T. W. Langford	1968-77	Raymond Hamlin
1901-18	F. B. Tippins	1977-80	Ken Katsaris
1918	Z. T. Hand	1981-96	Eddie Boone
1919-23	F. B. Tippins	1997	Larry Campbell
1923-25	E. A. Albritton		
1925-32	F. B. Tippins		

LEVY COUNTY

1845-47	William D. Andrews
1847	Robert Waterton
1848-49	E. Allan. Weeks
1852-53	Robert W. Randall
1854-55	Robert Waterson
1855-63	Joseph F. Prevatt
1866-67	L. J. Hogans
1872	W. B. Wimberly
1873-75	G. W. Hodge
1875-77	F. B. Faitonte
1877-80	H. Porter Jackson
1880	W. D. Finlayson
1881-83	J. S. Parker
1883-85	J. J. Mixson
1885-95	William H. Bigham
1895-97	E. H. Lambert
1897-1903	H. S. Sutton
1903-25	E. Walker
1925-29	L. L. Johns
1929-44	W. B. Whiddon
1944-45	J. W. Turner, Jr.
1945-55	George T. Robbins
1955-56	Fred Moring
1956-64	James W. Turner
1964-76	Pat Hartley
1976-80	Horace Moody
1981-88	Pat Hartley
1989-2000	Ted Glass
2001	Johnny Smith

LIBERTY COUNTY

1857-59	Seaborn J. Johnson
1859-62	Joseph Shepard
1863-67	J. T. S. Michaux
1868	Joseph Sheppard
1872	C. B. Edwards
1874-79	W. H. Neil
1879-83	R. F. Hosford
1885	I. G. Harrell
1887-90	J. P. Owens
1890	Samuel Edwards
1890-91	B. F. Owens
1891-93	G. M. Deason
1893-97	Jasper Ryle
1897-99	B. F. Owens
1899-1901	L. J. Owens
1901-1919	J. L. Forehand
1919-37	E. A. Chestang
1937-41	O. M. Revell
1941-45	J. M. Phillips
1945-57	S. G. Revell
1957-76	Link C. Rankin
1977-92	Harrell W. Revell
1993-97	W. L. "Bud" Burke
1997-2000	J. L. Bailey
2001	Harrell W. Revell

MADISON COUNTY

1828	William Dowling
1835	James Wallace
1839	Christopher H. Edmonds
1840-42	Sherrod Edwards
1842-44	William Bridges
1844-45	Elisha Surnmerlin
1845-47	Thomas Langford
1847-49	Adoniram Vann
1849-51	Thomas M. Anderson
1851-54	John H. Patterson
1853-55	Thomas M. Anderson
1855-57	John H. Patterson
1857-59	Thomas M. Anderson

1859-61	E. W. Vann
1861-63	E. W. Vann
1863-65	S. J. Perry
1865-67	J. W. Jones
1868-73	David Montgomery*
1873-76	G. W. Bogue
1877-81	Theodore H. Willard
1881-83	S. M. Hawkins
1885-89	S. A. Parramore
1889-97	E. F. Dickinson
1897-1905	E. J. Armstrong
1905-17	A. D. Stanton
1917-21	R. L. Millinor
1921-25	M. A. Parker
1925-37	G. L. Morrow
1937-49	Lonnie Davis
1949-72	Simeon H. Moore
1973-2000	Joe C. Peavy
2001	Peter C. Bucher

MANATEE COUNTY

1856-57	William H. Whitaker
1858-59	James D. Green
1860-61	John W. Whidden
1861-69	Joel J. Addison
1869-71	A. W. Garner
1871-73	Jessie Tucker
1874	William H. Altman
1874-75	James D. Green
1875-76	Jesse B. Mizell
1877-81	William C. Hayman
1881-96	Alexander S. Watson
1897-1904	Thomas R. Easterling
1905-12	Matthew H. Wyatt
1912-20	Josiah O. Gates
1929-39	Leon G. Wingate
1925-28	Henry J. Stewart

1930-36	J. P. Davidson
1937-42	Cliint J. Hutches
1942	Mrs. C. I Hutches (Eva Hutches)
1942-	S. Dewey Smith
1942-59	Roy F. Baden
1959-60	Herman E. Turner
1960-67	J. Kenneth Gross
1967-76	Richard W. Weitzenfeld
1977-84	Thomas M. Burton, Jr.
1985	Charlie Wells

MARION COUNTY

1844	William Strifel
1845-51	Edmund D. Howse
1852-55	Simeon Helvenston
1856-57	Norman A. McLeod
1857-59	Simeon Halvenston
1860-63	Daniel Cappleman
1864	L. D. Harris
1864-65	Samuel O. Howse
1865-68	Benjamin F. Priest
1869-70	M. A. Clonts
1870-73	John O. Matthews
1873-77	William G. McGrath
1877	Francis D. Carver
1877-81	Francis D. Pooser
1881-89	Anson B. Crutchfield
1889-93	Edwin T. Williams
1893-97	B. DuPre Hodge
1898-1905	Perry H. Nugent
1905-08	Henry Gordon
1908-21	John P. Galloway
1921-37	S. C. M. Thomas
1937-45	Gordon Moorehead

299

1945-46	S. C. M. Thomas		1861-64	D. B. Cappleman
1946-50	Edward J. Porter		1865-67	Francis Gunn
1951	R. A. McDaniel		1868-74	James G. Jones
1951-55	Donald McLeod		1875-77	James Roberts*
1955-57	David Baillie		1877-79	Richard Curry
1957-60	F. L. McGehee		1881-88	George A. Demerit
1960	Mrs. Agnes McGehee		1889-93	Charles F. Dupont*
1960-61	Charles "Dizzy" Thomas		1893-1901	Francis W. Knight
			1901-05	Richard F. Hicks
1961-72	Doug Willis		1905-09	Francis W. Knight
1973-1993	Don Moreland		1909-17	Clement Jaycocks
1993-98	Ken Ergle		1917-21	Angus H. McInnis
1998	Ed Dean		1921-26	Roland Curry
			1926-33	Cleveland Niles

MARTIN COUNTY

			1933-41	Karl O. Thompson
			1941-53	Berlin A. Sawyer
1925-26	B. H. Babcock		1953-63	John M. Spottswood
1926-33	M. M. McGee		1963-65	Henry V. Haskins
1933-42	C. E. Christensen		1965-69	Reace A. Thompson
1944-53	G. M. Hancock		1969-77	Robert L. Brown
1954-72	Roy C. Baker		1977-88	William A. Freeman, Jr.
1972-73	Robert L. Crowder			
1973-92	James D. Holt		1989-90	Allison DeFoor
1992	Robert Crowder		1990	Richard Roth

MONROE COUNTY

NASSAU COUNTY

1829	Lemuel Otis		1827	Harman Holliman
1830	P. B. Prior		1828	Lewis Bailey
1832-40	Robert R. Fletcher		1842-44	James Lord
1841	Benjamin A. Vun		1844-45	John Jones
1842	Samuel T. Vail		1845-63	Alexander J. Braddock
1842-44	B. K. Kerr			
1844	Edwin Page		1864-65	John Boothe
1845-47	John Coslin		1865-67	J. M. Bennett
1847-49	John V. Ogden		1868-69	Nathan L. Gano
1849-58	Robert Clark		1869	Henry Hazen
1858-61	Edgar A. Coste		1870	William F. Wood

Appendix

1872	Samuel T. Riddell	1921-22	C. O. Miller
1873-78	James D. Meddaugh	1922-24	J. C. Platt
1877-83	Peter Cone	1925-30	William Collins
1883-89	John A. Ellenmen	1931-33	Z. H. Simmons
1889-93	J. P. O'Neile	1933-38	Claude Simmons
1893-1900	W. F. Higginbotham	1938	Mrs. Eugenia Simmons
1900-06	A. J. Higginbotham		
1906-09	R. P. Carleton	1938-41	C. C. Simmons
1909-21	A. J. Johnson	1941-45	L. L. Conrad
1921-25	J. M. Adams	1945-57	Newton O. Stewart
1925-41	A. J. Higginbotham	1957-64	Jasper C. McPherson
1941-69	H. S. Youngblood	1964-77	John W. Collier
1969-78	H. S. McKendree	1977-80	Clayton Williams
1980-84	R. W. "Ronnie" Dougherty	1981-86	John W. Collier
		1986-1997	O. L. Raulerson
1985-92	Lawrence Ellis	1997-2000	Edward Miller
1992	Ray Geiger	2001	O.L. Raulerson

OKALOOSA COUNTY

ORANGE COUNTY

1915-21	B. H. Sutton	1845-46	William H. Williams
1921	J. M. Surnmerlin	1846-52	John Simpson
1921-30	P. J. Steele	1852-55	Elijah Watson
1930-33	L. H. Hughes	1855-61	John Clay Stewart
1933-41	J. P. Steele	1861-63	Andrew Jackson Simmons
1941-50	H. 1. Enzor		
1950	F. C. Campbell	1929-37	Issac Winegord
1950-53	J. A. McArthur	1865-68	John Ivey
1953-56	H. 1. Enzor	1868-70	David W. Mizell
1956-76	Ray Wilson	1870	John Evans
1977-81	Frankie L. Mills	1870-71	David Bradwell Stewart
1982-1996	Larry E. Gilbert		
1997	Charlie Morris	1871	Issac Winegord
		1872-73	Arthur Speer
OKEECHOBEE COUNTY		1873-77	William A. Patrick
		1877-82	Thomas W. Shine
1917-18	S. J. Drawdy	1885-1901	Julius Caeser Anderson
1919-21	William Collins		

301

1901-09	John Henry Vick		1923-33	Robert C. Baker
1909-13	James A. Kirkwood		1933	J. S. Wilson
1913-21	John Frank Gordon		1934-41	W. H. Lawrence
1921-33	Frank Karel		1941-45	L. R. Baker
1933-37	Harry Hand		1944-60	John F. Kirk
1937-41	Frank Karel		1960-68	Martin Kellenberger
1941-49	James Allen		1968-76	William Heidtman
1948-72	S. David Starr		1977-95	Richard P. Wille
1972-80	Melvin G. Colman		1995-97	Charlie McCutcheon
1981-88	Lawson Lamar		1997-2000	Bob Neumann
1989-92	Walt Gallagher		2001	Edward W. Bieluch
1992	Kevin Beary			

OSCEOLA COUNTY

PASCO COUNTY

1887-89	Thomas A. Bass		1887-91	J. A. Grady
1888	John T. Bass		1891-97	A. J. Odell
1889-93	Calvin Buckels		1897-1905	Henry Clay Griffin
1893-97	Joseph W. Miller		1905-17	Bart D. Sturkie
1897-1905	Charles F. Prevatt		1917-21	Issac W. Hudson
1905-08	Joseph M. Walker		1921-25	Bart D. Sturkie
1908-13	Charles F. Prevatt		1925-29	Issac W. Hudson
1913-21	Lon H. Ingram		1929-37	Charles E. Dowling
1921-33	Levin R. Farmer		1937-41	Otis A. Allen
1933-53	Young Tindall		1941-63	Leslie Bessinger
1953-67	Robert M. Buckels		1963-65	Basil Gaines
1967-68	Robert U. Best		1965-69	Leland E. Thompson
1969-84	Ernest P. Murphy, Sr.		1969-77	Basil Gaines
1985-88	Bob Fornes		1977-84	John M. Short
1989-92	Jon Lane		1984	J. M."Buddy" Phillips
1992-2000	Charlie Croft		1985-89	Jim Gillum
2001	Charlie Aycock		1989-2000	Lee Cannon
			2001	Bob White

PALM BEACH COUNTY

PINELLAS COUNTY

1908-20	George B. Baker		1911-20	Marvel M. Whitehurst
1920-23	Robert C. Baker			
1923	E. A. Stephenson		1920	Lorenzo Sloat

1920-26	William Lindsey		1919-25	John Logan
1926-29	Roy Booth		1925-29	A. H. Wilder
1929-30	Gladstone Beattie		1929-33	J. A. Johnson
1930	E. G. Cunningham		1933-41	W. W. Chase
1930-33	Roy Booth		1941-49	Dewitt Sinclair
1933-41	E. G. Cunningham		1949-50	Frank M. Williams
1941-51	Tod Tucker		1950-53	A. Hagan Parrish
1951-58	Sid Saunders		1953-56	H. P. (Pat) Gordon
1958-75	Donald S. Genung		1956	Joel C. Gerrard
1975-80	William T. "Bill" Roberts		1956-60	A. Hagan Parrish
			1960-76	Monroe Brannen
1980-88	Gerard A. "Gerry" Coleman		1976	Quillian S. Yancey
			1977-84	Louie T. Mims
1989	Everett Rice		1985-87	Dan Daniels
			1987	Lawrence E. Crow, Jr.

POLK COUNTY

PUTNAM COUNTY

1861	W. H. Durrance			
1861-62	Edward T. Kendrick		1849-52	Robert T. Boyd
1862-63	S. T. Watkins		1853-55	Nathan Norton
1863-65	C. W. Deeson		1855-56	James B. Brown
1866-67	Robert Wilkinson		1857-59	Howel A. Baisden
1868	Archibald Hendry		1859-62	Napoleon B. Mizell
1872	Felix J. Seward		1863	Steven J. Wall
1872	Thomas B. Ellis		1863-65	John L. Monro
1872-74	W. H. Pearce		1865-67	William B. Stephens
1874	William Durrance		1867-72	Thomas A. Shelley
1874	E. E. Mizell		1872-77	Joseph H. Mann
1875	J. L. McKinney		1877-82	Lemuel G. Sibley
1877-81	R. H. Peeples		1882-86	Thomas A. Shelley
1881-83	C. C. Gresham		1886-88	G. J. Zehnbauer, Jr.
1883	W. M. Bowen		1888-92	James H. Shelley
1885-87	R. P. Kilpatrick		1892-1901	John W. Hagan
1888-97	H. D. Ballard		1901-08	R. C. Howell
1897-1905	J. D. Tillis		1908-16	R. L. Kennerly
1905-09	J. R. Wiggins		1916-24	Peter M. Hagan
1909-19	John Logan		1924	William M. Canon
1919	J. M. Langford		19245-28	Raiford J. Hancock

1928-30	Peter M. Hagan		1919-42	Elmer E. Boyce
1930	Raiford J. Hancock		1942-49	Jurat T. Shepherd
1930-32	R. C. Howell		1949-70	Lawrence O. "L." Davis
1932-40	R. J. Hancock			
1941-44	Carlyle Hayes		1970-80	Dudley Garrett
1945-54	W. J. Revels		1981-89	Francis M. O'Loughlin, Jr.
1954	Myrtle G. Revels			
1955-88	E. W. "Walt" Pellicer		1985	Neil Perry
1989	Taylor Douglas			

ST. LUCIE COUNTY

ST. JOHNS COUNTY

			1846-47	M. O. Burnham
1821-23	James Hanham		1847-49	F. M. K. Morrison
1827-28	Squire Streeter		1850-51	C. L. Brayton
1828	Daniel G. Gardiner		1905-07	R. W. Lennard
1829	Francis J. Arice		1907-13	D. S. Carlton
1840-42	James Keogh		1913-20	William T. Jones
1842-44	George Acosta		1920-21	W. R. Monroe
1844-45	Francis Ferriera		1921	Augustus Rufner
1845-47	Joseph S. Sanchez		1922-29	J. R. Merritt
1847-48	James M. Gould		1929-53	B. A. Brown
1848	Michael Usina		1953-73	J. R. Norvell
1849-53	Rafael B. Canova		1973-85	Lanie Norvell
1854-55	Jacob Mickler		1985-2000	Robert Knowles
1855	James A. Mickler		2001	Ken Mascara
1855-57	Paul Sabate			
1857-60	Alberto D. Rogero		**SANTA ROSA COUNTY**	
1864-65	William Mickler			
1866-67	A. D. Rogero		1842-44	Jesse Carter Allen
1867	Charles E. Bohn		1844-45	Thomas V. Mims
1868-74	Ramon Hernandez		1845-49	William W. Harrison
1874-77	Alonzo Hernandez		1849-51	James R. Mims
1877-81	Adolphus W. Pacetti		1851-55	Isaiah Cobb, Jr.
1881-88	Raymond Hernandez		1855-59	James C. McArthur
1888-89	N. N. Floyd		1860-61	Isaiah Cobb, Jr.
1889-97	Charles Joseph Perry		1861-63	James M. Amos
1897-1901	Silas E. Davis		1864-65	John L. McClellan
1901-20	C. J. Perry		1865-67	A. B. Dickson

Appendix

1868-77	John W. Butler
1878-81	A. C. Benbow
1881-93	William J. Johnson
1893-97	John H. Collins
1897-1909	David Mitchell
1909-13	John H. Collins
1913-21	J. H. Harvell
1921-33	H. C. Mitchell
1933-43	J. T. Allen
1945-57	Marshall R. Hayes
1957-59	Bart D. Broxson
1959	Annie R. Broxson
1959-61	John Ray Broxson
1961-68	Wade H. Cobb, Sr.
1968-72	Leon Hinote, Jr.
1972-81	Harvell Enfinger
1981-85	I. A. "Jim" Powell
1985-92	E.M. Coffman
1992-92	James F. Coats
1992-2000	Jerry D. Brown
2001	Wendell Hall

SARASOTA COUNTY

1921-22	B. D. Levi
1922-29	Leon D. Hodges
1929-34	W. Albert Keen
1933-38	Clem B. Pearson
1939-53	B. D. Pearson
1956-72	Ross E. Boyer
1973-83	Jim Hardcastle
1985-2000	Geoffrey Monge
2001	Bill Balkwill

SEMINOLE COUNTY

1913-17	Charlie M. Hand
1917-21	E. E. Brady
1921-28	Charlie M. Hand
1929-37	James F. McClelland
1937-47	Charlie M. Hand
1947	R. C. Whitten
1947-53	Percy A. Mero
1953-55	J. Luther Hobby
1955-56	J. Denver Cordell
1957-68	J. Luther Hobby
1968-69	Peter D. Milliott
1969-90	John E. Polk
1991	Donald Eslinger

SUMTER COUNTY

1853	U. Z. Wood
1853-55	E. H. Crow
1855-56	George R. Mobley
1857	W. L. Story
1857-59	John W. Matchett
1860	William G. Parker
1860-61	William M. Christian
1861-63	R. H. Williams
1863-65	W. J. Ward
1865-67	B. P. Rouse
1868-69	Akin Stevender
1869	Bird Mobley (declined to qualify)
1870	Joseph W. Thurman
1871-73	Josiah S Dyches
1873-77	Mathew W. Dozier
1877-81	Josiah S. Dyches
1881-85	W. W. Chapman
1885-88	J. P. Galloway
1888-95	W. T. Chapman
1895-98	J. T. Warren
1897-1905	1 H. Lane
1905-17	A. T. Coleman
1917-19	L. J. Galbreath

1919-25	A. T. Coleman		1948-49	C. B. Barnes
1925-29	Carl ONeal		1949-53	Sim P. Howell
1929-45	W. T. Coleman		1953-64	Hugh Lewis
1945-46	M. W. Baldree		1964-69	Duke McCallister
1946-49	Mrs. M. W. Baldree		1969-72	J. M."Buddy" Phillips
1949-69	M. H. "Popie" Bowman		1973-97	Robert Leonard
			1997	Alton K. Williams, Jr.
1969-73	Fred Roesel			
1973-77	Don Page			

TAYLOR COUNTY

1977-81	G. E. "Ernie" Johnson
1981-96	James L. "Jamie" Adams, Jr.
1997	William O. "Bill" Farmer, Jr.

1857	S. R. White
1858-59	John Sherrod
1859-68	Edward Jordan
1868-71	Hezakiah Wilder
1872-73	Daniel Cox
1874-75	J. A. J. Cruce
1875-77	J. H. Sutton
1877	John F. McLeod

SUWANNEE COUNTY

1858	Noble A. Hull
1859-61	Robert G. Parker
1862-64	Elza B. Lealman
1865-68	William D. Green
1868-69	Richard Hurt
1869	John H. Baker
1872-73	Samuel U. Hicks
1874-76	George W. Allen
1876-77	W. H. Slate
1877-83	John R. Sessions
1887-89	W. H. Mobley
1889-93	Gus Potsdamer
1893-1906	J. W. Hawkins
1905-10	J. H. Rickerson
1913-14	Gus Potsdamer
1914-34	W. H. Lyle
1934-35	Joe E. Hinely
1935-41	Perry B. Cannon
1941-45	Tom Henry
1945-47	W. Arch Hunter

1877-83	Thomas Osteen
1883-84	G. B. Weaver
1885-87	B. A. J. Tucker
1887-93	G. W. Carlton
1893-98	A. J. Head
1898-1901	F. M. Lipscomb
1901-03	T. H. Stripling
1902	B. M. Knight
1903-05	Robert Smith
1905-21	J. H. Parker
1921-33	F. L. Lipscomb
1933	F. M. Lipscomb
1934-41	S. L. Wilson
1941-49	J. H. Parker
1949-53	W. A. Towles
1953-77	Maurice S. Linton
1977	Von Whiddon
1981-84	Grady Murphy
1985-88	Quentin Whittle
12/89-97	John Wesley Walker

1997	Lawrence E. "Bummy" Williams	1942-53	Alex D. Littlefield
		1953-57	James H. Tucker
		1957-68	Rodney B. Thursby
		1969-88	Edwin H. Duff, 11
		1989-2000	Robert Vogel
		2001	Ben F. Johnson

UNION COUNTY

1921-41	W. S. Brannen, Jr.
1941-45	J. E. Dekle
1945-49	Willie Croft
1949-53	L. C. Clemons
1953-85	John H. Whitehead
1985	Jerry Whitehead

WAKULLA COUNTY

1843	E. Madden
1844	R. H. Alexander
1845-53	Abijah Hall
1853-55	N. G. W. Walker
1855	R. H. Alexander
1855-61	Robert M. Spencer
1861-65	R. H. Alexander
1865-67	A. Hall
1868	Noah Posey
1872	C. K. Miller
1873	James M. Gaskins
1874-76	R. C. McMillan
1875	J. M. Gilchrist
1877-83	W. H. Walker
1883-89	C. S. Alligood
1889-93	R. S. Smith
1893-96	Henry Walker
1897-1901	R. L. "Bad Bob" Braswell
1901-12	J. W. Smith
1912-13	C. K. Smith
1913-32	Angus Morrison
1933-40	E. C. Ferrell
1941-44	C. S. Alligood
1845-56	E. C. Ferrell
1957-76	W. R. (Bill) Taff
1977	David F. Harvey

VOLUSIA COUNTY

1855	Hezikiah E. Osteen
1855-57	Elijah Watson
1857-59	Thomas J. Brooke
1859-60	A. J. Simmons
1860-61	James C. Marsh
1862-63	Cordin Barnes
1863-65	Ora Carpenter
1865-68	Reuben Marsh
1868-69	Alonzo A. Hoyt
1870-71	Andrew A. Alexander
1871-74	William F. Bucknor
1874-75	Christopher C. Hart
1875-77	Hezekiah E. Osteen
1877-85	William A. Cone
1885	Barton F. Brooke
1886	Uriah M. Bennett
1887	G. P. Healy
1888	William K. Turner
1889-91	Henry Stevenson
1891-95	Jefferson Davis Kurtz
1895-1908	John R. Turner
1908-16	E. L. Smith
1916-24	Lee Morris
1924-42	S. Edward Stone

WALTON COUNTY

1827-30	Michael Vaughn
1830-34	Alexander McKenzie
1834-36	A. Bellamy
1836-40	Daniel McLeod
1840-42	Alexander Campbell
1842-44	Giles Bowers
1844-46	William W. McCallum
1846-47	Enos Evans
1847-49	Anthony H. Brownell
1859-53	William W. McCallum
1853-57	Alexander C. Monroe
1858-60	John C. Campbell
1861-65	W. W. McCollum
1865-67	J. L. Campbell
1868-72	Samuel Rutan
1872	Calvin McDonald
1872	John A. McLeod
1873-77	Neil Campbell
1877-78	James H. Rice
1878-81	W. B. McLeod
1881	Joseph Malary
1881	J. W. Campbell
1882	Malcolm D. McLean
1883-89	J. C. McSween
1889-94	J. A. McLeod
1894-98	M. Manning
1898-1909	J. W. Campbell
1909-16	J. M. Bell
1916-17	J. B. Cawthon
1917-33	Thad Bell
1933-37	M. H. Prescott
1937-38	D. C. Adkinson
1938	Mrs. Celia Adkinson
1939-41	M. H. Prescott
1941-42	R. E. Gatlin
1942-45	Aubrey McDonald
1945-53	C. R. Miller
1953-57	Aubrey McDonald
1957-61	Curtis R. Miller
1961-70	Howard "Andy" Anderson
1970-77	L. S. "Sam" Campbell
1977-80	Jessie A. Carter
1981-2000	Quinn A. McMillian
2001	Ralph Johnson

WASHINGTON COUNTY

1826-27	Mortimer Bright
1827-30	John W. Bush
1831	William Hall
1840-42	Stephen Daniel
1842-44	John W. Cook
1844-45	Stephen J. Roche
1845-47	John W. Cook
1847-49	John R. Miller
1849-51	Levi F. Miller
1851-55	John A. Tabor
1855-57	John B. Pearson
1857-60	George F. Gainor
1861-63	Cary A. Taylor
1862	Abram Skipper
1864-65	William P. L. Home
1865	E. P. Melvin
1868	W. M. Owens
1872-74	George W. Cook
1875-76	S. H. Gainor
1877-80	J. C. Boykin
1881-83	L. D. Watts
1883-85	E. P. Melvin
1885-86	S. W. Davis

Appendix

1886-93	Thomas Y. Watts
1893-1902	Charles G. Allen
1901-04	J. A. McKeithen
1904-13	Charles G. Allen
1913-21	Henry Faffior
1921-25	G. W. Johnson
1925-31	Henry Faffior
1933-39	John Haffell
1941-45	H. M. Farrior
1945-53	Dan Brock
1964-69	George W. Watts, Jr.
1966-73	Bryant L. Thurman
1973-77	Theron H. Cook
1977-93	Fred Peel
1993-97	Danny Hasty
1997	Fred Peel

* African-Americans

BIBLIOGRAPHY

Primary Sources

Manuscripts

Baker Family papers, Palm Beach County Historical Society, West Palm Beach, Florida.
Frank Hatheway Diary, Special Collections, Robert Manning Strozier Library, Florida State University, Tallahassee, Florida.
Ledger of Wanted Notices, Collected by Sheriff Bill Joyce (1953-1969) of Leon County Florida. On file at the Leon County Sheriff's Office, Tallahassee.
Claude Pepper Diary, Claude D. Pepper Library, Florida State University.
Roster of County Sheriffs, Florida Sheriffs Association, Tallahassee, Florida.
C. C. Yonge papers, P. K. Yonge Library of Florida History, University of Florida, Gainesville, Florida.

Federal and State Documents, Published and Unpublished

Carter, Clarence E., ed., *The Territorial Papers of the United States*. Washington, D. C.: U. S. Government Printing Office, 1934-1962. Vols. 22-26 cover the Florida Territory.
"List of United States Marshals in Florida," United States Marshals Office, Middle District of Florida, U. S. Courthouse, Tampa, Florida.
"Roster of State and County Officers Commissioned by the Governor of Florida, 1845-1868." Jacksonville: Florida Historical Records Survey, Works Progress Administration, February, 1941.
Testimony Taken by the Joint Select Committee to Inquire into the Condition of Affairs in the Late Insurrectionary States. Florida. Washington: Government Printing Office, 1872.
United States Manuscript Census, Population, 1850, Calhoun, Franklin, and Leon counties.
Thirteenth Census, 1910.
United States Statutes At Large, 1822-1823.
Acts and Resolutions Adopted by the Legislature of Florida, 1861-1945.
Biennial Report of the Secretary of State of the State of Florida, 1915-1916, Part 3, Automobiles, 3-126.

Duval, John. *Compilation of the Public Acts of the Legislative Council of the Territory of Florida Passed Prior to 1840.* Tallahassee: Samuel S. Sibley, 1840.

Florida House Journal, 1939.

Florida General Assembly Acts and Resolutions, 1845-1860.

Florida Territorial Legislative Council Acts. 1822-1845.

Florida Senate Journal, 1877, 1939.

Holdings In Florida State Archives, R. A. Gray Building, Tallahassee
- RG 101, Correspondence of the Governors.
    - Ser. 32, Letterbooks, 1836-1909, vols. 1-7.
    - Ser. 577, Papers of Harrison Reed, 1868-1873.
        - Papers of George F. Drew, 1877-1881.
        - Papers of Edward A. Perry, 1885-1889.
    - Ser. 578, Papers of William D. Bloxham, 1897-1901.
    - Ser. 580, Papers of Francis P. Fleming, 1889-1893.
    - Ser. 581, Papers of Henry L. Mitchell, 1893-1897.
    - Ser. 596, Papers of William Sherman Jennings, 1901-1905.
    - Ser. 613. Papers of Park Trammell, 1913-1917.
    - Ser. 664, Papers of Napoleon Bonaparte Broward, 1905-1909.
    - Ser. 755, Correspondence of Thomas Brown, 1849-1853.
- RG 102, Correspondence of the Governors
    - Ser. 204, Correspondence of Doyle E. Carlton, 1929-1933.
- RG 151, Office of the Secretary of State
    - Ser. 261, Removals from Public Office, 1869-1888, 3 vols.
    - Ser. 1284, State and County Directories, 1845-1961, 35 vols.
    - Ser. 1325, Correspondence of the Secretary of State, 1831-1917.
    - Ser, 1326, Letters of Resignations and Removals from Office, 1844-1904.
- RG 156, Office of the Governor
- Ser. 13, Book of Records (Proclamations and Executive Orders), 1845-1992, 36 vols.
    - Ser. 260, Resignations from Public Office, 1868-1975, 10 vols.
- RG 350, State Comptroller
    - Ser. 554, Correspondence, 1845-1904.
- RG 910, Territorial Legislative Council
    - Ser. 876, Records of the Legislative Council, Unicameral, 1825-1838.

Journal of the Proceedings of the Constitutional Convention of the State of Florida Which Convened at the Capitol, at Tallahassee, on Tuesday, June 9, 1885. Tallahassee: N. M. Bowen, State Printer, 1885.

Thompson, Leslie A. *A Manual or Digest of the Statute Law of the State of Florida, of a General and Public Character, in Force at the End of the Second Session of the General Assembly of the State, on the Sixth Day of January, 1847*. Boston: Charles C. Little and James Brown, 1848.

Message of Park Trammell, Governor of Florida to the Legislative Regular Session. Tallahassee: Appleyard, State Printer, 1913.

"Register of Automobiles, 1905-1917," 2 vols., State Archives.

County Records

Anna Ethene Baker vs. Robert Clarence Baker Complainant, 4 vols, in Baker Family papers in Palm Beach Historical Society, West Palm Beach.

Escambia County (Pensacola, Florida)
 Case Files, 1832-1854.
 Superior Court Minutes, 1828-1841, Book I.
 Circuit Court Minutes, 1854-1870, Book B.

Orange County (Orlando, Florida).
 Circuit Court Minutes, 1847-1883, Book A.

Palm Beach County (Palm Beach Historical Society).
 Fine Book of Sheriff George B. Baker

Newspapers

Atlanta [Georgia] *Constitution*, 1924.
Bartow *Informant*, 1881.
Bartow *Polk County Informant*, 1886.
Cincinnati [Ohio] *Commercial*, 1874.
Fort Myers *News-Press*, 1938.
Gainesville *Cotton States*, 1864.
Gainesville *Daily Sun*, 1923-1924, 1930.
Jacksonville *Florida Times Union*, 1891-1945.
Jacksonville *Journal*, 1938.
Jacksonville *News*, 1848-1849.
Jacksonville *Tri-Weekly Floridian*, 1874.
Key West *Herald*, 1897.
Lake City *Columbian*, 1865.
Lakeland *Star Telegram*, 1923.
Marianna *Whig*, 1849.
Miami *Daily News*, 1924, 1933-1935.
Monticello *Family Friend*, 1860-1861.

New York *Times*, 1924.
Palm Beach *Post*, 1913, 1920-1933.
Palm Beach *Times*, 1920-1928, 1932-1933.
Palm Beach *Tropical-Sun*, 1913.
Pensacola *Florida Democrat and Workingman's Advocate*, 1849.
Quitman [Georgia] *Reporter*, 1876.
St. Augustine *Florida Herald and Southern Democrat*, 1840.
St. Augustine *News*, 1841.
St. Joseph *Times*, 1840.
St. Petersburg *Times*, 1934.
Savannah [Georgia] *Morning News*, 1870, 1874.
Tallahassee *Daily Democrat*, 1907, 1913.
Tallahassee *Florida Sentinel*, 1849, 1862-1866.
Tallahassee *Floridian*, 1832.
Tallahassee *Floridian and Journal*, 1849-1859.
Tampa *Tribune*, 1933-1945.
Thomasville [Georgia] *Southern Enterprise*, 1876.

Oral Interviews

Colonel M. F. Mann, Jr., Martin County Sheriff's Office, September 1,1999.
Vernon Peeples, August 3, 1997.
Ada Coats Williams, February 9, 11, 2000.

Secondary Sources

Addison, Ferguson. "The Addisons in Florida." Manuscript in possession of James M. Denham.

Adler, Jeffrey S. "Black Violence in the New South: Patterns of Conflict in Late Nineteenth-Century Tampa." In *The African American Heritage of Florida*. Edited by David R. Colburn and Jane L. Landers, 207-219. Gainesville: University of Florida Press, 1995.

Akerman, Joe. *Florida Cowman: A History of Florida Cattle Raising*. Kissimmee: Florida's Cattleman's Association, 1976.

Alduino, Frank. "The Noble Experiment in Tampa: A Study in Prohibition in Urban America." Ph.D. dissertation, Florida State University, 1989.

_____. "Prohibition in Tampa," *Tampa Bay History*, IX (Spring-Summer, 1987), 17-28.

Ayers, Edward L. *Vengeance and Justice: Crime and Punishment in the Nineteenth Century South*. New York: Oxford University Press, 1984.

Bacchus, James, "Shackles in the Sunshine," Orlando *Sentinel Star Sunday Magazine*, June 17, 23, 30, 1973.

Ball, Larry D. *Desert Lawmen: The High Sheriffs of New Mexico and Arizona, 1846-1912.* Albequerque: University of New Mexico Press, 1992.

_____. *The United States Marshals in the New Mexico and Arizona Territories, 1846-1912.* Albuquerque: University of New Mexico Press, 1978.

Berg, A. Scott. *Lindberg.* New York: G. P. Putnam's Sons, 1998.

Bergreen, Laurence, *Capone: The Man and the Era..* New York: Simon and Schuster, 1944.

Blake, James Carlos. *Red Grass River: A Legend.* New York: Avon Books, 1998.

Blum, John Morton. *V Was For Victory: Politics And Culture During World War II.* New York: Harcourt Brace Jovanovich, 1976.

Bosquet, Stephen C. "The Gangster in Our Midst: Al Capone in South Florida, 1930-1947." *Florida Historical Quarterly*, LXXVI (Winter, 1998), 297-309.

Brearley, H. C. "The Pattern of Violence." In *Culture in the South*, edited by H. C. Couch, 678-602.

Brown, Canter Jr. "The Civil War in Florida, 1861-1865." In *The New History of Florida*, edited by Michael Gannon, 231-248. Gainesville: University of Florida Press, 1996.

_____. *Florida's Black Public Officials, 1867-1924.* Tuscaloosa: University of Alabama Press, 1998.

_____. *Florida's Peace River Frontier.* Orlando: University of Central Florida Press, 1991.

_____. *Fort Meade, 1848-1900.* Tuscaloosa: University of Alabama Press, 1995.

_____. *Jewish Pioneers of the Tampa Bay Frontier.* Tampa: Tampa Bay History Center, 1998.

_____. *Ossian Bingley Hart: Florida's Loyalist Reconstruction Governor.* Baton Rouge: Louisiana State University Press, 1997.

_____. "Politics, Greed, Regulator Violence, and Race in Tampa, 1858-1859." *Sunland Tribune: Journal of the Tampa Historical Society*, XX (November, 1994), 25-29.

_____. "Tampa's James McKay and the Frustration of Confederate Cattle Supply Operations in South Florida." *Florida Historical Quarterly*, LXX (April, 1992), 409-433.

Brown, Richard Maxwell. *Strain of Violence: Historical Studies of American Violence and Vigilantism.* New York: Oxford University Press, 1975.

Brundage, Fitzhugh. *Lynching in the New South: Georgia and Virginia, 1880-1930*. Urbana: University of Illinois Press, 1993.

_____. *Under Sentence of Death: Lynching in the South*. Chapel Hill: University of North Carolina Press, 1997.

Buchanan, Patricia. "Miami's Bootleg Boom." *Tequesta*, III (1970), 13-31.

Buker, George E. *Blockaders, Refugees, and Contrabands*. Tuscaloosa: University of Alabama Press, 1993.

_____. *Jacksonville: Riverport-Seaport*. Columbia: University of South Carolina Press, 1992.

Burnett, Gene. "The Ashley Gang–Scourge of Florida." *Florida Trend*, XIX (August, 1976), 76-78.

Cable, George W. *The Silent South*. New York: Scribner's Sons, 1885.

Calhoun, Frederick S. *The Lawman: United States Marshals and Their Deputies, 1789-1989*. Washington: Smithsonian Institution Press, 1989.

Carper, N. Gordon. "The Convict Lease System in Florida, 1866-1923." Ph.D. dissertation, Florida State University, 1964.

_____. "Martin Tabert: Martyr of an Era," *Florida Historical Quarterly*, LII (October, 1973), 115-131.

Carr, Madeliene Hirsiger. "Jook Joints in Northern Florida." M. A. thesis, Florida State University, 1998.

Carswell, E[lba] Wilson. *Homesteading: The History of Holmes County, Florida*. Chipley, Florida: E. B. Wilson, 1986.

_____. *Washington: Florida's Twelfth County*. Tallahassee: Rose Publishing, 1991.

Carter, James A. "Florida and Rumrunning During National Prohibition." *Florida Historical Quarterly*, XLVIII (July, 1960), 47-56.

_____. "Florida and Rumrunning During National Prohibition." M. A. thesis, Florida State University, 1965.

Cash, Wilbur, J. *The Mind of the South*. New York: Alfred A. Knopf, 1941.

Chalmers, David. "The Ku Klux Klan in the Sunshine State: The 1920s." *Florida Historical Quarterly*, XLII (January, 1964), 209-215.

Chandler, Billy Jaynes. "Harmon Murray: Black Desperado in Late Nineteenth Century Florida." *Florida Historical Quarterly*, LXXIII (October, 1994), 184-199.

_____. "William Pope DuVal." *Tallahassee Historical Society Annual*, I (1934), 10-13.

Cofer, Richard. "Bootleggers in the Backwoods Prohibition in the Depression of Hernando County." *Tampa Bay History*, I (Spring-Summer, 1979), 17-23.

Coffey, Thomas. *The Long Thirst: Prohibition in America, 1920-1933*. New York: Norton, 1975.

Bibliograghy

Coles, David J. "'A Fight, a Licking, and a Footrace'": The 1864 Campaign and the Battle of Olustee." Master's thesis, Florida State University, 1985.

_____. "Military Operations in Civil War Florida." Ph.D. dissertation, Florida State University, 1997.

_____. "'They Fought Like Devils': Black Troops in Florida During the Civil War." In *Florida's Heritage of Diversity: Essays in Honor of Samuel Proctor*, edited by Mark I. Greenberg, William Warren Rogers, and Canter Brown, Jr., 29-42. Tallahassee: Sentry Press, 1997.

Covington, James W. *The Story of Southwestern Florida*. 2 vols. New York: Lewis Historical Publishing Company, 1957.

Crankshaw, Joe. "Florida's Jesse James Rode the Crest of a 13-year Crime Wave." St. Petersburg *Times*, Sunday Magazine, May 26, 1963.

Dabbs, Lester Jr. "A Report of the Circumstances and Events of the Race Riot on 2 November 1920 in Ococee, Florida." Master's thesis, Stetson University, 1969.

Danese, Tracy E. "Railroads, Farmers, and Senatorial Politics: The Florida Railroad Commission of the 1890s." *Florida Historical Quarterly*, LXXV (Fall, 1996), 146-166.

Davis, Jack E. "The Spirits of St. Petersburg: The Struggle for Local Prohibition." *Tampa Bay History*, X (Spring, 1988), 19-33.

_____. "Whitewash in Florida the Lynching of Jesse James Payne." *Florida Historical Quarterly*, LXVIII (January, 1990), 277-298.

Davis, William Watson. *The Civil War and Reconstruction in Florida*. New York: Columbia University Press, 1913.

DeCanio, Stephen. *Agriculture in the Postbellum South: the Economics of Production and Supply*. Cambridge: Cambridge University Press, 1974.

Denham, James M. and Canter Brown, Jr. "Black Sheriffs of Post-Civil War Florida." *Sheriff's Star: The Journal of the Florida Sheriffs Association*, XLII (September-October, 1999), 12-15.

Denham, James M. "The Read-Alston Duel and Politics in Territorial Florida." *Florida Historical Quarterly*, LXXVI (April, 1990), 427-446.

_____. *"A Rogue's Paradise": Crime and Punishment in Antebellum Florida, 1821-1861*. Tuscaloosa: University of Alabama Press, 1997.

Dodd, Dorothy. *Florida Becomes a State*. Tallahassee: Florida Centennial Commission, 1945.

Doherty, Herbert J., Jr. "Florida and the Presidential Election of 1928." *Florida Historical Quarterly*, XXVI (October, 1947), 174-186.

_____. "The Governorship of Andrew Jackson." *Florida Historical Quarterly*, XXXIII (July, 1954), 3-31.

D'Orso, Michael. *Like Judgement Day: The Ruin and Redemption of a Town Called Rosewood*. New York: G. P. Putnam and Sons, 1996.

Dovell, J. E. *Florida Historic, Dramatic, Contemporary*. 4 vols. New York: Lewis Historical Publishing Company, 1952.

Drobney, Jeffrey A. *Lumbermen and Log Sawyers: Life, Labor, and Culture in the North Florida Timber Industry*. Macon, Georgia: Mercer University Press, 1997.

_____. "'Where Palm and Pine are Blowing': Convict Labor in the North Florida Timber Industry, 1877-1923." *Florida Historical Quarterly*, LXXII (April, 1994), 411-434.

Ellis, Mary Louise. "A Lynching Averted: the Ordeal of John Miller." *Georgia Historical Quarterly*, LXX (Summer, 1986), 306-336.

_____. "Rain Down Fire: The Lynching of Sam Hose." Ph.D. Dissertation, Florida State University, 1992.

_____. "Surrender to Violence: Mob Justice in Southwest Georgia, July 1899." Master's thesis, Florida State University, 1989.

Erikson, John M. *Brevard County: A History to 1955*. Tampa: Florida Historical Society, 1995.

Fernald, Edward A. and Elizabeth D. Purdum. *Atlas of Florida*. Gainesville: University of Florida Press, 1992.

Florida Highways. XIII (February, 1945).

Florida Sheriffs Association Magazine and Directory, 1942.

Florida Sheriffs' Yearbook, 1929-1930.

Flynt, Wayne. *Cracker Messiah: Governor Sidney J. Catts of Florida*. Baton Rouge: Louisiana State University Press, 1977.

Foley, Bill. "Sparky's Still in Business." Jacksonville *Florida Times-Union*, April 20, 1977.

Friedman, Lawrence M. *Crime and Punishment in American History*. New York: Basic Books, 1993.

George, Paul S. "Bootleggers, Prohibitionists, and Police: The Temperance Movement in Miami, 1896-1920." *Tequesta*, XXXIX (1979), 3-41.

Gladwin, Irene. *The Sheriff: The Man and His Office*. London: Gallancz, 1974.

Goodnow, Mark N. "Turpentine: Impressions of the Convicts' Camps of Florida." *Internationalist Socialist Review*, XVI (June, 1915), 724-733.

Grant, Donald I. *The Anti-Lynching Movement, 1883-1932*. San Francisco: R. and E. Research Associates, 1975.

Grantham, Dewey. *Southern Progressivism: The Reconciliation of Progress and Tradition*. Knoxville: University of Tennessee Press, 1983.

Green, Fletcher M. "Some Aspects of the Convict Lease System in the Southern States." In *Essays in Southern History*, edited by Fletcher M.

Green, 112-123. Chapel Hill: University of North Carolina Press, 1949.

Guthrie, John A., Jr. "The Florida Supreme Court and the Intoxicating Liquor Laws: From Local Option to National Prohibition, 1885-1920." *Georgia Journal of Southern Legal History*, II (Spring-Summer, 1993), 99-137.

_____. "Hard Times, Hard Liquor, and Hard Luck: Selective Enforcement of Prohibition in North Florida." *Florida Historical Quarterly*, LXXIV (Summer, 1995), 23-29.

_____. *"Keepers of the Spirits:" The Judicial Response to Prohibition Enforcement in Florida, 1885-1935*. Westport, Connecticut: Greenwood Press, 1998.

_____. "Rekindling the Spirits: From National Prohibition to Local Option in Florida, 1928-1935." *Florida Historical Quarterly*, LXXIV (Summer, 1995), 23-29.

Hackney, Sheldon. "Southern Violence." *American Historical Review*, LXXIV (February, 1969), 906-925.

Hadden, Sally. "Law Enforcement in a New Nation: Slave Patrol and Public Authority in the Old South, 1700-1865." Ph.D. dissertation, Harvard University, 1993.

Hanna, Alfred J. and Kathryn Abbey Hanna. *Lake Okeechobee Wellspring of the Everglades*. Indianapolis and New York: Bobbs-Merrill Company, 1948.

Hawes, Leland, "Brutal Tale Emerges of Priest's Castration in the '20s." Tampa *Tribune*, August 2, 1992.

Hartman, David W. and David J. Coles. Compilers. *Biographical Register of Florida's Confederate and Union Soldiers*. 8 vols. Wilmington, North Carolina: Broadfoot Publishing Company, 1996.

Higham, John. *Strangers in the Land: Patterns of American Nativism, 1860-1925*. New York: Atheneum, 1985.

Hindus, Michael. *Prison and Plantation: Crime, Justice, and Authority in Massachusetts and South Carolina, 1767-1878*. Chapel Hill: University of North Carolina Press, 1980.

Hix, C. Stuart. *The Notorious Ashley Gang: A Saga of the King and the Queen of the Everglades*. Stuart, Florida: St. Lucie Printing Company, 1928.

Holmes, William D. "White Capping in Georgia: Carroll and Houston Counties, 1893." *Georgia Historical Quarterly*, LXIV (Winter, 1980), 388-404.

Horan, James D. *The Pinkertons: The Detective Agency that Made History*. New York: Crown Publishers, 1967.

Hoskins, F. W. "The St. Joseph Convention: The Making of Florida's First Constitution." *Florida Historical Quarterly*, XVI (July, 1937), 33-43;

(October, 1937), 97-109; (April, 1938), 342-350; XVII (October, 1938), 125-131.

Hovanyetz, Scott. "Outlaws of the Treasure Coast." Fort Pierce *Tribune*, March 30, 1997.

Howard, Walter T. *Lynching: Extralegal Violence in Florida During the 1930s*. Selinsgrove, Pennsylvania: Susquehana University Press, 1995.

_____. "Vigilante Justice and National Reaction: The 1937 Tallahassee Double Lynching." *Florida Historical Quarterly*, LVII (July, 1988), 32-51.

Hughes, Edward M., "Florida Preachers and the Election of 1928." *Florida Historical Quarterly*, LXVII (October, 1988), 131-146.

Ingalls, Robert P. "General Joseph B. Wall and Lynch Law in Tampa." *Florida Historical Quarterly*, LXVIII (July, 1984), 51-70.

_____. *Urban Vigilantes in the New South: Tampa, 1882-1936*. Knoxville: University of Tennessee Press, 1988.

Jackson, Harvey H., "The Middle-Class Democracy Victorious: the Mitcham War of Clarke County, Alabama, 1893." *Journal of Southern History*, LVII (August, 1991), 453-478.

Johns, John E. *Florida During the Civil War*. Gainesville: University of Florida Press, 1963.

Johnson, David R., *American Law Enforcement: A History*. Arlington Heights, Forum Press, 1981.

Johnson, Herbert A., and Nancy Travis Wolfe. *History of Criminal Justice*. Cincinnati: Anderson Publishing Company, 1996.

Jones, James P., and William Warren Rogers. "The Surrender of Tallahassee." *Apalachee* (1963-1967), 103-110.

Jones, Maxine D., "The African-American Experience in Twentieth Century Florida." In *The New History of Florida*, edited by Michael Gannon, 333-390. Gainesville: University of Florida Press, 1996.

_____, and Larry E. Rivers, David R. Colburn, R. Thomas Dye, and William W.. Rogers, "A Documented History of the Incident Which Occurred at Rosewood, Florida, in January 1923." Report submitted to the Florida Board of Regents on December 22, 1993.

Jones, Maxine D. "Without Compromise or Fear: Florida African-Female Activists." *Florida Historical Quarterly*, LXXVII (Spring, 1999), 475-502.

Kabat, Ric. "Everybody Votes for Gilchrist: The Florida Gubernatorial Campaign of 1908." *Florida Historical Quarterly*, LXVII (October, 1988), 184-203.

_____, and William Warren Rogers, "Mob Violence in Tallahassee, Florida, 1909." In *Florida's Heritage of Diversity: Essays in Honor of Samuel Proctor*, edited by Mark I. Greenberg, William Warren Rogers, and Canter Brown Jr., 111-122. Tallahassee: Sentry Press, 1997.

Jordan, Philip D. *Frontier Law and Order: Ten Essays*. Lincoln: University of Nebraska Press, 1970.

Karraker, Cyrus Harreld. *The Seventeenth-Century Sheriff: A Comparative Study of the Sheriff in England and the Chesapeake Colonies, 1607-1689*. Chapel Hill: University of North Carolina Press, 1930.

Knauss, James Owen. "William Pope DuVal, Pioneer and State Builder." *Florida Historical Quarterly*, XI (January, 1933), 95-139.

Knetsch, Joe. "Forging the Florida Frontier: The Life and Career of Captain Samuel E. Hope." *Sunland Tribune: Journal of the Tampa Historical Society*, XX (November, 1994), 31-42.

_____. "Hamilton Disston and the Development of Florida." *Sunland Tribune: Journal of the Tampa Historical Society*, XXIV (1998), 5-19.

Koeniger, A. Cash. "Climate and Southern Distinctiveness." *Journal of Southern History*, LIV (February, 1988), 21-44.

Lauriault, Robert. "'Can't to Can't': the North Florida Turpentine Camp, 1900-1950." *Florida Historical Quarterly* (January, 1989), 724-733.

Long, Durwood. "Florida's First Railroad Commission, 1887-1891." *Florida Historical Quarterly*, XLII (October, 1953); 103-124, and (January, 1964), 248-257.

McGovern, James R. *Anatomy of a Lynching: the Killing of Claude Neal*. Baton Rouge: Louisiana State University Press, 1982.

MacLean, Nancy. *Behind the Mask of Chivalry: The Making of the Second Ku Klux Klan*. New York: Oxford University Press, 1994.

Manatee County Sheriff's Office, 1855-1993. Dallas, Texas: Taylor Publishing Company, 1993.

Mancini, Matthew J. *One Dies, Get Another: Convict Leasing in the American South, 1866-1928*. Columbia: University of South Carolina Press, 1996.

Martin, Richard A. and Daniel L. Schafer. *Jacksonville's Ordeal By Fire: A Civil War History*. Jacksonville: Florida Publishing Company, 1984.

Matthews, Janet Snyder. *Edge of Wilderness: A Settlement History of Manatee River and Sarasota Bay*. Tulsa, Oklahoma: Caprine Press, 1983.

Mormino, Gary R., and George E. Pozzeta. *The Immigrant World of Ybor City: Italians and Their Latin Neighbors in Tampa, 1885-1985*. Urbana and Chicago: University of Illinois Press, 1987.

Mormino, Gary R. "World War II." In *The New History of Florida*, edited by Michael Gannon, 323-343. Gainesville: University of Florida Press, 1996.

Morn, Frank. *"The Eye That Never Sleeps": A History of the Pinkerton National Detective Agency*. Bloomington: University of Indiana Press, 1982.

Morris, Allen, and Joan Morris. *Florida Handbook, 1999-2000*. Tallahassee: Peninsular Publishing Company,1999.

Morris, William Alfred. *The Medieval English Sheriff to 1300*. Manchester, England: Manchester University Press, 1968.

Nasaw, David. "Review of David Margolick's *Strange Fruit: Billie Holliday, Café Society, and an Early Cry for Civil Rights*." New York *Times* Book Review, May 21, 2000, 38.

National Association for the Advancement of Colored People. *Thirty Years of Lynching in the United States, 1889-1918*. New York: Negro University Press, 1969.

Nulty, William H. *Confederate Florida: The Road to Olustee: Florida During the Civil War*. Tuscaloosa: University of Alabama, 1990.

Orange County Sheriff's Office, Orlando, Florida: 150th Anniversary History Book. Paducah, Kentucky: Turner Publishing Company, 1994.

Orrick, Bentley, and Harry L. Crumpacker. *The Tampa Tribune: A Century of Florida Journalism*. Tampa: University of Tampa Press, 1998.

Paisley, Clifton, *The Red Hills of Florida, 1528-1865*. Tuscaloosa: University of Alabama Press, 1989.

Patterson, Orlando. *Rituals of Blood: Consequences of Slavery in Two American Centuries*. Washington: Civitas, 1998.

Peoples, Vernon. "Alexander Bell." Manuscript in possession of James M. Denham.

Pickard, John B. *Florida's Eden: An Illustrated History of Alachua County*. Gainesville: Maupin House, 1994.

Polenberg, Richard. *America at War: The Home Front, 1941-1945*. Englewood Cliffs, New Jersey: Prentice Hall, 1968.

Powell, J. C. *The American Siberia or Fourteen Years' Experience in a Southern Convict Camp*. Chicago: H. J. Smith & Co., 1891; reprint ed., Gainesville: University of Florida Press, 1976.

Prassel, Frank Richard. *The Western Peace Officer: A Legacy of Law and Order*. Norman: University of Oklahoma Press, 1972.

Pratt, Kathleen Falconer. "The Development of the Florida Prisoner System." Master's thesis, Florida State University, 1949.

Prescott, Stephen R. "White Roses and Crosses: Father John Conoley, the Ku

Klux Klan, and the University of Florida." *Florida Historical Quarterly*, LXXI (July, 1992), 18-40.

Proctor, Samuel. *Napoleon Bonaparte Broward: Florida's Fighting Democrat*. Gainesville: University of Florida Press, 1950.

_____. "Prelude to the New Florida, 1877-1919," in *The New History of Florida*, edited by Michael Gannon, 266-286. Gainesville: University of Florida Press, 1996.

Reed, John Shelton. "Below the Smith and Wesson Line: Southern Violence." In his *One South: An Ethnic Approach to Regional Culture*, 139-153. Baton Rouge: Louisiana State University Press, 1982.

_____. "To Live and Die in Dixie: Contribution to the Study of Violence." *Political Science Quarterly*, XXXVI (September, 1971), 429-443.

Reiger, John F. "Deprivation, Disaffection, and Desertion in Confederate Florida." *Florida Historical Quarterly*, XLVIII (January, 1970), 279-298 and L (October, 1972), 128-142.

Remini, Robert V., and Robert O. Rupp. *Andrew Jackson: A Bibliography*. Westport, Connecticut: Greenwood Press, 1991.

Remini, Robert V. *The Life of Andrew Jackson*. New York: Harper & Row, 1988.

Revels, Tracy Jean. "World War II-Era: Changes in the 1940s." In *Florida's Heritage of Diversity: Essays in Honor of Samuel Proctor*, edited by Mark I. Greenberg, William Warren Rogers, and Canter Brown, Jr., 137-150. Sentry Press, 1997.

Richardson, Joe M. "The Florida Black Codes." *Florida Historical Quarterly*, XLVII (April, 1969), 363-379.

Rivers, Larry E. *Slavery in Florida From Territorial Days Through the Civil War*. Gainesville: University of Florida Press, 2000.

Rogers, William Warren, and Robert David Ward. *August Reckoning: Jack Turner and Racism in Post Civil War Alabama*. Baton Rouge: Louisiana State University Press, 1973.

Rogers, William Warren, and Canter Brown, Jr. *Florida's Clerks of the Circuit Court: Their History and Experiences*. Tallahassee: Sentry Press, 1996.

Rogers, William Warren. *Outposts on the Gulf Saint George Island and Apalachicola from Early Exploration to World War II*. Pensacola: University of West Florida Press, 1986.

_____. *200 Years of Independence: Tallahassee Celebrates the Fourth of July, 1976*. Tallahassee: Bicentennial Commission Committee of Florida State University and the Leon County Bicentennial Action '76 Committee, 1976.

Rorabaugh, W. J. *The Alcoholic Republic: An American Tradition.* New York: Oxford University Press, 1979.

Sabbag, Robert. *Too Tough to Die: Down and Dangerous with U. S. Marshals.* New York: Simon and Schuster, 1992.

Shofner, Jerrell H. *A History of Brevard County.* Melbourne: Brevard County Historical Commission, 1995.

_____. *History of Jefferson County.* Tallahassee: Sentry Press, 1976.

_____. *Jackson County, Florida: A History.* Marianna: Jackson County Heritage Association, 1985.

_____. "Judge Herbert Rider and the Lynching at LaBelle." *Florida Historical Quarterly,* LIX (January, 1981), 292-306.

_____. *"Nor is it Over Yet": Florida in the Era of Reconstruction, 1863-1877.* Gainesville: University of Florida Press, 1974.

_____. "Renewal and Reconstruction, 1865-265." In *The New History of Florida*, edited by Michael Gannon, 249-265. Gainesville: University of Florida Press, 1996.

Sinclair, Andrew. *Prohibition: the Era of Excess.* New York: Harper and Row, 1962.

Smith, Julia. *Slavery and Plantation Growth in Antebellum Florida, 1821-1860.* Gainesville: University of Florida Press, 1973.

Smith, Robert Wayne. "The Medieval English Sheriff in the Reign of King Henry II." Master's thesis, Florida State University, 1986.

Southern Commission of the Study of Lynching. *The Tragedy of Lynching.* Chapel Hill: University of North Carolina Press, 1933.

Sparkman, Steven L. "The History and Status of Local Government Powers in Florida." *University of Florida Law Review,* XXV (1972-1973), 271-307.

Spillane, Joe. "History of Alachua County Sheriff's Office." Draft copy in possession of Florida Sheriff's Association.

Stanaback, Richard J. *A History of Hernando County, 1840-1976.* Brooksville, Florida: Action '76 Steering Committee, 1976.

Tatum, Georgia Lee. *Disloyalty in the Confederacy.* Chapel Hill: University of North Carolina Press, 1934.

Thorton, J. Mills III. *Politics and Power in a Slave Society, Alabama, 1800-1860.* Baton Rouge: Louisiana State University Press, 1978.

Tolney, Steward E., and E. M. Beck. *Festival of Violence: An Analysis of Southern Lynchings, 1882-1930.* Urbana: University of Illinois Press, 1992.

Trelease, Allan W. *White Terror: The Ku Klux Klan Conspiracy and Southern Reconstruction.* New York: Harper and Row, 1971.

Van Landingham, Kyle. "James T. Magbee: Unionist, Undoubted Secessionist and High Priest in the Radical Synagogue." *Sunland Tribune: Journal of the Tampa Historical Society*, XX (November, 1994), 7-24.

Wallace, John. *Carpetbag Rule in Florida: The Inside Workings of the Reconstruction of Civil Government in Florida After the Close of the Civil War*. Jacksonville: Da Costa Printing and Publishing House, 1888. Reprinted., Kennesaw, Georgia: Continental Book Company, 1959.

White, Walter. *Rope and Faggot: A Biography of Judge Lynch*. New York: Alfred A. Knopf, 1929.

Wilbanks, William. *Forgotten Heroes: Police Officers Killed in Early Florida, 1840-1925*. Paducah, Kentucky: Turner Publishing Company, 1998.

Williams, Ada Coates. *Florida's Ashley Gang*. Port Salerno, Florida. Florida Classics Library, 1996.

Williamson, Edward C. *Florida Politics in the Gilded Age, 1877-1893*. Gainesville: University of Florida Press, 1976.

Wilson, Theodore B. *The Black Codes of the South*. Tuscaloosa: University of Alabama Press, 1965.

Wooster, Ralph. *People in Power: Courthouse and Statehouse in the Lower South*. Knoxville: University of Tennessee Press, 1969.

Work, Monroe N. ed. *The Negro Year Book: An Annual Encyclopedia of the Negro1931-1932*. Tuskegee, Alabama: Negro Year Book Publishing Company, 1982.

Wyatt-Brown, Bertram. *Southern Honor: Ethics and Behavior in the Old South*. New York: Oxford University Press, 1982.

Zimmermann, Hilda. "Penal Systems and Penal Reforms in the South Since the Civil War." Ph.D. dissertation, University of North Carolina, 1947.

INDEX

Adams, Frank, deputy sheriff of Monroe County 182
Adams, John Quincy, U.S. Secretary of State 14, 16
Addison, Joel J., sheriff of Manatee County 65, 66, 76
Adkinson, Celia, widow of Sheriff Adkinson, sheriff of Walton County 256, 257
African 274: Americans 124; bondsmen 33, 83, 86, 89, 153; chattels 34; free blacks 22, 23; free colored 44; mulattoes 23; Negroes 23, 48, 90, 137, 141; quadroon 48
Aiken, South Carolina 134, 135
Alabama Polytechnic Institute 192
Albury, Henry, sheriff of Hillsborough County 97
Alden, George J., Florida secretary of state 90
Alderman, Mrs. J. D., member of the state milk board 270
Alford, Nell, committeewoman for Democratic National Committeewoman 270
Allen, Louis, sheriff of Dade County 220
Allen, J. D. 155
Allies 273, 281
Allison, Abraham K., governor of Florida, president of the state senate 82
Alston, Willis 21

Alvarez, David Levy, sheriff of Bradford County 138
Amendments: Eighteenth 206, 215; Fifteenth 88; Fourteenth 88; Thirteenth 77; Twenty-First 216, 222
American Legion 280
American Sheriffs' and Peace Officers' Association International 214, 215
Anderson, Julius C., sheriff of Orange County 162, 163, 164
Andrews, Daisy 269, 270
Angebilt Hotel 253
Anglo-American Rumrunning Convention 221
Anna, Santa, Mexican general 48
Antebellum 40, 48, 66, 73, 89, 130: officials 33; patrols 57; sheriffs 33
Anti-Saloon League 204
Apalachicola Bay 70
Apalachicola Judicial District 36
Appomattox 71, 84
Armwood, Levin, deputy sheriff of Hillsborough County 139
Asher, Frank, head of State Safety League 250, 254
Ashley, Bill 222, 228
Ashley, John 216, 218, 219, 220, 222, 223, 224, 225, 226, 227, 228,
Ashley, Julius Warren, Joe 216
Ashley, Lugenia Clay 217

325

INDEX

Ashley-Mobley gang 218
asylums, 62, 63
Atlanta 72
Atlantic Coast Line 248
Atlantic Ocean 10, 16, 253
Auburn University 192
Avon Park 278
Axis powers 271, 279

back taxes 65
bailiffs 10, 17, 44, 191, 202, 245
Baker: Edwin; Estelle; Eva; George; Henry; Leola; L. R.; siblings of Robert C. Baker 210
Baker, George B., father of Robert C., sheriff of Palm Beach County, 212
Baker, Henry, deputy, sheriffs office, Palm Beach County 215
Baker, James, Judge and Solicitor 37
Baker, L. R., Jack, sheriff of Ocala 275
Baker, Robert C., "Bob," sheriff of Palm Beach County 168, 210, 211, 212, 213, 214, 215, 216, 218, 219, 220, 222, 223, 224, 226, 228, 232, 238, 239, 240, 248, 255, 274, 275
Baltimore 214
bank heists 216
Barber, Moses, Orange County farmer and cattleman 76, 110, 112
Barnes, George L., sheriff of Alachua County 96
Bartow *Informant* 127
Baseball 106, 212: contest 192; games 192; players 212; team 189

Bass 110
Bassett, Henry O., CSA soldier (Sixth Florida Infantry, Co. E), sheriff of Jackson County 71
bawdy houses 158
Beach Club 212
Beard, John, Florida Comptroller 19, 102, 103
beating on trains 180
Beauregard, P. G. T., CSA general 75
Bedlam 96
Bell, Alexander, captain in Florida militia, Democrat, sheriff of Hamilton County 67
Bell, Thad, sheriff of Walton County 245
Bell, Thomas, brother of Alexander, Confederate, Republican, sheriff of Hamilton County 67
Big Cypress Reservation 238
Billy Bowlegs War (1855-1858) 58
Bimini 221, 222
Black Codes 86-88
black suffrage 96
Blackburn, Elias E., marshal of northern district of Florida 21, 46, 47, 87
Blanding, Albert H., Lieutenant General 272
Bleeding Kansas 50
blind tiger 138, 155
Blocker, Haley, Leon County sheriff (1851-1857), stable owner, surveyor, Major, 80th regiment, Florida militia 33, 42, 44, 56, 57, 67, 70
Bloxham, William D., governor of Florida 119, 120, 128, 137

326

INDEX

Board of Control 158, 197
bone dry 206, 215
Boney, David J. W., CSA soldier (Second Florida U.S. Cavalry), sheriff of Hillsborough County 70
bootleggers 158, 220, 233, 255
bootlegging 216, 218, 222, 227, 255
Bourbon Democrats 123, 132, 144
Bowden, Fleming, sheriff of Jacksonville 197
Bowden, Frank 134
Bowie knife 87
Bowlegs, Billy, Seminole Indian chief 238
Braddock, Alexander J., sheriff of Duval County 38
Bradenton Country Club 272
Breakers Hotel 228
Brevard, Theodore G., state comptroller from Mellonville 36, 38, 44
Brewton, Alabama 173
British: government 216; officials 221
Broward, Napoleon Bonaparte, governor of Florida and sheriff of Duval County 143, 145, 164, 168, 194
Brown, Canter, historian 112
Brown, Daniel J., sheriff of Holmes County 67
Brown, J. B., CSA soldier (home guards), sheriff of Putnam County 72
Brown, Thomas, governor of Florida 49
Buckley, Frank 221
Buckner, William Francis, tax assessor of Volusia County 94

Buffum, Richard V., CSA soldier, sheriff of Hillsborough County 71
Buford, Rivers, Associate Justice of the Florida Supreme Court 259, 279
Bulloch, Robert 36
Bullock, W. S., judge 167
Bureaus: Criminal Identification 238; Customs Personnel 221; Federal Identification 276; Federal Investigation 231; Freedmen, Refugees, and Abandoned Lands 88, 101; Prohibition 221
Burnett, S. W., sheriff of Alachua County 66
Burton, Grady L., state attorney, tenth judicial circuit 274, 275
Bush, Warren S., sheriff of Columbia County 105

Cahoon, W. B., sheriff of Duval County 243, 244, 246
Cain, Dempsey, sheriff of Brevard County 110
Caldwell, Millard, governor of Florida 172, 275
Calhoun, Frederick S. 17
California 224
Call, R. M., county solicitor 135
Campbell, John C., CSA soldier (Sixth Florida Infantry), sheriff of Walton County 71
Campbell, Walter, deputy of Volusia County 272
Canal Point 228
Canty, Bill 138
Cape Florida 133
Capone, Al 252

327

INDEX

Cappleman, D. B., sheriff of Marion County 36
Caribbean Islands 220
Carlton, Doyle, governor of Florida 169, 239, 241
Carlton, George W., sheriff of Taylor County 142
Carson, S. M., deputy of Suwannee County 139
Carter, F. M. G., sheriff of Jackson County 101
Carter, George, sheriff of Citrus County 168
Carter, Jerry W., railroad commissioner, Mr. Democrat 251, 253, 258, 268
Catholics 155, 158, 159
Cato, Fernando, H. 251
Catts, Sidney J., Independent-Prohibitionist, governor of Florida 118, 156, 184, 206, 212
Cedar Key 58, 61, 67
Celtic 161
Census 17, 39: figures 199; county children 44; takers 87
Cerro Gordo 48
Cessna, W. K. 104
chain gangs 135
Chaires, Green, Leon County cotton planter 122
Chambliss, W. F., Flake, sheriff of Jackson County 173
Chance, Thomas, justice of the peace of Jefferson County 48
Chandler, Anna E., first wife of Robert C. Baker 214
Chapman, Foster, Escambia County constable, de facto jailer 24, 25

Chapman, Ward, L. F., of Raiford State prison 250
Chattanooga, Tennessee 71
Chester, B. W., sheriff of Gadsden County 147
Chickamauga, Georgia 71
Civil Rights movement 159
Civil War 32, 33, 34, 41, 52, 59, 62, 63, 70, 77, 82, 84, 89, 101, 108, 113, 124, 153, 216, 255
Civilian Conservation Corps (CCC) 277
Clark, G. D., sheriff of Calhoun County 245
Clark, Walter R., sheriff of Broward County 253
Cleveland, Grover, U.S. president 196
Clontz, sheriff of Marion County 94, 95, 96, 99
Clower, Jesse 137
Club Pier Casino 272
Costa, George, CSA soldier (auxiliary artillery in St. Johns County), sheriff of St. Johns County 72
Cobb Isiah, CSA soldier, sheriff of Santa Rosa County 44, 63, 64
Coe, Charles Francis, candidate for U.S. Senate 258, 268
Coleman, D. C., sheriff of Dade County 252, 253, 276
Coleman, W. T., sheriff of Sumter County 259, 270, 274,
Collier, Benjamin F., sheriff of Hamilton County 106
Collins, A. J., Florida sheriff 49
Collins, Vivian, Florida adjutant general 250

INDEX

Cone, Frederick, governor of Florida 171, 251, 256, 258, 259, 262, 268
Cone, W. N., sheriff of Columbia County 135, 137
Confederacy 59, 67, 74, 77, 87, 88
Conger, Georgia Robles, member of Florida Democratic Committee 270
Conoley, John Francis, Father 158, 159
Conscription 74: laws 66; officers 61
constables 23, 25, 83, 87, 89, 90, 104, 123, 130, 142, 143, 178, 181, 182, 234, 238, 271
constitutional convention 86, 123
convict lease system 89, 120, 122, 142, 184
Cook's Cabinet Shop 234
Cooper, James 96
Corbett, James J., Gentleman Jim, American boxer 196
coroner 64, 226
cotton-based economy 56
counties: Black Belt 83, 153; Red Hills 56
County Traffic Officer (CTO) 233, 234, 236, 237, 244, 254, 260, 262, 272, 273
Cow Cavalry 72
Cox, John D. 141
crackers 108, 216, 258
Craft, Isaac D., sheriff of Hillsborough County 165
Crane Hall 158
Crawford, George W., governor of Georgia 51
Crawford, Martin W. 24
Creel, Joshua 120
Crenshaw County, Alabama 135

Crosby, J. C., sheriff of Escambia County 44
Cross, H. C. 170
Cross, W. B., Palatka merchant 133, 134
Crowder, Robert "Bob," sheriff of Martin County 215, 227
Cuba, 17, 129, 195, 246, 251
Culbreath, Hugh 279, 280
Cunningham, E. G., sheriff of Pinellas County 253

Danner, R. G., Florida FBI agent 272, 273, 274,
David, Lonnie T., sheriff of Madison County 172
Davis, Ralph, Florida executive secretary 274
Davis, T. O. 225, 226
Davis, William W., author 152, 153
Dawkins, William H., deputy sheriff of Jefferson County 182
Dean, Charles S., sheriff of Citrus County 250, 274
DeBary, Frederick 84
Decourcey, Philip D., sheriff of Leon County 106
Delany, John, sheriff in Alligator, (Lake City) Florida 49
Desperadoes 112, 128, 164, 223, 225
Dishong, Owen, sheriff of Desoto County 137
Division of State Motor Vehicle Drivers Licenses 260
Dixie Highway 224
Dixon, A. B., sheriff of Santa Rosa County 97
Doherty, Jack, historian 159

329

INDEX

Dorr, Ebenezer, born in Maine, U.S. marshal of West Florida and sheriff of Escambia County (1841-1846) 21
Dorsey, William 120
Douglas, W. B., sheriff of Columbia County 246
Dowling, W. H., sheriff of Duval County 189, 190, 191, 192, 193, 201, 202, 238, 274
Dred Scott decision 50
Drew, George F., governor of Florida 95, 118, 119, 120, 122, 128
Driggs, J. S., sheriff of Duval County 118
Drys 159, 204, 220
Duncan, Moses, candidate for sheriff of Hamilton County 93
DuPont, Charles F., sheriff of Monroe County 124, 125, 126
Durrance, Sam, reverend, FSA chaplain 256
Duval Athletic Club 196
DuVal, William Pope, governor of Florida 12, 13, 14, 15

Edwards, Benjamin, CSA soldier, Florida sheriff 71
Edwards, Christopher H., sheriff of Madison County 39
Eight Box Ballot Law 124
Elks club 214
Ellenwood, James, Jefferson County justice of the peace 57
Ellis, W. H., sheriff of Jefferson County 61
Emancipation Proclamation 77
Empire House Hospital 72
Empire of Japan 281
English sheriffs 10

English, Colin, State Superintendent of Public Instruction 258
Epperson, Henry W., sheriff of Bradford County 138
Erie County, New York 196
Evans, Charles, U.S. marshal of the Western Judicial District 18
Evans, John, acting sheriff of Orange County 110
Everglades 58, 64, 197, 216, 218
Executive Investigation 137
Extortion 46
Extradition 252

Fallen, Patrick, jailer 135
Farris, Ion L., Florida state senator 202
Faultless Cleaners 157
Fee, W. I., Ft. Pierce undertaker 226
Fennell, Lewis Washington, "Uncle Wash", sheriff of Alachua County 189, 190, 191
fingerprint, fingerprinting 194, 214, 276
Finley, Jesse J., CSA general 71
Fisher, Alfred A., CSA soldier (home guards), sheriff of Leon County 42, 72
Flagler, Henry, railroad baron 128, 212, 217, 228
Fleming, Francis P., governor of Florida 119, 135, 136, 141, 164, 197
Fleming, James A., deputy of Monroe County 124, 126
Fletcher, Duncan U., Jacksonville mayor, U.S. senator 196
flogging 157

INDEX

Florida East Coast Railroad 212, 218, 248
Florida *Gazette* 8
Florida Highway Department 259
Florida Highway Patrol 236, 237, 254, 258, 259, 260, 262, 272, 273
Florida League of Municipalities 233
Florida Safety Council 254
Florida Sheriff's Association (FSA) 41, 178, 194, 202, 203, 210, 214, 216, 228, 232, 240, 245, 252, 259, 281
Florida Sheriffs Association Year Book (1929-1930) 240
Florida State Game and Fish Protective Association 214
Florida State Sheriffs Association 134, 203, 252
Florida's Ashley Gang 226
flying squadron 253
Folsum, George W. 34
Forbes, James Grant 16, 17
Fort Brooke 6
Fortune, Emmanuel, marshall of Jacksonville 109
Forward, William, Circuit Court Judge 37, 38
Futch and Floyd, train robbers 162

Gainesville *Daily Sun* 227, 242
Gainor, G. F., sheriff of Washington County 50
Galloway, J. P., sheriff of Marion County 202
Gandy, Herbert E., sheriff of Escambia County 173
Garner, Andrew, sheriff of Manatee County 96

Gautier, Peter, editor of the St. Joseph *Times* 36
Geiger, A. E., sheriff of Alachua County 42
Gibbs, Jonathan, Florida secretary of state 101
Gilchrist, Albert W., governor of Florida 170, 212, 236
Gill, King 34
Gomez tract 217
Gordon, Henry, sheriff of Marion County 137
Goss, Jesse H., circuit judge 96
Graham, Lee, deputy sheriff of Sumter County 167
Grant, Ulysses S., Union general, U.S. president 90
Gray, Robert, Florida secretary of state 253, 274
Green, A. M., sheriff of Escambia County 98, 118
Green, James D., cattleman, CSA soldier (Second Florida U.S. Cavalry), Republican, sheriff of Manatee County, Unionist 64, 65, 70, 72, 85, 86, 96
Green, Ralph, Sr., inventor of Florida's electric chair, Jacksonville physical 234
Gregory, E Scott, sheriff of Gadsden County 169, 202, 233, 234
Gresham, C. G., sheriff of Polk County 127
Griffin, Georgia 222
Guilford, James A. 49
Gulf Coast Blockading Squadron (GCBS) 61
Gulf of Mexico 16, 58

331

Guthrie, John J., Jr., authority on prohibition in Florida, professor 206

Hagan, Gertrude 170, 171
Hagan, P. M., sheriff of Putnam County 170, 171, 245
Hahn, Charles, secretary of the National Sheriff's Association 277
Hall, John P., sheriff of Clay County 119, 256, 271, 272
Hall, Perry, sheriff of Flagler County 239
Hammack, Frank, Miami FBI agent 271
Hammocks 108, 223
Hanham, James R., Florida's first sheriff 12, 14
Hanson, G. A., circuit judge 126
Hardee, Cary A., governor of Florida 212, 213, 214, 232
Hardee, Mrs. Enid Broward, committeewoman for Democratic National Committeewoman 270
Hardie, Dan, sheriff of Dade County 220, 221
Hardin, John B. 42
Hardwick, J.F. "Ned," Jr., deputy, sheriffs office, Palm Beach County 215
Harrad, Robert, constable of Putnam County 106
Harrell, Nathan A., sheriff of Lafayette County 104
Harrington Hall Hotel 202
Harrison, W. W., CSA solider (Santa Rosa Guard), sheriff of Santa Rosa County 72

Hart, Hubbard, northern entrepreneur 84
Hart, Ossian B., sheriff of Columbia County, governor of Florida 105
Havana, Cuba 17, 246, 251
Hawkins, D. L., deputy of Manatee County 66
Hawkins, J. W., sheriff of Suwannee County 140, 188
Hay, James R., sheriff of Hillsborough County 112
Healy, G. P., sheriff of Volusia County 133
Hemingway, Jason A., Columbia County preacher 21
Hemphill, Edward, Jacksonville lawyer 260
Henderson, Lucius 141
Hendrickson, Wilbur W., Miami deputy sheriff 219
Hendry, Archibald, sheriff of Polk County 96
Henry, John C., sheriff of Columbia County 129
Hermitage, the 12
Herndon, U. C., sheriff of Baker County 181
Hiers, L.M., sheriff of Hillsborough County 343
High Sheriff 112
Hijacking 220
Hilleary, A. U., sheriff of Alachua County 145, 147, 240
History of the Metro-Dade Police Department by Donald Thompson and Al Goodman 221
Hoard, James 181
Hobe Sound 217
Hodge, B. Du Pre, sheriff of Marion County 135, 179

INDEX

Hodges, W. C., Florida senator 249, 250, 251
Hogans, Reuben, CSA soldier (Eighth Florida Infantry, Co. I), Florida sheriff 70, 71
Holland, Spessard, governor of Florida 268, 269, 274
Holley, Caley, ex-officio timber agent, sheriff of Calhoun County 141
home guards 57, 72
Homosassa Springs 250, 259
Hoover, Herbert, U.S. president 159
Hoover, J. Edgar, director of the Federal Bureau of Investigation (FBI) 251, 258
Hope, Samuel E., Hernando County representative 97
Hotel Seminole 192
Hotel Thomas 240, 242
Houston, J. P. S., sheriff of Leon County 192, 193, 201
Howell, R.C., sheriff of Putnam County 166, 188
Howse, E. D., CSA soldier (home guard), sheriff of Marion County 72
Hudson, I. W., sheriff of Pasco County 203
Hunter, J. W., Florida state attorney 275
hurricane of 1926 169
Hutchinson, Henry, sheriff of Franklin County 106

impress property 61
Indians 108
International Association for Identification 215

International Sheriffs' Peace Officers' Association 215
Interstate Commerce Commission 144
Invisible Empire 152, 153, 156, 159
Italy 129, 271

Jackson County War, (1869-1871) 6, 101
Jackson, Andrew, Old Hickory, governor of Florida, U.S. president 6, 7, 8, 12, 14, 16, 17,
Jackson, Mississippi 120
Jackson, Rachel 12
Jackson, Robert A., sheriff of Hillsborough County 189, 190
Jacksonville *Florida Times-Union* 145, 171, 180, 189, 197, 227
Jacksonville Kennel Club 258
Japanese 270, 281
Jazz Age 281
Jefferson Beauregards 71
Jeffersonian Magazine 156
Jennings, William S., governor of Florida 165, 166, 167, 168
Jernigan, Aaron, homestead of 47
Jews, Jewish, 129, 155, 159
John Brown's raid 50
Johns Hopkins Hospital 214
Johns, Enoch 50
Johns, Thomas B., sheriff of Hamilton County 181
Johnson brothers, Gus, Alonzo, Raymond 112
Johnson, Andrew, U.S. president 84, 86, 88
Johnson, Arthur 170,
Johnson, Frank 234
Johnson, James 36

333

INDEX

Johnston, John W., sheriff of Hernando County 136
Jones, William, sheriff of St. Lucie County 203
Jordan, Edward, sheriff of Taylor County 67
Jordan, J. P., sheriff of Gadsden County 90
Joyner, John, deputy sheriff of Washington County 50
jukejoints, jooks, jukes 274, 275

Karraker, Cyrus Harreld 10
Keen, George G., sheriff of Columbia County 105
Keen, W. A., sheriff of Sarasota County 245
Kelly, John 48, 49
Kendrick, Edward T., CSA soldier, sheriff of Hillsborough 71
Kentucky 12, 19, 71
Key West 20, 58, 62, 86, 106, 124, 128, 239, 240, 246, 248
Kilpatrick, R. P., sheriff of Polk County 165
King, David W. 51
King, John W., sheriff of Jackson County 101
King, Sidney 164
King, Thomas, judge of Manatee County 66
Kitchen, A. P., Miami FBI agent 275, 277
Kiwanis 158, 214
Klanvocation 156
Klaverns 155, 156
Knights of Pythias 145, 179, 214
Knoxville, Tennessee 71
Koonce, J. C., native of Putnam County 167
Krimminger, John N. 104, 105

Ku Klux Klan 88, 105, 152, 153, 154, 155, 161,

Lake City Outrage 106
Lake Okeechobee 6, 218, 227,
Lamb, Robert W., sheriff of Bradford County 100
Land, Thomas Jefferson, CSA soldier, sheriff of Calhoun County 33, 71
Landholtes, Julian Warren, I.D. man, sheriffs office, Palm Beach County 215
Landis, Cary D., Florida attorney general 250
Lane, J. H., sheriff of Hillsborough County 167
Langston, William W., sheriff of Leon County 170
Lawrence, Red, motorcycle man, sheriff's office, Palm Beach County 215
Lawrence, W.H. "Hi," chief deputy, sheriffs office, Palm Beach County 215
Laws of Florida 198
Ledwith, Thomas, sheriff of Duval County 42
legislative council 8, 12, 14, 15, 17, 18, 25, 32, 35, 40, 42
Leon County Whigs 6
Levies 44
Lincoln, Abraham, U.S. president 56, 77, 88
Lindberg, Ann, wife of Charles 246
Lindberg, Charles A., U.S. pioneer aviator 246
Lipscomb, F. M., slain police officer of Taylor County 250
Little New Deal 251

334

INDEX

Littlefield, Alex D., sheriff of Volusia County 277
loco-foco 19
Lovering, Lee 202
Loyal Order of Moose 157
lunacy hearings 179
Lyle, W. H., sheriff of Suwannee County 203, 239, 240, 245, 246, 248, 250, 274
Lynn, Ray 224, 227

Magbee, James T., Florida judge 93
manhunt 160, 174, 224
Mann brothers 165
Marrero, Louisa 124, 126
Martin, James W., governor of Florida 157, 169
Martin, John W., governor of Florida 238, 258
Martin, Robert, sheriff of Columbia County 105
Marvin, William, district attorney, judge, and provisional governor of Florida 84, 85, 86
Maryland 10, 71
Mathews, John E., Florida senator 279
Mathis, W. B., sheriff of Lafayette County 182
Matthews, John O., candidate for sheriff of Marion County 94
Matthews, Roy Y., alias Roy Y. Matthews 218, 222
Maury, Francis, sheriff of Escambia County 50
May, Asa, sheriff's assistant of Jefferson County 48
Mayflower Hotel 256
McArthur, J. C., sheriff of Santa Rosa County 44

McClellen, A. J., sheriff of Calhoun County 138
McClendon, Julia P., mother of Robert C. Baker 210
McCook, Edward M., Union general 82
McCray, Lafayette Napoleon Bonaparte "Buck," sheriff of Jefferson County 106
McGovern, James, historian 173
McGregor, Louise, head of Democratic women's unit in Florida 270
McGuire, J. J., administrative assistant to J. Edgar Hoover 258
McKay, Robert 106
McKewon, T.J., sheriff of Calhoun County 205
McLaughlin, Dan L., sheriff of Hendry County 168, 169
McLeod, J. R., "Jerry", sheriff of Hillsborough County 268, 270
McMinn, Charles J., sheriff of Hernando County 45
McNeill, A. D., circuit judge 259
McNeill, John, CSA soldier, sheriff of Alachua County 71
McRaney, Daniel, circuit clerk of Leon County 42
Meredith, Bryant 34
Merritt, J. R., sheriff of St. Lucie County 216, 220, 224, 225, 226, 228
Mexican War 48
Miami Biltmore Hotel 251
Mickler, J. B., sheriff of Hernando County 164

335

INDEX

Mickler, Thomas, CSA soldier (Tenth Florida Infantry, Co. D), sheriff of Columbia County 70
Middleton, John Clarence 218, 222, 224, 225, 226
Miller, Albert 223
Miller, Levi, CSA soldier, sheriff of Washington County 42, 71
Miller, Ted 225, 226
Milton, John, governor of Florida 59, 60, 62, 63, 74, 75, 82
Mitchell, Charles, English boxer 196
Mitchell, Henry L., governor of Florida 119, 120, 121, 147, 196
Mitchell, Primas, alias Jim Jones 138
Mitchell, William G., sheriff of Calhoun County 94, 95
Mizell, David W., sheriff of Orange County 110
Mizell, John, judge 110
Mobley, Hanford 218, 222, 223, 224, 225, 226, 227
Mobley, Mary 222
Mobley, Wesley 222
modern national prohibition movement 204
Monroe, George W., sheriff of Jefferson County 106
Monroe, James, U.S. president 6, 12, 16
Montgomery, David, sheriff of Madison County 106, 107
Monticello *Family Friend* 61
moonshine, moonshiners 169, 194, 203, 220, 222, 223
Moore, E. Kathryn, second wife of Robert C. Baker 214

Moran, L. W., sheriff of Dade County 220
Morehead, Gordon, sheriff of Orange County 277
Morgan, Fletcher 279
Morgan, George W. 127, 128
Morris, Mick 170
Morris, William Alfred 10
Moseley, Alex, sheriff of Leon County 141
Moseley, William D., Democrat, Florida's first governor 25, 26
Motorcycle Squad 236
Mrs. Mathis 182
Murfreesboro, Tennessee 72
Murphree, Albert A., president of the University of Florida 158
Murray, Harmon, black gang leader 138, 141

Nasaw, David, historian 160
Nashville, Tennessee 12
National Association for the Advancement of Colored People (NAACP) 169
National Defense Program 273
National Sheriffs Association 6
Neal, Claude 173
New Deal 251
New York 16, 19, 20, 84, 106, 196, 262, 277
Newfoundland 195
Niles, Cleve, sheriff of Monroe County 239
Noble, Robert 39
Northwest Territory 6
Norton, Nathan, CSA soldier (home guards), sheriff of Putnam County 72
Nugent, P. H., Florida sheriff 181

INDEX

Office of Price Administration (OPA) 279
Old Sparky 234, 235
Old Testament 161
Otter Creek 141

Packwood, Frank H., deputy, sheriffs office, Palm Beach County 215
Padgett, Elmer, deputy of Ft. Pierce 215, 224
Padgett, O. B., marshal of Stuart 224
Padlock Road 129
Palm Beach Limited 218
Palm Beach *Times* 194, 238
Palm Beach *Tropical Sun* 212
Panhandle 84, 219
Paramore, S. A., sheriff of Madison County 142
parimutuel betting 238
Parker, William G., CSA soldier (Third Florida Infantry, Cos. E and K, Columbia and Suwannee Guards), sheriff of Suwannee County 72
Patterson, Henry 168
Patterson, John H., sheriff of Madison County 44
Paty, B. P., Florida gubernatorial candidate 268
Paul, Daniel J., sheriff of Holmes County 120
Payne, Jesse, sharecropper 172
Peacock & Company 155
Pearce, John A., sheriff of Leon County 134, 135
Pearl Harbor 270
Pearson, N., sheriff of Lafayette County 239
Peculiar Institution 56

penology 32
Pensacola *Gazette* 50
Pensacola *News* 158
Pepper, Claude, senator 258, 276
Perry, Edward A., governor of Florida 74, 119, 130, 133, 196
Perry, Madison Starke, governor of Florida 59
Pinkerton National Detective Agency 134
Plant, Henry B., railroad baron 84, 128
Point Lookout prison, Maryland 71
Pope, Wash 213, 214
popular referendum 199, 204
posse 10, 16, 49, 50, 101, 104, 108, 109, 110, 112, 127, 130, 131, 160, 162, 165, 170, 223
Potsdammer, Gottschalf, "Guss", prominent Jewish citizen of Lake City (Columbia County), sheriff of Suwannee County 129, 130, 139, 141, 201
Potts, Robert 48
Powell, J. C., captain of convict camp (Sing Sing) 129, 130
Pratt Mines prison, Alabama 134
Price, Emory H., Florida congressman 279
Price, John, judge 110
Price, John, sheriff of Duval County 188
Priest, A. T., sheriff of Citrus County 138
private clubs 206
Progressive Movement 132, 143
Prohibition Survey of Florida 221
prohibition 159, 203, 204, 206, 214, 215, 216, 220, 221, 222, 232, 236
prostitution 154, 277

337

Protestant, ecumenicalism 156
proxy 145, 180, 181
Pulaski, Tennessee 153

quarantine 142, 277

rabies 142
race riots 160
Raiford Prison 219, 222, 240, 250
Ramsey, J. P., sheriff of Dade County 274, 275
Ramsey, Perry Gilbert, sheriff of Alachua County 192, 203
Randall, Jack 138
Randolph, Nathaniel 108
Randolph, Thomas E., U.S. marshal of Middle Judicial District of Florida 19
Raffenburg, William 34
Read, Leigh, *appointed U.S. marshall of Middle Judicial District of Florida* 19, 21
Reconstruction 67, 78, 82, 83, 84, 86, 88, 94, 96, 97, 99, 101, 106, 110, 113, 132, 141, 152, 153, 154, 155, 157, 159, 160, 161, 162
Reed, Harrison, governor of Florida 89, 91
Reeve 10
reform school 144
regulators 96, 154
Reid, R. R., governor of Florida 34
Riblet, John Rihehart, Miami police officer 219
Richardson, Joe M., historian 153
Richmond General Hospital 71
Richmond, Kentucky 71
Rider, Herbert A., county prosecuter, judge 168, 169

Riggs, Tom, jailor, sheriffs office, Palm Beach County 215
Ringling Circus 272
Roach, Richard "Dick", deputy sheriff of Hillsborough County 106
Roberts, James A., constable and sheriff of Key West 106
Roberts, James B., sheriff of Escambia County 103
Robinson, Joseph W., deputy of Nassau County 139
Rodman, John, Port Colletor for St. Augustine 20
Rogero, A. M., sheriff of St. Johns County 102
Rogers, Calvin, constable of Jackson County 101, 106
rolling cage 187
Roosevelt Hotel 258, 279
Roosevelt, Franklin D., U.S. president 251, 262, 270, 273, 277, 280
Rose, Polly, committeewoman for Democratic National Committeewoman 270
Ross, Francis A., sheriff of Calhoun County 42
Rountree, Henry 93, 94
Royal Palm Hotel 251
rumrunning 220, 221, 222
Ruth, secretary, sheriffs office, Palm Beach County 215

sabotage 272, 277
saloons 204, 206
Salvation Army 226
San Francisco World's Fair
Sanchez, Joseph, U.S. marshall of Eastern Judicial District of Florida 8, 9, 19, 21

INDEX

Sanford, Henry S. 84
Sapp, Norton, sheriff of Lafayette County 119
Saunders, Richard, sheriff of Leon County 59, 67
Savage, H.B. "Barney," deputy, sheriffs office, Palm Beach County 215, 217
Saxon, Benjamin, candidate for sheriff of Polk County 93, 94
Scott, John 24
Scott, Winfield, S., U.S. general 48
scrub 112
Scully, W. T., deputy sheriff 181
Seaboard Air Line Railway 248
Sears, sheriff of Lafayette County 104
Second Seminole War 25, 48, 67
Seeley, Thomas, candidate for sheriff of Hernando County 93
Self, George W., deputy sheriff of Orange County 112
Seminole War 25
Seminoles 6, 20, 58, 214, 216, 218, 238
Seward, Zachariah, candidate for sheriff of Hernando County 93
Sharp S. S., sheriff of Hamilton County 136
Sheriff's Overseas Highway Convention 239
shire 10
Shofner, Jerrell H., historian 101, 152
Sholtz, David, governor of Florida 173, 206, 249, 250, 251, 252, 255, 259
Shuler, A. S., Jacksonville reverend 155
Silver Springs 84, 202
Simmons, A.K. 76

Simmons, Claude, sheriff of Okeechobee County 256
Simmons, Eugenia, first female sheriff in Florida, widow of Claude 256, 257
Simmons, Henry 168
Simpson, John 94
Sirmans, Mack 140
Skipper, Abram M., sheriff of Washington County 74, 75
Skipper, Sam 135
Slager, Charles, sheriff of Hillsborough County 112
Sledge, Lamar, slain police office of Jefferson County 250
slot machines 157, 274
Smith, Al, 1928 U.S. presidential candidate 159
Smith, J. M., Ft. Pierce chief of police 224, 225
Smith, James M., sheriff of Gadsden County 46
Smith, Waters, U.S. marshal of Eastern Judicial District 19
Southern Baptist church 158
Spear, Arthur, sheriff of Orange County 108, 109, 112
Spencer, Thomas K., sheriff of Hillsborough County 137, 139
Spencer, William C., sheriff of Hillsborough County 248, 249, 250, 251, 252, 255, 256
Spencer, W.S., sheriff of Hillsborough County 43, 67, 76
St. Joseph Constitution 22
St. Patrick's church 158
Stafford, John G. 34
Stanley, Steve 137
Starke, James D., CSA soldier 75

339

INDEX

Stearns, Marcellus L., governor of Florida 90, 98
Steele, J.P., sheriff of Okaloosa County 245
Stevens, William, sheriff of Putnam County 106
Stewart, Asa E., CSA soldier (Ninth Florida Infantry, Co. E), sheriff of Columbia County 71
Stewart, David B., sheriff of Orange County 112
Stewart, Jonathan C., sheriff of Orange County 44, 45, 68, 69, 70
Stone, Ed, sheriff of Volusia County 272
Stone, S. E., sheriff of Volusia County 248
Story, W. B., sheriff of Sumter County 39
Stoutamire, Frank, sheriff of Leon County 171, 250, 274, 279, 280
Stowe, Harriet Beecher 50
Stubbs, H. L., chief deputy of Ft. Pierce 224
Sulphur Springs dog track 268
Sutton, John H., sheriff of Taylor County 119
Sweat, Rex, sheriff of Duval County 248, 250, 251, 252, 253, 258, 260, 274, 275, 276, 279
syphilis 138
Tallahassee *Democrat* 156, 157; *Floridan & Journal* 66; *Floridian* 66; *Sentinel* 100, 106
Tampa *Morning Tribune* 266
Tampa Terrace Hotel 268, 280

tariff 50, 144
tarring and feathering 157
temperance campaign 204
Tennessee Coal and Iron Railroad Company 134
Texas 112, 120, 136
the Straightouts 196, 197
The American Siberia 129
the Antis 196, 197
The Florida Sheriff's Mutual Benefit Association 145
The Gold Coast 210, 220
The Great Depression 194, 253, 262, 271, 278, 281
The Leon County Temperance Club 192
Thigpen, Clinton, butcher, Franklin County sheriff 33
Thomas, J. B., Len, deputy of Ft. Pierce 224
Thomasville (Thomas County), Georgia 82
Thompson, Tee 183
Tidwell, B. F., ex-Confederate, Republican, sheriff of Madison County 101
Tiger, De Soto 216, 218
Tillis, H. M., sheriff Alachua County 147
timber agents 141
Tipping, Frank L., sheriff of Lee County 238
Trammell, Park, governor of Florida 184, 185, 238
Trelease, Allen W., authority on Ku Klux Klan 153
Trinity Methodist church 156
Tropical Park 252
True Americanism and the Truth About the Ku Klux Klan 155

INDEX

Truman, Harry S., U.S. president 280
Tucker, James R., sheriff of Jefferson County 42
Tyler, John, U.S. president 18
Tyler, William 68
Tyne, J. 49

Uncle Tom's Cabin 50
University of Florida 158, 240, 245, 253
Upthegrove, Laura, Queen of the Everglades 218, 224, 226, 228

Valdosta, Georgia 138
Van Loon, Warren E., FSA field secretary 256
Vann, Edward, CSA soldier, sheriff of Madison County 71
venereal disease (VD) 277, 278
Venetian Guards 61
Vick, J.H., sheriff of Orange County 183
Vicksburg, Mississippi 71, 72
Victory in Europe (VE-Day) 279
Victory in Japan (VJ-Day) 279
Vigilantes 96, 104, 152, 154, 161, 173

Walker, George K., acting governor of Florida 24
Walker, Joel T., sheriff of Jefferson County 42, 48
Walker, Robert Elias, Bob, sheriff of Levy County 160
Wall, Joseph B., brigadier general, Hillsborough County attorney, U.S. Attorney 165
Walls, Perry E., county treasurer of Hernando County 93

Walls, William W., head of Hernando county commissioners 93
Walton, Charley 134
Walton, George 12
Ward, James J., sheriff of Lafayette County 66
Watson, Tom, Georgia Populist leader 156
Watson, William, killer of two Florida sheriffs 49, 50
Watts, James B., Escambia County constable 24
Wellborn, Charles E. 135
Wells, Hortense K., first female candidate for U.S. Senate, Democratic National Committeewoman 270
Wells, R.J., sheriff of Alachua County 240, 246
Wentbrook, George E., sheriff of Escambia County 106
West End, Grand Bahamas 216
West, Thomas, sheriff of Jackson County 101
Wets 159, 220
Whidden, John W., sheriff of Manatee County 65
Whitaker, W. H., Confederate, sheriff of Manatee County 65
White, John F., circuit judge 136, 139
whitecappers, white capping 154
Whitehair, Francis P., Florida gubernatorial candidate 268
Wiggins, C. E., chief deputy of Ft. Pierce 225, 225
Williams, Ada Coats, author 226
Williams, Daniel, sheriff of Taylor County 67

Williams, F. M., Tampa police chief 233
Williams, Hub, Robin Hood of South Florida 112
Williams, Lewis, sheriff of Jackson County 49
Williams, R. C., Florida comptroller 63, 64
Williamson, Edward, historian of Florida's Gilded Age 118
Willingham, William W. "Ham" 112
Willis, William W., judge of Bradford County 99
Wilson, Henry, U.S. marshal of Southern Judicial District of Florida 20
Winegord, Isaac, candidate for sheriff of Orange County 112
Women's Christian Temperance Union (WCTU) 204
Woodmen of the World 214
Wooster, Ralph 33
World War I 202, 232
World War II 179, 271, 272, 273, 278, 280, 281
Worthington, William 16, 17
Wright, Arthur J. T., CSA soldier (Third and Ninth Florida Infantry), Florida sheriff 70
Wright, Arthur, sheriff of Columbia County 37
writ of habeas corpus 131
WRUF 240, 245

Yates, John 110
Yates, Needham 110
Ybor City 129
Ybor, Vincent, cigar manufacturer 84, 128
YMCA 156
Young Men's Democratic Club 153

In 1927 Hillsborough County sheriff L.M. Hiers prevented a mob from lynching a prisoner. During three nights of rioting at the county jail five people were killed and thirty-two were wounded. (Courtesy of Florida Sheriffs Association).

In times of emergency local militia men aided law officers, as seen here around 1908 in Pensacola. (Courtesy of the Florida State Archives).

County jail in Bartow around 1905. (Courtesy of Florida State Archieves).